"If I Am Alive Next Summer"

THE CIVIL WAR LETTERS
OF
CAPTAIN CHARLES ROBINSON JOHNSON
OF THE
16TH MASSACHUSETTS INFANTRY,
"THE IRON SIXTEENTH"

EDITED BY
Albert C. Eisenberg
and Michael Hammerson

WITH A FOREWORD BY
William C. Davis

HERITAGE BOOKS
2015

HERITAGE BOOKS
AN IMPRINT OF HERITAGE BOOKS, INC.

Books, CDs, and more—Worldwide

For our listing of thousands of titles see our website
at
www.HeritageBooks.com

Published 2015 by
HERITAGE BOOKS, INC.
Publishing Division
5810 Ruatan Street
Berwyn Heights, Md. 20740

Copyright © 2015 Albert C. Eisenberg
and Michael Hammerson

All rights reserved. No part of this book may be reproduced or transmitted in any form or by any means, electronic or mechanical, including photocopying, recording or by any information storage and retrieval system without written permission from the author, except for the inclusion of brief quotations in a review.

International Standard Book Numbers
Paperbound: 978-0-7884-5649-7
Clothbound: 978-0-7884-6192-7

1. Captain Charles Robinson Johnson

Table of Contents

Foreword	vi
List of Illustrations	ix
List of Maps	xiii
Preface and acknowledgements	xiv
Introduction	xvii
Chapter 1: The written legacy	1
Chapter 2: Charles Robinson Johnson, his letters, and the "Iron Sixteenth"	4
Chapter 3: A contemporary narrative of Johnson's service and death	8
Chapter 4: Off to War	10
Chapter 5: From Massachusetts to Fortress Monroe	12
Chapter 6: Fortress Monroe, 1862	36
Chapter 7: From the Peninsula to Suffolk	64
Chapter 8: The Seven Days' Battles	76
Chapter 9: Harrison's Landing and the 1862 Maryland Campaign	94
Chapter 10: Burnside and Fredericksburg	121
Chapter 11: 1863, to Chancellorsville	139
Chapter 12: Gettysburg	180
Chapter 13: After Gettysburg	204
Chapter 14: Johnson's Civil War Souvenirs	209
Appendix 1: Itineraries of Charles R. Johnson and the 16th Massachusetts	211
Appendix 2: Roster of Company F, 16th Massachusetts Infantry	222
Appendix 3: Extract from the Reports of the Adjutant-General for the State of Massachusetts for 1863 and 1864 giving a synopsis of the Service of the 16th Massachusetts Infantry during those years	231
Appendix 4: Official reports of the Battle of Gettysburg relevant to the role of the 16th Massachusetts Infantry	236
(1) Report of Brig. Gen. Andrew A. Humphreys, commanding 2nd Division, 3rd Corps	236
(2) Report of Brig. Gen. Joseph B. Carr, commanding 1st Brigade, 2nd Division, 3rd Corps	243
(3) Report of Captain Matthew Donovan, 16th Massachusetts Infantry	247
Appendix 5: Note on the Flags of the 16th Massachusetts Infantry	250
Appendix 6: Newly-discovered letters	252
Bibliography	259
Index	261

Foreword
by
William C. Davis

By now, enough collections of Civil War letters and memoirs have been published to denude several Canadian forests, and still more appear, each with its own unique contribution to the story. Every soldier was an individual and his own story was highly personal to him and his family in their own time, as it is singular today. Occasionally someone argues that we need publish no more of these, as we already have so many, and after all, there can only be so much difference between them. After thousands have come to print, what is left to say?

Then along comes something like *If I am Alive Next Summer*, the letters of Captain Charles R. Johnson of the 16th Massachusetts Infantry. On a per capita basis, the Bay State is probably represented in the field of published letters, diaries, and memoirs, more than any other state at the time. Literacy ran so high, and early commitment to the cause of the Union was so strong, that a legion of Massachusetts men recorded their experiences at the moment and afterwards. Johnson's letters home are especially important thanks to the 16th being one of the early regiments raised, mustering in July 1861 just days before the First Battle of Bull Run, almost the only significant major action in the East that the regiment missed during its three years' service. Those early regiments with the low numbers embraced the most patriotic and motivated soldiers of the war, and so it was with Johnson.

The story of how these letters came together in this book is a journey in itself, and is ably outlined by the editors, so it is only necessary here to add that this is one more example of just how much of this valuable primary material still remains in private hands, belonging to descendants or collectors, awaiting "discovery" by someone with an eye and an interest. Johnson's letters to his "Nellie" are replete with personal insights into camp life and company level command, but occasionally he witnessed something of epic importance. In parts of three letters he describes the March 8-9, 1862 Battle of Hampton Roads and the fight between the ironclads *Monitor* and *Virginia*. Few eyewitnesses from the land left behind better or more detailed descriptions. When it came to his own personal actions, Johnson provides equally detailed accounts of his regiment's fights on the Virginia Peninsula and in the Seven Days' Battles, and a continuous portrait of the life of an active regiment that spent much of its service on the move. Sadly his wounding at Gettysburg and subsequent death stilled his pen, or we could have hoped for more, for the 16th Massachusetts continued distinguished service until it mustered out in July 1864.

The editors have done an outstanding job of providing extensive background and context to illuminate the letters, making *If I am Alive Next Summer* almost as much a history of the regiment's first two years as it is Johnson's personal record. This is particularly useful as there is no regimental history of the 16th, and no memoirs by any of its officers or men - a sad omission for a hard-fighting regiment. Al Eisenberg and Michael Hammerson are to be praised for bringing Charles Johnson, his regiment, poor soon-to-be-widowed Nellie Johnson, and many more characters, to our attention in a work that will be a significant contribution to the literature of the Union Army, the Civil War, and the nation's struggle for definition.

*

List of Illustrations

No.
1. Captain Charles Robinson Johnson
2. Captain Charles Robinson Johnson
3. Johnson's U.S. Model 1850 officer's sword
4. Inscription on the throat of Johnson's sword
5. Johnson's dress epaulettes and japanned tin box
6. Johnson's Commission
7. Johnson's grave, Mount Auburn Cemetery
8. Col. Gardner Banks, 16th Massachusetts Infantry
9. Belt plate, buttons and G.A.R. hat wreath of Col. Gardner Banks, 16th Massachusetts Infantry
10. Lt. Col. William Blaisdell, 16th Massachusetts Infantry
11. 1st Lieut. John B. Brown, 16th Massachusetts Infantry
12. Charles Frederick Copeland, 1st Lieutenant and Quartermaster, 16th Massachusetts Infantry
13. 2nd Lieutenant Ward Frothingham, 16th Massachusetts Infantry
14. Chaplain Arthur Buckminster Fuller, 16th Massachusetts Infantry
15. Grave of Chaplain Arthur Buckminster Fuller, Mount Auburn Cemetery
16. Corporal Henry Scales Harrington, 16th Massachusetts Infantry
17. Captain Joseph S. Hills, 16th Massachusetts Infantry
18. Printed cover for Capt. Joseph S. Hills, Jan. 1863
19. Surgeon Charles C. Jewett, 16th Massachusetts Infantry
20. Captain John Pittman King, 16th Massachusetts Infantry
21. Major Daniel Sanderson Lamson, 16th Massachusetts Infantry
22. Captain Richard J. Lombard, 16th Massachusetts Infantry
23. Waldo Merriam, Adjutant and later Colonel, 16th Massachusetts Infantry
24. Captain John Chandler Putnam, 16th Massachusetts Infantry
25. Major Samuel Richardson, 16th Massachusetts Infantry
26. Lieutenant Henry M. Sturgis, Staff of Maj. Gen. Hiram G. Berry
27. Colonel Thomas Redding Tannatt, 16th Massachusetts Infantry
28. 2nd Lieutenant Payson Tucker, 16th Massachusetts Infantry
29. Assistant Surgeon Edward A. Whiston, 16th Massachusetts Infantry
30. 1st Lieutenant John U. Woodfin, 16th Massachusetts Infantry
31. Colonel Powell Tremlett Wyman, 16th Massachusetts infantry
32. Grave of Colonel Powell Tremlett Wyman, Mount Auburn Cemetery
33. Major-General Hiram G. Berry
34. Major General David Bell Birney
35. Brigadier General Joseph B. Carr
36. Brigadier General Cuvier Grover
37. Major General Samuel P. Heintzelman

38. Major General Joseph Hooker
39. Major General Andrew A. Humphreys (as Brigadier General)
40. Brigadier General Henry M. Naglee
41. Major General Daniel E. Sickles
42. Major General Daniel E. Sickles at the 1913 Gettysburg Reunion
43. First National Colors of the 16th Massachusetts Infantry
44. First State Colors of the 16th Massachusetts Infantry
45. Second National Colors of the 16th Massachusetts Infantry
46. Second State Colors of the 16th Massachusetts Infantry
47, 48. Programme for dedication of the Chapel Tent of the 16th Massachusetts Infantry, Fortress Monroe, Dec. 22, 1861
49. Birds-eye view of Fortress Monroe, Virginia
50. The army passing the Hygeia Hotel, Old Point Comfort, Virginia
51. The burning of Hampton by the Rebel Forces
52. The ruins of Hampton, Virginia
53. Federal troops at Hampton, Virginia
54. Rebel batteries on Sewall's Point, opposite Fortress Monroe
55. Battle between the U.S.S. *Monitor* and C.S.S. *Virginia*
56. Headquarters of General Heintzelman, commanding the Third Army Corps, at Howe's Saw-Mill, before Yorktown
57. The City of Norfolk, Virginia
58. The reoccupation of Norfolk by Union forces under General Wool, May 10, 1862
59. Gen. McClellan's Army on the march through the woods from Williamsburg towards Richmond
60. Heintzelman's Headquarters at the Nelson House, Battle of Glendale
61. The Battle of Charles City Cross Roads, June 30 1862
62. Heintzelman's Headquarters at Malvern Hill, by the river
63. Harrison's Landing, on the James River, the new base of the Army of the Potomac
64. General view of the encampment of the Army of the Potomac at Harrison's Landing
65. Part of the fortified camp at Harrison's Landing
66. Left defense of the camp at Harrison's Landing, Kimmeridge's Creek
67. The U.S.S. *Vanderbilt*
68. Heintzelman's Headquarters, Fort Lyon, defences of Washington, D.C.
69. Heintzelman's Headquarters at Alexandria, Va., September 3, 1862
70. Reconnaissance balloon, James River
71. Warrenton, Virginia
72. General McClellan surrendering the command of the Army of the Potomac to General Burnside
73. McClellan's adieux to his officers at Warrenton, Virginia
74. Fredericksburg, Virginia, viewed from Falmouth
75. Fredericksburg: Union troops crossing the river during the bombardment
76. Street fighting during the Battle of Fredericksburg
77. "The Mud March", Jan. 20-24, 1863
78. Suffolk, Virginia
79. President Lincoln reviewing the troops at Falmouth, Va.
80. Camp of the 12th Massachusetts Regiment at Falmouth, Va.
81. Abandoning the winter camp at Falmouth
82. Franklin's Crossing, Fredericksburg
83. Union troops crossing the Rapidan at Ely's Ford
84. The 2nd and 3rd Corps repelling Jackson's assault at Chancellorsville

85. Gettysburg: view to the rear of the 16th Massachusetts' position on July 2, 1863
86. Gettysburg: view to the left (south) of the 16th Massachusetts' position on July 2, 1863
87. Gettysburg: view to the immediate front of the 16th Massachusetts' position on July 2, 1863
88. Gettysburg: view to the right (north) of the 16th Massachusetts' position on July 2, 1863,
89. Gettysburg: right hand flank marker of the 16th Massachusetts
90. Gettysburg: view (south) along the front of the 16th Massachusetts' position on July 2, 1863
91. Gettysburg: memorial for the 16th Massachusetts Infantry

List of Maps

	Page
Fortress Monroe and the Yorktown Peninsula, 1862 .	65
Battle of Glendale, June 30, 1862 . . .	86
Battle of Malvern Hill, July 1, 1862 . . .	91
Route of the 3rd Corps from Falmouth to Chancellorsville	142
Chancellorsville, 5 p.m. and 7.15 p.m., May 2, 1863 .	146
Chancellorsville, 9 p.m., and position of Berry's Brigade, 9.30 p.m., May 2, 1863 . . .	150
Chancellorsville, 5 a.m. and 7.30 a.m., May 3, 1863 .	153
Chancellorsville, 9 a.m. and 12 p.m., May 3, 1863 .	155
Chancellorsville, 5 a.m., May 6, 1863 . .	158
Route of 16th Massachusetts from Fredericksburg to Gettysburg, June 11 – July 1, 1863 . .	179
Gettysburg, July 2, 1863 – the attack on Humphreys' Division	185
Gettysburg, July 2, 1863 – retreat of Humphreys' Division	187

Preface and Acknowledgements

*

It is with some surprise, the editors realise, that this book has been close to thirty years in the making – not through our being separated by 3,000 miles of the Atlantic, but because two busy careers have dictated that it should be so. However, since independently acquiring the various elements of Charles Robinson Johnson's effects nearly a third of a century ago, and finding our common interest through the medium of our mutual friend, the late John L. Heflin of Brentwood, Tennessee, we have never lost sight of our resolve that Johnson's story, which he took such care to record and which his family clearly took care to preserve, should be told. Our commitment to telling it was reinforced by the realisation that, inexplicably, there was virtually nothing published about his regiment, the 16th Massachusetts Infantry, despite its three-year hard-fighting record with the Army of the Potomac and its nickname, "The Iron Sixteenth". We have not set out to make this a regimental history, since the subject of the book is Johnson, but we have endeavored to use Johnson's story to illustrate the career of the 16th, certainly up to the time of his death, and in summary form for the remainder of its service, to serve as at least a partial history of the regiment until some future author can write a detailed one.

Although much of the research was done by the authors, this, as always, could not have been achieved without the help of a number of people:-

- Richard Dobbins, Historic Data Systems Inc., for permission to use the roster of Co. F, 16th Massachusetts Infantry, and photographs of men of the regiment, on his invaluable website, www.civilwardata.com;
- John Heiser, Historian, Gettysburg National Battlefield Park, for kindly agreeing to review and correct the introductory chapter on the Battle of Gettysburg, and for his advice in helping us to understand the very confused course of events associated with the retreat of Humphreys' Division from the Emmitsburg Road to Cemetery Ridge on July 2; and for providing a copy of the photographs of General Sickles at the 1913 Gettysburg Reunion, published here with permission of the Gettysburg National Battlefield Park;
- John D. Imhof, author of *Gettysburg, Day Two: A Study in Maps (Baltimore, 1999)*, for permission to adapt his Maps 32 and 38 for inclusion in this volume;
- the late James Kegel, author of *North With Lee and Jackson*, who made the assembly of all Johnson's letters possible by spending several days on our behalf copying the photocopies of those letters not in either of our collections, held at the United States Army Mititary History Institute at Carlisle, Pa.;

- Peter Lockwood, of the United Kingdom Civil War Round Table and Civil War battlefield tour guide, for providing seven superb photographs of the area where the 16th was engaged during the battle of Gettysburg (figs. 85-91);
- The late Col. Edward D. Milligan, USM (retired), for copying Johnson's miltary documents at the National Archives. His tragic death in January 2010 following an automobile accident deprived a great many Civil War students, both in the United States and abroad, of an indefatigable and invaluable helper and researcher and a good friend;
- Eileen M. O'Brien for permission to use her photograph of the grave of Regimental Chaplain Arthur Buckminster Fuller at Mount Auburn Cemetery, Cambridge, Mass., viewable on the Findagrave website;
- Donald Pfanz, Historian, Fredericksburg-Spotsylvania National Battlefield Park, for kindly agreeing to review our introductory chapters on the Battles of Fredericksburg and Chancellorsville, and preventing us from making a number of basic factual errors;
- William Prince, for permission to publish the three Johnson letters in his ownership - Oct. 5, 1861; Nov. 28, 1861; Dec. 1862 (no date);
- Robert Shenk, of the Civil War Preservation Trust, for permission to use the Trust's detailed map of the Battle of Glendale (viewable in full colour on their website, www.civilwar.org);
- Charlene Bickford, a good friend of Al and Sharon Eisenberg, without whose invaluable help during the later stages of editing the manuscript during a period of great difficulty for Al and Sharon, it would have proved difficult or even impossible to see the work through to completion.

In addition, the following repositories gave permission for the use of material in their archives and collections:-
- the Commonwealth of Massachusetts Art Commission for permission to reproduce the illustrations of the four surviving flags of the 16th Massachusetts Infantry in the State House Flag Collection;
- The Massachusetts Commandery, Military Order of the Loyal Legion, and the U.S. Army Military History Institute, owners of the two photographs of Johnson published in this book, references Massachusetts MOLLUS Photo Collection, Vol. 104, p. 5355, bottom right (standing view) and middle (bust view). We learned with sadness of the death of Arthur W. Bergeron of USAMHI, who had been of signal help in obtaining the photographs for us, during the final stages of putting together the manuscript;
- the Massachusetts Historical Society, for permission to use the anonymous contemporary manuscript account of Johnson's wartime experiences in their collections (see Bibliography, *Brief Memoranda of our Martyr Soldiers*) and their copy of the programme for the dedication ceremony of the Chapel of the 16th Massachusetts;
- Mount Auburn Cemetery, Cambridge, Mass., for permission to use their photograph of the grave of Colonel Powell T. Wyman.
- Of Johnson's letters, the following are transcribed from photocopies on deposit in the William Prince Collection, U.S. Army Military History Institute, Carlisle, Pa., and reproduced with Mr. Prince's kind permission (the location of the originals are unknown):
1861 – September 3, 15, 22, 26, undated; October 5, 13, 17, 20; November 4, 17, 22, 24, 28; December 4, 12, 29.
1862 – January 2, 9, 16, 22, 26; February 6, 21, 24; March 2, 5, 9, 12, 13, 16, 20, 25; April 13, 21, 30, undated; May 4, 8, 9, 11, 21, undated; June 11, 15, 19, 24, 26, 27; July 7, 10, 11, 14; August 8, 23; September 1, 11, 14, 17, 26; October 6, 8, 13, 20, 29; November 4, 9, 12; December 10, 15, 21, 27, undated.
1863 – January 6, 14, 17, 24, 28; February 8, 17, 19, 23, 25 or 26, two undated; March 5, 8, 11, 16, 26, 30; April 28; June 2, 16, 20, 24, 30
All other letters in the collections of the editors.

Photograph & illustration credits and sources (Illustration numbers):
American Civil War Research Database (www.civilwardata.com): 10, 11, 12, 13, 16, 17, 19, 20, 21, 22, 23, 24, 25, 26, 27, 28, 29, 30, 31, 34, 35, 36
Battles and Leaders of the Civil War: 49, 50, 52, 55, 56, 60, 62, 65, 69, 79, 81, 82, 83
Commonwealth of Massachusetts Art Commission: 4, 44, 45, 46
Editors' collections: 3, 4, 5, 6, 8, 9, 18, 37, 38, 39, 40
Eileen O'Brien: 14
Gettysburg National Military Park: 42
Harper's Weekly: 51 (Aug. 13, 1861), 53 (Apr. 19, 1862), 54 (Nov. 2, 1861), 57 (Apr. 19, 1862), 58 (May 24, 1862), 59 (June 7, 1862), 61 (Aug. 9, 1862), 63 (July 19, 1862), 64 (Aug. 23, 1862), 66 (Aug. 23, 1862), 70 (Sept. 6, 1862), 71 (Sept. 13, 1862), 72 (Nov. 22, 1862), 73 (Nov. 29, 1862), 74 (Dec. 20, 1862), 75 (Dec. 27, 1862), 76 (Jan. 3, 1863), 77 (Feb. 14, 1863), 78 (May 2, 1863), 80 (May 16, 1863), 84 (May 23, 1863)
Library of Congress: 68
Massachusetts Historical Society: 47, 48
National Archives and Records Administration: 22, 41
Peter Lockwood: 85, 86, 87, 88, 89, 90, 91
United States Army Military Historical Institute: 1, 2
United States Army Historical Center: 67

INTRODUCTION

*

There came a great rattling and clanking as if a giant in armor had been aroused. Shouted commands ripped through the air, and the punctuated pounding of drums, scores of them, resounded across the fields, on boulder-strewn ridges and behind stone-piled fences. Rank upon rank of blue-coated men fell into line, cheering as their color guards unfurled their national and state flags, which, let loose from their constraints, rolled free and snapped in the warm summer breeze. The late afternoon sun peeking through clouds gleamed off the bright metal of the riflemuskets, and for a brief moment the war was grand and spectacular as the men all had thought it would be, when once upon a time they had rushed laughing to the enlistment stations to become part of it.

Upon those ridges and behind those fences and boulders, other men in blue shook their comrades from their slumber, and scrambled to their feet. Together these farmers, tradesmen, mechanics and clerks gaped in awe at the great sight. The Union Army of the Potomac's Third Corps was moving out beyond the almost two mile long defensive line it anchored. From a bird's eye view, the Union position looked like a gigantic fishhook. With the eye of the shank on the south, the Union line ran north from the boulder-strewn treed Round Tops, Big and Little, toward the little road junction named Gettysburg. The hook of the line curved to the east around Cemetery Ridge and then to Cemetery Hill, just to the south of town, and finally to Culp's Hill, where the line doubled back to the south.

Despite the orders of Major-General George Gordon Meade, commander of the Army of the Potomac, Major-General Daniel Sickles, a former New York Democratic Congressman and the first man in America acquitted of capital murder by reason of temporary insanity, marched the 10,000 men of the Third Corps into broad, ripening fields of wheat and orderly rows of peach orchard. They sought to occupy higher ground, which was normally safer ground, but on this extraordinary afternoon would become killing ground.

Sickles' superior, General Meade, known to his men as 'that damned, goggle-eyed old snapping turtle,' was astounded at this movement commenced without his orders.

Along with artillery commander Henry Hunt, Meade rode up to General Sickles, demanding to know the meaning of this madness. Sickles replied that Meade had allowed him to dispose his troops as he saw necessary, and that moving to higher ground fitted those orders. Upon hearing that answer, Meade angrily pointed out that the ground in Sickles' front indeed was higher, all the way to the mountains miles from the western horizon. Sickles offered to pull back his troops, but Meade discarded the notion because the Confederate attack was developing. In an attempt to secure greater safety for his men, Sickles had created a dangerous salient a half mile in front of the Union line, causing a bulge in the lines vulnerable to attack on three sides. Like a bubble waiting to be popped, the Third Corps stood out, inviting the assault of the Confederate forces gathering on Sickles' front, on higher ground, as the glowing red sun began its drop during the balmy late afternoon. And to the north, upon the ridge line that Sickles had left behind, Major-General Winfield Scott Hancock, the Second Corps commander, observed to his staff, "Wait a moment, you will see them tumbling back."

In Company F of the 16th Massachusetts Volunteer Infantry, in the First Brigade of the Second Division of the Third Corps of the Army of the Potomac, twenty-seven-year-old Captain Charles Robinson Johnson of Cambridge, Massachusetts, roused his company. Grasping their rifle muskets, and swinging them onto their shoulders, the soldiers stepped into line at Johnson's command. Facing the sun in the west, he led them forward in obedience to the orders of his regiment's commander, Lieutenant-Colonel Waldo Merriam. They marched into the maelstrom of Gettysburg's second day of combat, assigned to a place along the Emmitsburg Road, which ran southeast/northwest to and from Gettysburg and in front of them to places whose quaint peaceful names, "the Peach Orchard" and "the Wheatfield", only underscored the irony of war.

Yet to the men of the 16th, volunteers all since the very first days of the rebellion, their enthusiasm to save the Union far outweighed the horrors of war. On April 12, 1861, rebels in Charleston, South Carolina's harbor opened fire at dawn's first light on Fort Sumter, one of the very few military installations in the South still in the hands of the Federal government. The fort stood in the middle of the harbor and the ring of batteries the rebels had established along the shore poured out their issue, hot and heavy. The bombardment went on for a long eighteen hours before the fort's gallant commander, Major Robert B. Anderson, from the border state of Kentucky, hauled down the Union flag and surrendered to the rebels. Civil war had come to the United States, and throughout the northern states young men raced to answer President Abraham Lincoln's call for 75,000 troops to put down the rebellion.

With the abandon and bravado of youth, they flocked to the recruiting offices to save the Union, to avenge the insult to their country's flag, and to "see the elephant." The adventure of their lives lay before them, and how could they possibly shrink from this one chance to experience it?

Charles Robinson Johnson felt the passion rise in his own blood and sought to enter the war as an officer. A thin, handsome man with short, carefully combed, blonde hair, a delicate, patrician face, and the affectation of a Napoleon III-style mustache and goatee, at age twenty-five Johnson was somewhat older than those who rushed to fill the blue ranks of the gathering Union armies in 1861. A man of wealth and stature, little did he know that he would play a part – and make the ultimate sacrifice - in the greatest battle to take place on the North American continent, and that the outcome of the battle would lead to the establishment of a United States truly united and free. His is a story worth telling.

=====================

CHAPTER 1

*

THE WRITTEN LEGACY

Following the war, Oliver Wendell Holmes, Jr., a former Union officer and later Supreme Court Justice, said of the soldiers of his generation, "We have seen the incommunicable experience of war." Yet communicate they did, in the letters they wrote prolifically from the field, and afterward, as they described their personal experiences and the histories of their regiments, in an outpouring of books and articles, and just gathering around the fire, which continued to capture the imagination of Americans long into the 20th century, and beyond, as letters, diaries, and documents tucked away in little-visited places were discovered once again. The veterans of the Civil War fervently sought to describe the terrible, awesome sights they had seen. Neither before nor since had a single event in American history produced such a mass of literature from its participants.

Perhaps the soldiers feared that nobody would believe or even remember their war stories if they failed to recount the experiences they had endured. But in describing their service, they reached across the great distance of time and humanized not only for their own generation but for future ones as well a defining moment in American history.

Despite the distance of nearly 150 years between the end of the war and today, there are many stories left to tell. For whatever reason, some regiments on both sides of the Mason-Dixon Line had no one to step forward to write their history, leaving significant gaps in the record of the conflict. Among the units that never produced an account of its service, either in the form of a regimental history or memoirs of its men, was the 16th Massachusetts Infantry, a hard-fighting regiment largely from the Lexington-Cambridge area. In spite of the high level of education of its officers and some of its men, none of its members felt compelled to write down and publish the story of the "Iron Sixteenth," as it was known. The Report of the Adjutant-General of Massachusetts for 1864, in addition, notes that it cannot give an estimate of casualties as "the regimental reports have been lost." The story of Captain Johnson and the 16th Massachusetts has thus lain dormant and neglected while other regiments went on to proclaim publicly their exploits in the Civil War through books and articles.

Yet the regiment's experience was not entirely lost. In the relicts of Captain Charles Robinson Johnson lay a treasure trove of letters waiting for someone to rediscover and publish them so that future generations might learn something of the regiment and its service.

Fortunately, in the late 1970s, Johnson's letters finally came to light, when a college professor who taught at Northern Virginia Community College offered them for sale; presumably the family had died out or no longer had an interest in them. The letters were in excellent condition and, from their coverage, probably essentially intact. Inevitably they covered only the period from the summer of 1861 through the battle of Gettysburg in July 1863. These surviving letters provide, for the first time, an opportunity to present at least the first two-thirds of the 16th Massachusetts' service, thus giving Civil War students substantial new information about the regiment's experience during its three years of war. Further information about Johnson and his regiment has also been researched to augment the picture drawn by Johnson. Our discoveries included a fascinating biographical manuscript unearthed from the Massachusetts Historical Society collections, probably written by his widow, which provides a brief, though readable and touching, account of Johnson's service and experience.

The letters and the Historical Society's manuscript provide the only known substantial personal record of the Iron Sixteenth. A little further material which surfaced through searches of the Internet provide some more insight into the history of the regiment.

The surviving letters total 159. When the grouping was broken up, a high proportion found their way into the hands of two dedicated researchers and collectors of Civil War memorabilia, Albert C. Eisenberg, of Arlington County, Virginia, and Michael Hammerson of London, England. Fortunately, before the letters became divided, the entire set was photocopied, and copies of all found their way to the U.S. Army Military History Institute at Carlisle Barracks, Pennsylvania, via collector William Prince. Thus, in original manuscript or in photocopy, the grouping has essentially remained together. In addition, there exist the official documents in the National Archives pertaining to Johnson, the official battle reports in the extensive *Official Records of the War of the Rebellion*, Federal pension records, and a little more written ephemera, all of which were important in helping to fill out the story. These are interspersed through the narrative in their appropriate places.

Following the sale of Johnson's letters, a collection of his personal items appeared in the catalogue of a Tennessee dealer, the late John L. Heflin, in the late 1970s. This consisted of his engraved presentation Model 1850 foot officer's sword, inscribed with his name, regiment, and the sentiments of his employees, along with his gaudy epaulettes in a japanned tin box, and his commission signed by Massachusetts Governor John A. Andrew, who almost two years after Johnson's commission caused the formation of the famous black regiment, the 54th Massachusetts Infantry. Finally, two photographs of Johnson were located in the collection of the U.S. Army Military History Institute at Carlisle Barracks, Pennsylvania.

A few words as to editorial method. The transcriptions of the letters retain Johnson's original spelling and grammar throughout, including his frequent habit of omitting the 's' from plural words. While it would be tiresome for the reader to put [sic] after every aberration, there were some occasions when the editors considered it helpful to add it, if only to reassure the reader that it was Johnson's original spelling or grammar, rather than a mistake in the transcribing. In the case of letters which only survived as photocopies in the U.S.A.M.H.I. collection, the top or bottom line was occasionally missing; this is indicated as necessary. Places where a word or phrase was illegible are indicated by a line of periods (..........) approximating very broadly to the length of the word. Words or phrases crossed out by Johnson are retained but also lined out. 'Superscripted' written letters at the end of a Johnson abbreviation have been lowered to the line and are followed by a period. Where extracts from published accounts are given in the explanatory narrative, a space filled with three periods (...) indicates that text not considered relevant has been omitted. Johnson also frequently omitted full stops at the end of sentences; these have not been put in by the editors, but to aid in clarity these omissions have been marked by a wider space between the last word of one sentence and the first word of the next.

The editors considered it important that they should research as many of the references to people, places and events as possible which might not be familiar to the readership, or need explanation to understand the context in which they are mentioned; these have been explained or expanded upon in the footnotes. Since, in the editors' view, footnotes at the end of a book are a considerable annoyance involving much page turning and interruption of the narrative, they have been placed at the foot of the page to which they relate. If a footnote merely states "not known" – or one is not given - this indicates either that research failed to find a reference, or that it was impossible to identify a person such as a relative or friend referred to in the letters, often by only a forename, since no other family papers are known to exist.

Finally, Johnson often signed off his letters very hurriedly, reducing his intended "Yours affectionately, Charles (or Charley)" to an illegible scrawl or dashed-off line. In these instances, the full intended words are shown italicized in parentheses.

h

CHAPTER 2
*
CHARLES ROBINSON JOHNSON, HIS LETTERS AND "THE IRON SIXTEENTH"

Born on April 7, 1836, in Boston, Massachusetts, Johnson grew up in Lexington, Massachusetts. He graduated from Boston High School, and studied chemistry at the Scientific School in Cambridge. He married Ellen Walcott, "Nellie," on September 16, 1857, the Rev. A.L. Stone presiding.

The couple had a son, "Berk," short for Berkley, who was four years old at the time that Johnson went to war. Johnson was a partner in the E.A. & W. Winchester Company located at 15 South Market Street, in the Faneuil Hall area of Boston. This site is now the U.S. National Park Service headquarters for the "Freedom Trail," which encompasses the Revolutionary War era Battle Road as well as Concord Bridge, Walden's Pond, and numerous historical icons of the birthplace of the American Revolution, not to mention the more than 1,000 colonial period homes still standing.

Johnson's company dated back to 1809. It manufactured soaps, candles and other sundries. Census records for 1860 noted Johnson as a maker of such items. The company's four "partners" listed in the 1860 Boston directory included the 25-year-old and soon-to-be-Captain Charles Robinson Johnson, his father C. Berkley Johnson, S.S. Winchester, and T.B. Winchester. Charles Johnson was the manager of the firm's factory. The last listing for this company is found in the 1868 Boston directory.

Johnson's letters to his wife reveal a great deal about himself. A businessman of some means, young Johnson was clearly erudite and observant, although in his writings he had a habit of leaving the "s" off of plural words. He depicted in great detail his experiences and the events going on around him. He wrote faithfully and prolifically. Few subjects escaped Johnson's comment, from the clatter of battle and the unsavory character of a general's headquarters, to the frost on a man's beard during a winter march.

Johnson clearly loved his family, repeatedly inquiring about the welfare of Nellie and Berk. He also held a typically Victorian attitude toward women's roles in their households, as he instructed his wife how to arrange family and business affairs in his absence. He refused to allow her to visit him in camp, even though other officers had secured passes for their wives and families to enjoy reunions with loved ones from home during times when the army was inactive. Certainly, money was not an issue, and his father and brother visited him in camp on at least one occasion. Perhaps Johnson feared to place his young wife in the coarse, unwholesome environment of a soldier's camp.

Johnson remained deeply committed to his cause and to his responsibilities as a soldier and an officer. Yet, although he was a product of a Boston society favorable toward abolitionism, his letters show that he had a narrow, even hostile view of African Americans. He felt they could neither make good soldiers nor appropriately exercise the full rights of citizenship upon emancipation.

This attitude was not uncommon in the North and even, ironically, among the patriotic citizens of that most abolitionist of cities, Boston. Notable among such men were the officers of the 20th Massachusetts Infantry, many of whom were from the blue-blooded families of Boston society; though known as the "Harvard Regiment," reflecting the high proportion of its officers who were alumni of that institution, its solid fighting reputation was perhaps slightly counterbalanced by its other nickname, "The Copperhead Regiment," which reflected the strongly anti-abolitionist sentiments of many of its officers.

Such attitudes damaged the Union cause abroad, where Confederate and Union emissaries fought a four-year diplomatic war of their own, notably in England and France, the two world powers of the time, to secure or prevent foreign recognition of the South. Confused Englishmen reasoned that, if the North was not, in fact, fighting to free the slaves, then it could only be fighting for empire against the gallant and oppressed South, heirs of the English Cavaliers of old, fighting for their liberty and independence against the 'mercenary' armies of the North, a high proportion of whose soldiers were of German or Irish origin. With such mixed messages crossing the Atlantic from the North, and with the severe economic impact which the war was having on trade and industry abroad, European sentiment was strongly pro-Southern, and there was until relatively late in the war a continual danger that European armies would intervene on the side of the South.

The 16th Massachusetts came into being during the spring and summer of 1861. It was mustered into the U.S. service on July 12 of that year, enlisting 1372 men into its ranks during its service. Most of them were tradesmen, laborers, and blue-collar workers, with a smattering of sailors, farmers and professionals. They came mostly from Middlesex County. A few hailed from beyond Massachusetts borders, including a couple of men born overseas.

The 16th Massachusetts left the state for Baltimore on August 17, 1861. Then it moved to Camp Hamilton, near Fortress Monroe, in Hampton, Va., where it remained until September 1, at which time it went to the Peninsula of Virginia. During its garrison duty here, near Fortress Monroe, on March 8th and 9th, 1862, Johnson stood on the shoreline, an eyewitness to the epic naval battles involving the Confederate ironclad C.S.S. *Virginia* against the U.S.S. *Congress* and the U.S.S. *Cumberland* on the first day, and the U.S.S. *Monitor* and the C.S.S *Virginia* the following day.

Following the naval battle, the 16th joined in the preparation of McClellan's forces for the Peninsula campaign. In the spring of 1862, the regiment became the first Union unit to enter the cities of Norfolk, Portsmouth and Suffolk. On June 13, the regiment joined the Army of the Potomac before Richmond and on June 25 it encountered the enemy in extending the picket lines, losing 3 killed, 19 wounded and 5 missing in the action. Leading his troops into battle for the first time, Johnson demonstrated the leadership expected of an officer, proudly remarking in a letter home that his men had stood the test well. Johnson himself displayed courage and coolness under fire and never flinched from his duty.

Later that month Johnson was heavily engaged in the Seven Days' battles. Following Lee's attacks north of the Chickahominy River against the isolated Union right wing, the Union forces began to withdraw to a more secure position along the James River south-east of Richmond. The 16th participated in the battles of Glendale on June 30 and Malvern Hill on July 1, where on both occasions it helped thwart Rebel efforts to intercept the withdrawing Union forces. The 16th lost 4 killed, 24 wounded and 32 missing during the two days of fighting. At Glendale, the regiment lost its Colonel, Powell Tremlett Wyman.

The regiment went into camp at Harrison's Landing, where McClellan gathered his beaten army following the end of the Seven Days' Battles.

Johnson felt the need to keep his letters as a record of his service. In his first letter home to his wife Nellie, he made clear that he wanted his letters to be set aside so that the family could benefit from them. His instructions, fortunately, were followed, leaving to his family, and now to us, a rich record of his experiences as an eyewitness and participant in some of the most stirring moments in American history.

Remaining at Harrison's Landing, the fortified encampment where the Army of the Potomac rested after its withdrawal from combat with Rebel forces following the Seven Days' Battles, the regiment was moved to Northern Virginia during late August, participating in the 2nd battle of Bull Run, a serious Union setback. Here the 16th suffered 5 killed, 64 wounded, and 41 missing. Suffering from jaundice, Johnson was not present. Four months later, at Fredericksburg on December 13, 1862, the regiment was present at, but not actively engaged in, the battle and the bloody assaults of other Union units against well-entrenched Confederates on high ground above the city. From there the unit went into winter quarters, where it remained until the following May, except for participation in the abortive "Mud March" of late January 1863, where Major General Ambrose Burnside's army succumbed to the terrible weather conditions, until the movements of the Chancellorsville campaign. At Chancellorsville (May 1st-5th) the 16th found itself supporting the XI Corps, which was smashed by "Stonewall" Jackson's surprise flank attack on the Union right on Saturday, May 2, 1863. In the fight, the 16th lost 82 men killed and wounded, one of whom was Johnson, who suffered a wound to the jaw, for which he received twenty days' home leave – meaning, unfortunately, that there are no letters covering the battle. On July 1, 1863, the 16th reached Gettysburg, Pa., following a hard march to catch and defeat Rebel forces which had crossed the Potomac and invaded Maryland and Pennsylvania. On the late afternoon of July 2, it stood against the furious assaults of Rebel General James Longstreet, taking heavy losses. Johnson went down with two more wounds during the fight along the Emmitsburg Road, which this time were to prove mortal.

From Gettysburg, the Iron Sixteenth fought in most of the major battles of the Army of the Potomac, including the Wilderness and Overland campaigns of 1864, and finally the early stages of the siege of Petersburg. On July 12, 1864 its term of service expired, and the Iron Sixteenth returned home to Boston, leaving behind 16 officers and 134 enlisted men who were killed in action, or had died of wounds or were lost as prisoners of war, plus another 93 enlisted men who perished from disease and other non-battle causes.

Johnson's carefully-preserved letters provide only a partial narrative of the regiment's service. As noted above, jaundice kept him away from Second Bull Run, and so he missed much of the action there and reported little of it. His regiment was present, though basically inactive, at Fredericksburg, and he wrote only a terse note from that field. At Chancellorsville, on May 3, 1863, he sustained a wound from a minie ball which ploughed through the flesh of his lower jaw nearly to his ear. The wound was dressed in the field, and he was granted 20 days' convalescent leave, returning to his regiment in late May from his home in Massachusetts; during that leave, his second child was conceived - a child he never lived to see. As a result, there is no letter from him concerning his participation in that battle.

When he returned to the 16th, his wounds were still not healed. No doubt his debilitating experience fed a growing melancholy that began to appear in his letters by June of 1863. He sounded morose and weary, seriously and extensively writing to his wife about resigning from the service, if he could find an honorable means to do so. Yet he never dwelled on the possibility that he might not return home, other than to use the phrase taken for the title of this book in his letter of July 11, 1862.

In June the Army of the Potomac followed Lee north as the Rebel army invaded Maryland and Pennsylvania. On June 30, 1863, Johnson's personal correspondence comes to an abrupt end at Taneytown, Maryland, just eleven miles south of Gettysburg. Johnson penned a couple of terse, hurried last letters to his wife, two days before the unit saw action at Gettysburg, where on July 2, 1863, the 16th went into action on the Union left center, taking its position along the Emmitsburg Road. During Longstreet's furious assault on that part of the Union line in the late afternoon Johnson went down with wounds to the head and groin.

After his rescue from the battlefield, while in temporary tent hospital quarters, he penned two letters to his commanding officer, one asking for convalescent leave, which was granted, and another from his home in Lexington, informing his superior that he had reached home. His wounds almost certainly became infected, and he died at his home in Cambridge on July 17, 1863, his family at his bedside. In the family plot in Mount Auburn Cemetery, Johnson and his entire family rest with other American heroes. The last gravestone in the family plot bears the date 1991.

The Appendices to this book include three battle reports concerning the role of the 16th in the fighting of July 2. None mentioned Johnson's wounding, but much later, in the official Adjutant General's report on the battle of Gettysburg and the officers who were killed or wounded, Captain Johnson is finally given his due:-

"The name of Captain C. Robinson Johnson will awake in the heart of every soldier of the Sixteenth a feeling of respect and love, which can only die when the last patriot of the Sixteenth is no more. His life was so full of noble deeds and heroic acts that his peaceful death adds to his brilliant record. In camp, on the march, on the field of battle, he was the same. His heroic fortitude, his gallantry, his kindness of heart, reared for him a living monument in the hearts of all soldiers of the command."

CHAPTER 3
*
A CONTEMPORARY NARRATIVE OF JOHNSON'S SERVICE AND DEATH

In the course of our research, a remarkable manuscript, most likely written by Johnson's wife or father, was discovered in the archives of the Massachusetts Historical Society. This describes Johnson's service during his two years with the 16th Massachusetts. The account was loose in an album containing similar documents describing the service of several hundred Massachusetts officers who had died during the war. The first part of the manuscript, which can be found in *Brief Memoranda of our Martyr Soldiers Who Fell During the Great Rebellion of the Nineteenth Century*, compiled by Henry Ingersoll Bowditch, affixed to page 77, is transcribed below; but, for the sake of continuity of the narrative, the parts relating to his experiences at Chancellorsville and Gettysburg and his death, have been put with the Chapters dealing with those battles. It opens:

"Charles Robinson Johnson, the son of C. Berkley Johnson and Sarah B. Johnson, was born at Boston, Mass. on the 3rd April, 1836. He graduated at Boston High School. Went through a course of study in chemistry at the Scientific School, Cambridge. Afterwards became a partner in the house of E.A. & W. Winchester, Boston, which position he left in all the ardor of youth and patriotism to join in the battles of his beloved country.

"From the commencement of this war Capt. Johnson took a deep interest in the affairs of his country. He commenced on the 25th of Apr. 1861, at their request, to drill a few of the young men of Lexington, Mass, so as to be in readiness in case of an emergency. One by one joined the squad 'till their number was considerably increased and they determined to have "Old Lexington" represented in our country's call for companies to assist those who had so hastily left their homes. Capt Johnson thus labored hard and faithfully to recruit a company of three months men, which for some reason was disbanded shortly after it was organised.

"But not discouraged, they set to work again and raised a second company and was about ready to leave when orders were issued from Govt. to accept no more three months men and as they had enlisted for three months the men would not serve for three years. So the second company after much hard labor and expense to recruit the men were allowed to leave, the company was left a skeleton, the officers still holding their commission of which Capt. Johnson held the command. On the first of July Capt. Johnson was ordered to appear at Camp Cameron, Cambridge with not less than thirty five men at the end of the week he entered the Camp. He had not a man left of his second company when he received his orders to appear at Camp Cameron.

"To get his third company he labored with untiring energy. Being fourth July week he was unfortunate in not getting the complement of men in the time required by the Govt. His time was extended under the circumstances. By extraordinary exertions and expense he finally obtained the full complement of men - 101 - in due time. His company was organised, accepted and lettered Company F, 16th Regt. Mass. Vols., July 12th, 1861, which command he held until his death.

"On the 17th of August the Regt. broke camp, marched into Boston took the cars and left for Balt., at which city they arrived 19th Augt. Went into camp at Camp Patterson. On the 20th was ordered to McKim Encampment. They remained in Balt. 'till the first of Sept. when they were ordered to Fortress Monroe, Camp Hamilton, where they remained 'till the 8th of May when they left their old camp for livelier scenes. On the 10th of May the 16th Regt. entered Norfolk. They were the first whole regiment to enter Norfolk, Suffolk & Portsmouth. Early in June they left Suffolk, preceded up to White House, and from thence up the Peninsular. Here they were marched into Grover's Brigade, Hooker's Division and Heintzleman's Corps. Three fine Generals all under our noble Genl. McClellan. On the 18th of June the 16th were under their first fire - woodland skirmishes near the Fair Oaks battle ground, here they lost fifty nine men killed, wounded and missing. Thus commenced the gallant 16th under command of the accomplished officer Col.Wyman.

"Capt. Johnson was in all the Seven Days' fight & Genl. McClellan's retreat from before Richmond. Was in the battles of Second Malvern Hill, Manassas, Chantilly, Fredericksburg, Chancellorsville and lastly Gettysburg. At Chancellorsville he received a wound by a minnie ball ploughing through the flesh of his lower jaw nearly to his ear. Had his wound dressed on the field then walked fifteen miles to get conveyance to Washington - here he obtained a furlough of twenty days which time he passed at home. Left home before his wound was healed reached his Regt. at Falmouth in time to march with it to Pennsylvania to meet the rebel army under Genl. Lee who was then invading that state."

The document continues with descriptions of the circumstances of Johnson's wounding at Chancellorsville and Gettysburg, his journey home on each occasion, and subsequent death. As stated above, these parts of it are given at the ends of those chapters.

CHAPTER 4
*
OFF TO WAR

Johnson was a 26-year-old Bostonian, and a partner in the E.A. & W. Winchester company of that city when he joined the Union army at Cambridge on July 12, 1861. He was mustered into the U.S. Service at Boston that same day. Johnson's letters are to his wife Nellie, whom he married on September 16th, 1857. The couple had two children: a boy, Charles Berkeley, born September 7, 1859, and a girl, born February 8, 1864, seven and a half months after Johnson's death from wounds received at Gettysburg.

In 2004, 27 years after the letters were bought, copied, and dispersed, Michael Hammerson discovered an article in the July 31, 1861, *Boston Daily Courier*, page 2, column 5, describing the ceremony held to present Johnson with his inscribed sword, his epaulettes, and his sash. The sword, epaulettes, and the box in which they were stored have survive, but the sash is lost; being made of silk, it may have disintegrated. The article reads as follows:-

"SIXTEENTH MASSACHUSETTS

LETTERS OF THE CIVIL WAR.
JULY 31, 1861.

" *The employees of the Messrs. Winchester, the well known soap and candle manufacturers, met at the New England House yesterday afternoon, for the purpose of presenting an elegant sword to Capt. Charles R. Johnson, of Company F, Sixteenth (Wyman's) Regiment. Mr. Johnson, since the war began, has formed two companies; but the gold lace gentlemen at the State House have prevented their acceptance. The company which he is now destined to command is the third that he organized, and it is composed of able and brave men. Capt. Johnson is a joint partner in the house of E. A. & W. Winchester. He is a man of education and fortune; a national democrat, who, at the last Congressional election, marched sixty-five Unionists to the polls, who voted for Mr. Appleton. As the Captain entered the room, attended by his friends, Messrs. S. S. Winchester and Eben Fogg, he was cheered by the company. Mr. Fogg spoke as follows:*

'*Captain Johnson: On behalf of the operatives in the establishment with which you have been connected, I have the pleasure of presenting you with a sword, sash and a pair of epaulettes, which they beg you to accept as a slight token of their esteem and good wishes.*

'*While we regret your departure, we honor you for the patriotism which has led you to volunteer for the defence of our common country. That your efforts and those of the other* brave sons of Massachusetts may be speedily crowned with complete success, and that you may return in safety to your friends, is our sincere prayer'.

"Capt. Johnson feelingly responded, 'that he felt proud and grateful that those with whom he had had daily intercourse for the past six years, had so kindly remembered him; that as he had buckled on the sword at his country's call, he should not take it off until the holy purposes of the war were accomplished, and that the motto on the sword was henceforth his motto, and that whether he returned, or fell in the conflict, the recollection of this day would be a green spot in his memory.' James Dennie spoke thus:

'Your action today speaks volumes for your appreciation of the patience, self denial and perseverance which Capt. Johnson has under gone to place himself in the proud position he now occupies, for when one like him, in the full enjoyment of happiness and prosperity, is about to leave family, friends and a competency to risk his life in the defense of his country, you may indeed feel proud of him, and I speak but the glances of your moistened eyes when I know you all wish him God speed, and pray that ere long he may again be the representative of that firm (Winchester) which has so long been a symbol of the highest mercantile honor and integrity'. Grandville Mears, Esq., was introduced and said:

'Capt. Johnson, I need not assure you of the pleasure I experience in being present on this occasion, assembled, as we are, to give those with whom you have been long associated, and best know your sterling worth and manly courage, an opportunity to testify by this noble gift, not only their warm, friendly attachment to you, but their devotion to our beloved Union.

'In times like these, you, sir, as well as every American, experience a thrill of pleasure which words faintly express, in witnessing the patriotic devotion of America's adopted sons rallying under the Stars and Stripes in defense of that country which we trust will ever be the "Land of the free and home of the brave."

'In our country's early history, how many bright jewels from Erin's green isle adorn its pages; and now, true to the instincts of their noble sires, their sons of the Sixty-ninth have added the key stone to that glorious arch.

'We have heard of a traitor Johnson at Winchester, we now have a patriot Johnson from Winchester. Should it be the good fortune of you and those of your command to meet him, I trust he will soon be convinced the resemblance is only in name.

'Go forth, my young friend, like Saul, feeling assured that, like him, God is with you, and when you draw that trusty steel, may its motto and the prayers of its donors nerve your arm to glorious victory.'

After which, by invitation of the Messrs. Winchester, the operatives partook of a bountiful collation at the New England House.

The sword bears this inscription: 'Presented by the employees of Messrs. F. A. & W. Winchester to Capt. C. Johnson, Co. F, 16th Regt. Mass. Volunteers, July, 1861,' and the motto is: 'Draw me not without cause, Sheathe me not without honor.' "

CHAPTER 5
*
FROM MASSACHUSETTS TO FORTRESS MONROE

The Roxbury City Gazette for August 22 announced the Regiment's departure: "On last Saturday afternoon, the Sixteenth Regiment of Massachusetts Volunteers left Camp Cameron, at North Cambridge, for the seat of war. The baggage wagons, ambulances, and hospital wagons, numbering thirty-two, were sent in advance of the regiment, and arrived in Boston at 9 o'clock, A.M. At 9 1/2 the regiment was formed in line, in marching order, and heavily equipped. In the cartridge box of each solder were forty rounds of cartridges. Each soldier also carried two days' rations. The regiment altogether takes seven days cooked rations and sixty thousand cartridges.

"At half past eleven the regiment started on its march from North Cambridge to Boston, which was accomplished in quick time, the weather being cool and favorable. The regiment was accompanied by the brigade and regimental bands, each of them alternatively furnishing the music. Arriving in Boston, they marched through Cambridge, Charles, Beacon Park, Tremont, School, Washington, Summer and South Streets, to the Old Colony Depot, being all the way vociferously cheered by the crowd.

"The whole number of men in the regiment, according to the report of last Friday, was 1,033. Of these six were left behind, slightly sick, but will soon be able to rejoin the regiment. Five of the men were taken along as prisoners, having attempted to desert.

"This regiment is one of the best provided and equipped that have been sent to active service."

h

Camp McClellan   Baltimore Aug 25 [1861]

Dear Nellie,

We have been blessed with beautiful weather since I last wrote to you and every thing seems to go smoothly along. The nights here are very cool and the days are very comfortable we have had no very warm weather as yet. Lieut Mayo[1] has been roaming about the city today and he says the Sundays are better kept here than in Boston, there is a fine of five dollars for every cigar sold and he could not find a restaurant open. It is about time now for church call 4 1/2 oclock and I am going to hear Mr Fuller[2] discourse so I expect to be interrupted every moment. You may want

---

[1] 1st Lt. Charles H. Mayo, of Roxbury; commissioned Aug. 1, 1861; mustered out Aug. 10, 1862; commissioned 2nd Lt., 3rd Mass. Heavy Artillery,Sept. 10, 1863; dismissed July 26, 1864.

[2] Arthur Buckminster Fuller (1822-1862), Regimental Chaplain. Chaplain of a church in Watertown, Mass.

to know how I am situated, the appearance of my tent and the arrangement of it. I have for my domicile what is called a wall tent with a fly over it which makes its [sic] rain proof; in the centre of it is one of those square table which father gave me on which I am writting [sic]; over my head hang my overcoat and other clothing, on a cord suspended between the two upright poles of my tent. I have my mess chest on my right and my bed folder upon my left and am sitting with my back to the opening of my tent which look[s] down company street[3] . Watermelon, cantelopes & peaches are very cheap   watermelon can be bought for 2.00 a hundred and you buy the best at five cts a piece, cantelopes three cents   peaches little dearer. Nellie I believe I left behind your daguerrotype[4]   if I did please send it on   also send me some letters and newspapers. Give my love to all my friend father, mother, Berk (little) and write to me often directing to Camp McClellan, Baltimore. Yours
     Charley

****

           Camp McClellan Aug 29 [1861]
Dear Nellie,
  It is a rainy day and not much drilling to do so I will send you a few lines. We had a serious accident today which I fear will result in the loss of one of the men of the regiment; one of the sentinels accidently shot another sentinel the ball going through the lungs. I think by the appearance of things that we shall make a long stay here and while here their will be no danger of our regiment being in any danger. The weather is still quite cool which is unusual here at this season. There is nothing of interest taking place at our camp   it is nearly the same routine every day, I have but little praise to give to Mr Smith either for the fit or the material of my coat. It is about time for supper so I shall close. I saw an officer from Gen Banks[5] division   and he thought that they [sic] would soon be another battle.
    Yours affectionately,
    C Robinson Johnson
    Commander Co F

****

---

at outbreak of war, he enlisted on August 1st, 1861, and resigned on Dec. 10th, 1862, on account of sickness. He had just received his discharge, when he learned that his regiment was about to go into action at Fredericksburg. Crossing the river in the boats with the forlorn hope, he joined the skirmishers of the Nineteenth Massachusetts, who were then fighting their way through the streets. He was shot dead, rifle in hand, in front of a grocery store on Caroline Street. Fuller was one of eleven Union Chaplains to die in battle in the war. The renowned mathematician, R. Buckminster Fuller, was his grandson. His sister, Margaret Fuller Ossoli (1810-1850), was a leading author, feminist and abolitionist of the era; her posthumous memoirs were compiled and edited in 1852 by Ralph Waldo Emerson.

[3] The space along either side of which the company's tents were laid out.

[4] Johnson habitually calls a photograph by this name. The daguerreotype, invented in France in 1839 by Louis Daguerre, had been rendered obsolete in the early 1850s by the ambrotype, tintype and albumen print. However some, like Johnson, continued to call any photograph by that name, although he is undoubtedly referring either to a tintype or a carte-de-visite, a small albumen print highly popular during the war for photographs of the soldiers; millions were made, and still exist.

[5] Major-General Nathaniel P. Banks (1816-1894), at that time commanding Banks' Division, Army of the Potomac.

Camp McClellan   Sept. 1/61

Dear Nellie,

    Sunday has come round once more & I sit down to scratch off a few lines to you. I received a letter from you Friday eve last in which you said you had not received a letter from me that week, which shows that they must be careless at the store in regard to forwarding them to Manchester; if I had your address at Manchester, it would expedite your receiving letters and save three cents[6] . I shall only commence this letter now waiting until evening to finish it. After dinner I expect to take a walk around the city and as it is a perfect day I think I shall enjoy it amazingly. We have very cool mornings here with but little to relieve the monotony. The other day (being officer of the day) I arrest [sic] a secesh[7] outside of the lines who had been bothering the sentinels the last week he was sent to Fort Lafayette[8] . I think I shall make a practice of not saying anything about military movements which come to my notice in any other way than through newspapers but it is the opinion here that there will be fighting before long, the pickets of each army are so near that to use the common expression they can shake hands with each other.

****

Sept. 3, 1861   Old Point Comfort[9]

Dear Nellie,

    I commenced a letter last Sunday morning leaving it unfinished intending to complete it in the even after I had finished or return from my walk in the afternoon, having have leave of absent until six and half o'clock P.M. I left the camp to take a stroll around the way a little while after dinner intending to visit some of the various camps about the city. I paid a visit to a camp occupied by the Mass. 17 & Nim's battery[10] which was from three to four miles from my camp. While there I heard rumors of our regiment leaving for fort Monroe and the seventeen taking our place, and on going to the Lieut. Colonel of the seventeenth I found the rumor to be true, we were order to fort Monroe. I hurried back to camp immediately, found my baggage all packed up, part of the tents struck and your unfinished letter in the trunk with the other articles. At six o'clock we left camp McClellan and went on board the steamboat Louisiana and nothing occurred unusual until next morning when we heard loud noise from the machinery and the boat stopped; on examination they found the cylinder head [knocked] out and bolts to stuffing box broken and we consequently dropped anchor waiting for something to come to our assistance. We had not waited long when the Adelaide came in sight and came alongside when our company and three others went aboard of her; hawsers fasten[ed] both steamboats together and we

---

[6] i.e. the cost of a postage stamp.

[7] Contemptuous Northern abbreviation of "Secessionist".

[8] In New York Harbour, used during the war as a prison, particularly for political prisoners, spies, etc.; conditions there were harsh.

[9] The extreme southern tip of the Virginia Peninsula, the location of Fortress Monroe and, later in the war, the base for exchange of prisoners-of-war in the east.

[10] 2nd Massachusetts Battery, Light Artillery

went at about 6 miles an hour arriving at our destination, fort Monroe[11], in the afternoon, where after considerable delay we embarked. We are very near the enemy, though I do not realize it, the outer picket guard are only one mile from my tent and the enemy have control of all land outside that. Sewall's point[12] is plainly seen from where I am and the rebels have a strong battery there, in fact they have batteries all along the sea opposite to us. I am quartered in a tent belonging to an officers of Turner's Regiment[13] who has gone to Cape Hatteras. our tents and baggage have not arrived yet. There are about us a part of Turner's regiment comprised mostly of Germans who have done every thing for our comforts that was in their power. I hope we shall get paid off soon as money is getting to be a scarce article with us, officers have to buy what they eat and being without money is being almost without food. The news of the taking of fort Hatteras[14] is very cheering I hope it will soon be followed by similar successes.

    From yours,
     Affectionately,
      C. Robinson Johnson

(Dear Mother, I received this last night, please lay Charles' letters that I send you one side as I want to keep them as we shall enjoy reading them, and showing them to Berkley. I guess Berkley knows this is his birth day for he is talking at a great rate, he puts five or six words together, as fast as can be. This pattern is eight cents a yard, delain[?] width. Love to all from your affectionate daughter, Nellie)

****

            Old Point Comfort Sept. 8/61
Dear Nellie,
  The letter was commenced at Baltimore and I was not able to finish it owing to the order which the regiment received to strike tents and pack; I being absent when the order was given; the commencement of this letter was put into my trunk & my trunk on to the baggage wagon[15] or I should have sent it on as it was. I was Officer of

---

[11] An old but strong coastal defence work which remained in Federal hands throughout the war. Its location at the tip of the Virginia Peninsula enabled it to cover the entrance to the James River. It was the base friom which the 1862 Peninsula Campaign was launched.

[12] Across Hampton Roads from Fort Monroe, held by the Confederates

[13] The 20th New York Infantry ("The United Turner Regiment"), also garrisoned at the time at Fortress Monroe.

[14] Guarding the entrance to Pamlico Sound and the North Carolina ports, it was captured in a Federal amphibious operation on Aug.29, 1861.

[15] According to the 1861 U.S. Army Regulations, "baggage to be transported is limited to camp and garrison equipage, and officers' baggage. Officers' baggage shall not exceed (mess-chest and all personal effects included) as follows:

	In the Field	Changing Stations
General Officers	125 pounds	1000 pounds
Field Officers	100 "	800 "
Captains	80 "	700 "
Subalterns	80 "	600 "

the Day[16] yesterday & last night that is regimental officer of the day; their is also a Field Officer of the Day who duties it is to visits the picket guard and have the general care of the whole field their being three regiments here encamped together viz. the 20th N.Y.[17] & the Naval brigade. Our pickets have been fired at several times but without any results, our pickets find every night something to fire at but nothing has as yet been captured except an empty boat that I really know of there are always plenty of rumors afloat. The picket guard are the outer guard and are commanded by a Captain and two Lieutenants divided into three post the Captain have immediate care of the centre post; it is a situation requiring great vigilance and none of the officers commanding are allowed to sleep. There seemed yesterday some movement of the enemy at Sewall's point and on the opposite short. The weather here is not very warm except at midday then the sun is very hot. I should have sent you by last letters two small pieces of the secesh flag which waved over Fort Hatteras[18] and also some threads out of a Lieut. Col. Sash who was captured there it will be an old string when you receive it. The mosquitoes here are very thick and annoying. I received your letter[19] of Sept. 5 and also some paper. I received also a letter from *[illegible]* which I shall answer. I received your photograph[20] Thursday. Write often and I will try to do the same.

    From yours
     affectionately
      Charley

---

[16] While the 1861 Regulations do not define what an Officer of the Day is, various sections give his duties. He must "see that the officer of the guard is furnished with the parole and countersign before retreat"; he "visits the guards during the day at such times as he may deem necessary, and makes his rounds at night at least once after 12 o'clock"; upon being relieved, he "will make such remarks in the report of the officer of the guard as circumstances requiure, and present the same at headquarters"; he "is charged with the order and cleanliness of the camp"; he "satisfies himself frequently during the night, of the vigilance of the police guard and advanced post. He prescribes patrols and rounds to be made by the officer and non-commissioned officers of the guard".

[17] The "United Turner Regiment", of predominantly German soldiers. From June 1861 to May 1862, it had just returned to Fortress Monroe after participating in the capture of Forts Hatteras and Clarke, N.C. on August 28-29. The name derives from the German Turner Society of St. Louis; Turners taught gymnastics and physical culture to young German-Americans. This, in turn, was named after the celebrated gymnastic school, or Turnschule, attended by many who had fled to America after the revolution of 1848 and formed a gymnastic society, or turnverein, later called the St. Louis Turnverein. At the outbreak of the Civil War it had over five hundred enrolled members. Entire companies of volunteers, and almost entire regiments, were made up almost exclusively of Turners; the Seventeenth Missouri was known as the Western Turners' Regiment.

[18] The first major combined operation of the war. Marines from Flag Officer Silas H. Stringham's Squadron and 900 soldiers (including the 20th New York - see footnote 16) under Major General Benjamin F. Butler took the two forts on August 28-29, sealing off Hatteras Inlet, N.C. against commerce and blockade running and securing a valuable coal and supply base for the blockading U.S. Fleet. Johnson's note in the same letter about sending two pieces of the Confederate flag which flew over Fort Hatteras suggests that he had a friend in that regiment.

[19] Regrettably, no letters to Johnson from his wife or father survive. This may be explained by his observation at the end of his letter of August 12, 1862 that he burned all letters when the regiment marched.

[20] One of the rare occasions when Johnson uses the word "photograph", rather than "daguerreotype" (see note 4).

****

Old Point Comfort,   Sept. 15th [1861]

Dear Nellie,

    I received yesterday your letter of the 11th for which I am thankful. I receive from you about two letters a week sometimes more I use to receive papers every other day until lately when they have not come so often. I received the paper having the death of Mr. Tibbett's wife & other news; it contained more real news than any I have as yet received. I was officer of the picket guard Thursday; the duties lasting 24 hour. One picket guard is divided into the centre guard which I had the command of one guard stationed on what I call the Foxhill road[21] & the third at Hampton Bridge[22] , opposite the ruin of the town of the same name. I had a beautiful day & splendid moonlight night & the post of some of the sentinels are delightful. We have no tent but simply some brush thrown up as shelter for the guard house, and the sentinel are placed on the skirt of woods and brush out of sight from the enemy outside. (I have just received a letter from you & two papers; a letter from mother containing $5.00 & three papers from father all of which came at the right time as it is Sunday, and I shall have a fine opportunity to read them after dinner) The post of some of the sentinel are delightfully situated and the scenery from them would make a pretty picture. The delightful weather & scenery and the general quietness which existed put me so much in mind of Lexington that I felt a little homesick, one of the post is situated on a bank overlooking a creek or small river while farther down towards the mouth lies the ruins of Hampton, plainly visible it is a melancholy sight to see on such a pleasant locality for a town nothing but deserted ruins where once existed the prettiest village of Virginia. It would take but little imagination to carry one back to Lexington & forget the object of history here. Yesterday I went on top of a large building which was used as a female seminary and is capable of accommodating I should think a thousand scholars. The rebels left behind seven [.........] and in the room apparently occupied by an artists studio were unfinished paintings and drawings evidently the work of a novice. Todays is one of those days which we have sometime enjoyed together in Lexington not a cloud is to be seen and a gentle breeze from the water make it cool and delightful. Thank mother for her letters and father for his newspapers no mention was made in mother letter of five dollars which it contained. Nellie I would not pay an exorbitant price for board as I do not wish to depend on my friends at all I hope to be able to send you some money soon but I do not know how soon we shall get paid I have been obliged to borrow I have plenty now I am glad Berk is getting along so nicely. My love to my friends.

                                              Yours affectionately,
    Charley

Friday night we were warned to be ready in a minutes notice as it was expected that the enemy would attack Newport News[23] that night.

---

[21] No roads of this name are shown on the detailed maps of the area in Plates XVIII. 1 and 2 of the *Official Military Atlas*.; but see Joseph Kinsley's letter of October 2, 1861.

[22] Probably the main bridge immediately south-east of the ruined town, crossing Hampton Creek and running towards Fortress Monroe.

[23] The southernmost tip of the Yorktown Peninsula, 7 miles west of Fortress Monroe and, like it, also heavily defended by the Federals.

[Old Point Comfort]
Virgingia [sic]
Sept. 17 [1861]

Dear Nellie,
I am still located outside Fortress Munroe with but little prospect of changing locality. It is about 8 o'clock in the evening and my labors for the day are done, the wind is blowing quite hard with occasional flashing of lightening but it is an agreeable ending of a very warm day. At noon here unless there is a good breeze it is very warm but I do not notice it any more than I would warm weather at home. There has nothing happened [*next page photocopied incompletely*] my usual custom, ...rd's Hampton which ....vated from our pickets .... small river, across this [is a] bridge completed within [abou]t 3 rods of the opposite [side] but the commun[ica]tion is kept up by placing ....d cart midway between [the] bridge and shore and [connec]ting the bridge with the ....cart & handcart with ...... by planks .... at night are drawn in; [the] end of the bridge towards [the] opposite shore is barr[ica]ded to resist any attempt [by the] enemy to cross it, also [there] are two earth Battery's [draw]n up commanding the *[line missing]* way into Hampton and about the ruins; this town as I have said before was the prettiest town in Virginia and inhabited by wealthy (& retired from business) people, containing private boarding schools & private institutions of learning, & if I can believe reports the air was fragrant with the odor of roses in summer, which were largely cultivated here. I was told that there were at least seventy houses burnt & property valued at over million dollars; in a town containing only 2500 inhabitants is a large amount. There is but very little sickness here .... by sickness only .... by accident. I wish [you] would write father [and] tell him where to direct [you]r letters, for I do not [.............]eve I shall write to [........] me but you. I receive [the] papers from you to day .... Weekly Pictorial &c [for] which I am much obliged .... can write me as [of]ten as you feel a mind to [I] enjoy receiving letters [fro]m home.
From yours
Affectionately
Charley

****

Sunday Sept. 22 [1861]

Dear Nellie,
I received a letter from mother and one from you dated Sept. 20. I wrote a letter to you last week on Sunday & Tuesday and you should have received two letters instead of one last Thursday. We are having today one of our easterly storm and it remind me very much of some of the rainy Sunday which we often passed together at E. Cambridge. I had beans for breakfast but no brown bread & Evening Gazette without saying anything about the absent of you & Berk. I believe house keeping is the only life for a married man to live for I never look back to the winter we spent at Mrs Welbasky's for pleasant reminiscences; but I can recall any number of pleasant times enjoyed at Lexington & E. Camb. Today I recall forcible my usual Sunday breakfast and I hope I may be able to enjoy many more of them. I walked this morning to the fort, the rain have ceased for a time, I took it easy, walking slowly, most of the way beside the sea shore; though I have been on the same road often yet it seems new

today. The tents of the three regiments outside the fort are along the same line the 16th being the farthest away and on the extreme left so I have to pass the other two regiments on my way to the fort. After getting outside the line of tents a short walk bring you to the bridge which connects the peninsula which the fort is on with the main land, after crossing the bridge their is a narrow strip of land, which looks as if the water would cover it in a gale, which encloses a very pretty basin of water about as large as Sandy Pond on one side and on the other side is James River which is here from five to six miles wide. The scenery here is quite pretty increased by the large number of vesels of all descriptions anchored here, small tug-boats and mammoth men-of-war. On leaving the ismuth and entering the small square from which is the entrance of the Fort I thought myself in some foreign place, the square was occupied here and there by groups of darkies with marines & soldiers of different regiments passing to & fro & a detachment of regulars marching out of the fort was a seen unusual to me in this country. I mention a singular coincidence   there is a Capt. Johnson of Co. F Naval Brigade, so you see there are here two Capt. Johnson's of Co. F. There are plenty of figs growing here but the most of them are outside of the picket and we only get them when some of the contraband bring them into camp. There were two shots cannons fired from the Rip Raps[24] last night but do not know what at. The mail is about to start, must close, direct all letter here until further notice.

    Yours affectionately   Charles

****

    Camp Hamilton, Va.[25] *[undated - late Sept/early Oct. 1861]*

Dear Nellie,

It is fast day and we past it the same as we do our Sundays. There has nothing of interest transpired. We have had two regiment arrive here in the last 24 hours; and there is rumors that there will be barracks put up here to winter the troops. Those pickles which you sent me from Manchester are very nice, I have still some left. I have not as yet tasted of mother pickles, but they look good. I received a letter from you & one from Winnie & Austin dated the [............]. You must not believe all the papers say we are doing as I have seen several false reports lately. I hope to be paid off soon it will be only up to Aug 31 a little over a month and shall not be able to send you much money this time. There is something unusual occurring towards Sewall's Point between two steam boats I believe both have the flag of truce up. I have not time to write anymore if I send this letter today. Tell mother that her cake is very nice and tell father when he send me another box if he ever does to put in a box of pens. I must now take the men to bathe for which purpose we have a delightful beach very handy to the camp.

    from yours Affectionately   Charley

****

    Oct. 2/61   Camp Hamilton

Dear Nellie,

It is the end of the first quarter and I have had considerable business to do

---

[24] A small island half-way between Fortress Monroe and Confederate-held Willoughby's Point on the south side of Chesapeake Bay. On it was located Fort Wool, used mainly by the U.S. Army as a military prison.

[25] Located between Hampton and Fort Monroe, on the neck of land between Hampton Creek and Mill Creek.

and consequently have neglected to write to you or any body else   Their has been but little of interest transpired with the exception of one of the pickets belonging to the 20th N.Y. regt. being shot in the leg by some rebel scout which is the first incident of the kind that has happened since I have been here. Sunday morning I arrayed myself in my best clothes expecting to go on board the frigate Roanoke[26] but on arriving at the wharf where the landing is made I learnt that she had sailed the day previous. The square at the entrance to Fortress Monroe always presents to me something unusual which is the only place I have as yet been in that forcible reminds me that I am away from home; there are generally assembled here Sunday mornings soldiers and marines from every regiment & frigate mingled with the colored servants and contrabands making a strange and heretofore an unusual sight in this country. I am detailed for guard (picket) tomorrow so I shall not be at home tomorrow. I leave the camp for the picket at nine o'clock tomorrow morning and do not return until nine o'clock the day after, if it is a pleasant day I shall enjoy it. I received today from you a box containing, 1 bottle coffee, 1 box of milk and 1 bottle of medicine, also a letter, a bundle of papers from you and 1 from father. I received from father every thing which he sent me as by his letter and I will see that it is well dealt out to the men. Lieut Tucker[27] will leave here soon to recruit what men we need   he has been on the sick list nearly all the time that he has been here; he will probably call to see you. Let father know I have received those articles which he sent me   shall write him in a day or two. Excuse the shortness of this letter, I shall write a longer one next time.

                from yours   affectionately   Charley

=====================

(Johnson's narrative is here supplemented by a letter discovered in the Cambridge, Mass., Chronicle for October 12, 1861, page 2, column 1, sent in by "J.W.K.", identified as Joseph W. Kinsley of Co. A. A typical letter of the time submitted by a soldier to his home newspaper, it nevertheless adds to the picture of life in the regiment in the area of Fortress Monroe)

                                      Headquarters, 16th Regt. Mass. Vols.
                                              Camp Hamilton, Oct. 2, 1861.

Mr. Editor:

Having an opportunity, I shall improve it by giving you a brief account of the doings of the "Sixteenth."

When I wrote last, we had just arrived here and had not got fairly settled; but now we are considering ourselves old settlers, in consideration of the large number of troops coming and going. We have now some six thousand men in and about the fortress, but General Wool wants to concentrate about forty thousand troops here, and then he

---

[26] U.S.S.Roanoke, a 46-gun screw frigate commissioned in 1858, was present at the Monitor-Merrimac fight on 8th March, 1862. It was decommissioned 17 days later and converted into a Monitor - the only one to have three turrets. The combined weight of the turrets was too heavy, the draft too great, and the freeboard too low to allow either inshore or ocean operating, and her whole wartime service was spent guarding Hampton Roads.

[27] 2nd Lt. Payson Elliot Tucker, a 27 year old lawyer from Cambridge, was commissioned on July 12, 1861 into Co. F of the 16th. He resigned on September 21, 1862. He was also a member of GAR Post # 68 (Dorchester), and died on June 20, 1896 in Brookline, Massachusetts

commence operations on the coast, and further more our Colonel assures that we shall quarter in Yorktown this winter. Yorktown is a city about ten miles from here, where are encamped a considerable number of troops; they are nearest to us of any body of rebels.

But little of interest is transpiring here at present. Now and than a scouting party goes out to see what is going on in the suburbs. The first scouting party sent out from this regiment was from Co. A, under command of Lieut. Samuel McKeever, with nine of his company. We went to Hampton at night, and after prowling around amongst the ruins for several hours and finding no one, we returned to resume our search the next morning. So at daybreak we again crossed the bridge and soon were upon the spot we had visited the night before. Here we saw where the Fourth Massachusetts Regiment was quartered; and in an old house used by them for a guard house, we found written on the walls the names of many of them. We also saw the battery, nearly a mile long, built by them and others who were encamped there at the time. There are no troops there now, and but few white persons, and they have to hold a protection from Maj. Gen. Wool. There are also several colored families living there, some of them occupying the mansions formerly occupied by their masters. We also found large quantities of corn, fruit, &c., growing there, much of which will go to waste, as no one is allowed to carry any off, although almost every one that goes there tries to find some relic; and many letters, books, etc. are found and carefully preserved or sent home to friends. But it is very seldom any one is seen there, except those who belong there, although on the picket guard, at a post about a mile from Hampton, on what is called the Fox Hill Road, a corporal from the Twentieth New York regiment was fired upon and shot in the hip. A scouting party was immediately sent out in search of the person or persons who had done this, but they could not be found. The party returned much disappointed.

Thursday, Sept. 26, being East Day at home, was duly observed here, by order of General Wool. We had services by the Chaplain at 10 o'clock, drill being dispensed with for the day. The next day, we were visited by the "line storm." which was pretty severe, a heavy wind raging at the time, depriving some of their tented homes for the night, also driving many small vessels ashore, although doing but little damage except to keep back the steamer a short time, with our mail, which, by the way, is eagerly watched for, and gratefully received by both officers and men. Hundreds of papers and letters arrive for different companies. In one paper received some time ago, we saw a statement that we have been paid off on the 18th ult., although we knew nothing of any such occurrence, but I suppose it was thought that this, like other reports, would be some consolation, and perhaps would answer the same purpose as if it were true. As yet we have not received any pay from government, although we have been sworn into the United States service over three months, and our company were in camp two months previous to that, at Spy Pond and Watertown. But hoping payday is not far distant, I remain, until then,

    Yours, &c.   J. W. K.   Co. A, Sixteenth Regt. Mass. Vols.

****

Old Point Comfort   Oct. 5 /61

Dear Nellie,

I have not written as often as usual as I have been very busy. I was officer of the picket guard yesterday but nothing worthy of mention happened; one of the pickets was considerably alarmed, but without cause; there was not a gun fired during the night. Nellie I received yesterday from you a letter dated Sept. 30th which I carefully perused I should like to see Berk very much, but do not expect to see any of my family for sometime to come; you must not entertain the idea of visiting me though I should be very happy to see you, it will be one of the happiest days when I shall return to visit you, but I think an officer can not attend to his duties as well when he has an attraction which he might want to see oftener than his duties would allow him to. You would be oblige to board a mile away from camp and perhaps would not see me more than once every other day. There are rumors that there will be next week a large addition to our force and when we have a large force here we may make a start at any moment to attack the enemy, which would suit the men. Lieut Tucker you will see before you receive this letter and he can give you any information you may wish to obtain. I would endeavour to obtain from the state the money which it allows to wives whose husbands are in the army, if you consult father he will tell you how to go to work to obtain it. We have not as yet received any pay though it is a month over the time which we should have been paid off. We are all out of money but have been able to borrow enough to get along with, and, I am happy to say, there has been but little grumbling among the men on that account. I may go to Newport News tomorrow and if I do I shall have something new to write about. The weather here is occasionally cool but pleasant. I shall send home my iron bed as soon as I receive from Lieut. Tucker a hammock which he is to send to me. and you might use it for Berk it is low. My love to all.

      From yours Affectionately   Charley

=====================

                Old Point Comfort   Oct 9th /61

Dear Nellie,

  It is about eight o'clock in the evening the wind blowing hard and quite cool but I am quite comfortably situated and I shall soon have a little stove in my tent. I shall not write any more tonight as since I commences [sic] this I was oblige to leave off to do something more important. Last Sunday I went to Newport News on a little pleasure trip and enjoyed it much. It is now about six o'clock in the morning and raining hard which will make the third day of the storm which corresponds in every shape to our N.E. storms. It blows hard and rains hard. It is about seven miles from water from Old Point Comfort to Newport News the steamer that runs between the two places is commodious, kept neat and a moderate fast sailer. You past by Sewall's Point and with the aid of my opera glass could see the battery but not very distinctly the rebel flags was plain enough but an earth battery does not show very plain as their is no contrast between it and the objects around it. On Craney Island which is about six miles from Sewall's Point and seven from Newports News in the direction of Norfolk there is a large rebel camp it would to appearance accommodate more than 5,000 men, they have there a tall flag-pole and a large secesh flag flying on it. Newport News or that part of it on which our breastworks are is a high bluff and to all appearance it was covered with woods and I believe some fields of wheat when our troops first occupied it, we have now an extensive breastwork, capable of containing ten thousand men, and a number of large cannons mounted. On the water side we have our largest cannons consisting of two rifled and three columbiads, the rifled cannon can throw a ball or shell across to the other shore. You probably will see the letter which I wrote to father yesterday about our being in expectation of an attack and being up half night. Last night the men were ordered to sleep on their arms and one or two companies sent out reconnoitring. I for my part think there will be no attack and the prospect of a fight small. I received today a letter from you and your mother Altree[?] also two papers from somebody. I receive considerably more papers from father and he & you had better come to some understanding so as not to send papers of the same date. Nellie I have my breakfast at 1/2 past 6 o'clock, dinner 12 o'clock supper as [sic] six o'clock. I hope you wont have to pay over $15.00 per week as payment will come in very shortly by that I mean you cannot tell when you will be paid off. I may find time to write this evening to Mr. Soule and your mother if possible.

I understand that we shall be paid off tomorrow. I shall send some money home and I would deposit it with father and draw on him whenever you want any. Tell father this money is for services rendered up to Sept. 1 and I shall have some more pay rolls to make out in about ten days.

From yours affectionately   Charley

****

Sunday Oct. 13 [1861]   Camp Hamilton

Dear Nellie,

I received a letter dated Oct. 10th and two papers from you today and were carefully perused. The band is playing near my tent which it does every pleasant evening. We are having today a sample of a clear fall day the mornings quite cool. Yesterday I went to Hampton after timber to make the men comfortable taking fifteen men from company B with Lieut Flagg[28] of the same company. I believe I have before mentioned that the bridge ends two rods from the opposite shore and the communication is completed by means of one or two loose plank which are taking in night times, the end of the bridge near Hampton is barricaded and behind the barricade is posted our picket. On arriving on the Hampton side I had six men and a sergeant posted on the outskirts as sentinels to warn us of danger the remainder of the men were divided into two working parties to procure boards of which we gathered two four horse loads. The expression of all the private what a pity the place was burnt and what a beautiful place this must have been. It must have been a melancholy sight for the inhabitants to have witnessed the conflagration for it is a sad sight now to wander among the ruins of the houses. I noticed a sewing machine the wood work burnt off but iron work not much injured. There are some houses in the outskirts still standing and one which I entered appeared to have been finished this spring too late to be occupied. There is a rumour that Gen Magruder[29] is being tried at Richmond by court martial for the burning of it. There were ten of our men captured by a party of horseman at Newport News while gathering wood outside camp a company was sent to retake them but did not succeed. The alarm or rather the suspicion of an attack has disappeared and we are about our usual work. How much furniture did Amos Lydia take and what pieces. How much do you pay board per week The firm has allowed you Nellie 30 dollars a month which you can draw every month on the first day commencing on the 1st of October. I shall send to father at your disposal about $75.00 dollars per month but it will not come regular nor oftener than once in every two months I would save as much of it as you can so as to lay up a little if possible, for we can't tell what may happen. The firm is very generous and it is more than I expected from them not that I doubted there generosity but it is more than I asked for. Hoping this will find both you and Berk well I will bid you good night.

              Yours Affectionately   Charley

What girl have you now?

---

[28] 2nd Lieut. Cassander Flagg. Mustered Aug. 1, 1861; Captain, July 23, 1862; Mustered out July 27, 1864

[29] Major-General John Bankhead Magruder, CSA (1807-1871). He rose to fame after his early defeat of the Federals at Big Bethel, Va. (June 10, 1861) and, with a greatly inferior force, successfully stalled McClellan's advance up the Peninsula in May 1862, but his failure to perform satisfactorily during the Seven Days' Battles in June-July 1862 resulted in his being transferred to the Trans-Mississippi Department, where he remained until the end of the war.

****

                                                Oct. 14 /61   Camp Hamilton

Dear Father,

    I was obliged to make use of you as a broker to pay off the families of the men[30] or rather as a means to convey it to them. I at first refused to have any thing to do with it but was obliged to being urged so hard; as it was some $200 and odd dollars was sent home through another channel. This is the 2nd letter I have written on the same subject the first was hastily written in order to finish it in time to reach the mail but it was a failure. I received the bundles of papers which you sent and will distribute them to the men. In my first letter[31] I believe I sent thanks to the firm for their generosity in allowing the sum which you named to my wife, and I hope we will be able to live considerably inside of it. I believe I left off with

no. 32, Sallie E. Denton		20.00
no. 33, John Mack	$	10.00
" 34, Timothy Connolly		10.00
" 35, Kate Keily		10.00
" 36, Patrick Quenny		10.00
" 37, Sarah Howard		15.00
" 38, Mary Farrell		10.00
" 39, Patrick McCabe		10.00
" 40, Mary Weston		<u>10.00</u>
		85.00

Summary

Nellie (for)	151.00
For Lieut Tucker	27.00
from Lieut, Mayo[32] to C.B.S.	100.00
From the men to various parties, as per 1st letter	542.33
For C.B.S.	<u>9.25</u>
	829.58
Amt. in this letter account for	<u>85.00</u>
	914.58

Also the following

No. 41,	Mrs Sarah Harington	15.00
" 42,	James Buckley	15.00
	Thrown in	<u>.02</u>
		944.60

There has been about 1200 dollars sent home from our company in various channels. From

        Yours affectionately

---

[30] Presumably employees of the E. & A.W. Winchester Company serving in the army.

[31] The first letter seems not to have survived. Not all the men referred to here have been identified, and few of the names appear in Company F. Charles F. Denton was discharged March 14, 1862 at Fortress Monroe; John Farrell was discharged for disability Oct. 22, 1862. Eight men named John Mack served from Mass.; only John F. Mack, 5th Mass. Light Artillery, enlisted during 1861 (Sept. 28, 1861). Patrick Weston, 26th Mass. Inf., was killed in action at Fair Oaks June 18, 1862.

[32] 1st Lieut. Charles H. Mayo. Mustered out Aug. 10, 1862. The Johnsons evidently knew him well.

C. Robinson Johnson
There will be at least $15,000 in specie sent to Mass. from this regiment.

****

Oct. 20 [1861]   Camp Hamilton

Dear Nellie,
    I received a letter from you yesterday which I was glad to read. Being in the same place there is nothing but the usual routine day in and day out so you must expect that my letters will be growing shorter & shorter each successive time while we remain here Today attend church in the fort which is the first church I have been inside since I left home, the episcopal service was used; the church is a modern one, gothic style with an organ, aisle carpeted so that I felt as if I was at home again. There were a few ladies present. I dined at the hotel which reminded me of my former travels and had a good dinner. We are quietly doing our work, all alarm has subsided and we continually repeat one day what we did the day before, perhaps with a rumor that add a very little excitement as seasoning to our work, rumors don't pass for much here. The officers and men have considerably leisure time and no man can complain of having to much to do. I am glad you are so comfortably settled and would like to look in on you. Berk must be quite a companion for you by this time he must be quite a walker if he takes after me. Well Nellie I shall bid you good night, if I have anything more to write tomorrow morning I may add it to this. Give my respect to Edmund & Lottie also your father and mother.
        Yours   Charley

Rec'd orders to cook 24 hours rations and to be ready to march at a moments notice. Just received a letter from you.

****

Camp Hamilton   Oct. 20 / 61

Dear Father,
    I received your favor of Oct. 17th yesterday and am glad the money arrived safe. I have sent by express today $10.00 more to on account of draft no. 43 payable to Susan McDonald. I received today your package of letter paper & c and if you send me any more bundles I wish you would put in it a box of steel pens as it is hard work to obtain good steel pen here; the paper & envelopes will come to a good use. I am glad to hear that business is so good and hope it may continue so. I received also last Friday a letter from Mr. Soule which I shall answer at the first leisure moment. There has been lately a large accumulation of transports and war vessels which gives to the harbor quite a lively appearance, they are no doubt preparing for a large expedition[33] for one transport here the Great Republic has 500 horses aboard and another transport has numbers of seige [sic] cannons. There are many rumors flying about but none speak of the removal of the 16th to any other locality. Give my respects to all.
      From yours respectfully   C. Robinson Johnson
P.S.
    I forgot to state that I gave Charley Mayo his order, also I received yesterday a letter from Austin. Please see that Lieut. Tucker get the $27.00 due him from me if he has not already received it.

---

[33] The expedition to Port Royal, S.C., which departed from Fortress Monroe on October 29th.

****

Oct. 23rd /61

Dear Nellie,

It is now about ten o'clock in the evening   I am the officer of the Day or I should have been to bed before this. I received a letter from you today of Oct. 17. Yesterday I received your box with its contents and have eat the cake already, it was good; the butter arrived in excellent condition so did everything, the grapes even. I am sorry that Aunt Lydia has taken so much furniture as with as much care taken of it as possible it must be considerably worn when we shall need it again, it cost a large sum to furnish a house and I shall want to go to housekeeping when I return and that furniture must do us. You will please see that they have us insured   In any case of business nature I would always consult either your father or mine about it if you have not time to write me; they have had large experience in the ways of the world and we had better take advantage of it. You might send three pairs of those draws and buy me two striped flannel shirts. Two pairs of those long stockings will be enough. I would like to have made for me at Smith one blue vest with army buttons to button tight up to the neck. You might give my wing coat to some one. I shall in very cold weather want a thick pair of gloves. I mentioned in my last letter that we were ordered to be ready in a moment's notice but the order was countermanded. It is my opinion that the 16th will winter here unless something turns up, our regiment is ranked high and they have some object in keeping us here. There is a large expedition fitting out here and the harbor is filled with men of war and transports. I received last Monday a letter from you of Oct. 15. Give my respects to all. The naval expedition will sail today so it is rumored and I am glad to see some expedition under way and ready without the destination being known.

Yours   Charley

****

Camp Hamilton Sun.   Oct. 27 [1861]

Dear Nellie,

Writing from the same locality so often has deprived me of anything to write about. I took dinner at the old Hygeia House[34] where they set a very good table besides have the presence of ladies to make it appear more civilised. I had oyster soup, roast beef with sweet potatoes stewed tomatoes and good bread & butter ending with a bread pudding, everything on the table looks neat and everything is well cooked and served, by the way this used to be a very fashionable hotel. The large fleet mentioned in my last letter is still here but we expect it to sail every day. I thought I had written that the men relished the pickles very much   I made three meals of them. There is but very little prospect of our doing anything unless we advance to attack the enemy as he shows no disposition to attack us, it is a general rule with them not to attack but to wait in one place selected by themselves. Have Berk daguerrotype[35]

---

[34] The Hygeia Hotel at Fort Monroe was located among the buildings outside the Fort, between the defensive ditch and the wharves. Useful contemporary sketch maps of the area are to be found on pp.28 and 33 of *Images from the Storm*, the memoirs of Robert Knox Sneden of the 40th New York Infantry.

[35] The term was not uncommonly used during the Civil War to refer to photographs - particularly tintypes and ambrotypes - even though the Daguerrotype process, invented in 1839 and utilising a sensitised silver plate, had effectively been superceded by c.1850 by the wet plate process. It was perhaps used in the same casual way that older people still use "wireless" and "gramophone" today.

taken in his new clothes and send it on. I think their is no doubt but we shall be here thanksgiving day and we shall be glad to receive anything from you. I saw a man picking some flowers today in a small garden near the fort he had quite a bouquet and a good variety. I received a letter from father and a newspaper from I don't know whom. I am glad to hear that you are so well. We shall advance in all probability our pickets soon. We had a review by General Wool[36] yesterday their were over three thousand troops present it made a very imposing sight. We are told that we are the favorite regiment of General Wool and we have had General Mansfield[37] present at several dress parades which makes me think he has a good opinion of us. We have every day about the same duty to perform and consequently have but little to write. Received this morning (Monday) a letter from you for which I am thankful.
                    From Yours   Charley

                    ****

                                        Camp Hamilton   Nov. 1 [1861]
Dear Nellie,
    You tell my father that the box of ale arrived safely and will be enjoyed, I dont know but I owe the thanks to the firm as I see it is from E. & A.W. on the box. You have learnt before this that the naval expedition has sailed[38] and we are waiting here anxiously to hear the result as I suppose the whole north is. I took a little trip into the enemies country the other night, I was officer of the picket having a Lieut from the Delaware Regiment[39] with me, I had heard that a Rebel Colonel had brought over the Back river a Miss Susan Poole and would come after her in the morning, to carry her back. I took eleven men and started at eleven o'clock in the evening and did not return untill [sic] eight o'clock next morning was much pleased with the conduct of the men though we were unsuccessfull in obtaining the colonel yet it served to show that in the presence of danger our men could be cool. There will be great suffering in this part of Virginia this winter as the farms are all forsaken by the males who have left behind in some case their families and their slaves. One darkey[40] said that there were a powerful lot of white women about and he could not see how they were to get along this winter as they had nearly all they had on hand eat up, his master left 1st May to join the rebel expecting to be gone a month; one woman (white) told me that her husband was forced to go and she had not heard from him. Their are plenty of pig

---

[36] Major-General John A. Wool (1784-1869), the oldest officer to hold an active command during the Civil War, commanded the Department of Virginia, with his Headquarters at Fort Monroe, until his retirement on August 1, 1863.

[37] Brigadier General Joseph K. Mansfield, commanding the XII Corps, Army of the Potomac. Born in Connecticut in 1803, he served on coastal construction under General Zachary Taylor in the Mexican War, was appointed Brigadier General in 1861, and fortified the south side of the Potomac, and after First Bull Run took command of the XII Corps. Killed in action at Antietam Sept. 18, 1862.

[38] The Port Royal Expedition, q.v. note 33

[39] The 1st Delaware Infantry, U.S.A., also stationed at Fort Monroe at the time.

[40] Possibly one of the many escaped slaves who had sought Federal protection at Fort Monroe. It was on May 27, 1861, while in command at the Fort, that Major-General Benjamin F. Butler issued his famous declaration that escaped slaves, as the former property of rebels, were to be deemed "contraband of war".

wandering through the woods outside the pickets and I saw a large number of cows also yet milk is scarce and high. I do not think it worth while to make any cotton shirts at present untill we know where we shall be for <u>certain</u> in the next year or two. You might make Mr Soule a present of something both useful and ornamental if you can find such an article. You can judge yourself how much to spend, I would give him something pretty. Give my regards to Mrs Soule & Miss Sherriff and all enquiring friends.
      from yours affectionately   Charley

All officer who have wife present have been notified that there will be no more room than is absolutely necessary to accommodate the troops this winter and consequently one of our officers wives who have been with the regiment since we left camp Cameron has returned home. Received from you letters dated Oct. 24, 27 & 28.

        ****

        Camp Hamilton Va. Nov.4 [1861]
Dear Nellie,
  I received a letter from you and one from Edmund yesterday; also a bundle of papers and one of paper (writing) and a book of drafts from father. Tell father not to send any more writing paper as I have as much as I can conveniently take care of the government furnishes paper to the officers for business purpose; it would not do to have too many things on hand for if we should get orders to march I could not carry them with me. Tell father I sent him a duplicate draft No. 36 which was filled out wrong in the margin I copied it from my book which has on one page the person sending on the other the person to whom the draft is payable; have father thank Steven for those envelopes he printed and sent me[41] tell him they will last me a good six months. Tell your mother (Altra) I have her letter laid one side and shall reply sometime. There are a large number of rumors about, those in relation to the Naval Expedition are bad; rumor says the fleet landed its forces at Ball bluff[42] or some place 25 miles this side of Charleston S. Carolina, you will hear of it by the newspapers before this reaches you; if it be true. Tell Edmund I know nothing about a tent being purchased or about to be for the Chaplain the preaching is now done in the open air, may be they mean to purchase a large tent to hold services in. Tell Edmund not to feel slighted if I don't answer his letter immediately as I shall not find so much time now I must read some. I shall be happy to receive Berk daguereotype. This letter is written in a hurry don't criticize it much.
    from yours Affectionately   Charley

        ****

          Sunday Nov. 10 /61
Dear Nellie,
  I have received your letter of the 3rd, 5th and 7th of Nov. also a box containing some clothes preserves, cake and Berk's daguerrotype from you and a letter from father dated Nov. 7 for all of which I am thankful. I intended to have Aunt Lydia pay

---

[41] An example survives with Johnson's letter of Feb. 24, 1862

[42] Possibly Bull's Bay, about 20 miles east of Charleston. Johnson may have heard the name and confused it with Ball's Bluff, Virginia, scene of a recent engagement on October 21st in which Union forces were defeated with severe losses, including Lincoln's friend Col. Edward Baker.

for the insurance on the furniture and crockery which she is using. I agree with you in your opinion of Berk's daguerrotype it is perfect. When I have leisure I shall send home to you some of my clothes, you want me to write what I think about the war lasting, I cannot form any opinion except from what I learn from the newspapers; the Southern army is only enlisted for one year, I think, which would make the term of their enlistment expire next spring or summer when it will be difficult for the south to either enlist recruit or to reenlist those men whose time has expired again, which would reduce their army certainly one half, our troops are enlisted for three years or for the war; next spring we shall be finely disciplined and drilled with our forces diminished only by battles (which temper the men). The character of the Southern people are more earnest but not so enduring as the Northern[43]. The war when it first commenced was in their opinion to be a short one and they may have looked forward to suffer privations but not so long. This winter their will be a great deal of suffering among them and I think that they will not be willing to endure another winter like this. The war is carried on in their own states and unless they can transfer it to the Northern states a large amount of territory and large number of towns must be laid waste which will reduce their people and finances to such a low state that there will be no hope of their forming a powerful state of themselves in this century. I am officer of the day and do not feel like writing. Excuse all mistakes. I should have said that in a year from this time their will be a cessation of hostilities to say the least if not next spring, the south may be in earnest but it was not prepared for a long war and I don't believe that it can prepare itself either. We must not suffer any large defeats to revive their spirit and if we do nothing else but remain where we are it will exhaust them. But I think that there will be great energy on our side during the winter resulting I hope in several successful engagements[44]. My books ought to be worth about $200.00. Give my respects to all.

From Your Affectionately   Charley

****

Camp Hamilton   Nov. 13 [1861]

Dear Nellie,

I received a letter from you yesterday of Nov. 10 and one from Austin of the same date. Nothing has happened since I last wrote. Our pickets are extended a mile further from camp in the midst of thick woods. The forest here are magnificent, pine trees grow as straight as a mast to great heights often 50 feet (before you will find a branch) from the ground. We have had good news from the naval expedition which you will hear & read before this arrives to you. The band is now playing near my tent and I am enjoying it while writing. We have our tents floored and otherwise fitted up for winter a good stove which we obtained from Baltimore and with little more fixing we can pass the winter comfortably here. You made an improvement on Charles

---

[43] A sentiment interestingly reminiscent of the prophetic warning given to the Texas Secession Convention by its Governor, and hero of State Independence, Sam Houston: "I tell you that while I believe with you in the doctrine of state rights, the North is determined to preserve this Union. They are not a fiery, impulsive people, as you are, for they live in cooler climates. But when they begin to move in a given direction where great interests are involved such as the present issues before the country, they will move with the steady momentum and perseverance of a mighty avalanche. And what I fear is they will overwhelm the South with ignoble defeat."

[44] These sentiments anticipating an early end to the war were commonly expressed on both sides.

May[o]s[45] night caps over mine   it fits him well and he wears it a great deal. There has been two resignations of officer[46] and there are now two or three under arrest for small offences. The officers are trying to start a small club to promote sociability among themselves using a large tent outside the camp line as their room. Four companies of the German regiment were out scouting in the direction of Little Bethel and had three shells fired at them without doing any harm, they fired at a small body of horsemen, they think with some effect[47] . The longer I stay here the shorter will grow my letters as there is nothing to write unless rumors which if they have foundation you will see them in the papers before I could inform you of them by letter. Give my regards to all. I ment [sic] to have thanked Lettie for her cake and preserves which are very nice   her apple jelly is as good as ever.

        From yours Affectionately   Charles

        ****

              Camp Hamilton Dec. 1st /61

Dear Nellie,

I have received your letters of the 21st, 26th & 28th. Our men have all received new frock coats similar in style to the officer but of cheaper material and blue pants and when they appear on dress parade they wear white gloves which makes a fine appearance. The officers in consequence of the fine show made by the men are getting epaulets and army hats so you will have to send back my epaulets[48] as soon as possible. If we are able to return looking as well as we do now Massachusetts will be proud of us. The harbor is comparatively deserted but vessels arrive and leave nearly every day. I have almost made up my mind that we shall do nothing here this winter but you can't tell what may happen. If father (Johnson) travels anywhere he must come here. He can see and learn more here than any where else. Two companies have gone from our regiment to Newport News by land to examine the telegraph wires. Nothing has transpired unusual   their as[sic] been no arrivals of troops lately. I will look after your photograph. I think the first I had is in my trunk. I expect to receive my pipe by next Wednesday   shall be disappointed if I don't. I suppose Berk grows fast and if I stay away six months longer it will be hard work to recognise him among a crowd of children. Give my regards to all and if anything happens between now and tomorrow morning I will add the account of it to this. Monday morning. This morning there was firing on James river for two hour [sic] owing to the attempt to run the famous Yorktown pass the blockade at Newport News, we were successful in driving her back   I have not heard with what damage.[49] Tell father I received his 100

---

[45] See note 32

[46] Capt. Benjamin A. Bridges, discharged Nov. 3, and Lieut. William A. Smith, discharged Nov. 4.

[47] Probably the 20th New York Infantry, "The United Turner Regiment", stationed at Fortress Monroe. No action is recorded for this period in Frederick A. Dyer's *Compendium of the War of the Rebellion*.

[48] These still survive; see illustration No. 5.

[49] The *Yorktown* was a sidewheel New York-Richmond passenger steamer, seized by the state of Virginia and converted into the C.S. warship *Patrick Henry*. During the early months of the war she was located in the James River to guard against Federal attacks from Newport News. On Dec. 2, Commander John Randolph Tucker, CSN, took the ship to a mile and a half above Newport News and opened fire on the Federal Squadron at long range, hoping to lure out some vessels, inflicting some minor damage but failing to achieve the main aim. It accompanied the Virginia during the battle of Hampton Roads on March 8 and

newspapers yesterday.

From Yours affectionately   Charles

****

Camp Hamilton Dec. 4/ 61

Dear Nellie,
    Since I last wrote we have had some cold weather; Monday night we had rain, snow and hail and the following morning our tents were well coated with ice and snow; the ground white with the same covering giving a winter look to every thing; Tuesday was still colder all the puddles of water were frozen solid; water in my tent was slightly skimmed. I go on picket tomorrow. I received a letter from you, father and Austin and some papers from father. Everything remains the same as when I last wrote . no arrivals, and no interesting event has happened. I did not write anything about Charlie Mayo being unwell as I thought he had better tell his own story. He had an attack (slight) of bilious fever he will soon be fit for duty. This ink is so pale that I can hardly see what I write. Regards to all   etc.

****

Camp Hamilton Dec. 8/61

Dear Nellie,
    Ben has arrived bringing my pipe and cap with a letter from Steven; I am very much pleased with the pipe. I have received a letter from you dated Dec. 1st, one from Austin and one from father. Charley is improving slowly but it will be a week or ten days before he will be fit for duty. The officers of our regiment have an entertainment to the officers of the 20th (the regiment which looked after us when we first arrived here) and Naval Brigade. The reporter of the N. York Herald was there and in the next letter from here in that paper there will be an account of it. Tell Austin he must write to me if I don't write to him. We have been enjoying mild weather the last few days together with beautiful moonlight night. We were fortunate in having while on picket mild weather; our picket fired on what they supposed to be a man lurking in the woods, a large portion of the pickets are station on a road through the woods cut expressly for the purpose, the stations are far apart which makes it a lonesome place to be in at night. For the first time our mail has not arrived though it is due at six o'clock in the morning, and it is now 8 o'clock in the evening   what has detained the steamboat is the anxious enquiry. The steamboat arrived last night bringing a letter and a paper from you and a paper from mother. I wish you would ask Steven to print me some blank about 50 similar to form 13 Subsistence Department Army Regulations.

Headed

Provision Return   Captain C.R. Johnson   Company F 16 Regiment Mass. Vol for ------ days, commencing ------ day of ------ 186--, and ending ---- day of ----, 1861. If he can send them on so as to have them in ten days, I can use two of them. Give my regards to all

from yours affectionately   Charles

****

9, 1862, attacking the *Congress* and the *Monitor*. In October 1863 she became the Confederate floating Naval Academy, and was burned on April 3, 1863, on the evacuation of Richmond.

A sombre note is struck by the Boston Daily Journal for December 11:- "A Fort Monroe letter in the New York Herald states that Private Patrick Flarity of Company F, and private John Dillon of Company H, Sixteenth regiment Massachusetts Volunteers, have been convicted of sleeping on their posts while doing picket duty and sentenced to be shot, and that Gen. Wool has approved the sentences."

Both, however, must have been reprieved. Flarity (more correctly Flatery) reappeared after being missing in action at Glendale on June 30, 1862, and was discharged for disability on Aug. 18, while Dillon was mortally wounded at Second Bull Run, Aug. 29, 1862, dying of his wounds on Oct. 26, 1862.

****

Camp Hamilton   Dec. 12/ 61

Dear Nellie,

I received a letter from you of Dec. 5th and 8th and also one from Winny. I dont feel like writing a letter so this one will be very short. Charley is improving slowly but still at the hospital, he walk to the camp every day and take a ride to the fort. Their is but little chance of my having my dagueratype taken so you must not look for it. I am in good health. The weather has until yesterday been inusually[sic] mild but its is growing colder. I saw that conundrum in the paper before I received your letter I wish you would send me the third volume of Scott's tactics[50] . I had forgotten about little Nellie writting but no doubt it is very good. I was officer of the day yesterday, relieved this morning. I think it is best not to subscribe to the Congressional Globe[51] for this Session. Give my regards to all. Tell father if any of the drafts have not been drawn please let me know it.

Yours affectionately   Charley

****

Camp Hamilton, Va.   Dec. 15 /61

Dear Nellie,

I have received your letters of Dec. 11th & 12th. You remind me in your last letter of a promise I made you that in case I receive a furlough you should come on to meet me. The prospect of getting furlough is very small and if I succeeded it would not be for a longer time than 12 days and there could not be any notice giving you until I received it. How could you, on my arrival at Baltimore if I telegraph to you to meet me at Philadelphia, start immediately for Phila. without somebody to travel with you; and unless you did start immediately, I should be spending my time at Philadelphia to no purpose. I don't think that will be much danger of your having opportunity of seeing me this winter. Friday we received news that Charleston had been burnt by the slaves[52] by the way of Norfolk. Saturday the steamer G. Morris from Port Royal

---

[50] *INFANTRY TACTICS* by Lieutenant-General Winfield Scott. At one time the standard Infantry manual for the U.S. Regular Army, it was first published in 1840 and was reprinted in 1861, and was widely read by officers on both sides. An abridged Confederate edition was published in Raleigh, N. C., in 1862.

[51] *THE CONGRESSIONAL GLOBE, CONTAINING THE DEBATES AND PROCEEDINGS IN CONGRESS*, published in Washington, D.C. since 1833.

[52] An entirely false rumor.

reported Charleston in a blaze thus confirming the news received Friday from another source. The burning of Charleston by the slaves will strike terror throughout the south it is the severest blow that secession has yet received, and it is a staggering blow. The slave are ignorant and heretofore docile showing no sign of containing any fierce or evil disposition towards their masters but the fear in the vicinity of Savannah & Charleston, which their masters have lately show for their own safty [sic] may have imparted courage to the most daring of the slaves The burning of Charleston may excite slaves in other parts of the south both in cities and in plantations to do like deeds and if the burning of Charleston is soon followed by another conflagration it would not be surprising if it spread like an epidemic throughout all the slaves of south transforming the docile slaves into savages ready to commit the most revolting act as the occasion offers[53] . When we consider that the slave population are three to one of the white in some parts of the south in peacable time and when we next consider the large number of whites in the army of the south away (especially in the interior) from their plantations thereby giving strength to the slaves the act, the burning of Charleston, may be only a preface to more terrible facts. We can't imagine if the conclusions or rather the programme which I have mentioned should be enacted what would be the condition of the South it must be anarchy; besides it will tend to make all heads of Families all husbands in the army desirous to go to protect their families and wives from a danger which at any moment may leave them houseless and homeless as the least danger with which they are threaten, thereby weakening the rebel army. I have no doubt the experience of Bull Run is being improved now, nothing will be done until we are ready; when our gunboats on the Mississippi are ready to move down to sweep the obstructions on their way in conjunction with the army following on shore then and not before will there be any attempt to advance upon Mannasas[54] , the victory must be first gained at Columbus, which would expose the force in Tennesee to be attacked in front by our army in Kentucky on the flank and rear by our land forces near Columbus, our armies in Kentucky united in Tennesee with the Missippi [sic] land force would threaten Western Virginia and also threaten to get in the rear of Mannasas, while our forces at and about Washington would threaten the front of Beauregardes[55] forces. Charley is improving rapidly he is not yet fit for duty. Give my regards to all.
From Charley

****

---

[53] A revealing insight into Johnson's contemptuous attitude towards the slaves, shared by many Northern officers at the time, notably those of the 20th Massachusetts Infantry, known as the Harvard Regiment but also nicknamed the Copperhead Regiment because of the predominantly anti-Abolition sentiment of their officers. At this stage of the war, the attitude of most Northern soldiers was that they were fighting to preserve the Union, not to free the slaves. It was commonly believed, in America and Europe, that slave revolt and massacres would be the result of Emancipation, but the freed slaves in fact themselves confounded such predictions, and there was no serious recorded instance of violence or revolt following the Emancipation Proclamation.

[54] Manassas Junction, Virginia, where the Army of Northern Virginia was camped during the winter of 1861-2.

[55] Full General Pierre G.T. Beauregard, CSA. A national hero following his authorising the firing on Fort Sumter on April 12, 1861 as Commander of Confederate forces in Charleston, S.C., he added to his laurels by defeating the Union army at the first major battle of the war, Bull Run, on July 21. His later military career was clouded by a serious falling-out with President Jefferson Davis and he was ordered to the West in January 1862.

Camp Hamilton, Va.   Dec. 18 /61

Dear Nellie,

I received your letter yesterday of Dec. 15. There is nothing of interest transpiring here, a small scouting party from the picket while on this side of S.W. Branch had a shell fired at them but without doing any harm. We have brigade drill every day in the afternoon   I like them. Hardy case is a doubtful one   I dont know whether the sentence will be carried into effect or not   some think it will while others are positive it will not. We have had for a long time very mild and pleasant weather with as bright, clear and moonlight nights as I ever saw; if the spring here is a [sic] early as the autumn is late winter will be but a short one. I received a letter from Minnie and also one from George Kimball. I have given up messing together and gone into a large Officer's mess; the reason of my doing so was lack of room and making a kitchen, dining and bed room out of a small tent kept every thing in disorder.

Charley is improving slowly, has not yet returned to duty. I am going to board the inside of my tent which will make me quite comfortable during the winter and if it was not for going on Picket I should have a very easy time, picket duty is not very bad except that you cant sleep for about thirty hour.
[No further pages of this letter survive]

****

Monday Dec. 23rd /61   Camp Hamilton, Va.

Dear Nellie,

I have received your letters of Dec. 17 & 19   in the former you hoped I would not be on picket when it arrived but I was and read it while on picket. I have received your epaulets that you have worried so much about. Yesterday was the dedication of the Chaplain's tent and the line officers also had Hon. Chas. Train[56] to lunch. Enclosed you will find two programmes of the dedication. Mr Soule send me his card as well as you so I have two of his cards. I shall, I hope, receive your box tomorrow. Charley is improving slowly, took a little cold the other day which may put him back a little   he is not sick a bed but sets up nearly all day but is [s]till quite weak owing to the medicine the Dr gives him. You must not expect me home this winter as I am at present so situated with one Lieut sick and another absent that I shall not be able to apply for one *[a leave]* for a month to come and they will be so many applications before me that mine will be refused. Today it is raining the first rain which we have had for some time and I expect we shall have many rainy days now. On dress parade there was order read in relation to the kindness which the Charles St. Living Circle had shown to this regiment. I will copy it and sent it to mother as soon as I can get it. Saturday a company of the 20th Germans were out after wood from Newport News and they I believe were fired upon and on calling the roll Sunday morning found one of the men missing, the four companies of 20th N. York (Germans) which are at Newport News when out scouting hoping to find the missing man and while near Newmarket bridge   were fired upon by the enemy who I believe attempted to surround them   they sent to Camp Hamilton for the remainder of their regiment here to assist them which immediately went and succeeded in driving the rebels with we think some loss   one dead rebel was found and there is no doubt of their carrying off other [sic]; our loss was four wounded and none of them dangerous   two were in the arm (fleshy part), one in the neck which strange to relate is not a serious one[57] .

---

[56] Charles Russell Train (1817-1885), Representative from Massachusetts. See illustration nos. 47 & 48 of the programme for the ceremony.

[57] In the skirmish at New Market Bridge, Dec. 22, six men of the 20th New York were wounded.

****

Camp Hamilton   Dec. 25 /61

Dear Nellie,
    I received your box Monday after the mail had gone every thing in good condition. I wish you would send me as soon as possible some of my old carpet to put on the floor of my tent   I want a piece 7 ft by 10 ft good measure. When I receive my carpet I shall be as comfortable and warm as if I was at home. my tent is now boarded on the inside and I shall paste newspapers over them which will keep out the wind; I shall have two small bunks   one for myself and one for my servant. Those provision forms are what I wanted and will be very useful. I received a letter from you today but no papers. I am Officer of the Day today and write this in a hurry. The rebels came this side of Newmarket bridge yesterday and set fire to two house leaving 8th Alabama regiment marked in the sand, some of the 20th went on the other side of the river and set fire to two house to balance accounts. At the same time we were telegraphed from Newport News that the enemy were approaching and the regiments on brigade drill among which was our [sic] were ordered to advance immediately, I was in the camp with my company working on a large log house intended for a guard house, but the order was soon countermanded.

        Yours Affectionately   Charles
Give regards to all
Charley is improving slowly

****

Camp Hamilton, Va.   Dec. 29 /61

Dear Nellie,
    It is Sunday evening and I do not feel like writing so you must be satisfied with a very short letter. Your cake is very light and nice also the doughnuts meant to have mentioned it before. I was quite surprised to received your daguerertype; quite a pleasant one. We had a little miniature naval battle this morning which will learn our gun boats to be more on the alert, a rebel gunboat attacked the Newport News boat making her relinquish a schooner she had in tow capturing the schooner and carry it off followed after it had had a good start by 9 gunboats, which fired at every opportunity The worst of it is that the rebel gunboat came between the Newport News boat and our side of the river and was within easy shelling distance from our camp. The Rip Raps send a few missile at Sewell's point and they appeared to have been in a very good range[58] . Hoping this will find Lettie family well as well as your self I remain yours respectfully. meant to have said affectionately
    Charley

****

---

[58] The Confederate ship was the C.S.S. *Sea Bird*, Flag Officer W. F. Lynch. The Federal schooner was carrying fresh water to Fortress Monroe.

CHAPTER 6
*
FORTRESS MONROE, 1862

Camp life between New Year 1862 and the start of the Peninsula Campaign continued in very much the same way, the monotony relieved by the historic battle between the ironclads U.S.S. Monitor and C.S.S. Virginia on March 9th, witnessed by Johnson and his colleagues in the regiment.

h

                                                          Camp Hamilton Va.   Jan 2 /62

Dear Nellie,

      I have received two letters from you and one from mother since I last wrote. I was unfortunate in being officer of the day both on Christmas and New Years which were both kept as holidays here, we are not having any drill. I shall be very brief as I have nothing to write and want to forward this by this afternoon mail. We are enjoying fine weather, not very cold, and with scarcely any rain, very much like March windy and dusty. Charley has not yet got out of the hospital. Lieut Rogers formerly of Co H has been attached to my company and Lieut Tucker has been transferred to Co H. You had better give up all hopes of seeing me this winter as it about impossible to obtain a furlough.

                        Yours affectionately,   Charley

Give my regards to all; how is your father and mother you have not mentioned them lately in your letters. You might send me two or three bottle of currant wine if it is good

                                             ****

                                        Jan. 3rd / 62   Camp Hamilton

Dear Nellie,

      I write this letter to night to let you know that I have received your box and to tell you that probable I shall not write next Sunday as I go on picket tomorrow and being relieved on Sunday shall be to tired to write. A large scout was sent out today on a reconnaissance and discovered I am told that the rebels had left Big Bethel carry away their guns which they had in their battery located there. Your carpet is down and I am quite comfortably fixed in a room or tent about 9 fts by eight which so small is easily kept warm. It has this moment commenced sprinkling and I anticipate

unpleasant weather on picket. I have no objection of your sending me another daguerrotype of yourself in a different position you need not be afraid of sending too many. My hammock is open and placed for the bottom of my bunk which makes a very comfortable berth. I have received a letter dated Dec. 31 from you also some papers from father. I suppose that we shall for the next three months at least be here without anything except to perfect ourselves in drill to do unless Burnside expedition comes down this way then it is possible that we may take part.
Jan. 6th
By a piece of absent mindedness this letter which was to have been sent Saturday was left in my pocket until this minute. I went on picket Saturday morning, and came off Sunday knowing I should be to tired to write Sunday. I write this Friday evening to tell you that I should not write Sunday with the reasons. Nothing has transpired. I have received your letter of Jan. 1st and will answer it in my next.
     Yours affectionately   Charley
One of the prisoners from Richmond[59] says that there are two disaffected S. Carolina regiment and that they loudly cheered the Union prisoners when the [sic] passed them.

****

         Camp Hamilton   (January) 9th /62
Dear Nellie,
  I have received your letter of Jan 5th also one from Austin. Nothing occurring here; rumors of all sort have been circulating but I believe have no foundation. Charley may & may not leave his comfortable home here pay you strangers a visit though I should consider it as making myself very uncomfortable to be obliged to sleep between brick walls leaving out the danger of sleeping so high above the ground. What strange notions civilians have that to be happy and comfortable they must have brick house and sleep up in the third story, there is nothing like a well arranged tent if you don't like the locality why you can change your position without any trouble. If Lynn is fashionable when I return home instead of hiring a house and paying a large price hire a small piece of ground pitch my tent and enjoy myself and I shall be able in that way to own a house at all the fashionable watering place as long as they continue so. You can't help seeing that I am hard up for something to write. Tell Austin I am much obliged to him for his letter and ask him to write often. There has been a drawing of Camp Hamilton by one of our regiment sent to be put into one of the pictorial and I was obliged to agree to take 20 copies to secure its being engraved shall send the copies to you. Give my regards to all inquiring friends. from
     Yours affectionately,   Charley
P.S. Tell mother that there are about twenty officers at my mess. Send out a book on artillery by Major Anderson[60]   at some convenient time   Charly Mayo has been detailed as signal officer and will be stationed at the fort.

****

        Camp Hamilton, Va. Sunday Jan. 12 /62
Dear Nellie,
  It has been a lovely day as mild as in the middle of May, I have been without a

---

[59] Old Point Comfort, Fortress Monroe, was the official base for exchange of Prisoners throughout the war.

[60] *EVOLUTIONS OF FIELD BATTERIES OF ARTILLERY* by Major R. Anderson (New York, 1860)

fire sitting with my door wide open all day, occasionally hearing a bird sing. You would be astonished at the quietness which generally prevails in the camp, in my camp you could easily imagine yourself at Lexington with nobody within sight or hearin [sic]. Last night Burnside expedition[61] sailed and before this letter reaches you, you will have heard of its luck; we imagine that it has not gone far from here either on the N. Carolina shore or somewhere nearer. I had the pleasure of seeing most of the officers of the 24th[62] which was a great pleasure. I received two letters from you to day dated Jan. 7th and 9th and from them I learn that you expect to visit Callie   I no doubt you will enjoy yourself and will be an aid to getting through winter. Rumors of all descriptions about but none say that we are to do anything, the men are to all appearances better satisfied to remain than they were but they still desire to see a little active service, we have come to the opinion that we are not to see a fighting the expression "did you ever no a sixteenth regiment in a battle?". I am blessed as usual with a good apetite and health. Charley is out of the hospital and has been placed on detached service and will be located for the present at the fort   he is attached to the signal corp which will take him away entirely from the company. I have a great many newspapers sent me   now received a bundle for the men from father also a letter from father. We are to build a gymnasium perhaps two   one for each wing 75 ft by 25[63]. We have under way a bake house to cook our own bread; each company has a good size wood cook house with a large chimney and cook the old style hanging the pots on a crane.

    From yours affectionately   Charles

****

Jan. 16 /62

Dear Nellie,

  It is getting late and you must be satisfied with a short letter. I have been very busy the last week or two as their is a great deal of work to be done at the end of every quarter. We have been visited with a rain, sleet and snow storm of several days duration covering the ground with three inches snow. The roads, through the woods, are in a frightful condition and must grow worse unless we have very cold weather, what do you think of mud a foot in depth? We have it here and will have it deeper in spring. We are building a gymnasium for the men of the regiment for their health and amusement during the rainy season. I am afraid that I shall have to say no to your wish as I have not any accommodations we shall have wet and bad weather for moving about during the next two or three months. You will have learnt before this reaches you that Charley will not be home, it will be a great disappointment to Hattie. Hoping this will find you all well.

  I remain Yours Affectionately   Charley

Give my regards to all. I go on picket tomorrow morning weather now clear &

---

[61] The expedition, under Brigadier-General Ambrose E. Burnside, to capture Roanoke Island, N.C. was one of the relatively few Federal successes of the early part of the war. It was quickly followed by the capture of Beaufort and New Bern, establishing an invaluable coaling and supply station on the enemy coast which remained in Union possession throughout the war.

[62] The 24th Massachusetts Infantry, participating in Burnside's Roanoke Expedition.

[63] An interesting reference to the steps taken to ensure the health and recreation of the soldiers, not often mentioned in the literature.

moonlight. Nellie, you can send back by Corporal Harrington[64] a pair of thick long legged boots. You can find the necessary size by looking at any of my old boots.

****

Camp Hamilton, Va. Jan. 19 /62

Dear Nellie,

I received your letter of Jan. 14th on picket. While on picket we made two prisoners one a rebel sutler the other a rebel deserter. The patrol which left in the afternoon on its return reported to me that they was told that two spy had left the rebel camp and were about Foxhill. The patrol I sent out a[t] 12 o'clock, midnight, awoke two negroes who acted as guides leading them to Mr. Topping's House about three miles from our picket, the sergeant of the patrol rapped on the door and it was three or four minutes before the door was opened, the sergeant asked the lady who opened the door if Mr. Topping was in She said no and pledged her honour as a southern lady that he was not there, the sergeant not satisfied asked permission to search the house, which was reluctantly granted. The house is one of the best at Foxhill well furnished and containing a large number of beds. The sergeant and one private enter the house leaving three outside to watch they entered every room and found nothing to excite their suspicion, they came to a bed which did not differ from the rest in appearance but which they tumbled about and between the mattress and feather bed had found the man they were looking for, whom they brought into us, I searched him and found nothing of any consequence about him. At four oclock in the morning sent out patrol to search his house, they succeeded in finding his pocket book which contained several rebel passes permitting him to pass from place to place 3 one dollar Confederate scrip all of different banks a certificate from Col Magruder that his mule had drawn a piece of ordnance from Hampton to Yorktown and various papers. After searching Mr. Topping's house they went to another house rapped on the door asked who lived there then asked the woman if her husband was in she answered no, when he entered saw under the table a pair of recently muddy shoes, heard some noise overhead, asked the woman who was up there she answered, her mother-in-law, Sergeant said I will go up and see her she immediately said I will go up and bring her down, she then asked the sergeant if he would harm her husband if he should find him, he said, no, she went up returned with her husband who stated that he was a deserter of the 2nd Virginia Regiment of Volunteers Col. Mallory he was brought into us. I carried both prisoners down to fort the sutler was locked up the other was permitted to return to his home to induce other to do the like. The rebel troops have not been paid for five months are well clothed and comfortably provided for and moderately equipped but have no uniformity of dress, considerable drunkenness prevails and but moderate discipline kept up he told all he knew about the situation of the rebel troops and there batteries. The same night we were on picket there were fourteen shots fired at the pickets at Hampton. I offered Genl Wool 3 gold dollars for the 3 bills but he thought best to keep them.[65] Charles Mayo will not

---

[64] Henry Scales Harrington, A resident of Stoneham, Massachusetts, and a 30 year-old Painter, Harrington enlisted on July 12,1861 as a Corporal. He mustered into Co. F., and re-enlisted on December 23, 1863. He transferred out on July 11,1864, entering Co. E, 11th Massachusetts Infantry. Harrington was listed as Missing on March 31, 1865 at Hatcher's Run, VA, but was taken prisoner and released. He was Mustered Out on May 15, 1865. During his service, he rose from First Sergeant to 1st Lieutenant.

[65] It seems unlikely that a company officer would offer money to his commanding general for some souvenirs. This suggests that Johnson, or his family, were acquainted with Wool, though Johnson makes no other reference to any such relationship.

probably have anything more to do with my company. Every thing quiet here. Mud! no end to it and no depths of it; rains worse   it will be reckless to try to cross the street. I have received your letter of Jan 17 also a box of good things which I will enjoy also a very warm sack from Mrs Gladden and some ginger bread from Mrs Leeds. I have never had occasion to try on those stockings you made the weather is so mild here; last night was very warm. My regards to all.

from yours affectionately
Charles

[in pencil]
Intended sending this yesterday but was hindered from doing so as I went to Taunton (12 miles) with Tud had a good sleigh ride, all well
your affect daughter   Nellie[66]
Saturday

****

Camp Hamilton Va.   Jan. 22 /62

Dear Nellie,
I have received your letters of the 17th & 19th. There has nothing happened since I last wrote and news, I mean local news, is scarce. Charley Mayo is very comfortably located at the fort and likes his new place very much, his duties are not so arduous as they were when he was attached to the company. I have now as usual only one lieutenant. The news from Kentucky is very cheering[67] . I received from home a large box containing sack from Mrs Gliddon and some gingerbread from Mrs Leeds, also peanuts cake gelatine and two bottles currant wine which has not improved any. The weather is and will be unpleasant for the next two months, the roads are in a horrible condition. You must excuse the shortness of the letter as nothing has transpired since I last wrote worth noticing. The troops in the Constitution[68] are at present encamped on the beach to air themselves, there seems to be some doubt as to their destination. Give my regards to all remember me to Callie and Fred.

From yours Affectionately   Charley

****

Camp Hamilton V.   Jan. 26, /62

Dear Nellie,
I have received your letter of Jan. 22nd. Today is the first pleasant day we have had for a long time, the weather not very cold and the roads are improving. The mail or rather the steamboat has not arrived so we have not had either papers or letters. I think that there is no danger of our regiment seeing active service certainly not till spring. There has been since I last wrote not a rumor, no news, every thing is perfectly

---

[66] This indicates that Nellie forwarded Johnson's letters to his father.

[67] The success of Union forces under Brigadier General George H. Thomas at Mill Springs, Jan. 19th.

[68] This cannot be the *U.S.S. Constitution*, commissioned in 1798, the second oldest serving ship in the U.S. Navy which spent the entire war as a training ship at Newport, R.I. It is presumably the name of a transport ship carrying troops through the area; Johnson's letter of March 5, 1862, refers to "the steamer *Constitution* on her way to Newport News."

tranquil except the wind which has been lately very violent. We have had no news from Burnside's expedition and wait patiently for it Give my regards to all.

      Yours affectionately   Charley

         ****

                Camp Hamilton, Va. Feby. 2/62

Dear Nellie,

  I have received your letters of Jan 29th and 31st. I have to write the same old story, nothing new, even more quiet than usual. I understand that the Constitution will sail this afternoon for Ship Island[69] . Lieut Rogers[70] formerly of Co. H is now attached to my company. I enjoy picket duty more than usual now owing to having two dragoons[71] with me, and I make use of one horse to visit my picket which is quite a pleasure compared with wading through water and mud. Picket duty now is unpleasant one owing to prevailing unpleasant weather rendering the going awful. and the nights cheerless. I don't expect any more pleasant weather for six weeks to come, the roads are so bad that sometimes four horses can't start an empty wagon. You must excuse the shortness of this, but it is impossible to find any news to write. Give my regards to all.

      Yours affectionately   Charles

         ****

                Camp Hamilton, Va. Feb. 6 /62

Dear Nellie,

  I have just received your letter of Feb. 2nd and glad to learn from it that you are all well. The weather still continues unfavorable for any outdoor work with an occasional pleasant day to create a desire that it may continue pleasant. The roads are growing "no better fast" and the quartermaster is afraid that unless they improve every wagon will be used up. We rarely have any drills now, a school to learn those who can't either read or write is about to commence under the chaplain and the chapel tent is to be fitted up with benches for that purpose. I shall have again to apologise for the shortness of this owing to the quietness which prevails here. Give my regards to all. I remain

        yours affectionately   Charley

         ****

                Camp Hamilton Va. Feb 6th / 62

Sir,

  Fearing that my petition for a leave of absence was not explicit enough I take

---

[69] An island in the Mississippi Delta, used by Federal Naval forces as its base for the campaign to capture New Orleans.

[70] Francis P.H. Rogers, from Waltham. 2nd Lt., Aug. 1, 1861; 1st Lt. March 1, 1862. Killed in action at Fair Oaks, Va., June 18, 1862.

[71] There were two regiments of Dragoons, or heavy cavalry, in the U.S. Regular Army at the outbreak of war, but these became the 1st and 2nd U.S. Cavalry. Cavalry units on duty at Fort Monroe at the time were Cos. A and B, 1st New York Cavalry, and the 11th Pennsylvania Cavalry. Johnson is probably using the term as a generic refence to cavalrymen.

the liberty to enclose a few of the reasons why I desire it. It was my duty as a member of the firm to carry on the factory, which is part of their business, having exclusive control over it. Business being dull, I obtained their consent, not without difficulty, to occuy the position which I have the honor of possessing. Since I have left some difficulties have been experienced, and the firm have written letters desiring me to pay them a short visit as the foreman was in want of information in regards to the leys; which is a most important part of the manufacture; any waste or mismanagement would involve a serious loss. Besides the firm are about to make changes in the steam power which was contemplated and recommended before I left and as it is my intentions to retake my old place when the war is over, the firm desires to consult me in regard to it. Account stock has been taken and I have sold some personal property since I left and am not informed how I stand. Private property valued at $1500.00 which I left stored owing to a misunderstanding of my letters have been loaned to different irresponsible parties. I have other reasons (concerning my relation with the firm) but the above seem to me to be sufficient to warrant a hope that my petition will be granted. The difficulties at the factory involves large sums of money which I am as confident I can remedy as that my absence will not be noticed. I am sorry to take up so much of your valuable time, therefore close.

  I am Sir Yours Respectfully
    C. Robinson Johnson Capt Comdg Co F, 16th M.V.
To:
  Wm. D. Whipple, Assistant Adjutant General[72]

****

         Camp Hamilton Va. Feb. 21, 1862

Dear Nellie,

  On my arrival I received your letter written the Sunday before I arrived, it was read with pleasure. There has been some improvements in camp since I left in the conveniency of travelling; the officers have now in front of their tents genuine brick sidewalks, connecting the whole line of tents with each other and if we remain here much longer and I know nothing at present why we shouldn't we shall have a very pretty village with flower beds around the officers quarters and brick walks and side streets. I became acquainted with some ladies, who were going to Richmond, on board boat from Baltimore, which made the trip pleasant. New orders have been issued whilst I was away, changing reveille from 1/2 past six to 1/2 past five consequently I shall not be able to sit up so late as I have been accustomed. Nellie, I want you to write very often for the next month at least, perhaps it may take some time to get back to my old business to relish it. To day is pleasant and I think that the roads have improved somewhat.

    Excuse the looks
      Yours Affectionately   Charley

****

(With stamped envelope, printed "Care Messrs. E. A. & W. Winchester, No. 16, South Market Street, Boston, Mass.", and hand-written "Mrs. C. Robinson Johnson". Printed in top left-hand corner, "From Captain Chas. R. Johnson, Co.F, 16th Reg't. Mass. Volunteers"

---

[72] Document in the National Archives

Fortress Monroe   Feb. 24 /62

Dear Nellie,

I have come off picket to day and being off Duty took the opportunity to show Austin[73] around the fort as well as other Lions[74]. The morning promised magnificent weather, but before noon the wind increased to a gale which has made the walking very disagreeable as the sand is blown in your face any way you may turn. This letter is written at the Hygeia House as I had not time to write from the camp. The wind has disturbed the arrangement of the tents our Chaplain's tent has taken wing and flown I am afraid that other tents may follow Father need not have worried about the bitters as I have not opened any of the bottles yet. I have been sorry since I left that I did not spend my last evening in Boston at home as it seems to me that I was away from home during my visit. Austin is well and appears to enjoy himself. Excuse the shortness of this letter next will be longer. I have made up my mind that father will go without you and mother. Give my love to Berk.

From yours affectionately   Charley

****

Camp Hamilton, Va.   March 2 /62

Dear Nellie,

I owe you many apologies for my neglect in omitting to write to you. I have received three letters from you and have sent two myself. Father arrived here Thursday morning and instead of staying only twelve hours has staid until now, leaving tonight for Baltimore. Austin seems to like camp life and manages to pass away his time pleasantly. I have succeeded in keeping father on the go most of his time; he has been fortunate in having fine weather, but cold, since he arrived. You must ask all the questions you wish of Austin, he has been on picket with me, also on a wooding party outside the picket. I have myself been quite busy making out muster rolls; the company are putting up new tents, which has to be looked after; not taking in consideration the time with father. As soon as I get settled into my old routine you will hear from me as usual. I shall send this by Austin. In regard to buying the engraving you mentioned, I have seen two small one here which I think would please you better, and if I can obtain them, I will send them on. I received McClellan's dream[75] in one of the papers which you sent me that same day that I received your letter containing it. Father brings in some curiosities, the stones which Austin brings you carry to some lapidary have him cut it like diamond and it will make a very pretty stone. I shall write you oftener than last week. Give my regards to all.

Yours affectionately,   Charley

****

Camp Hamilton Va.   March 5th /62

Dear Nellie,

It is half past seven o'clock in the morning and in 3/4 of an hour I start for picket. By this time father has arrived home; I wonder if he notice that as the steamer Constitution was on her way to Newport News the rebel from Sewall's point fired three

---

[73] Not identified

[74] The reading is not in doubt, but the reference is not known.

[75] A contemporary broadside

shells at her. Monday evening there were eight heavy guns fired by the rebels at Craney island the purpose of which I don't know, rumor stated that it might be the successful launch of the Merrimac[76]. We have had one beautiful day since father left, but it was cool. Monday night for a half hour the rain came down with as much violence as I ever remember of seeing it starting some small leaks in my tent, I went out of my tent with the impression that it was a violent hail storm but found myself mistaken. I forgot to mention that the guns on Craney island[77] are so powerful that at the distance we are from them Mrs Rogers state that the concussion jarred the crockery. Nellie, notwithstanding the rumors of a large reinforcement soon to arrive we now have here at Camp Hamilton less troops by one regiment than we have had all winter and consequently our turn to go on picket comes oftener, it is now once in ten days. I intended to have written you a long letter last evening, but had an invitation to play a game of Whist with Drs. Jewett[78] & Whiston[79] accepted it got interested did not retire until late. Give my regard to all friends. Yours   affectionately
    Charley

****

Camp Hamilton, Va.   March 9 /62

Dear Nellie,

I have a great deal to write and have but little time to do it. In the last twenty four [hours] we have been afflicted severely. The long looked for Merrimac made her appearance yesterday afternoon a little after one o'clock and long shall I remember it. Saturday was a beautiful day mild and pleasant and I took the opportunity to go to the fort; while at the fort I heard that the Merrimac had made her appearance and it was soon made manifest by the booming of heavy cannon I immediately returned to the camp and found that orders has been issued to have every man furnished with 1 days extra rations and stand in readiness to march at a moments notice. Having every thing arranged I turned my attention to watching the conflict, which was a warm one as you shall see, As soon as it became evident that Newports News was the object aimed at, General Mansfield signalize for aid, but before he receive it the action had commenced. The Merrimac assisted by gunboats from Richmonds & Norfolk numbering I am told as high as eight made directly for Newports News sustaining the united fires of the Congress & the Cumberland and the shore battery which did not affect her in the least, passing right by the Congress without replying to the well directed broadsides which she was pouring into her, made directly for the Frigate

---

[76] The old U.S.S. *Merrimac*, rebuilt by the Confederates as an ironclad, C.S.S. *Virginia*. The havoc caused among the U.S. Fleet by this revolutionary warship on March 8th, and her historic encounter the next day with the Northern answer to the threat, the U.S.S. *Monitor* - the first battle between ironclad warships - are well documented, and Johnson gives an eyewitness account of the battle in his next two letters.

[77] They must indeed have been powerful, being some 10 miles south of Fort Monroe, across Hampton Roads, near Portsmouth.

[78] Charles C. Jewett, regimental surgeon through the 16th's entire period of service. A resident of Holliston, Massachusetts, he enlisted on August 1, 1861 as a Surgeon. Three days later he was commissioned into Field & Staff of the 16th Massachusetts, and later Mustered out on July 24, 1864. Jewett attended to Johnson following his wound at Gettysburg.

[79] Assistant Surgeon Edward A. Whiston. A 22-year-old Physician residing in Framingham, Mass., he enlisted on August 5,1861 as an Assistant Surgeon. On the same day he was commissioned into Field and Staff of the 16th Massachusetts. He was discharged for promotion to Surgeon on March 5, 1863, joining the First Massachusetts Infantry. He was Mustered Out on May 28,1864

Cumberland, coming right under gun firing her broadside clean through her near the water mark steam around to her bow and gave her two broadsides of which raked fore and aft the ball going clean through her and then open with canister the slaughter at this moment must have been frightful both boat were very close in shore under the land battery, the groan of wounded and dying could be distinctly heard in the camp on shore, to cap the climax she began to sink, but not sinking fast enough to suit the rebel they drove the beak of their boat into her twice which nearly split her open. The officers and crew of the Cumberland fought nobly continue to fire, even while the vessel was sinking, with remarkable precision every shot striking but owing to build of the Merrimac every shot as it struck would glance from its side in the air and fall harmless. The Congress was run ashore to save but all her officer were taken prisoner, the sailor being permitted to leave. The land battery fired admirably wasting no shot but without effect. While all this was taking place the Minnesota was being towed followed by the Roanoke to the assistance of Newport News, and as each passed Sewall's Point the battery their would open on them, which our men of war would return as well as our gun from the Rip Raps. The Minnesota got a ground fortunately out of the reach of the Rebel fort where for a while she had to combat several large gunboats with only the aid of few of our gunboats. The Roanoke after seeing the disasters at Newports News exchanged a few shot with Sewall's point then retired to the protection of the fort. The firing at Newport News at 1/2 past four began to slacken the Rebel paying particular attention now to Minnesota which unless some[80].
The Mail leave now finish it in my next.

      Yours Affectionately Charley

****

Camp Hamilton, Va, March 12 /62

Dear Nellie,

  The last letter I wrote was brought to an abrupt close as the mail had left unusually early so I handed it to Mrs. McKiver[81] who was about starting for Boston. The letter had not been re-read as is my usual custom, all I hope is that you can understand part of it if not the whole. About an hour after the letter was sent I received orders to furnish my men with three days rations and be prepared to march at a moments notice. An hour after the order was sent me five companies including mine from the 16th were on the way to Newport News. I will now return to where I left off in my last letter. I believe the frigate Cumberland had been sunk and the Congress surrendered and the rebel gunboats were paying their attention to the Minnesota who was at their mercy being aground   At this stage of affairs the Roanoke sailed back under the fort. For over an hour the Minnesota was with the exception of a few very small gunboats the single object of attention when the frigate St. Lawrence and large gunboat came to their assistance and the combat was continued until about eight o'clock, the flashing of the guns and the explosion of the shells being extremely vivid, when the sound of the cannons gradually ceased. A little before eight a bright light was seen, it was at first supposed that the Minnesota had been fired but as the light grew more glaring we could distinguish that it was the Congress. All through the

---

[80] This seems to make little sense. The small piece of text from "some" to the end of the letter is written on a separate page, presumably the fourth page of the letter, and it might at first glance be assumed that there may be a page missing. However, Johnon explains in his next letter (March 12th) that he was cut off in mid-sentence by the necessity of catching the post.

[81] Spelt thus, but presumably the wife of 1st Lt. Samuel McKeever of Cambridge.

evening explosions from her loaded guns and loose shells were frequent resembling minute guns and it was mournful to hear them at nearly one o'clock the final explosion took place which sent in to air about every thing of the ship that remained above water making the earth shake. Half of each company was ordered to be awake all night, I went to bed about 9 o'clock, being awoke at twelve o'clock. Before I went to bed a rumor was circulated that the Monitor had arrived, but it was such good news though we all sincerely hoped it yet we did not dare believe it. Every thing passed of quietly after the explosion of the Congress at 4 o'clock, the Company all turned out under arms to be in readiness for an attack which was almost known to be about to take place; but nothing transpired until about nine o'clock when the Merrimac with two large steamer advance directly towards the the [sic] poor though not entirely helpless Minnesota   at the left of the Minnesota towards Pig Point a small black object looking no larger than a ship launch was visible; while around the Minnesota were little tug boats armed mostly with one gun (these boat are able to look after them selves owing to their speed and smallness) but nothing good [could] be seen that we felt we could call the Monitor and our feeling were bitter against somebody that had left us as it seemed entirely at the mercy of the enemy; but following event proved us in the wrong. The Merrimac gradually approached the Minnesota having these two armed steamers sailing so as to intercept all escape, apparently not noticing the little black object when the speed of the rebel seemed to slacken and the Merrimac after firing one or two shots at the our [sic] frigate sent one at this small affair which did not seem to them (probable) very formidable fire, until the Monitor in spite of what had occurred on the previous day sailed directly for the Merrimac, which circumstance alone must have shown to the rebel the great confidence the Monitor had that she could hold her own with her. As soon as we could see what the black object was actually steering for our terrible foe a great weight was taken from us and our confidence in her ability to defend increased as the fight progressed. As soon as the Monitor open one of her gun the Merrimac power was known it sent the two rebel steamers under point Sewall leaving the Merrimac alone. The Merrimac having eight guns the Monitor only two made the contest appear unequal but our guns were heavy we could tell when she fired by the shrieking of her balls which was plainly heard. I must confess when the Merrimac delivered two broadsides at close quarters into the Monitor that I expected to see the Monitor either sink or become disabled but at the latter part of the fight that when the Monitor had so manoeuvred that the Minnesota could bring her eleven inch gun to bear bringing the Merrimac under two fires I began to feel confident of the result which was increased by the Monitor going completely around the Merrimac pouring rapidly her solid shot while the rebel seemed helpless and soon after steamed away for Craney island. There were several exciting moment one when it was evidently the intention of the Merrimac to run down our boat but was skillfully avoided. I must now close shall send a letter by next mail. Received a letter from you and Austin; all well and safe Expect the Stevens Battery here[82] . Give my regards to all.

      Affectionately   Charley

****

         Camp Hamilton, Va.   Mch. 13/ 62

Dear Nellie,

  My company has left for Hampton Bridge for Picket duty I have just been

---

[82] Unit not identified. The two Union units with that designation were not posted to Fort Monroe.

relieved from Officer of the Day and shall join my company this afternoon. I believe I left off in my last letter describing the engagement between the Monitor and the Merrimac which as you know resulted in the retiring of the Merrimac. Before the Merrimac retreated the Monitor sailed round her several times driving her shots into her. I shall now close the engagement and commence with the company as it left Camp Hamilton for Newport News. I left at 3 o'clock in the afternoon arriving at six o'clock after a rapid march; the road being in some places so bad that we had to go in single file; though the majority of the way the roads were good. We slept in the open air without tents or covering otherwise than a blanket, where the ground had the marks of the effects of the Merrimac's shots the ground being ploughed in several places pieces of shell laying about and we found one that had not exploded still filled with powder and might be used again. On going to the beach I could see only a small portion of the bow of the Congress and the masts of the Cumberland while the shore was covered with fragment of charred wood pieces of furniture parts of state rooms, clothing and boxes; farther up the shore kegs of pickles had been found in large numbers. The next morning we change our locality and succeeded in borrowing a few tents, not enough for my company to make ourselves comfortable. The only thing that happened beyond our usual routine was an exciting chase after some cattle who by being driven so far and fast had got wild scattered in all directions pursued by cavalry and infantry with numberless dogs; my regiment killed three which was quite lucky as we needed some meat, it was confiscated property did not cost U.S. anything. After staying at Newport News two nights we started in the morning for Camp Hamilton. arriving at eleven o'clock; since we have been here we have had more to do oweing to the twentieth regiment formally *[formerly]* at this camp being at Newport News. Colonel Wyman[83] is now commander of the camp. While we were away the gunboat Whitehall burnt up[84] ; she laid abreast of our camp, and our officers who were here at the time plainly heard the groans of the persons who were in her, she exploded at about 1 a.m. with terriffic noise. *[rest of letter missing]*

****

(Simeon Smith, a 44-year-old Fish Dealer from Waltham, Mass., enlisted on June 29, 1861 as a Private and mustered the same day into Co. H, 16th Massachusetts Infantry. He was listed as missing on August 29, 1862 at 2nd Bull Run, and was discharged for disability on October 2, 1862 at New York City. On March 14th he wrote home, mentioning the Battle at Hampton Roads on the 8th-9th and giving some interesting insights into the fear in which the C.S.S. Virginia was held, and into life in the regiment)

---

[83] Col. Powell Tremlett Wyman. Born 1828. Cadet at the US Military Academy 1846 - 1850; Bvt. 2nd Lt., 1st U.S. Artillery, July 1, 1850; served in Florida against the Seminole Indians 1850 and 1854-7; Adjutant, 1854-7; at Fort Moultrie, 1857-8; Fort Monroe Artillery School, 1858-9; leave of absence, 1859-60. Resigned July 13, 1860, and in Europe until outbreak of Civil War; Col., 16th Massachusetts Inf., Aug. 5, 1861; killed in action June 30, 1862 at Glendale, Va. On July 15, 1862, Brig Gen. Joseph Hooker sent a letter to Governor Andrew of Mass., regretting Wyman's death: "At the Battle of Glendale... he was the personification of gallantry, and rendered services which will cover his name in renown. The enemy... came pouring down on my right, the extreme of which Wyman held... The success of the enemy, at that moment, would have destroyed the army. The loss of Wyman falls heavily upon me." Buried in Mount Auburn Cemetery, Cambridge, Mass. The monument over his grave reads: "To the memory of Powell T. Wyman, Col., 16th Reg., Mass. Vol. Infantry. Erected by the Officers and men of the Regiment / He was a glorious soldier, and his death in every sense was that of a hero in a holy cause / Killed in Battle, June 30, 1862, aged 34 yrs."

[84] A tug, accidentally burned on March 10.

Camp Hamilton (Fortress Monroe)
Mar 14th, 1862

Bro. Thomas

Not being very well to day I thought I would devote a few moments in writing to you [.] I have had a severe cold for a few days past but am getting better[.] My Health generaly is as good as usual, and I hope this will find you and all our friends well. I have nothing particular to write[.] I will state I saw those Naval Battle fought on last Saturday and Sunday, wich I supose you have seen acounts of in the papers. on Saturday the rebel Steamer Merimack atacked the Cumberland ran into her and sank Her of Newport News point. She then atacked the Frigate Congress overpowered her and she surendered after a short but desperate fight. one of the sailors told me it was no use to contend with Her as no vessel of Wood could possibly stand against so formidable a foe. Both vessels suffered seven in kiled and wounded. She next atack the Minesota, and she getting aground, could not work her guns to advantage she also got a good Pepering of Shot & Shell, however by the timely arival of the Ericsson Iron Batery wich engage the Merimack on Sunday morning, giving her all the worst of the Fights, that last seen of her she was Steaming for Norfolk, suposed to be badly cripled by the better Monitor. She is a brick and in my opinion if it had not been for Her timely arival wee should all have fared hard as wee were so Encampd that She could have Sheled us with perfect ease. It has ben all excitement here ever since as wee have ben expecting an atack from the Enemy untill to day. all is quiet. this Soldiering is a curious life, filed with anciety, and sometimes hard; but a good man that is always ready to do duty will find its not the worst Buisness in the service and a Gentleman, perhaps I have had a chance to know as I have Cooked on particular occaisions for the Staff down to the Field officers[.] on every occasion I have always ben used well. My regular duty is cooking for our Co. Capt. [Gardner] Banks is a very pleasant officer[.] Some our boys have got sick of the life, I tell them they ought not to get home sick, long as the maried men don't complain[.] as for myself I feel contented, though long to see my Family and had I once suposed this war would have been such a long one, I should not have left my Family although I hope they get along comfortable as I send them the Most of my earnings. I hope to be at Home by fall, though Most of our Co. think by July, but in my opinion they will be disapointed as I see but little prospects of a speedy peace. I should write oftener if wee had convenience as you will see that my writing is poor as we have nothing but a ruff board to write on poor pens &c.

P.S. I will write to my wife in a day or two[.] wee are expecting to get paid of every day, therefore I will hold on a few days then sent her some money. please tell them I am well and hurd from them on arival of Mr. Stedman a member of our Co. from Waltham. He was at home on a furlough. Please write let me know how buisness is &c[.] now kind Brother I must close hopeing to meet you all once more ere long.

Your Brother in Haste   Simeon Smith[85]

****

Camp Hamilton Va.   Mch. 16th 1862

Dear Nellie,

I have received your letters of Mch. 11 & 13th. Since I last wrote there has been no changes and quietness has prevailed as far as action or combat is concerned but the camp has been flooded with rumor and we have been under marching order about half the time the men keeping their equipments on and officers going to bed

---

[85] Authors' collections

with clothes and boots on. I meant to have mentioned the pleasant evening I spent at the Delaware regiment[86] at their theatre; but the naval battle was so much more interesting that I have deferred it. The theatre is a large log house the seats for the audience rising one above the other. a regular stage with scenery of which I believe they have four sets, orchestra consisting of the regimental band. The ladies parts are taken by the actors. The acting was good and the whole past of very pleasantly. I send you one of the programmes which was reduced to the present state by being in my vest pocket while marching to Newport News. All the ladies have left and every person here without business are also obliged to leave. I hope that before the Merrimac again makes her appearance the Monitor will have some other battery to assist her as the Merrimac has 4 guns to her one. You can send on the sash as it is if the difference in color is not to great. I have received Austin letter. Give my regards to all

Yours Affectionately

Charley

****

Mch. 22 / 62   Camp Hamilton, Va.

Dear Nellie,

I received your letter of Mch. 18th yesterday with pleasure. You will soon hear exciting news from this quarter; but I believe we are not to participate. A large arrival of troops has increased our force largely, having received a division from what direction I shall not tell you; it surprises us here to see how quiet the papers our [are] about it not even mentioning that there is a rumor afloat concerning it. I was told today that no letter would leave the fort for seven days. We intended to have made an attack on a certain locality but the night fixed was so very stormy that it was not attempted. You can make up your mind to my remaining at Camp Hamilton whatever occurs. Tell Austin that I have altered the arrangement of my tent have the bunk placed perpendicular to its old position; made wider and placed lower, it seems to give me more room and comfort. Sunday morning; I have just returned from visiting the lately arrived regiments.[87] The first night of there arrival was a severe night the troops were without shelter and exposed to a sever rain most of them took refuge in stables and other building our regiment accommodated about 500 with lodgings and coffee. We have about 12 additional regiments, from every Northern state. I received a letter from you this morning. We are now enjoying a magnificent day, mild without wind; it is the clearest day we have had for a long time. These new regiments are without tents and have arranged their rubber blankets over boughs and stick making a respectable dog house accommodating two which serves to shelter them from rain and wind. You may expect to hear news from this quarter in a fortnight. Give my regards to all.

Yours affectionately,   Charley

****

Camp Hamilton Va.   Mch. 25 /62

Dear Nellie,

I received to day your letter of Mch. 22nd. I am sorry to disappoint father but I

---

[86] See footnote 59

[87] The 1st Michigan Infantry, 5th Maryland Infantry and 58th Pennsylvania Infantry arrived at the Dept. of Virginia, Fortress Monroe, during March 1862.

may stay here; the reasons are against our moving. All the regiments arriving are brigaded and unless we form a brigade of the regiments here we shall probably remain for some time at least. You need not be surprised to hear that Genl McClellan[88] has arrived at fort Monroe. I don't know nor can I conjecture the number of troops arrived or to come but they are here in large numbers and are continually coming. I saw sixteen large river steamboat entering Hampton Roads together, it was a magnificent site. I go on picket tomorrow and if the weather is pleasant I shall enjoy it. I saw yesterday Ward Frothingham[89] who staid at the Bowling alley Lexington he is now corporal in the Mass. 22nd. We have now here the Mass. 9th, 18th and 22nd and expect the first, eleventh and thirteenth, making including our regiment seven from Mass. Dr Cogwells rode over from Newport News, Sunday call to see me enquiries all ways very particularly after Callie. Lt Tucker will write his mother to to let you have one of his new daguerertype. I commenced messing together yesterday I mean Lt. Rogers, Tucker and myself have our meals together. You are to direct your letters here until you get notice to do otherwise. Give my regards to all.

        Yours Affectionately   Charles

****

      Mch. 26 /62   Camp Hamilton Va.

Dear Nellie,

You must be satisfied with a short letter to day as I was very busy last evening, looking after men and officers who had just arrived and were exposed without any covering to strong wind and heavy rain. I did not retire until late and then not to my own bed it being occupied by a lieutenant in the 87 N. York regiment[90]. There is a rumor that we shall advance soon, if so, any letters will be very irregular we are having a large reinforcement arriving here. I did not save anything for a relic except two little pieces of paper which I found on the shore which I enclose. If I should relate all the rumors that I hear it would astonish you, but probably some of them may be true, we are to have 50,000 troops here and are to advance at a rapid rate taking breath at Norfolk, I mean Richmond. I have received your letter of Mch 16th. Lieut Tucker is attached to my company

The attack made on Gen'l McClellan by some in the newspapers is wicked and proceeds from a malignant disposition and the man who makes is enemy of his country. I almost believe politics would permit any means to accomplish the end which its desire. I am in excellent health and if we advance don't believe all you hear or all you read ever. I send you two engravings of Camp Hamilton, one for yourself and one for father. This two pieces of papers were from the Congress.

      Yours affectionately,   Charley

****

     Camp Hamilton, Va.   Mch. 30th /62

Dear Nellie,

---

[88] Maj.-Gen. George B. McClellan, Commander of the Army of the Potomac.

[89] 2ne Lieutenant Ward Frothingham was a 33 year-old Farmer from Lexington. Wounded and captured at Gaines Mill, Va. Captured again at Ft. Stedman, Petersburg, March 25, 1865.

[90] It is unclear why; the 87th New York was in the Washington, D.C. area until April, when it was ordered to the Peninsula.

I have received your letter of the 26th also a box of luxuries. This box was not so fortunate as its predecessors. The jar of pickles was broken and was obliged to throw them (the pickles) away owing to small peices of glass being through them, I have written two letters every week and if you have not received them one must have been mislaid. We have had continual arrivals of troops since I last wrote   they now camp beyond Hampton. I ~~rode around~~ went horseback to visit the various encampments yesterday but few if any have tents but shelter themselves with rubber blankets made for the purpose; two sticks with cruckets are placed in the ground and a pole laid in the cruckets, which answers for the ridge pole, two blankets are tied together laid over the pole and fastened to the ground which protects two person from perdicular [sic] rain, one end is closed with brush or peat or may be with another blanket, this manner of protecting themselves is generally adopted; instead of a ridge pole they often bend twigs fastening both ends in the grounds which give a semi-circle appearance; a great deal of ingenuity is displayed. There must be 70,000 troops beyond Hampton[91] including all arms; between Hampton and Newmarket there are nothing but troops. Hampton from a deserted place has suddenly become alive with business, almost everything is now landed there having two wharf at which are continually three or four steamers besides canal boats; in the river are anchored waiting their turn all descriptions of vessels stern wheel, side wheel, propeller steam boats, with canal boats, lighters besides the small tug boats continually moving around. In the ruins of Hampton are temporarily encamped troops and soldier have taken chimneys and every nook to shelter themselves in; the quiet streets are filled with government wagons mostly drawn by six mules, soldiers on foot, horseback, single and by company, cannons, caissons, battery wagons and everything that relates to war.

Genl McClellan is said to be here. With all the preparation now being made for an advance with officers here of all ranks nobody can tell where, when or how the blow is to be struck, which direction the troops are going, whether they will all advance on Norfolk capture it and then advance by way of railroad to Petersberg [Petersburg, Va.] to Richmond by land and by James River with our fleet, or whether parts of the troops will be left to take Norfolk while the larger part proceeded directly by the same means to Richmond or whether they are all or part going by the way of Yorktown   everything is a conjecture and it speaks well of the General that a movement of such magnitude can be planned, prepared and the purpose and place not known until the blow is struck.

Concerning our regiment we know nothing   neither does the Colonel   we may attack Norfolk with what regiments we have here independent of the newly arrived regiments. I suppose you understand that I am missing in my old fashion way and have only three in the mess. I forgot to state that there [are] several Mass. regiments here and I understand that General Hooker's division[92] is to come here also in which

---

[91] The report of John Tucker, Assistant Secretary of War, stated that 121,500 men were transported to Fort Monroe in a period of less than three weeks during late March and early April in preparation for the Peninsula Campaign (Sears, 1992, 24).

[92] Joseph "Fighting Joe" Hooker (1814-1879), at the time Brigadier-General, 2nd Division, III Corps, Army of the Potomac. A West Point graduate, Hooker was a highly regarded officer during the Mexican War, receiving brevets for gallantry through Lieutenant Colonel. For some reason he resigned the service, then returned as a Brigadier General. During the Peninsula campaign, a press wire read, "Fighting—Joe Hooker", as a result of which the nickname stuck. He fought in many of the war's major battles up to the engagements in the fight for Chattanooga and Atlanta, at which point he asked to be relieved, feeling he was slighted in his service. He exercised department command until his retirement in 1868, and died at Garden City, New York in 1879. He was a hard-fighting general whose personal relationships and

there are several Mass. regiments including the 1st. Saturday afternoon it commenced to rain the storm gradually increased till evening the rain poured steady until this morning when it held up; I am much alarmed about the condition of the soldiers beyond Hampton they had made preparations to meet the rain as it fell but none in case of a flood as I fear that some of the field on which they are will be partially flooded, but a soldier can stand more than you people can imagine. When I was in Boston I thought, or people tried to make me think that the war was about over and I acknowledge that when on State St. reading those despatches (which as they travel seem to increase on the bulletin board I thought that with such rapid strides we shall be soon to the gulf of Mexico, Boston papers seem to ornament the facts and stretch them beyond limits, I have now before me the Boston Traveller and the manner in which they write their telegram give them a higher color than the papers which I read.

The men of our regiment are taking a great deal of pride in their looks and take pleasure in comparing themselves with the troops now arriving, in visiting their friends in other regiments they go in full dress and white gloves and have been taken for regulars which makes them quite proud. I have bought me a new sword to take with me when we go into active service. It is a regular artillery sword[93] with a steel scabbard little longer and heavier than my other, my other scabbard being of leather is not strong enough for rough work; I obtained it from the United States cost $5.00, I am about prepared for a start have my loose articles mostly packed in a box, for it would seems strange if we are kept here and not allowed to participate in any of the active engagements. I should think that you would be lonely at Lexington but in pleasant weather. Ruth would have a fine place to play. I would suit myself in regard to where I spent the summer, I shall not send home but $140.00 which may not be enough to balance what was due the firm but shall make it up next pay day. I loose about $25.00 a month by not drawing pay for a servant as I employ an enlisted man he is so short that I don't want him in my company and he is a good servant so I keep him, the officer generally are not very particular upon this point and draw any way though they have unenlisted man as a servant. This seems a very long letter for me so I close. Give my regards to all.

     Yours affectionately   Charles

Monday Morning
There are a forest of masts and smoke funnels in Hampton Road this morning. If there are any rubber articles made to put up quickly to shelter one from the rain very light, they must be no heavier than a rubber blanket as I shall be obliged to carry it on my back I should like one. There is a rubber [piece *crossed out*] goods that you can crawl in if they are light I should like one. My sash is all right. More troops arrived this morning. Received your letter of Mch. 28 this morning.

****

          Camp Hamilton, Va.   April 3rd, /62
Dear Nellie,
  I received yesterday your letter of Mch. 30th as well as one from Austin. I think that you are mistaken as to my not answering your questions, when a direct question

---

behaviour are reputed – without any real foundation - to have brought the word "hooker" into the language.

[93] This is not Johnson's surviving sword, which is the Model 1850 Foot Officer's sword normally used by Infantry officers. Johnson provides unusual direct evidence of an infantry officer using the longer, and more robust, sabre, which would have been heavier and more unwieldy to use in the less mobile infantry battle conditions.

is asked, it gets an answer. Last night or rather early this morning we had our first thunder shower, the thunder was heavy but appeared some way off as the lighten[ing] failed to illuminate my tent, for a short period poured heavy drops of rain. It is a lovely morning; last night shower has washed the roads clean and everything has that fresh, bright appearance which we often notice at home after a thunder shower. One of my men died day before yesterday under peculiar circumstances[94]; last Monday night he was found by a patrol from our regiment in the guard house of a neighbouring regiment drunk, and was left there for the night, sending for him the next morning he was placed in our guard house he obtained more liquor by some means, so at noon he was very happy laughing and talking as drunken men will. The sergeant having care of the prisoners, as far as keeping them to work, took the prisoners out, excepting this drunken man, leaving him alone in the guard house; the sergeant of the guard having occasion to confine a man put him into the guards house, notice this drunken man look peculiar in the face, spoke to him, receiving no reply, then sent immediately for the doctor, who said on his arrival that he must have been dead some time. To show you how sudden must have been his death it will be necessary to describe the guard house to you, it is a large log house with a door at one end; nearly in the centre a partition is made upright logs, dividing it into two part, the front part nearest the door is used by the guard and the rear part, having a door in the partition opening into it, which door is made fast by a padlock, is used to confine the prisoners. The logs used to make the partition are not placed so near together but that you can look from one part to the other between them, in fact there is quite a large hole with bars across, where you can see everything occurring in the next room. When you consider that as well as having a look at the prisoners, all sound in one part can be distinctly heard in the other and that the part used for the guard always has somebody in it is show that his death was too sudden for him to cry for assistance. The company immediately subscribe $57.00 to pay the expense of sending on his body, what is left after paying expenses is going to his son which will be nearly $35.00. His body was escorted part of the way to the boat according to military rule having the band with us, it makes a very solemn impression to see a military funeral; proceeding the body is the escort with reverse arms after the body came the company or whoever wishes to accompany it, the whole procession marching in common time the band playing a dirge; the officers march in the rear of all with swords reversed. I have a little white kitten which I keep in my tent, it is her fault that the above line are blotted as she is walking over the paper and trying to play with my pen as I write. She crawls all over me.

They have a balloon here now[95], it was inflated Monday afternoon but did not go up and has been up since [sic] although we have had some favourable weather. There continues to be the same constant arrival of troops now as when I last wrote no forward movement has as yet taken place. I receive the papers now quite regularly. The flowers in the gardens around the officers' quarters are in full blossom and everything indicates the commencement of spring. As I have no more time I will close. Give my regards to all. I could not get a rose bush from Hampton for father, could not find any. This kitten would please Berk, but it would scratch him. I expect in my next letter from you to hear of your visit to Lexington.

---

[94] The only man in the Company shown as dying on April 1, 1862 is Private Thomas Flynn, whose cause of death is given as "died of disease" at Camp Hamilton.

[95] The Balloon Corps, established through the efforts of Professor Thaddeus S.C.Lowe, provided valuable information for the Army and was used extensively, and to great advantage, for monitoring enemy troops during the Peninsula campaign. Its existence was short-sightedly terminated in 1863.

Yours affectionately

****

Camp Hamilton, Va,   April 7th. /62

Dear Nellie,

I have received your letters of the 1st and 3rd of April. In regard to a boarding-house, you cannot be too particular, it will be difficult to obtain a place such as you want, I am afraid with all your caution that you will at last agree upon a place that will not be as agreeable to you as you expect. I do not object to Lexington, because it will be so pleasant for both you and Berk to spend the pleasant days at the house and from Lexington you can make visits on your friends. I would enquire about Mr. Mulliken if I decided to go up whether he kept a good table or if the family were agreeable   also if they are to take boarders and how many; wherever you go I would satisfy myself on these point. You forgot to mention although the last letter was written on my birthday anything about it. The harbor on Hampton Roads have been until the last two or three days crowded with vessel and night time you can imagine that you see two heavens one above and one on the horizon in front of you for there was but very little difference in appearance; lately there has been a decrease in number. I have this moment received a letter from father, quite a long one. Instead of writing you a letter yesterday I was hunting up news and seeing sight and worked so hard that on my return to camp was too tired to write Saturday   at sunrise commenced the forward movement; the large army consisting of a strong 100,000 men commanded by Gen. McClellan in person started I suppose for Richmond. During Saturday continual booming of cannon was heard and we were all anxious to learn the cause or rather the particulars as the cause was evident; we were very desirous of learning how determined a stand the rebel were making and at what place;[96] toward six o'clock the reports began to slacken and, at last, gradually ceased. Sunday morning we listened but heard only now and then the cannon's echo and concluded that the rebels had retired from the position which they had held yesterday. I will give you as I heard it an account of Saturday's doing of the grand army. Our army pushed forward without meeting any oposition except the occasional firing of the rebel pickets retiring, until they arrived at what was called Winn's Mills (but I am of the opinion that it was at Harrold's Mill) where the rebels showed fight. On the arrival of the head of our column opposite Winn's Mill the Rebel band came out of their entrenchments and played Dixie; we brought the two batteries to bear on them, Griffin's[97] and 5th Massachusetts; on our batteries opening on them at every good shot that they made the rebel would jump on the parapet and cheer. We had five or six killed before that place   this is all that I have learnt of Saturday experience of our army. Sunday morning early the army started again and Sunday noon lay before Yorktown where today (Monday) I suppose they have commenced to shell it. Now I must relate my Sunday excursion, leaving out entirely the various little mishaps such as the giving out of one of my stirrups and awkward figure which I cut endeavouring to ride a hard horse under difficulties. Sunday morning I obtained permission to go beyond Hampton and after considerable difficulty succeeded in obtaining a horse and a very poor saddle. Adjutant, Quartermaster and myself at 10 o'clock started taking the road to Yorktown. After passing Hampton nothing interesting is seen excepting here and there a tent left behind, and stores left with a small guard; along the road would be

---

[96] On the east bank of the Warwick River, about 3 miles south of Yorktown

[97] Johnson must be in error here; there was no Union battery with this title.

stray soldiers among them was a large sprinkling of Duryea Zouaves of 5th N. York regt. who have been stationed at Baltimore for eight months; they have a flashy uniform made in regular Algerine Zouave style pantaloon of bright red color, turban and every thing to correspond, they have been very comfortable all winter and the change is considerable for them; it may be the same with us. I have strayed away from what I commenced to write about that is that we met nothing of interest until arriving at Newmarket Bridge with [sic] is only two miles beyond Hampton this bridge has obtained considerable fame with us as it was the scene of a little skirmish last winter[98] and as being the boundary in a measure of our territory as we rarely ventured over it there being no bridge, the bridge is in itself insignificant as it is only a rod long but association connected with it make it worth describing. After crossing Newmarket bridge and travelling seven long miles we arrived at the scene of our disgraceful defeat, Big Bethel[99] which is really a strong place by nature and the earthworks are skillfully laid out but the earthworks themselves are very light and low and seem to me entirely unable to protect the troops a rod behind them. The earthworks extend a long distance and I should judge much more form[id]able than when our three months troops attacked them. The old church from which it derives it name Big Bethel is still standing with windows broken and other signs of disability, but it is strange that it was not burnt during the engagement being made of wood. Leaving Big Bethel the next place we arrive at worth noticing is Harrolds Mills, at which place I think the rebels made a stand Saturday, this is by nature much more formidable and the rebels have have [sic] much more extensive works than at Big Bethel and it surprises me that they should leave it without making more resistance. To enable you to better understand how the fort are situated it is best perhaps for me to inform you that the country generally is level except where there are stream of water, then the stream seems in some places to have cut it way through leaving high perpendicular bluff on either side of it it is on these bluffs that they erect earthworks and also works raking the approach to them. The sweep at Big Bethel is limited compared to Harrold Mills as the roads before it crosses the creek wind with the creek exposed for some distance to an enfilading fire; as you come down the road you face a bluff without any fortification appearing on it, and there is where they have exercised their cunning, for if a force should march directly by the road, without having flankers out either to the right or left they would not discover the batteries until they had descended the bank and had turned either to right or left and in case of retreat would be exposed to sharpshooters besides being under a raking fire sometime; the desertion of this place by the rebels and falling back on Yorktown show at that place they intend to risk everything and it is no doubt well entrenched, but they have got to meet a stronger power than their trenches will make them, in our army. In the army now in motion there is at least 216 field peices small to be sure compared with those which they have in their works but nevertheless could throw such an incessant shower of shells that it must make their work untenable. In the attack on Yorktown our gunboats will participate and are already before the place, they all carry heavy guns and of long range and the rebel defences must be strong to withstand for any long time the combined attack of our army and navy. Leaving Harrold Mill we pushed our way among forges, battery wagons, ambulances and

---

[98] See note 54.

[99] In the first notable fight of the War, on June 10, 1861, eight miles north-west of Fort Monroe, a hopelessly inexperienced attacking Federal force under Maj. Gen. Benjamin Butler was quickly routed by a Confederate force of one-third its size under Col. Daniel H. Hill. Though the engagement was little more than a skirmish in comparison with later actions, the defeat was a humiliation for the North.

government wagon, which as you approached our army began to appear in large numbers, towards Yorktown, between which and Harrolds Mills their are no fields works of any account; long line of rifle pits in the woods on the right of Harrolds Mill to check a flank movement was all that I noticed. At two o'clock we arrived near the Hd. Quarters of Gen. McClellan[100] and was among the army (as it use to be called) of the Potomac; as luck would have it we came across the 20th M[ass].V. and I had the pleasure of seeing Harry Sturgis[101], Capt. Putnam besides other Mass. boys; while we were there two or more men with shovel came in from the front from throwing up works to protect our gun which were being placed within two miles of Yorktown. Gen McClellan was making a reconnaissance while I was there; I also had the pleasure of seeing three generals. We found very difficult to obtain any dinner for our horses but at last found several wagons seemingly well supplied with oats and hay from which by permission our horses had a good dinner, after the horses had finished we learned that they had been eating from Gen. McClellan's wagons for the use of himself and staff. Near Harrolds Mills I forgot to mention that the rebel barrack were located - could not tell for how many troops they were built for, some of them had been consumed while others were untouched by fire, further on right in the rear of Gen McClellan head quarters situated in the woods and completely surrounded by them was another collection of log house made to accommodate 5,000 troops these by some means had not been touched and are now occupied by 5,000 regular troops. Considering that an immense army had just passed over the road it was surprising what excellent order our troops must have kept, I notice nothing on the road with but trifling exceptions that would appear to have been left behind by carelessness, I counted six horse dead lying by the road. We now had a long ride of twenty miles before us not liking the idea of being in a strange country by night we started at half past three for home, leaving the army before Yorktown with the impression that they would have hot work tomorrow but confident of success. A rebel soldier absent on a furlough, return to his barracks to report for duty which instead of being occupied by his regiment was occupied by N. York 37, he was taken prisoner before he was aware of his mistake (he came across too). 25,000 men are reported at Yorktown and constant arrivals increasing the force. I perhaps better state that I arrived home at seven o'clock tired having been over forty miles horseback. Capt Putnam says that after this battle he shall return as he is unable to stand it, a most remarkable thing is that he feel his lost hand as though it was there[102], he says yesterday that the regiment did considerable double quick and his hand felt as if a knife was stuck into it, his lost hand feels swollen sometimes his fingers itch and he wants to scratch where there is nothing to scratch. The army before Yorktown has all the various facilities for learning the movements of the enemy a balloon ascensions was made Sunday morning the rebel fired shells at it but did no injury. The rebel log houses are made different from ours being made of slabs and show some ingenuity. We took

---

[100] About three and a half miles below Yorktown, east of the road to Hampton.

[101] Lt. Henry M. Sturgis, formerly 20th Mass. Infantry, recently assigned to the staff of Gen. Hiram Berry. A resident of Boston, Sturgis was a 23 year-old Clerk when he enlisted on July 10, 1861 as a 2nd Lieutenant. He was commissioned into Co. H, 20th Massachusetts infantry. He was promoted to 1st Lieutenant On November 10, 1861 and resigned on July 7, 1862. He died in Boston On January 30, 1881

[102] Capt. John Chandler Putnam, born in 1835 and a resident of Boston, was a 26 year-old Clerk when he enlisted on July 10, 1861 as a Captain in Co. H, 20th Massachusetts Infantry. Following his severe wounding at Ball's Bluff, Va., where he lost right his arm, he returned to Fort Monroe on 30 days' leave, but never returned to active duty, receiving a commission in Co. A of the Veterans Reserve Corps on October 29, 1863. He resigned on January 15, 1865. A member of GAR Post #113 in Boston, he died in Santa Barbara, California, on June, 24, 1879

our lunch where three days ago a rebel force was located without any danger of seeing any of them. I send you home two confederate bills, saw some for five cts, these that I send come from Richmond and are of the best quality. Some signs of the Merrimac was evident yesterday   rebel steamers were seen of Sewall['s] Point yesterday, and this morning saw three steamer near Craney Island with eye without aid from opera glass. The mail has left the camp and I must send this down to the fort for if it don't go today I suppose you will be disappointed. We are enjoying beautiful weather   apple trees, peaches in blossom besides various flowers in full bloom. We have now and then a thunder shower.

Give my regards to all.   Yours affectionately,   Charles

****

Camp Hamilton, Va.   April 9, /62

Dear Nellie,

Received your letter today of April 6th as well as some papers. We have been unfortunate in having at this moments severe rain storm, it has now lasted 48 hours with but little signs of its clearing off, it has rendered the roads between here and Yorktown almost impassable, most of the provisions are landed at Shipping point[103] which is not more than five miles to the army but notwithstanding there has been great difficulty in obtaining sufficient food for the soldiers, who must be suffering from the severe weather being exposed, a large number of them, without tents to face it. When you consider that the large number of team which it requires to supply so large an army it is not surprising that the roads should in rainy weather be terribly cut up. They are making corduroy roads[104]   to Shipping point to facilitate transportations. This rain may be a good thing for us as it must affect the rebels (as well as us) more seriously if they have not prepared themselves by accumulating stores as they have a much longer road to travel. What I wrote father is confirmed from another source, concerning the withholding of Gen McDowell's[105]   Corps d'armee from Gen. McClellan after he was promised it. Gen McClellan will be obliged to alter his plans or leave part of his original idea unattempted, it might have been his plan to place Gen. McDowell's Corp d'armee (which consists of three divisions of 17,000 men each), on the one side of James River landing at Suffolk, capture Norfolk with the aid of Gen. Burnside, then advance along the Suffolk railroad to Petersburg and from there to Richmond as well

---

[103] Ship Point, on the west bank of the Poquosin River, Chesapeake Bay, about ten miles from Hampton and five from Yorktown.

[104] Laid with a foundation of horizontal logs at right angles to the direction of the road and levelled with a gravel or other surface.

[105] Maj.-Gen. Irvin McDowell (1818-1885). Educated in France, McDowell received the brevet of captain for gallantry in the Mexican War. He was appointed a Brigadier General at the Civil War's outbreak, but although with 23 years service he never had a field command. He is best known for being in command of Union forces at the First Battle of Bull Run, July 21, 1861, where his inexperienced troops broke, leading to a seemingly resounding defeat which, as events proved, were more damaging to morale than to the progress of the Union cause; indeed, it could be argued that the defeat was so decisive that it led the Confederates to underestimate their enemy, with eventually fatal consequences. He was later made a Major General commanding the 3rd Corps at Second Bull Run, where the result was another Union debacle and where McDowell himself narrowly escaped a court-martial for disobedience that ended the career of fellow Corps commander Fitz-John Porter, through political influence. As a result, he suffered virtual exile to commands in the Pacific northwest. He died in San Francisco, and is buried at the Presidio.

as clearing all the rebel batteries on James River on the south side, while McClellan went up the Peninsula clearing the batteries from his side of James River to Richmond on the North arriving after Gen McDowell had prepared himself to intercept all retreats, with an army at the North, one at the South and gunboats all around Richmond it would be soon taken and a large quantity of plunder bagged. Yorktown is represented as being very strongly fortified, having rifle pits and batteries from York across to James River, making it very difficult to outflank them, but notwithstanding all that we are endeavouring to throw some divisions in there rear to surround them, and I believe the work is progressing although the weather would appear to check all movements. We have rifle pits opposite their earthworks half a mile off in which are stationed Berdan's Sharpshooters[106] with telescopic rifles with which they pick off anyone that shows himself, the rebels also have their sharpshooters who are not to be despised, the rebel have lost a large number, total amounting to fifty killed and wounded; our sharpshooters shot three deserter from the rebels, who deserted in the night, killing 2 and wounder severely the other. The kitten, who I have named Miss Slidell, from her being so saucy[107], has given up playing with my pen and is sitting on my shoulder, she is perfectly white with the exception of her tail which is black and white. She also has two black stripe between her eyes, she would play to rude with Berk and probably scratch him. Thursday morning, it has ceased raining but is still cloudy and very cold, early this morning, we had snow, hail and rain together. I shall need some new shirts soon, those I now have are getting very short. Lieut Tucker sends his regards. We have heard here of the defeat of Beauregard[108] and if we are able to have the same success through the summer that we are having now next autumn will see the end of the war, but there is to be some desperate fighting yet. I like the idea very much of your boarding with John and hope that you will be able to. Give my regards to all.

              Yours   Ever   Charles

****

                                         Camp Hamilton Va.   April 13th /62

Dear Nellie,

I received your letter of April 9th yesterday; you did not in it acknowledge having received the letter which contained two rebel bank bills, and the account of my visit to York Town, We have now had three successive pleasant day and consequently the roads are improving. Friday morning the Merrimac, accompanied by seven other boats, paid us a visit at a respectable distance. The roads at her first appearance was crowded with sails, which were removed rapidly by the aid of tugs, outside. The Merrimac laid near Sewall's point abreast of our camp, occasionally approaching quite near to us, giving the best view of herself that I had had, her decks were crowded with

---

[106] The 1st and 2nd United States Sharpshooters, organised by Col. Hiram Berdan, gained a reputation for deadly accuracy with their Colt's Revolving Rifles and late their Sharp's Rifles. It has been asserted that they killed more Confederate soldiers than any other Union regiment.

[107] Perhaps a private joke, or even a reference to the behaviour of the eldest daughter of John Slidell, one of the two Confederate envoys seized from the British mail steamer *Trent* the previous December by the U.S.S. *San Jacinto*, an action which nearly brought England and the United States to war. She is said to have defiantly slapped the face of the U.S. Lieutenant who had come to take her father off the ship. The incident was presumably well-known in the North.

[108] The Battle of Shiloh, or Pittsburg Landing, Tennessee, April 6-7, 1862

men and she looked as formidable as she is. During the excitement in removing the vessels, two rebel steamboats approached near enough to our shore to seize three transports[109], which were in the mouth of Hampton Creek, the rebel steamers might have been easily persuaded to have remained at a proper distance by a field battery if it had been supposed that they were to have paid us a visit in that manner. After the boats had been captured two batteries of six pieces each were stationed on the shore. It seemed to be the desire of the rebels to have the fight come off in the range of Sewall's point battery and they manoeuvred accordingly. Nearly all of Friday was spent by them in coaxing us to come out, but we had but one object in view that was to prevent the Merrimac from visiting the blockade, which we reasoned she desired to do in order to visit Yorktown and play the old harry with our gunboats there. Directly opposite our hospital within a half mile lay the Naugatuck[110] and on her left an iron gunboat which I heard called 5 different names; about three o'clock the Merrimac fired a shot at them which fell considerably short, The Naugatuck replied with her long ranged gun sending her shots over the Merrimac, and at this position several shots were exchanged, by both gunboats with the Merrimac; this was exciting sport for us as our gunboat laid abreast of us and so near that we could see them load and fire and as if the Merrimac had been some closer or had the range of our cannons in all probability some of her some of her shells would have visited us, as it was I saw the water ploughed up by the Merrimac shots as they came towards us. One shot was fired by the Merrimac, her last shot, which seem to explode the instance it left her gun, and by her subsequent movements we thought she had burst her gun as she immediately steamed for Norfolk leaving her escort behind who followed in an hour or so. Saturday at 8 o'clock their fleet again made its appearance but at more respectable distance, and it was said that the Merrimac was not with them, but I feel confident that she was, nothing was done on our part but watch and on theirs to remain stationary in the position they first took in the morning; I made[?] not a sight of one of them; their plans must have miscarried and new one plotting. Every days delay makes us stronger and in ten days I hope we shall feel confident to attack her. We now have confidence in our ability to sink her if we could have her where we want, that is in some place where we could work; our commodore is determined not to attack her off Sewall's point or about there, as there is not water enough to manoeuver his large vessels as well as the risks of their getting aground. If we have the means on hand which I am told we have, she is certain to be sunk if she ever passes fortress Munroe. Hear firing every day in the direction of Yorktown but don't expect any decisive results as yet. I have had my whiskers cut off my chin and resemble General Burnside very much!![111] Capt Putnam was on here I mean at Camp Hamilton I obtained his photograph Monday morning, received your letter of April 11th, no signs of the Merrimac. Give my regards to all

       yours affectionately   Charley

---

[109] Under the protection of the C.S.S. *Virginia*, the C.S.S. *Jamestown* and *Raleigh* captured three Union transports on April 11, 1862.

[110] A Revenue Cutter, built in 1844 by John Stevens as an experimental single-screw boat, fitted out as a twin-screw ironclad as a demonstration ship for the "Stevens Battery". Its protection included flooding the fore and aft compartments to partially submerge the hull, though this gave it a draft of 9'10". A gun explosion on May 15, 1862 at Drewry's Bluff ended the experiment and the boat was returned to the revenue service.

[111] Ambrose Everett Burnside (1824-1892) was instantly recognisable for his bald crown and his luxuriant and well-groomed side-whiskers, the latter giving rise to the term "sideburns" still in use today.

****

[not dated: April 1862]

Dear Nellie,

Have received your letters of April 11th and 13th. I am glad of the arrangement you have made for the summer, and no doubt you will enjoy yourself much. Father has not said a word about your drawing too much money, has not referred to it in any way. My kitty is missing now expect it will turn up tomorrow. Gen McClellan will soon commence the bombardment of Yorktown, he has but few gunboats to help him, but he will get along with what he has, faster perhaps than the politicians want him to[112]. Since I last wrote we have had splendid weather, mild and even warm, sit in shirt sleeves noon time. I want a good servant, suppose I shall have to take a contraband if I can get one, but they steal terribly. Everything is remarkably quiet here, no signs of the Merrimac, they feel confident at the fort that she hogged herself, plenty bent her back, when she was aground she seemed chary of her appearance. After Richmond and Norfolk are taken I think Congress will disband some regiment, as the war will, after one or two more large battles, be a guerrilla war. Tonight the officers assembled at the gymnasium, a large building, and had quite a dance, three violins for music. Berk will have altered some before I next see him   six months or more makes a great change in one of his age. There were nine men in our batteries killed last night before Yorktown   I believe there is considerable firing on both sides. The weather here is getting to be very warm at noon, equal to our July weather. Give my regards to all. I wish you would send me some tartaric acid and essence of lemon to make lemonade, ask father about it and obtain information how to make it. Mr Tucker sends his regards.

From yours affect[*ionately*   Charles]

****

Camp Hamilton, Va.   April 21st 1862

Dear Nellie,

I received your letter of April 17th yesterday. I did not write yesterday as I had just returned from picket duty and felt too tired, it does not make any difference in regard to its going as it would not have left here any sooner had it been written on Sunday. We have had delightful weather lately until Saturday when it commenced to be showery and at last settled in a north east storm, becoming quite cold as well as rainy. Friday we went, I mean my company, after rails about three miles beyond Hampton, beyond the house at which the three drummer boys were taken some time ago. The day was delightful, roads good and the country pleasant, with but little to do, excepting loading wagon which was quickly done, leaving the time which they were absent on our hands to pass in as pleasant a manner as possible and consistent with our duty. On the same farm was a barn filled with tobacco, belonging to a secesh major. I detail a certain number of men to obtain some for the use of my company; on there return I took two men and proceeded to examine the barn and outhouses, which were filled with the newest inventions for carrying on large farms. The house in which the tobacco is stored was apparently made expressly for the purpose, rafters extend across the building like innumerable ladders; from one rafter to another are laid small

---

[112] McClellan had clearly infused his soldiers with his own belief that the politicians in Washington were actively colluding to hinder his military progress.

sticks on which are hung the tobacco, two leaves are fastened near the roof by another leaf and then are laid astride the stick to dry, they being culled and separated according to quality. On standing on the floor and looking upwards nothing but tobacco was discernable, the building maintained two presses, also new hogsheads ready to pack the tobacco into. The tobacco was marked No 1 Long bright and No 2 Long bright, our men helped themselves to No 1. In the numerous outhouses which you always find on large farms about here I found every thing necessary to carry on large farms, such as two large horse mowing machines, large thresher for four horses, some planting machine and black smith shop, showing that the owner of it had plenty of means, as well as the ability to keep up with the times, in applying the modern labor saving machines. The farm consists of over 1,000 acres, and kept busy about 50 slaves; the house was in good repair and kept neat by a family now living in it, who moved from Hampton, being situated in a grove, keeping it shady and cool. This farm is the finest I have as yet seen, having a large ice house on it showing evidently that the owner was able to live luxuriously. Saturday night while on picket heard heavy firing of musketry which lasted half an hour, have not yet heard the cause. They have caught the man on the white horse, described in the letters writting on the advance on Yorktown. Saturday afternoon quite a spirited fire was kept up from the Rip Raps on a new rebel battery erected nearly opposite to the Rip Raps[113], assisted by some gun boats; the rebels threw one shot between the Rip Raps and fort Munroe . We don't obtain much news from York town, hear occasionally the booming of cannons, expect Tuesday or Wednesday that we shall open on them but the rainy weather may delay. We are without any rumors about ourselves, got tired of getting up any more. Give my regards to all from

         Yours Affectionately   Charley

I have some of the tobacco from the barn mean to send some to S.S.W. T.B.W., and John Alfree some of the leaves were broken bringing in to camp. If I feel satisfied that it will make good segars, I shall send it on. The men like the quality and are making segars from it. Have a light sack coat and a pair of cheap light blue pants made at Edmunds tailor. I may send home my thick flannels soon.

        ****

        Camp Hamilton, Va. April 23 / 62

Dear Nellie,

  The mail has been very irregular lately receiving today two mails among which were three letters for me two from you and one from mother. We are enjoying fine weather now, but you can find that out by looking at the papers. The officers meet very often of an evening at the gymnasium, and dance, music by two violins. You must expect a short letter this time as I can find nothing to write. It is astonishing how difficult it is to learn of the movements taking place before Yorktown, some days we will hear heavy firing but can't find out the cause, the night we were on picket we heard heavy musket volleys but have not found out yet the cause. It was reported that three gun boats ran past the forts (Rebels) during a thunder shower Saturday evening. Notwithstanding I hear nothing from Yorktown, yet the troops there are hard at work placing seige guns in place, and are getting along very rapidly, we placed 18 this morning, and have considerable over a hundred in position, McClellan told the workmen that when every thing was ready he would take it in four hour, he dresses

---

[113] An island in Hampton Roads, about two miles off Fort Monroe, where Federal soldiers were sent to hard labor for disciplinary offences.

very plain, hardly a mark to distinguish his rank, and is untiring in his exertions. I shall send home the tobacco I have spoken of and let them judge for themselves; it is so dry that I am afraid it will all crumble up before it arrives at it destination. I think it would smoke well in a pipe or do to make into cigars.

Thursday morning: Heavy firing can be heard in the direction of Yorktown and attempt may be made soon by our army to take some of there batteries. The pickets on both sides sometime lay down their arms and have a talk together, the rebel seem unconscious of the fall of island no. 10[114] which is not so liable to be taken as Yorktown (so they say). We are arranging our camp for the summer and shall have a very pretty camp, the main street will have a row of trees along the sidewalk, and the spaces between the officers tent can be laid off in parks with trees and flowers. I am looking anxiously for the box expect it every day. You may buy Annual Scientific Discovery[115] of this year. Give my regards to all. Austin will have a vacation soon, have father let him come out here.

       From Yours Affectionately   Charles

       ****

          Camp Hamilton Va. April 30th /62

Dear Nellie,

Nothing has happened since I last wrote every thing especially in the last 24 hours very quiet, have not even heard any gun at Yorktown since night before last, when they were firing at intervals through the night. McClellan plays a deep game which must be very perplexing to the rebels, leaving them in doubt as to where and with what power we shall strike; we have in masked batteries within a mile of there earthworks guns of the heaviest calibre, some are as heavy as 240 lbs, also a large number of mortars, and notwithstanding all the firing of the rebels not one of these batteries have fired, there whereabouts may be suspected by the rebels, but there extent we have never revealed and will not I suppose until McClellan, is ready to take Yorktown. I imagine McClellan is very nearly ready, and may be waiting for Gen McDowell to arrive some where. I have not told you of the improvements taking place in camp I have in front of my house trees planted along the sidewalk, and between my tent and Capt Donovan's[116] , we have a very pretty little park, called Wyman's Park, below a plan

---

[114] The capture of Island No. 10, Tennessee, and New Madrid, Mississippi, by Federal forces during late March and early April 1862 opened the Mississippi River to union forces as far north as Fort Pillow, Tennessee.

[115] The Scientific Discovery Annual.

[116] Matthew Donovan, 1st Lieut., Aug. 1, 1861; Captain, Sept. 27, 1861; Major, June 30, 1864.

If I am alive next Summer 63

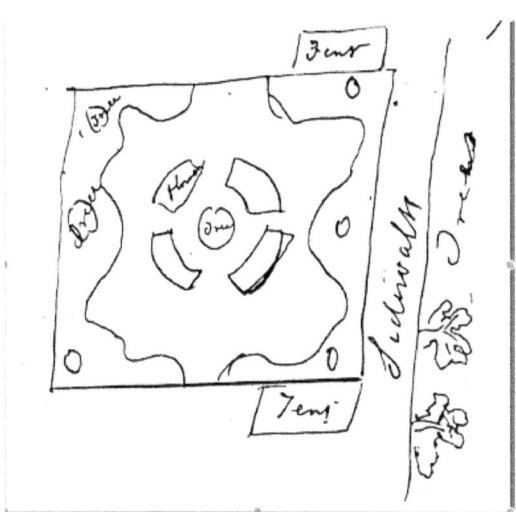

those round spot represent trees and the space around them is grass sods   I am about to enlarge my dwelling, giving somewhat more room, shall commence tomorrow if I have good luck shall have it finished before I write my next letter to you. I received your letters of 25th & 27th Tuesday. I have not seen Charles Rogers nor Capt. Stuart[117], the latter is not here now. My pay roll for two month go in tomorrow. The weather is very changeable lately now it is rainy or rather showery. Give my regards to all. I am at work on my tent.

Yours Affectionately   Charley

****

---

[117] Neither have been identified.

CHAPTER 7
*
FROM THE PENINSULA TO SUFFOLK

The move to Yorktown (from the History of the 1st Massachusetts Infantry)
"Ship Point had been fortified by the rebels, and some formidable earthworks were thrown up to prevent the landing of our forces. They were evacuated upon our approach, however,... At the landing were large numbers of troops just disembarked from a fleet of steamers, piles of quartermasters' and commissaries' stores, and ordnance great and small. Bands were playing merrily as we marched into the woods; and regiments lay over the fields in every direction, awaiting orders. The locality was found very unfavourable for the troops, on account of its low, swampy character. At any time during the day, water could be obtained by digging two or three feet; and at night or just before sunrise... fogs and mists enveloped land and water alike. A change of quarters was therefore made on the afternoon of Saturday the 12th; and after a march of about six miles, the regiment encamped a few hundred feet in the rear of the Poquosin River, upon dry land high and dry, in the midst of a growth of young pines. The appearance of the vicinity was not uninviting. There were several well-built houses, surrounded by cultivated plots of ground; and the residents, though not communicative, were civil and respectful. Most of the men had disappeared, having joined ... the rebel army. The women and children who remained... were not insulting. Until Wednesday the 16th the troops were occupied in building a wharf, loading and unloading vessels, and making themselves comfortable in their tents. All the regiments composing the brigade were encamped close by; and both Gens. Hooker and Naglee had their headquarters in our immediate vicinity. Fresh troops were pouring in daily, and marching in the direction of Yorktown, and the occasional discharge of artillery... showed that its investment had already begun... Never was an army in better spirits or better condition than that which Gen. McClellan gathered before Yorktown. Unlimited confidence was felt in him.

"As the Yorktown batteries approached completion, and one after another heavy mortars and two hundred pound Parrotts were placed in position, the rebels manifested continually increasing uneasiness. During the 3d of May they kept up an incessant din with guns of every calibre and awakened the expectation of an assault along the whole line. Wishing to know what it might portend, Gen. McClellan made a balloon ascent directly in front of the First's regimental line. As soon as the balloon ascended above the tops of the trees, it was greeted by a perfect storm of missiles... so that he was obliged to come down... During the night the firing was kept up in a furious manner... but about three o'clock in the morning it suddenly ceased. The pickets listened but could hear nothing... they crept slowly and cautiously forward, and met with no opposition. Finally,

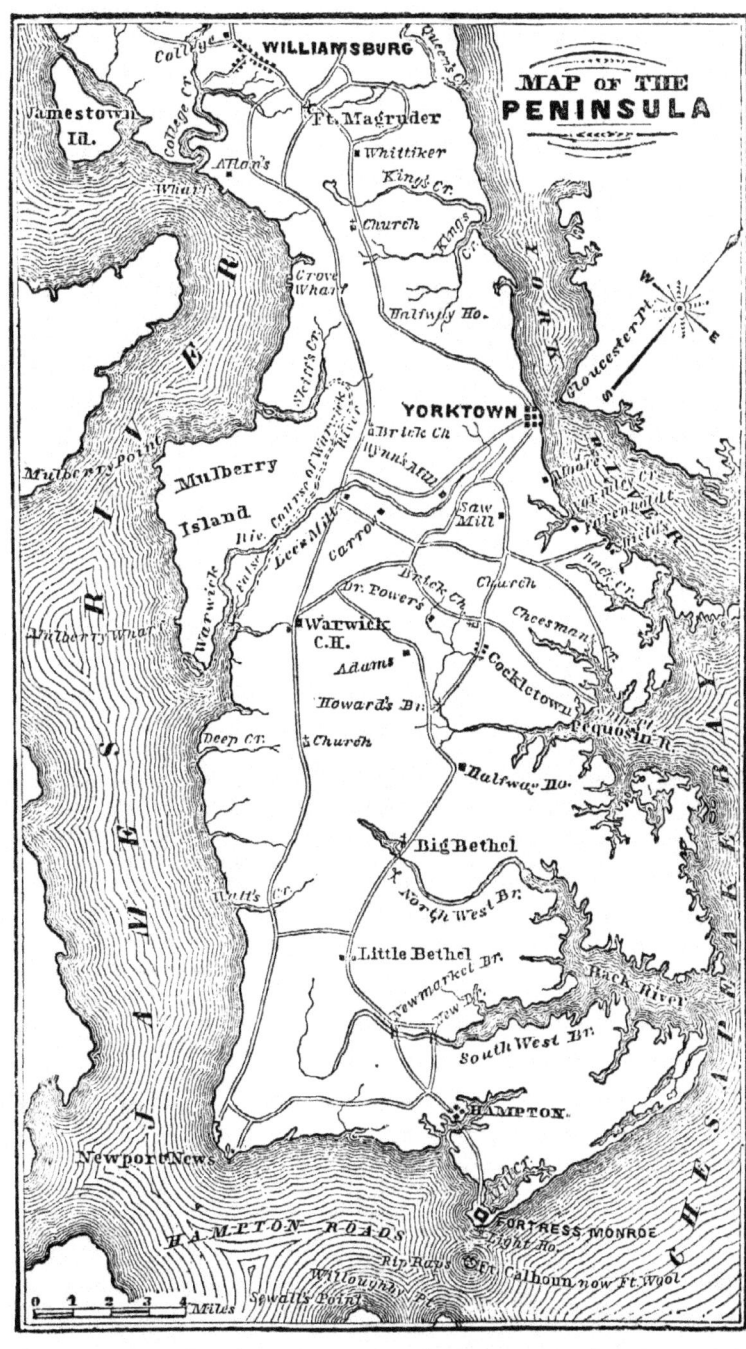

Fortress Monroe and the Yorktown Peninsula, 1862
(from "McClellan's Own Story," New York, 1887)

they reached the hostile breastwork, jumped into the ditches, scrambled up the ramparts—the rebels were gone!"

****

May 4th /62 Camp Hamilton Va

Dear Nellie

I have received your favor of May 2nd, and am glad to learn that you are all well. I am writing this letter in my new house which is very comfortable and roomy, size 14½ ft by 10½ ft; 7 ft high; it is made of boards covered with canvass, and has three windows in it, two sashes of which are on their way to Baltimore to have panes of glass placed in them/ I[t] will cost me about 8 dollars to build it in good shape there some little work yet to be done, which I shall finish tomorrow.

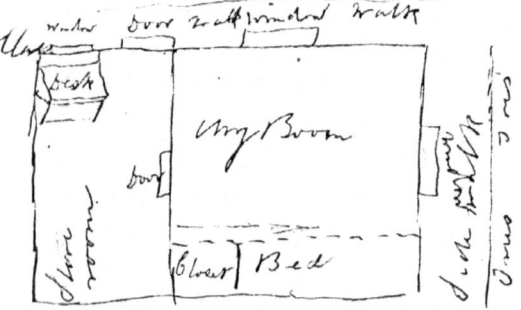

Received news of the evacuation of Yorktown to day. Merrimac was in sight nearly all day, expect she may go up James River to night. All manner of rumors are afloat, but fall on the ears of the 16th as balls on the side of the Monitor. You must excuse the shortness of this letter, as I have no reliable news, and want read up on Court Martials. I am on a General Court Martial Colonel Andrews President, I have nothing to do but to give my opinion on the guilt of the prisoner and the amount of punishment. I shall in all probability skip one picket duty, by being on it. Give my regards to all.

Yours Affectionately   Charley

Tell father that C H Mayo has sent on a draft of 75.00. I shall forward the money with the next lot.

****

Thursday May 8 [1862]   Camp Hamilton Va

Dear Nellie,

We march immediately, for Norfolk I imagine, don't expect much resistance all well.

Yours Affectionately   Charley

****

May 9 /62

Dear Nellie,

Had every thing packed up yesterday in boxes our baggage was reduced to what we could carry in our hands, which in my case consisted of one change of clothing. While we were packing up the Monitor Naugatuck and 4 or more large war vessel were shelling Sewall's Point, firing very rapidly, the rebel replying slowly, our guns or rather shells set something on fire judging from the black smoke which arose after an half hour shelling. The reply of the rebel slacken gradually until it entirely ceased, when from Norfolk came the Merrimac or a vessel like her and our boats retreated, while this last part of the drama was enacting we were on our way to the transports. Our boats retreated without firing a shot, being a part of their plan, which is to draw the Merrimac near the fort where the water is deeper and they can get at her better.[118] After staying on board the boat all night we were ordered back to camp, and I am now writing this in my new house. I suppose you know that the regiments have passed in review before General Lincoln, I mean President, the other day, he is yet here. The Monitor has been exchanging a few shots with Sewall's Point and now lies abreast of it trying to tempt the Merrimac to chase her the Merrimac was in sight this morning but have not seen her since. The firing yesterday was very heavy and rapid. The Galena[119] and two other gunboats went up James river yesterday, have not heard any reliable news yet from them except firing[120] . We are getting very indifferent here now don't seem to care what is done. Heard the Monitor firing, at least I was told it was the Monitor didn't take trouble to see, I have arrived at the state of mind that it is indifferent what turns up. I am all well, I am now Officer of the Day, though being on Court Martial I have no business as the court has only adjourned temporarily.

    Yours Affectionately,   Charley

****

Norfolk, Va.   May 11, 1862

Dear Nellie,

  I am penning this letter in the public jail at Norfolk, by that I don't intend to imply that I am a prisoner but that part of our regiment is stationed there. After writing the last letter and the mail had been closed, we received orders to start again with two day supplies. We started embarking on board of the Nellie Baker, the same one that used to run between Boston and Nahant. After embarking we lay in the roads until early in the morning. I forgot to mention that the Rip Raps shelled Sewall's Point for two or three hours in the evening. Early in the morning, we disembarked on the enemies shore at a place called Ocean View a part of Willoughby's point and from that time commenced the labor. It was nearly ten o'clock when we started to march. I had a small carpet bag containing a change of clothes for Lt. Tucker and myself, dressing case and writing desk which was light, and I supposed the men would be able to take turn in carrying it, I had also on my back my cape from my overcoat, woolen blanket,

---

[118] On May 8, the U.S.S. *Monitor, Dacotah, Naugatuck, Seminole* and *Susquehanna* shelled the Confederate batteries at Sewell's Point with a view to ascertaining the practicability of landing troops there for an attack on Norfolk. Information was obtained that the Confederate evacuation of Norfolk was under way and that the Virginia would be going up the James or York Rivers, giving rise to Federal hopes that she could be drawn into deep waters where she might be rammed by high-speed steamers; unfortunately for the plan, she did not.

[119] An experimental ironclad, one of the so-called "Pook Turtles" after their inventor, it was severely damaged six days later in an attack on Drewry's Bluff, its armor proving to be defective. It was reconverted to an unarmoured steam sloop during 1863-4.

[120] A movement suggested by Lincoln himself for the increased protection of McClellan's forces, which resulted in the forcing upriver of the CSS *Jamestown* and *Patrick Henry*.

rubber blanket, and overcoat. The day was intensely warm and the roads frightfully dusty. and 1 [one?] regiment was two hours ahead, we were were obliged to strike to overtake the foremost regiment a fearful gait, which with the dust and heat of the sun wilted the men, some men threw away their knapsacks, and more threw away their blanket and overcoat, the men carrying my valise let it drop and I undertook to take it and with the assistance of two or three men managed to carry it to the first stopping place where I took out one change of stockings and left the valise with its contents. I also threw away my cape. As luck would have it one of the men having a light knapsack helped himself to the dressing case and writing book which he is to turn over to me. After relieving myself as well as the men of some of their weight we started forward after after [sic] ten minutes rest and soon heard the enemies cannon which were situated the other side of stone bridge which we found in flames on our reaching it, consequently right about and retraced our steps a good ways striking a new road which led in a round about manner to Norfolk, part of the way double quick and at one rest the men had ordered to throw off knapsacks which was willingly done, but notwithstanding the killing gait was telling terribly on our men who were obliged to lay down on the road side in great many instances. We soon heard of a battery ahead which we must take by storm as we had no artillery, it not having time to unload from the vessels so on we went the men nearly ready to drop and we were soon inside the entrenchments which were very strong and finely constructed extended 7 miles and a half although I have been told they were five miles long and mounted ninety guns, but I give you the smallest or lowest estimate, which is that there were thirty guns the majority of them not spiked. After the regiment arrived inside the entrenchments there was a long rest and I began to feel as if I could go no farther as I had been drinking considerable water and had nothing pass for four days with but little appetite. I began to feel sick but on visiting the doctor I obtained a dose of whiskey which like to have made me vomit and afterwards a dose of brandy and having releaved myself and rested began to feel well and when the regiment was ordered to fall in to march to Norfolk I felt as well as ever. We were the first regiment which entered Norfolk which we did at seven o'clock in the evening without any opposition, the enemy eight thousand strong having left two hours before. There was some hearty greetings of the stars and stripes but generally but little said. Our rigement was divided the right wing going one part and the left wing the other part of the city. we the left wing occupying the jail and one of there armories. The Merrimac is either blown up or captured. I can't find out which[121] . The rebels burnt up the Navy Yard, blew up the dry dock, destroy a gun boat they were building like the Monitor. Our fleet is laying opposite Norfolk and everything in our possession. A great many deserters about the city and are being picked up every minutes. I saw one belonging to the Atlantic Artillery[122] consisting of 110 men, who told that they had all deserted but 41. Coffee selling here for 1.00 to 2.00 per lbs. butter 70 cts, boots as high as twenty five dollars, tobacco is cheap. There is evidently a lack of confident among the Rebel officers in their men, as those that left here were forced off in some instances by the point of the bayonet. My knapsack has not arrived yet. I send you some rebel papers and some peanuts.

                        Yours Affectionately   Charley

****

---

[121] With the fall of Norfolk, the C.S.S. *Virginia* lost her base and, realising that her draft was too great to retreat up the James River, Flag officer Josiah Tattnall had no alternative but to order her to be blown up on May 11th.

[122] Co. B, 18th Battalion, Virginia Artillery.

Portsmouth, Va.   Tuesday May 13 [1862]

Dear Nellie,
    The mail have not yet commenced arriving regular as yet   consequently have received neither papers nor letter since last Friday. The last letter was written you in the public Jail, Norfolk, this is written at the Ferry Station at Portsmouth, where my company is on guard, and will be until seven o'clock tomorrow morning. On the evening of the same day that my last letter was written, the remainder of our regiment left Norfolk for the Gosport Navy Yard[123] in which we now are. On arriving at Gosport Navy Yard three companies our among the number were order to patrol the city and suburbs, being ordered to escort every citizen to his house who was found out after nine o'clock with instructions to keep them there.   Col. was afraid of an attempt to burn the city by some of the desperate secessionist and also that the enemy might strike a blow as a parting farewell, but everything pass of quietly. The men met the order detailing our co. patrol duty with promptness, although some of them and in fact more than half were up on the previous night, and all had only hard bread and hard travel since they started. I had slept the previous night among the men on a bench without any covering being continually disturbed by orders for more men for guard duty. Our men were walking all night long   so was I, and got my foot or rather feet all blistered up, so that it was very painful for me to walk. I picked up a colored man on our approach to Norfolk, and he has proved himself a jewel, does everything that is required in good shape and has the happy faculty of always borrowing what I want. I have spent more money here in trying to obtain something to eat than I ever expected. I obtain an ordinary dinner for a gold dollar. And happening to want a bottle of brandy to have on hand in case of an emergency was obliged to pay four dollars. Yesterday I succeeded in getting some stewed oysters and some rye. Coffee which is not so bad, charge twenty five cents for a stew   I have no overcoat with me, but I make out to keep warm. Norfolk is a very large place and so is Portsmouth, the latter place is nearly as large as Charlestown, with a considerable Union feeling the stars and stripes being loudly cheered as we went through the town.

[last word written on top of first page - no ending or signature]

****

General Grover's brigade was detailed for provost-duty in and around Williamsburg on the 8th of May, and remained until the 15th.

****

Portsmouth Navy Yard   May 16th [1862]

Dear Nellie,
    I have but little to write only general information, and am besides not in the vein to write. I received your letter of May 11th today as well as some papers from father. Portsmouth is really a pretty city and a person if acquainted might enjoy himself nicely. We have a very pretty place in Navy Yard where we are encamped, on a grass plot near Commodore House, and was about making myself comfortable and now we are to move at six o'clock tomorrow morning, I suppose to occupy Suffolk. I am rather glad to keep on the move and the men are, and if the march is conducted

---

[123] The Navy Yard at Norfolk.

properly I shall enjoy it. There will be no prospect of a fight at Suffolk as there is no rebel troops near there, they having all left for Richmond. Flowers are growing here very profuse, and there is a splendid variety. The extent of the Navy Yard increase every time I walk over it, Charlestown is a baby navy yard compared to it. How our Government could have deserted it I cannot see, as it must have been a power or - rather - an immense source of supplies to anyone who hold it. The rebel have destroy every shop but two, and every dwelling but three one of them being let furnished. I send you a sword found in the rebel storehouse at Portsmouth, I have been told that some of the cavalry are armed with similar swords, there is also a sample of the balls used by the crew of the Merrimac in their boarding pistols. I am well, and enjoying myself. The weather is warm but is not hot. Excuse the shortness of this as I have some business to attend to. Give my regards to all. When I have more leisure I will write about the people.

  Yours Af[fectionately] C[harles]

****

           Suffolk Va Monday May [19?], 1862]

Dear Nellie,

  Last Saturday morning early we left Portsmouth or rather Gosport Navy Yard on our way to Suffolk. We were blest as we seem always to be with weather suitable to the occasion; the ground under foot was wet and the rather frequent occurrence of mud puddles was the only draw back. I traveled with a large pair of shoes and did not suffer with sore feet as I did on the previous march. Saturday we marched twenty miles through a level and marshy country, but sprinkled with fine farms, the roads were crossed in three places by running brooks about half foot deep, through which our troops waded. We had with us two pieces of artillery and two companies of cavalry. Saturday night we slept (that is the men slept on the ground I always sleep in my hammock which my servant carries on his back whilst marching) about five miles from Suffolk. Sunday morning we made an early start and arrived at Suffolk about 9 o'clock, and proceeded near an old rebel camp, with barracks capable of holding two thousand men, but which we did not occupy, sleeping as usual on the ground, the wagons remaining loaded and were in fact sent half a mile to the rear, oweing to the fact that 4,000 rebel troops were within 15 miles of us, strongly posted and not knowing but they might, learning the smallness of our force, attack us. I was Officer of the Day from day night[sic] and know that no attack took place. Suffolk is all secesh of the stiffest class, and to day there are no store open, but they will open tomorrow, as Colonel Wyman has issued a proclamation which insists that the store be opened. At noon today we moved to the fair ground where we have pitched our tents and there seems some likelihood of remaining. After we had about completed pitching tents we were visited with a smart shower, making large puddles of water too numerous to make marching pleasant. I suppose we have no support near us, that is nearer than Portsmouth, as the railroad is not in running condition, and twenty five miles is a good march. We have obtained some eighteen sabre quite good, some pistols and muskets. The representative of this county in the Confederate Congress, when he left his house, buried in the cellar of an outhouse all or a majority of his crockery ware, which we discovered and dug up, it was of a very expensive kind. There does not appear to be an union man in town, the people keeping themselves in door and out of sight. One company on picket is insulted by three cheers for Bull Run and another by secession flags being repeatedly thrust out of windows. Nothing however effects us wherever we have been the best of order has always prevailed, and the most rabid secesh cannot complain justly of the absence of good order. There will always be in this generation a dislike of the North by a large quantity of citizens but as ones interest is the object of most peoples lives if we can succeed in making them believe that they will be more prosperous in the union than out every thing may work smooth. There is a great scarcity of butter and in fact I see none offered for sale. We have not had any for three days. There is repeated inquiries if there will be any ice sent from the North showing which way the wind blows, and also if people will be permitted to visit N. York to purchase goods, as there is a great dearth of useful articles through the South.

****

Suffolk Wed 21 [May] 1862

Dear Nellie,
    I am now on picket duty at a very picturesque spot about a mile from Suffolk. The station is at a mill, by which runs a road leading south to Blackwater and north by a branch to Richmond. I received today with great pleasure two letters from you and about eight papers from father all of which were perused with interest. I perceived by the time of your letter that you imagine I am about used up, which is anything but the truth, as at this moment I never was better in health and spirits than now. Since I last wrote to you nothing has happened to write about. The vegitation and the trees look finely and in the woods you are surprised at the variety of flower especially on bushes. We are enjoying delightful weather now rather warm, but endurable. I am order to go to Norfolk on the General Court Martial which will give me a chance to see the country. I do not know as I wants anything that can be sent me and on the whole I am very comfortable, ham egg without butter has been my bill of fare every meal since I have been here. May 23 The Court Martial which I was on assembles again at Norfolk, at which place I am now making some additions to this letter. I came from Suffolk in a handcar[124] in a driving rain, having six men divided into two reliefs for power. On my arrival I found that the court had adjourned, and returns [i.e. to Norfolk] again in an hour. I am trying to write this with a poor pen. Give my regards to all.
               Yours Affectionately   Charley

****

Sunday May 25 [1862]   Suffolk

Dear Nellie,
    I have received your letter of May 21st and also the Watchman. We shall receive the mail regular now the bridge which the rebels burnt we have succeeded in repairing, and the cars run right into Suffolk once every day. There cannot be obtained at any price butter and I am learning to do without it. Strawberries are plenty and cheap at Norfolk but hard to obtain up here, green peas are plenty but still it is hard to obtain a good dinner or any meal, it may be owing to the lack of butter. Notwithstanding that we are supposed to be in the Sunny South, the weather is as cold and raw tonight as any weather we have had north. There has been a constant arrival of deserters from Petersburg mostly Virginians, they all tell the same story, that they are not well fed and are becoming disheartened. They say that the approach to Richmond this side of James River is not obstructed, and I imagine that Gen McClellan may try it when he is ready, if he has any idea of doing so Richmond will not be taken before a fortnight, we can afford to wait as the demoralisation of the rebel

---

[124] A self-propelled railroad vehicle, powered by hand-working a geared lever mechanism.

will go on every day, and there supplies decrease. The deserters say they have a large force at Richmond they say 200,000[125] , but the soldiers will not fight as they have done. The approach to Richmond by the Peninsula is represented as being very formidable. I go on picket tomorrow to the Mill, a very pleasant place. Magnolia trees grow here in abundance and are now in full bloom. I use the Citric acid as lemonade very often, the Drs say it is good for rheumatism and quite healthy. People of the town are becoming more polite, and at the fall of Richmond will evidently give up all hopes of the South as separate government. Norfolk is governed very strictly no produce can be sent there nor can the goods belonging to the various sutlers be sold to the public. At Fortress Monroe there is butter and other necessary articles waiting to be sent as soon as permission is granted. No article can be taken from Express office without written permission from Hd. Qrs. Lieut Tucker sends his regards and thanks you for the case of his clothing. It is impossible to obtain any newspapers either here or at Norfolk, government having prohibited there being brought or sold; the only papers I receive are those from father. Give my best regards to all.
    Yours   Charles

       ****

                Suffolk May 29 [1862]
Dear Nellie,
  I received your letter of the 26th today, in which you are much alarmed at the news; don't be frightened. We are enjoying delightful weather, no day has as yet been insupportable. If the sword sent has not arrived I am afraid it will not. The commissary sergeant has obtained some butter from Old Point [Comfort] for the use of the regiment, no articles being allowed to be sold to the inhabitance, for 35 cts. I suppose the news of Genl Banks defeat[126] will cause the secessionists to be saucy but it will be short lived. If the Rebel army before Richmond suffers a severe defeat a large part will desert, but may nevertheless act as guerrillas which is a specie of warfare very annoying and which the rebels from the knowledge they possess of the country have the advantage. The people here are very quiet and show but little disposition to do damage whether the recent news will make them show their hand time will tell. News is very scarce and unless I leave the camp on picket duty rarely have any other time. You must excuse the shortness of this letter as I have nothing to write. The news from home only make our men more disposed to meet the enemy. Nothing can be taken from the express office without permit from Hd Qrs and it is difficult for the sutlers to obtain any supplies for their regiments. On picket the other day I saw an ancient negress who would make the fortune of any minst[r]els. She evidently was little weak about the brains but her conversation was sharp and smart, but her

---

[125] McClellan was notorious for greatly over-estimating the strength of the opposing forces to a figure well in excess of his own strength - partly owing to faulty intelligence, and partly owing to his conviction that reinforcements were deliberately being withheld by politicians hostile to him at Washington. Figures of up to 150,000 had been accepted uncritically from Virginia civilians who had served in the state militia and claimed to know the numbers of troops under Johnston; the maximum available to General Joseph E. Johnston, commanding the Confederate forces at the start of the Seven Days' battles, was probably some 75,000. Johnson's figure of 200,000 may well be the result of ever-inflating rumour among the Union troops (Sears, 1992, 96-99).

[126] The Battles of Front Royal, Va. (May 23, 1862) and Winchester, Va. (May 25, 1862), in which Maj.-Gen. Thomas J. ("Stonewall") Jackson decisively defeated Federal forces under Maj.-Gen. Nathaniel P. Banks.

peculiarity was in her motions and her habit of loud singing as she walked along, such tunes as "I am going to heaven in de morning" singing without any cessation in a remarkable loud key. Cows are harnessed in carts here and are mostly used by the poorer negroes and white folks. The people commence to show themselves more and a walk through the main street in the afternoon of a pleasant day give one an idea of comfort and home, every house has a large entry and most all with a porch in front as the street mentioned has on either side large shade trees, the porches are well protected from the sun and are occupied by the families of each giving an appearance of great sociability, which no doubt exists among them. If we were in a country of friends the officers would have an opportunity of imposing themselves, through the hospitalities of the citizens, who I understand when the city or town was occupied by the rebel troops were continually giving parties and paying visits to the camp especially during dress parade. I suppose there is not a young girl in town that has not a dozen beaux in the rebel army. I don't anticipate the paymaster as soon as usual, the time for his appearance is already passed, he is looked for eagerly by the officers and men. I had it proved to me how careful it is necessary a person to be who he talks to and what he says, on my visit to Norfolk I met only two citizens and they were in the Adjutant General's office, the conversation was general, and yet to my surprise, in the N.Y. Herald of the 26th, a correspondent states that he is indebted to Capt Johnson for news from Suffolk. Lieut Tucker sends his regards. Give my regards to all. How is business with the firm, is it good. I suppose everyone is well as I hear nothing to the contrary.

[*Yours Affectionately Charles*]

Peanuts are cheap and fine here

****

The New York Herald for May 26, 1862, did indeed cite Johnson as its source. A column headed "The latest from Suffolk" announces that "Through the courtesy of Captain C. R. Johnson, of the Sixteenth Regiment Massachusetts Volunteers, who arrived from Suffolk this morning, I am in possession of some interesting information relative to the condition of affairs in that locality." and goes on to paint a vivid, and even amusing, picture of relations between occupiers and occupied in Suffolk at this period. The conversation was clearly a little less "general" than Johnson perhaps perceived, and the article is worth quoting in full:

"The force under Col. Wyman has made a very favorable impression upon the citizens of the place, and by their fine bearing and uniform good conduct the men now in occupation have completely disarmed the prejudices which greeted them when they marched into the city. The petty acts of spite, such as the removal of well buckets, and other means of annoyance to the soldiers, have disappeared, and a much better feeling is manifested. Yesterday the Mayor and members of the City Council had an interview with Colonel Wyman, and assured him that, notwithstanding that the people of Suffolk were unwavering in their sympathy for the Southern cause, the delicate consideration exhibited by the officers and men under his command towards the citizens had inspired them with such confidence that they were willing to co-operate with him in the conduct of city affairs, and would afford him all the aid in their power. The impression prevailed in Sufffolk before its occupation by Union troops that when the Union soldiers entered the place there would be no respect paid to persons and property; that the stores and dwellings would be indiscriminately entered and ransacked, and any amount of atrocities perpetrated. The city authorities desire to bear testimony that the most perfect order had prevailed, and that no cause of complaint had been given to the inhabitants. There is a marked improvement in the spirit and tone of the female portion of the

denizens of Suffolk. All through the portion of Virginia occupied by the Union forces the women have been found the most intractable and troublesome in their expressions, and the rule has held good in regard to the ladies in Suffolk. When Colonel Wyman entered the city the ladies thought it absolutely incumbent upon them to give their noses an extra elevation, and when in the dewy twilight officers or men would walk through the streets where the sweet creatures were trying to enjoy the mild air of the evening upon the stoops or at the doors, there would be an instant movement to the rear, skirts would flutter a moment in the wind, and the damsels incontinently disappear behind a door. Each day's experience has undoubtedly tended to dissipate the prejudices, fears and repugnance of the fair dames of Suffolk, and now of an eveneing they maintain their wonted places at the doors or walk the streets, giving no sign either of alarm or disdain. It is a good sign of an improvement in the condition of a captured town when the women give evidences that they are growing sensible, by leaving off unnecessary airs. The people of Suffolk do not pretend to disguise their contempt for the South Carolina troops. From the accounts which they give of the conduct of the representatives from the Palmetto State, the volunteers must have been a sweet set of boys. They were drunk nearly all the time, and appear to have had no more idea of the demands of common decency and the requirements of society than a parcel of Hottentots. Officers and men were alike drunkards and and thieves, and rendered themselves perfect pest wherever they went. The opinion prevails among the inhabitants of Suffolk that, if the rebels are driven out of this state, Virginia will furnish no more soldiers for the war."

****

Suffolk, June 2 /62

Dear Nellie,

The mail now arrives regularly every day, and I receive the newspaper from father generally every mail, they are quite valuable, being the only one which I can obtain. The weather has not been intensely hot as yet, although the heat of the sun is very oppressive. Friday night 1st was truly Southern, for we rarely have such nights at the north. We had been threatened with thunder showers during Friday afternoon and half past eight in the evening we were visited with one, and from that time until the next morning the lightening and thunder were incessant. The thunder or rather the noise resembled one continual roll increasing then almost dying away like a swell on an organ. A scouting party consisting of a Capt. Lieut and eighteen men were surrounding by a superior force of the enemy, and after a short fight each man looked out for himself eight of them having returned, the remainder are supposed to be either killed or captured, this occurred in the afternoon of Friday[127] , which news occasioned the doubling of the picket, our company being detailed to reinforce one picket station, they not having any duty to do took shelter in a house and were in a measure protected from the rain. I was detailed Friday morning to take charge of a detachment of regular artillery during the absence of its officer[128] and had good

---

[127]The identity of the action is uncertain. The only incident of this nature recorded in Dyer (1903) is a "Picket Affair, Seven Pines" on Friday, May 30th, 1862, involving the 96th New York Infantry and the 85th Pennsylvania Infantry; the casualties are given as 8 killed, 7 wounded, 1 missing. However Suffolk, where the 16th was stationed from May 17 - June 13, and presumably close to where the action described took place, was on the south side of the James River, close to Fortress Monroe and some 70 miles from Seven Pines, north of the river near Richmond, and Johnson makes clear, later in the letter, that the affair took place about fifteen miles away.

[128] Possibly from Battery D or L, 4th U.S. Artillery, stationed at Suffolk at the time.

quarters during the night having a good night's sleep. While absent during the night about twelve o'clock the wind blew down my tent wetting a great many articles. The scouting party before mentioned were attacked about fifteen miles out, a flag of truce sent that way yesterday returned last night, and reported that, both officers and eleven more men captured and and one killed. We have not suffered as yet from the climate the health of the men being good. We do not drill any having so much other duties to do. I am rather ashamed of Nass [?] having permitted herself to be frightened so easily. Give my regards to all. I suppose this will find you enjoying yourself in some cool place.

                Yours afftly   Charles

****

                                            Suffolk Va   June 6 /62

Dear Nellie,

I have been on picket for the last 48 hours and not having the means to write postponed it till today. I receive your letter dated June 2 /62 and I assure you all your letters arrive safely. I have received papers regularly every day. I told father he might expect me home the first of Oct. he sent word back that he would be happy to see me. Rumors are flying about in great numbers which is owing to absence of newspaper. The army before Richmond has suffered severly without doubt, the excursion of Gen Jackson and the success met with by him[129] having put courage into the rebels, but if with the fighting they have had the news that Gen Jackson's army was captured it would cause them to evacuate. Reports are flying around that the rebels have met a severe reverse, losing 15,000 (thousand) men, a large quantity of rolling stock, arms, ammunition and stores, I am waiting to see it proved by the papers, although I place no reliance in it. I send home [$]275, $150.00 is to meet the draft of C.H. Mayo, the remainder is for you, you will see that my clothing bill is paid. Next pay day shall send home more. I draw for a servant now, amount extra to $49.00 in two months. I have kept $100.00 with me to be provided in case of an accident and owe nothing, so that I stand pretty well, this pay being up to the first of May. We shall probably remain here some time, though we are prepared to march at a moment's notice. I suppose always that Birk is is [sic] all right, and like all first children he is A.1 (now don't be mad). Give my regards to all, hope this will find all friends well.

            [*Yours Affectionately*   *Charles*]

****

---

[129] This refers to Confederate Major-General Thomas Jonathan Jackson's highly successful Shenandoah Valley Campaign, aimed at preventing Federal forces in the valley and in the area of Fredericksburg from being sent to reinforce McClellan's Army of the Potomac on the Peninsula.

CHAPTER 8

THE SEVEN DAYS' BATTLES

"About the middle of June, the Brigade was reinforced by the Sixteenth Massachusetts, which came up from Fort Monroe with full ranks and new clothes. It was composed of excellent material, and had a chance to show its metal very soon after its arrival. On the 18th, having been ordered to make a reconnaissance to the front, Grover sent the Sixteenth forward. They went in with all the headlong dash of new troops determined to make a record, ran over the rebel pickets and tumbled the picket reserves out of the woods into the open fields beyond, where the main line of rebel works brought them up with a round turn. They lost fifty-nine men, and the fact that of these seventeen were killed shows the short range at which the fighting was carried in on the dense brush."
(From the HISTORY OF THE SECOND NEW HAMPSHIRE INFANTRY)

h

Wednesday June 11 [1862]　　　White House

Dear Nellie,
    I take this first opportunity to drop you a few lines to let you know I am well and in good spirits. We are now with McCinnam's [sic] army[130] . We are at present 18 miles from our rear guard or reserve for the …….. army and 27 from Richmond. We landed at place called White House[131] this morning and we expect to start for the army　　I want you to understand that we are in first rate spirits. Give my ………. *[remainder missing]*

****

Fair Oaks Battle Ground[132]　　　June 15th /62

Dear Nellie,
    It is again Sunday and I am as this note will inform you happy and in good health. Our camp is situated in part of the battle ground among scenes that would fill

---

[130] The 16th Massachusetts joined McClellan's Army of the Potomac on June 13.

[131] White House Landing, the Federal supply base on the Pamunkey River.

[132] The regiment had not taken part in the battle (May 31-June 1), joining the Army on the battleground on June 13, as noted above.

with horror any civilian but which a soldier ~~look~~ witnesses with indifference incomprehensible. There are still some men yet in the woods unburied and and the heavy rains have caused parts of bodies to be exposed which are suffering decomposition which in a still day or the wind in a favorable direction fills the air with the usual disagreeable odor attending decomposition. Cartridge boxes, clothing and large numbers of muskets are seen in every direction, my servant dug up with a knife a fine rifle everything complete and in excellent order but sold it to a boy before showing it to me. The rebels must have suffered terrible as we buried 2600 of them[133] and they are continually find more bodies in the woods and ditches. The second day must have been a terrible disappointment to them, as the battle of Fair Oaks was a test of strength of the two armies in regard to their fighting qualities. The rebels having every advantage opening their dams, flooding the Chickahominy causing it to rise nearly 12 fts in a very short time, (and it was fortunate for us that we succeeded in getting any troops across) thereby in a measure cutting off reinforcements; having us in this situation they launched into our advance division their best troops, and not withstanding what the papers have said about the behaviour of Casey division[134] they must have done some fighting as according to accounts a large number of rebel dead were found in front of the situation they occupied when first attacked. The first day they had the best of it, they fought well but they had not accomplished as much as they hoped. The second day we attacked them, making some splendid charges which completely routed them driving them two miles in advance of our first position, and if McClellan had been able to have crossed the Chickahominy River, I no doubt we would have followed up the .... by entering Richmond. When we consider of the superiority claimed by the rebels over us in courage, and their .... declarations and statements, that in a fair field right away from our gunboats, one Southern man was equal to an indefinite number of Yankees, and takeing into consideration proportion was immensely in the rebels favor, and then compare the results with what must have been the expectation of the rebels deduced from what they expressed themselves able to do, the balance is immensely in our favor, our army is [in] excellent spirits and have been strongly reinforced since the fight, their army must necessarily be demoralized, and they are not receiving any reinforcement and it even has been said by captured rebel soldiers that it was intended to make that the decisive battle, and that being defeated they doubted whether there would be another large battle, but the rebels will fight yet but it is the fight of a cornered man. We are in Genl Grovers[135] Brigade, Hookers Division, Heintzelmans Corps d'Armee[136] , our

---

[133] Johnson is in error here. The total deaths on both sides did not reach this figure: 790 Union and 980 Confederate soldiers died in the battle.

[134] Major-General Silas Casey (1807-1882) joined the U.S. Regular Army in 1826; his three-volume "Infantry Tactics" was the army's standard manual for infantry. His Division had been overrun by the initial Confederate attack. Fair Oaks was Casey's last battlefield command, and he spent the rest of the war in the defences of Washington, D.C.

[135] Born in Maine, Cuvier Grover had a younger brother who was a governor, and another brother who was a Senator of Oregon. He graduated from West Point, served in New Mexico, and was appointed Brigadier General in 1862. He led the First Brigade of Hooker's Second Division, transferred to General John Pope's Army of Virginia at Second Bull Run, and later served in the Gulf area at Port Hudson. He won Brevet ranks for Fisher's Hill and Cedar Creek. He later became Colonel of the 1st U.S. Cavalry. He died at Atlantic City on June 6, 1865.

[136] The 1st Brigade, 2nd Division, 3rd Corps, Army of the Potomac, in which the regiment remained until March, 1864. Major General Samuel Peter Heintzelman was a West Point graduate. He won a brevet for

brigade consists of 1st 11th 16th Massachusetts, 2nd New Hampshire & 26th Pennsylvania, and is as good a brigade as their is. Jimmy called on me as our regiment was marching to our camping ground and I have not seen him since he is looking well. We are in the advance and have to do picket duty every third day, the rebel pickets are about half a mile from us, and we are within six miles of Richmond. One Brigade does the picket duty 1 regiment doing the outpost duty the other regiments acting as reserve. We have so far lived well although much reduced in our baggage carrying only what our servants carry on their backs. I am going to bed after dinner while my man washes a pair of drawers I not having but one.

    I shall now give you a little sketch of our journey from Suffolk. Sunday afternoon the [8th] we had orders to cook three days rations preparatory to march, our tents were immediately struck and all the baggage prepared to be sent. Two companies left that night by [railroad] cars for Portsmouth and the remainder myself among them started early Monday morning by cars each car be densely packed and arrived at Portsmouth in good condition. There not being sufficient cars only portion of the regiment went in the first train, and those companies which arrived in Portsmouth first remained in the city, until the arrival of the remainder of the regiment; the consequent was, as each man had just received two months pay, an universal drunk, the soldiers having to obtain their liquor by stealth, by paying enormous prices. The regiment and baggage embark in two steamer the Star and Robert Morris on the former was myself we took the lead and kept it. We steamed for Fortress Munroe, passing Fort Norfolk, Craney Island and Sewall's Point, all places rendered famous as defending the approach to Norfolk. If our vessels had succeeded in passing Craney Island, they would have found a severe obstacle in their further approach to Norfolk. The rebel had driven piles clear across the channel with the exception of about six rods, and this was all the entrance to Norfolk and when their vessel had all retired inside of these piles they had an old frigate The State[137] I believe it was called arranged with valves and filled with ballast which they intended to have sunk in this opening to shut up all approaches to the City by water. We arrived at Old Point [Comfort] in the evening cast anchor and remained there during the night. The weather which when we started was pleasant gradually changed windy cold rain so on our starting from Old Point the next morning it was raining hard and the wind blowing fresh. The unpleasant weather put a damper on the full enjoyment of the scenery which otherwise would have been appreciated; we passed Ship Point, Yorktown & Gloucester [Point and] West Point, and entered Pamunkey river which is usually very narrow but the heavy and continued rains has made it a very respectable river, and the scenery about was delightful. As we shortened the distance between us and White House Landing, the vessels or transports became more numerous and the masts were as numerous as in Boston harbor. We arrived at White House at seven o'clock laying in the stream our steamboat was soon surrounded by bum boats selling hot coffee at 25 cts for cup which much to my surprise they got and seemed to sell it as fast as they could deal it out, as soldiers were cold and damp, having plenty of money they would have paid fifty as willingly as 25. Wednesday morning we landed, my company was detailed to look after the baggage, and was divided into two parts,

---

gallantry during the Mexican War, and rose to Major General by May 1862 but, as one observer said, "He somewhow just missed being an effective corps commander." Following his mediocre service during the Peninsula Campaign and 2nd Bull Run, he commanded the defences of Washington D.C., then the Northern Department, and then commanded in Texas until his retirement in 1869.

[137] Johnson's information is at fault here; there was no ship of this name in either Navy.

one under Lt Rowe[138] to remain with the baggage that went by rail, and the other part under Lieut Tucker & myself to accompany the wagons by the road; the roads were represented so bad that the wagons six in number carried only forage enough for the horses. At two o'clock in the afternoon we started, with magnificent weather, but we found the roads full as bad as described, but notwithstanding the country around was delightful, our road led through the woods a great portion of the way, which made it more pleasant to me, I having a horse which kept me above the mud may acount for my enjoying myself so much. We pushed forward until 10 o'clock in the evening but the roads were so bad we had not made very good speed compared to what we could have done under favorable circumstances. I posted my guard had my hammock swung on a zigzag fence, my company cooked some coffee and disposed themselves for the night. The night was beautiful and the country about luxuriant with vegetation, we were encamped on an open adjoinging [sic] a fine farm; the road we were on not having been traveled much by the army the land looked in excellent condition, and we I think presented as picturesque scene as is often found, six white covered wagons surrounded by horses tied to the wheel while in the bushes adjoining the flashes of three or four fires surrounded by men in all positions while to our rear in a little grove was also tied horses who would occasionally express their joy of being released from their days work by neighs all those combined with a clear full moon made a beautiful picture which I shall not soon forget. Our camp was bounded on three sides by woods, and a brook running through the woods served to water the horses. At daylight next morning we got ready our breakfast and started found better road and a fine country and at nine o'clock arrived at the Chickahominy river, before arriving at which we crossed a swollen brook by wading the men stripping up their pants. You have read descriptions enough of the river which swollen as it is is still very insignificant stream, we crossed at what is called Bottom's bridge. After crossing the Chickahominy river we proceeded some two or three miles farther to Savage Station to await the arrival of our regiment, and at which place we encamped the following night and started with our regiment to our present encampment. I have just received three letters from you and any quantity of papers from father comprising one weeks mail. Has Charley Mayo resigned, I heard he expected to obtain a place in an express company. I suppose my situation will fill you with fear for my safety but you must not be alarmed you have of course been expecting that I should be placed in some such situation. I shall for fear you may be unreasonably alarmed not tell you what is going on here. The rebels made a reconnaissance yesterday, we captured two Captain, we had seven men wounded[139], now I was mile away and when I say we I mean the Potomac Army. Direct to 16th Regt Mass Vol Gen'l Hooker's Division Army of the Potomac. Give my regards to all. In good health

    Yours affectionately   Charley

****

The Boston Daily Journal for June 23 reports a telegram sent to Governor Andrew on the 18th: "The Sixteenth Regiment of Massachusetts Volunteer Infantry made a reconnaissance in force yesterday afternoon, through the wood in front of their position at Fair Oaks, in order to ascertain the nature of the ground beyond. It drove in the enemy's pickets, until the rebels were reinforced to an extent which compelled it to

---

[138] 2nd Lieutenant Hiram Rowe, died May 10, 1863 of wounds received at Chancellorsville.

[139] Skirmish at Tunstall's Station, about 7 miles from White House Landing. Dyer states that the 42nd New York Infantry suffered 4 killed and 8 wounded.

retire. Co. A was not engaged in the fight. The following is a correct list of the killed and wounded of the other companies... Co. F: Wounded - Thomas Whalen, Chas. Sturnes, Thos. W. Coombs, Daniel Claford. Missing - Lieut. Rogers, supposed to be mortally wounded; Corporal J. Allen, Edward McAndrews, Thos. J. Reynolds, Patrick McCartney, Patrick Weston, J.D.S.Freeman"

****

June 19 /62   Fair Oaks

Dear Nellie,
     I write this short note to let you know I am well. Our regiment made a reconnaissance yesterday[140] to discover the situation of the land. We had to penetrate the woods nearly a mile until we reached the opening on the other side, driving the rebels before us. Our regiment lost more than it ought to have considering the nature of the skirmish. The loss in my company is among the heaviest Lieut Rogers was severely wounded and left on the field[141] near the enemies rifle pits *[line illegible]* his loss we have four privates wounded & five missing, the missing are probably wounded. The order was given to retreat which never reached me, I did not retire until I heard firing nearly in our rear. We received one heavy volley without much harm, much of the loss was by the enemies sharpshooters, who filled the woods and had all the advantage of us. Lieut Tucker was on detached service and did not go with the company. In my next letter I will write more.
     Yours in good spirits affectionately   Charley
We had 16 killed & fifty four wounded & missing in our regiment.

****

Sunday June 21 [1862]   Fair Oaks

Dear Nellie,
     I received your favor of June 18 this morning. My duties have not been very easy and I take advantage of every opportunity to get some sleep. Last night the enemy were annoying our pickets, which are in sight from my tent, causing great deal of firing. Yesterday afternoon they showed themselves in force and for about 15 minutes there was every prospect of a general engagement, vollies of musketry were exchanged our forts opening on them with shells and cannisters, which caused the rebels to retire, supposed to have been three regiments of them. We were under arms from three o'clock until nine this morning expecting a renewal of the attack but none took place. We go in duty as reserve picket at half past three o'clock this afternoon for twenty four hours. We have been under arms innumerable number of times it is rather harassing for the men, but they take it good naturedly. Our regiment is gradually becoming use to the sound of shells and musketry, and I think will behave like veteran. The 11th Mass march into our camp yesterday and gave nine rousing cheers for the bully sixteenth as they call us. I probably shall resign by the middle of

---

[140] Skirmish at Fair Oaks, June 18, in which the 6th New York Independent Battery Lt. Arty., 73rd New York Inf., and the 69th, 72nd and 81st Pennsylvania Inf. were also engaged. Union losses were 16 killed, 28 wounded and 15 missing; if Johnson's figures at the end of the letter are approximately correct, all the casualties appear to have been suffered by the 16th. According to Dyer, the 16th was also engaged that day, by itself, in a skirmish at Nine Mile Road (which led north-west and then west from Fair Oaks towards Richmond), losing 7 men killed and 57 wounded.

[141] As noted in footnote 70, Lieut. Rogers died as a result of his wounds.

next September if I can do it honorably, and go back to business again. I should like to have you send me a small compass (pocket) as if I do any more skirmishing in the woods it may be the means of saving my life, if it had not been for the sun I was as likely to have gone into the enemies camp as my own, it being very difficult to go directly through thick undergrowth. I am writing this letter in a chair made out of a cracker box. And have my tent to my self, Lieut Tucker being on Provost Guard and detached from my company. Mother may send me a small box of cake if she sends it soon it will probably find me here. Excuse the shortness of this epistle, and my regards to all.

       Yours affectionately   Charley
Send me some postage stamps can't buy them here.

****

       Fair Oaks June 26 /62   Thursday
Dear Nellie,

  I received a letter from you yesterday and one from mother which were acceptable. We have a great deal of duty to do and are consequently frequently in skirmishes. Yesterday there was a skirmish on a large scale[142] and to me of a most disagreeable character, we drove the enemy a half mile back in the woods and held our first position, against all the attempts of the enemy to recover them. Seven companies of our regiment were under severe fire late in the afternoon, but my company was not with them, the remaining three companies were active as reserve for the centre of our line, and it was not a very agreeable place as there was no excitement and little danger, we were obliged to fall back from our own shell, one of them breaking the arm of one of my men whom I was at the time talking with. I am in good spirits, but rather tired, and do not feel like writing the weather being such together with the duties, that I am inclined to sleep every opportunity. I hope to get mother box soon. Charly has I understood sent in his resignation but it will not be granted it is a difficult thing to obtain a resignation now. There has been all afternoon a very severe cannonading on the right of our line, and at this moment I hear our troops cheering what for I know not. I am quite jolly and in good heart. Charley is staying in my tent, and has delivered your message. I intend to resign in the middle of Sept. if I can do it honorably. Excuse the shortness of this. Give my regards to all. Friday morning: Last evening heard that our right wing had turned the rebels left, give them a good defeat[143] , consequently there was a good deal of cheering. This morning early heavy fire commenced from nearly the same direction, I supposed Mac was following up his success. Three o'clock as usual get up and remained under arms when awoken was enjoying splendid sleep, I thought it cruel. Send me some postage stamps you can't buy them here. Yours affectionately
       Charley
We are under arms now only expecting the rebels may make an attempt to break through here. We have some fighting generals around us, Gen Hooker, of division is always where the fight is thickest, and keeps up a continual grind. Genl Grover[144] our Genl is a brave and fine man.

---

[142] Engagement at Oak Grove, in which Union forces suffered 626 casualties (Dyer).

[143] The Battle of Mechanicsville, June 26th.

[144] Brigadier-General Cuvier Grover (1828-1885), commanding the 1st Brigade.

****

Fair Oaks /62 Saturday June 27[145]

Dear Nellie,

  There has been in the last two days great deal of excitement and numerous rumors which you nor anyone else can find out the foundation of. There has been heavy fighting on our right extending nearly to our center and I can't find out the results; that is I don't obtain the same information from any two people. I am in excellent spirits and as for writing the descriptions of any of the skirmishes I shall find it difficult until I have more leisure although you can find a better account in any of the newspapers, as I know only of what occurred directly about me. I shall not be able to obtain mother box at present, though I receive all the letters regularly, owing to the cars all being used for government. Did you receive, or rather did father, the $250.00 which was sent him, part of which was for you.

July 2 [sic]

Dear Nellie, I am on James River about 6 miles from Fort Darling[146] am well and in good spirits. Been fighting every day for the last three days.

    Yours Affectionately   Charley

****

"When the army was encamped there [a position on the Williamsburg Road, nearly in the centre of White Oak Swamp], the entire region was inundated by the severe and unusual rains. The Chickahominy, in portions, had ceased to be a river, and seemed like a vast lake. The roads, in every direction, were little better than ditches, and were quite unserviceable until they were all corduroyed. The ground had been excavated in many parts to form redoubts, or make lines of rifle pits. The plains, during and after a rain, were one compact surface of glutinous mire. In dry weather, they were baked hard by the intense heat of the sun, showing only here and there stagnant puddles, covered with a green slime.

  Thousands of dead bodies, of animals and men, some under ground, but more above, covered with from three to six inches of earth only, filled the air with an insufferable stench, which with the exhalations rising from putrid water and decaying vegetable matter soon began to tell on the health of the men. They were also compelled to drink water in frequent instances flowing from brooks and streams where wounded men had fallen and died or where the dead had been buried without proper consideration; and this but added to the prevalent depression of strength and spirits. It seems hardly credible, but hundreds could attest, that the first night Gen. Grover's brigade went out on picket, knowing nothing about the condition of the ground, the reserves slept upon their arms wherever they could find a spot, and in the morning discovered that their nearest companions had been the bloated and maggot-ridden bodies of dead soldiers, lying yet uncovered where they had been shot down; and that the disgusting vermin from their putrefying carcasses had found its way under their own blankets, or clothing, and even among their rations. Many a relief squad stumbled over what they supposed by the sleeping form of some soldier utterly worn out, and too

---

[145] Johnson is mistaken; June 27th, 1862 fell on a Friday, and the letter following is dated June 28th.

[146] Part of the Confederate defences on the James River, about 7 miles below Richmond, at Drewry's Bluff.

exhausted to move, whom morning revealed locked in the arms of a sleep that knows no earthly waking. During the hurry of battle, no attention can be paid to the killed... In and around the White Oak Swamp camping ground of the First lay bodies by the dozen. Black, festering, and alive with worms, it is impossible to move or touch them; and they could only be covered where they lay. During one forenoon, twenty-nine of these were thus disposed of, in the midst of odor so rank and nauseuous, that members of the working party were obliged to go away and vomit in spite of every effort to prevent it. Day and night the atmosphere was charged with a fetor stronger than any bilge-water that was ever taken from a vessel's hold; and at times it became so powerful and penetrating, that nothing but inflexible military discipline kept the men where they wre obliged to endure it.

Wednesday forenoon, the 18th of June, the rebels made two feints, in force in front and to the left of our position. It seemed to be the universal impression that they were coming at last for the grand final struggle so long anticipated; but, just as they approached with rifle-shot distance, they counter-marched, and turned off in another direction. To ascertain, if possible, what movements they might be making, the Sixteenth Massachusetts regiment was ordered to go out on reconnaissance in the afternoon, with the rest of Grover's brigade as a support.

The members of this regiment were full of alacrity as the prospect of a brush, for they had never before been under fire, and did not entertain that wholesome respect for rifle-balls and cannon-shot inmotion which experience invariably gives to the bravest and most reliable veterans. After the march began it was difficult to restrain their men, so eager were they to dash on, and unearth the skulking rebels from their forest hiding-places. In course of half an hour, they were pretty hotly engaged with a body of men at least as numerous as their own, and some thought much superior. The rebels lay behind logs and bushes, or were hidden by trees and stumps, whence they poured in a rapid fire upon our men in plain sight, advancing upon them. The contest was kept up somewhat over an hour, when, by order of Gen. Hooker, the word was passed round to withdraw, which was done with evident reluctance and without the least confusion.

Never did men behave better under fire than the soldiers of the brave Sixteenth. They were not only full of enthusiasm for the fray, but went into it with a dash, and carried it on with a pluck, which would have done honor to veteran troops. The only pity was that the men, scorning to imitate the hide-if-you can practice of the rebels, and thus fight them with their own weapons, exposed themselves without compelling the enemy to do likewise, and in consequence suffered severely. Two officers and five men were killed, and fifty-seven men were wounded.

At midnight on the 24th, orders came to the division to be ready at seven o'clock on the 25th , with three days' cooked rations in their haversacks, for an advance toward Richmond. At daylight, every man was up; at half past six, the line was formed; and at eleven precisely, the companies were filing over the field and into the woods, where the rebels were supposed to have located their picket reserves.

This supposition became a certainty soon after eight o'clock, as our skirmishers came upon the outposts of the enemy, and began that irreglar firing which ususually precedes a sharp engagement. Very soon the main body of the regiment came up, and the conflict waxed hot.

The Massachusetts First at this time had the advance, supported by the

Pennsylvania Twenty-sixth and New Hampshire Second, the Massachusetts Eleventh and Sixteenth being in reserve. They were obliged to advance through a... swamp, with water above their knees, when the rebels opened fire...

They were entirely without cover, also, and knew nothing of their location and surroundings, except what they were learning, second by second and inch by inch, while the rebels were perfectly familiar with the ground, and had to aim low,... protected by their rifle pits, almost sure of hitting somebody.

Not a man flinched, however; not a face turned back; but, firing and advancing, the whole line went forward, until the panic-stricken rebels were driven out of their own pits, and began a rapid retreat across an oat-field just in front.

...they came back again, and the First, not having been immediately supported, fell back a short distance, when a fresh onset was made, the rebels driven out... and the First... continued to hold their rifle-pits..

The attack upon this pit, where the enemy had every advantage of cover... was one of the the most daring exploits of the day; driving the enemy out of it twice in succession, and holding it for nearly ten hours... with an obstinate determination.

After the rebel rifle-pits had been taken, fighting began along the whole line. On the right, it was principally with artillery at long-range, but at the centre and on the left, it was till about two or three o'clock, mostly with muskets and rifles.

Repeated attempts were made to flank our position, during one of which the Massachusetts Sixteenth and Eleventh, and the Pennsylvania Twenty-sixth, were exposed to the one of the hottest fires of the day; but the coming of Gen. Berry's brigade, and repeated discharges of... howitzers, kept the enemy at bay...

The fighting began at 8 o'clock, a.m. and was kept up... all day. Sometimes the roll of musketry and the thunder of artillery were incessant.

After nine o'clock, an onset was made upon our lines; but a sheet of fire burst... such as flesh and blood could not stand, and the Union forces were left masters of the ground... Dear was the cost, however, as far as the First Regiment was concerned, Gen. McClellan was on the field, close by our division, a great part of the day, and personally directed one of the later movements.

Gen. Heintzelman, Hooker, and Grover were also on hand, cool, fearless, and resolute, contributing no little... to the success of the day.

Such of our wounded as could bear removal were at once sent down to White House, and put on board hospital steamers for transportation to Fortress Monroe. On Thursday the 26th, our dead were all buried on our own camp... and addresses were made by Col. Cowdin, Capt. Baldwin, and Chaplain Fuller of the Sixteenth...

Following the action of the 25th early on the the next day, an assault was made upon the Union right. Anticipating trouble, White House had been abandoned as a depot of supplies... and its... stores removed or destroyed. This was unknown to the rebels. Hoping to reach them, Longstreet and Hill fell suddenly upon McCall's position, surprising the Pennsylvania "Bucktails," while on picket, and capturing several companies of the reserve... they furiously assaulted McCall's line... hoping to... divide the right wing from the left. After a severe and protracted engagement, Gen. Morell's division came up, and the rebels were driven back... and rose by the dozen from their sick beds and besought wagoners or ambulance drivers to take them abroad, or followed feebly in the direction of the retreating columns... Meantime the rebels had drawn up a battery on the Union right, which opened the fight... Skirmishers then appeared in front, and soon a line of battle emerged from the woods at point-blank range. Every inch of the ground was commanded by our guns, which poured such a destructive fire into their ranks that they fell back... They then tried the flanks, but... every precaution had been taken in that direction... Finally... seeing that our men were steadily... falling back, they massed their troops and moved forward to the assault. From the whole line... they received discharges at such a disadvantage that they at last retired to the woods... The First regiment supported Battery K, Fourth United States Artillery, and guarded a portion of the railroad beyond the station, all the afternoon... The troops were kept constantly in motion... marching... and countermarching if along any portion of their line the enemy appeared in force. Surprise was therefore impossible, and... soon after dark the firing ceased. All night long the retreat continued. The roads were crowded with soldiers, horses, cattle, wagons and batteries; and before daylight the opposite bank of White Oak Creek had been reached, the bridges were destroyed and cannon posted commanding all fords...

This point was reached, passed and held in force by our batteries, and... the enemy did not appear upon our rear and flank until noon of the next day. Many of our troops had been drawn up in line of battle... since morning. At twelve, they were seen covering the crest of Poplar Hill, which had been our former camping ground, advancing so as to overtake our rear. They had no sooner arrived within cannon-shot than they were admonished by nearly fifty guns not to come any farther. Immediately planting our own batteries in front of the position, then commenced a furious cannonade, answering us... under cover of which their infantry attempted to cross the stream but... were driven back.

Below, the stream was too wide and deep to allow passage, and above, the ground was heavily wooded, and swampy, so that nothing was left for them but to hold the hill... this they did until long after dark.

Simultaneously, with the assault of Stonewall Jackson's forces on Poplar Hill, Longstreet's, A.P. Hill's, Magruder and Huger's columns commenced the passage of White Oak Swamp by the Charles City Road. It was the determination of those generals to penetrate the Union lines and cut off our retreat... they did not approach the vicinity of our pickets until late in the afternoon... Then they came on... closed in mass, almost on the double-quick. The Union forces had been resting for several hours, and moreover had chosen a position which afforded considerable advantage for... heavy guns, and received them with a destructive fire... Following up our advantage, the Union troops charged upon them; and the entire line would have been routed, had not Gen. Lee called up his reserves. Another advance was attempted, but... it was simply impossible to stand in such a situation... At first the Union soldiers did not attempt to follow them as they retired, but allowed them to reform, yet after hours of fighting they had not gained an inch of ground. The... battle-ground was covered with their dead and wounded; darkness was creeping through the woods, and our lines had been reinforced and extended... they became demoralized and turned back.

During their attacks, the Sixteenth Massachusetts Regiment was fiercely assailed, and Col. Wyman their commander killed, while scores of his brave men were left wounded and helpless on the field. As they went on to a fence fronting the rebel

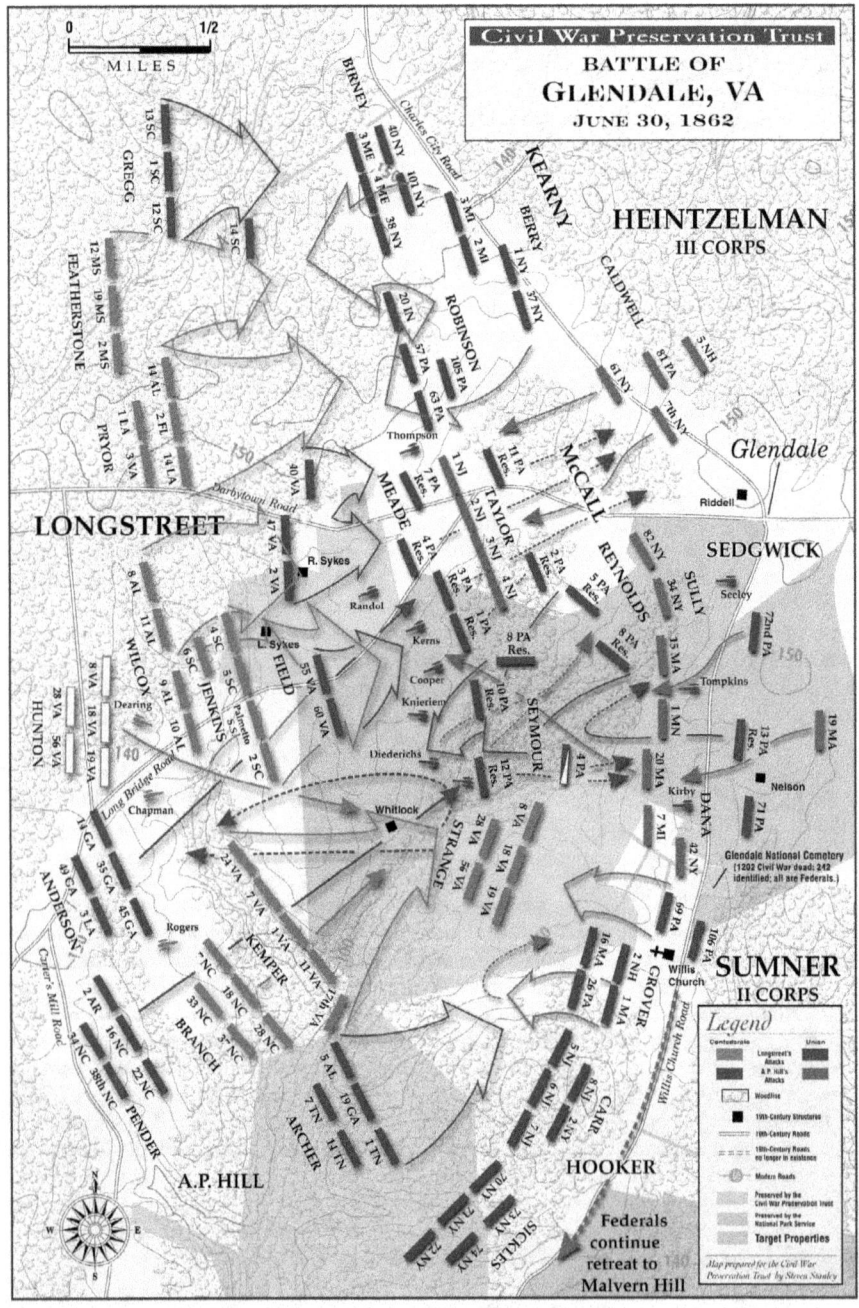

Battle of Glendale, June 30, 1862: Hooker's Division was at the southern end of the battlefield, but was not in Sumner's II Corps *(Map provided by the Civil War Preservation Trust)*

centre, they became mixed up with the First, and for a time both... fought together side by side. The Brigade was then formed for an advance; and Gen. Grover in person led them forward, one on either flank dressed in blue, and one in front dressed in gray. Supposing that the flank regiments were Federals, they continued to advance, when... a destructive fire was poured upon them from the front and and both sides.

The regiments in blue were rebels dressed in our uniforms. The fire was returned... but to remain there was certain death, and Gen. Grover gave his command to get out as soon as possible. How any succeeded in doing so is a marvel; for bullets were flying about... and men were dropping in dozens. The woods were so full of smoke, that it seemed like a thick fog. Branches of trees... were fallling to the ground... surprise, confusion, uncertainty, prevailed upon the men for a moment; they had been entrapped and were in danger of being captured... but, before there was hardly time to think, they were out of it... And... with a loss of nearly seventy... they were in their old position again.

The rebels were demoralized but a prominent general gathered what troops he could... and, forming them hastily in the woods, moved forward... with but forlorn hope... the combatants stood there, pouring their shots into each other... and... engaging in personal combat with bayonets, swords, knives or clubbed muskets. The Union soldiers had already advanced farther than they had been commanded to. They had been ordered only to prevent the rebels from breaking through the to the road... But they had driven the enemy several hundred yards... All night long, our men who were left behind heard... the groans of the dying and the calls of the wounded for water and help.

No sooner had darkness fallen than the Federal army began its movements towards the James River again. Before morning... the whole wagon-train was parked along the James under the guns of the <u>Galena</u> and <u>Mahaska.</u>

The rebel divisions of Wise and Holmes had made an attack on Porter's corps, near Malvern Hill, during the afternoon of the 30th, but having been hastily summoned to the assistance of Gens. Longstreet, Hill, and Huger, when they were so hard pressed, had afforded just the opportunity desired by Gen. McClellan to establish his communications with the gunboats and transports on the James, and thus obtain a new base of supplies."

(From the HISTORY OF THE FIRST MASSACHUSETTS INFANTRY)

****

                        June 28 /62   Camp near James River
Dear Nellie,
    I received the other day your letter with Berk's dag'type which I shall cherish. I am writing now to you not because I have anything to write, but that it has been my custom to send a letter by Monday mail. Our new Colonel took command yesterday[147]

---

[147] Although this letter is left in the sequence as dated, there must be some doubt as to when it was actually written. Col. Powell T. Wyman was killed in action at Glendale on June 30, 1862. The appointment of Thomas Redding Tannatt, previously 1st Lieutenant, 4th United States Artillery, wounded with that regiment at Malvern Hill on July 1, who succeeded him, was dated July 14th. 28-year-old Tannatt, a West Point graduate, died December 20, 1918.

he has created a favourable impression and appear to be one who don't talk much although he may be or felt little awkward in his new situation. We are enjoying now fine weather, not very hot, the 'johnnies'[148] have been very quiet, but they are at work somewhere and I hope our generals are about which I no doubt they are. Why don't they draft at home and send immediately into the field for drill and to get use to camp life those 300,000 men; the south won't stand still, we can afford to wait better than they, but we want the troops to be ready when they move to check them and to be able to take advantage of any mistake which they may commit. Yesterday was a lovely day, Saturday afternoon and evening we had frequent showers and the sun arose Sunday bright, but everything had a fresh appearance, the damp ground caused the wind to be cool and invigorating. There are delightful spots near here, where in peace time I should enjoy taking a walk with you & Berk. I have before mentioned that a little distance from our camp, is a small pond situated in a valley and consequently must be over look by high hill, this pond is not round but the part I have seen is shaped like a new moon in fact it resembles a river as much as any thing; on the side of this pond is a beautiful grove of pine trees, very shady cleared from all obstructions and has the appearance of having been used for that purpose by its owner. If the woods were not partly filled with horses and one did not meet constantly sentinels together with other incidents of warfare continually taking place before you, it would not require much imagination for one to carry himself back to time when such a place as this could be fully enjoyed and appreciated. I live now on tomatoes nothing else and enjoy them exceedingly, price 12 cts for qt, cost I suppose at Baltimore nothing. Lt Tucker is still confined to his tent but is improving. Charley seems to be well. Littells Living Age for which I am to thank someone, send more. You don't write as often as you did. Give my regards to all.

[*Affectionately Charles*]

****

"...early on the morning of the 29th Grover's Brigade was under arms in its camps, prepared, as the men prepared, as they supposed, to take the customary round of camp and picket duty. At the last moment before marching an intimation was given the Second [2nd New Hampshire Infantry]... that the men had better take their shelter tents along... in this matter they were more fortunate than many of the regiment, who marched off leaving their camps standing. The brigade marched to the trenches and relieved the New Jersey Brigade.

A mile or more to the rear, the Corps of Sumner, Heintzelman and Franklin halted and took position to cover the withdrawal of the rest of the army... across White Oak Swamp. Sumner posted his corps on Allen's Farm, between Orchard and Savage Stations, with his left upon the railroad, where it connected with Heintzelman, whose line extended across and covered the Williamsburg Road.

Grover's brigade was on Heintzelman's extreme right, next to Sumner... The brigade had not been in position an hour when, through the haze of smoke which enveloped everything in the direction of Fair Oaks, shadowy forms were seen upon the railroad, indicating that the rebels were feeling their way forward, in pursuit... it was about eleven o'clock when the silence was broken by a report of a cannon, followed by

---

[148] "Johnny Reb" was the Union soldier's generic nickname for his opponent, often shortened to "Johnnies" when referring to the rebel soldiers generally. In the same way, the rebels called their Northern counterpart "Billy Yank, or "Yankees" - though never "Billies".

the rush and explosion of a shell a little distance to the right. A lively artillery duel was immediately on. Several shells swept over into Grover's brigade, wounding a number of men. Then came the shrill rebel yell, with a rattle of musketry, lasting but a few minutes, when a swelling chorus of good Yankee Rah's told that the rebels were repulsed...

[Sumner moved back to Savage Station.] After a time, Heintzelman also withdrew, but instead of halting further back and stopping with Sumner and Franklin until night, he pushed on and crossed White Oak Swamp. But for the [Confederate] failure to rebuild Grapevine Bridge... this might have been a costly error.

Heintzelman's withdrawal commenced at three o'clock... [and on the morning of the 30th] the entire army... was across White Oak Swamp. From the bridge to Malvern Hill... is between four and five miles, and the various corps were disposed so as to cover this line for the protection of the immense army trains which, stretched out in a single line would have extended forty miles...

Heintzelman, commanding the only full corps present, designed placing his troops so as to cover the Long Bridge Road and... the Charles City Road... But while Kearney was getting into position, McCall[149] moved down the Long Bridge Road, across which he posted his division, a considerable distance in advance of Kearney's left. This threw Hooker out of position and made the separation of Heintzelman's two divisions advisable. Hooker was accordingly posted along the Quaker Road, Grover's brigade upon the right and its right upon a narrow cross road or lane affording a short cut between the Long Bridge and Quaker Roads. Sedgwick was in an open field to Hooker's right. Hooker strangely enough, was not even aware of McCall's presence on the field, until about 11 o'clock.

Meantime, four rebel columns were pushing forward against as many different points on the line of retreat: Holmes' division on the New Market or River Road; Longstreet and A.P. Hill on the Darbytown or Central Road; Huger upon the Charles City Road; Jackson made desperate efforts to force a passage at White Oak Bridge, but was stubbornly held to his own side of the creek. Longstreet's column... was the attacking party in the bloody battle known as Glendale, Charles City Cross Roads, and Fraser's Farm.

Hooker's division, once in position, enjoyed a rest of several hours in the grateful shade of forest trees.... Commencing before noon, heavy artillery firing was heard in the direction of White Oak Bridge, but everything was quiet in the vicinity of the cross roads until nearly four o'clock in the afternoon, when the advance of Huger came within reach of Slocum and was touched up by the latter's artillery. Longstreet, who for some time had been waiting to hear from Huger, at once advanced upon the Long Bridge Road and threw his columns upon McCall. After a stubborn fight of nearly an hour... his little division was forced back...

---

[149] George Archibald McCall was born in 1802, one of the oldest of West Point graduates. He fought in the Seminole Wars, and served in the Mexican War, for which he received brevet ranks under Zachary Taylor. He was commissioned Major General in 1861 and commanded a division of the Army of the Potomac. He fought notably in the Peninsula campaign, but was captured at the battle of Glendale and was confined in Libby Prison. He was paroled and resigned shortly thereafter in 1863. He died in 1868, and was buried in Philadelphia.

The Second New Hampshire had no hand in the bloody repulse which the rest of Grover's brigade inflicted upon the rebel force that pursued the fragments of McCall's left... Orders came... to rejoin the brigade. The hour of its absence had been big with exciting events. Longstreet had overwhelmed McCall, only in turn to be savagely repulsed and thrown back by Hooker's right assisted by two or three of Sedgwick's regiments.

Arriving at the head of the little cross road, one of Hooker's aides was met, who swung his hat and shouted exultantly, "General Hooker has whipped the enemy handsomely, and he wants you to join the division... The regiment filed into the cross road, up which it marched a little distance, then went into line to its left, with three regiments of the brigade, which were there in position. The Eleventh Massachusetts had been detached and sent to the extreme left to reinforce the Excelsior Brigade. The Sixteenth Massachusetts and Twenty-sixth Pennsylvania were along the line of a rail fence on the crest of a low ridge, and the Second took position to the rear, and in support of, the Sixteenth.

Longstreet was following up his success over McCall by vicious assaults... along the Union lines... At length the blow fell upon Grover. The rebels suddenly advanced upon the front of the Sixteenth, delivering a very sharp and destructive fire. Col. Wyman fell from his horse, shot through the heart, and his adjutant and lieutenant-colonel, with many men, also went down. The right wing being most exposed, was badly cut up, and soon gave back in confusion. But when the Second sprang to their feet, and with bayonets at a charge, slowly advanced up the slope in line, the reassured men at once rallied...

The Sixteenth, aided by an oblique fire from the Twenty-sixth, on their left, speedily broke the rebel attack, whereupon Grover proceeded to clear his front of the enemy. The Second advanced to the crest, while the Sixteenth withdrew by the right and retreated to get together. The Twenty-sixth went off in wild charge down the slope, partially crossing the Second's front, pushing twent or thirty rebels out of the holes and from behind rocks, and entering the woods from which the attack on the Sixteenth had come. Grover pushed directly forward from the left with the First Massachusetts, passing a long distance to the front, until the regiment rant into a cross fire in the darkness, from which it suffered a severe loss.

...It was now getting to be quite dark...But there was no further attack. The battle was over, except for the firing of pickets and the occasional collision of scattered detachments.

The horrors of that night at Glendale can never be forgotten by those who lay there in the line during the long, weary hours. The ground between the two lines was thickly strewn with the rebel wounded, but few of whom were within reach of succor, and the shrieks and groans and cries for help which came up from that valley of death were appalling. Hooker wrote, in his official report: From their torches we could see that the enemy was busy all night in searching for his wounded, but up to daylight the following morning there had been no apparent diminution in the heartrending groans of his wounded. The unbroken, mournful wail of human suffering was all that we heard from Glendale during that long, dismal night.

During the night, the troops were all withdrawn to Malvern Hill, where Hooker's division arrived shortly after sunrise. In the early hours of that day, there was

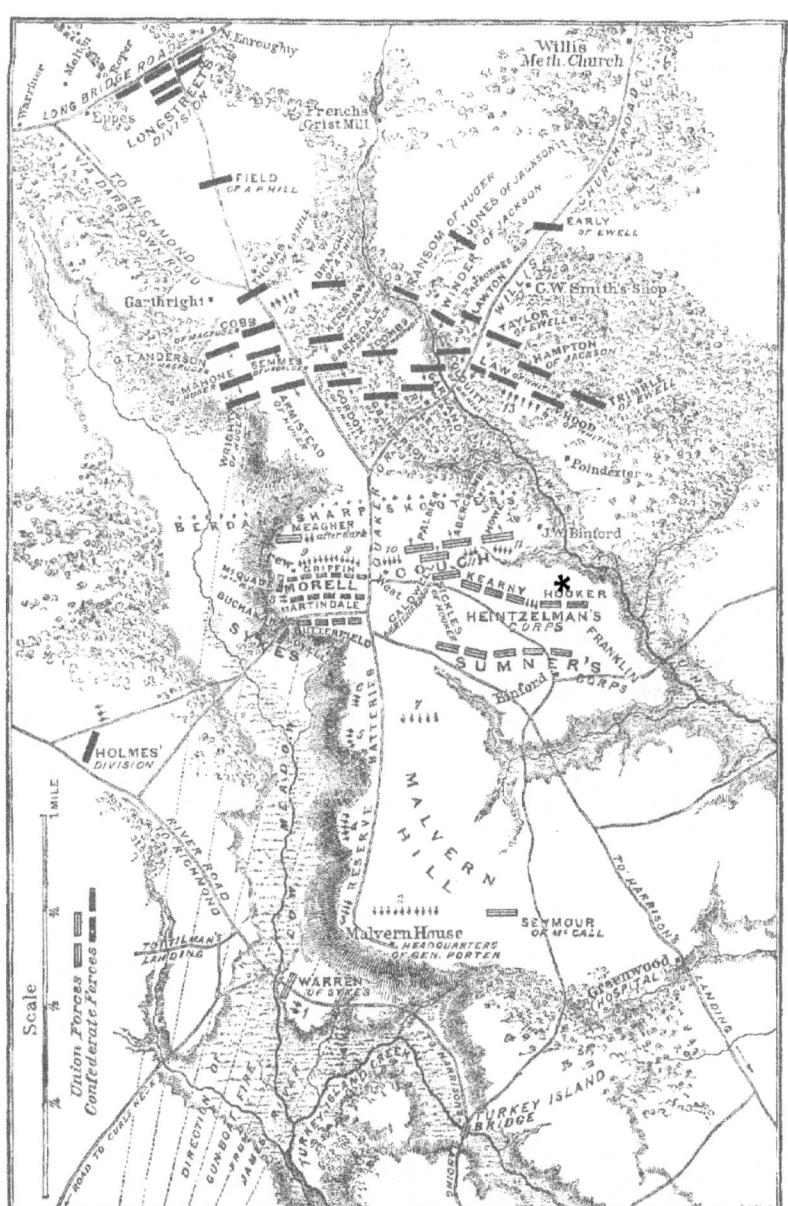

Battle of Malvern Hill, July 1, 1862: Hooker's 2nd Division, 3rd Corps, is shown at *
(from *Battles and Leaders of the Civil War*)

witnessed upon Malvern Hill one of the most impressive pageants of the war, several entire army corps being massed upon its broad, open slopes.

Shortly after Heintzelman's arrival, and while his troops were resting upon the plateau in front of the Quaker Road, advance parties of rebels made their appearance on that road, emerging from the woods, and were followed in time by a battery, which... opened fire. Almost its first shot struck a group of mounted officers surrounding General Hooker, the shell passing through the body of Captain Beam, commanding one of Hooker's batteries. Probably ten thousand men saw the incident and wondered how long Hooker would stand that. Not long!... Guns were wheeled into position... and within five minutes what was left of the rebel battery was tearing for the rear.

The position of Heintzelman's corps that day was on the left center. Grover's brigade was in a very comfortable position, in a rather open wood; and the situation was rendered peculiarly attractive to men who had been drinking swamp water or weeks, by several springs of clear, cool, wholesome water... Upon this higher ground the Excelsior Brigade was in line as support... It was a very strong position... made... still stronger by piling the forest debris into a breastwork.

...the fighting commenced between three and four o'clock in the afternoon, and when it closed, Lee had suffered one of the bloodiest and demoralizing repulses of the war. Assault upon assault was directed against the Union left, the brunt falling upon Porter and Couch, and again and again the rebels were driven back with terrible slaughter... Hooker's front was not involved in any of the assaults; but at a time when Porter was hard pressed, Heintzelman sent the Excelsior Brigade to his assistance...

The battle ended, the retreat was resumed, against the passionate protests of some of the Union generals. It commenced to rain early in the night and soon the roads wee in a very bad condition. That unmolested march of only a few miles to Harrison's Landing had a more depressing effect upon the rank and file of the army than all the marching and fighting they had done since leaving the lines in front of Richmond. It began to dawn upon them that they were taking part in a grand skedaddle for cover, instead of some brilliant feat of aggressive strategy. Up to this time the average impression had been that the army had only strengthened confidence of the men.

All the conditions were conducive to straggling, and it was a bedraggled mob that poured out upon the broad, open river bottom at Harrison's Landing... That magnificent army was disgracefully huddled under the cover of the gunboats, and at once set to work in all haste to cover its front with intrenchments, while its commander was frantically calling for reinforcements. Lee hung around for a few days, then leisurely withdrew to Richmond.

(from the HISTORY OF THE SECOND NEW HAMPSHIRE INFANTRY)

****

A finer position than that afforded by Malvern Hill for defensive purposes could not be desired... By experienced military men, it was hardly believed that the rebels would be so fool-hardy as to assault us again in such an advantageous position... But... at four o'clock in the afternoon the rebel divisions began to form in front of and within the woods in plain sight of our lines...

The artillery opened first on both sides; but as the enemy used wholly field guns, most of their shot fell short, while the 32- and 100- pound shells from our siege pieces and guns struck in their very midst... For some reason Magruder directed his assault towards our left wing, which was the strongest part of the whole line. As they advanced, the men were exposed to a fire in front and on the left flank from our posted artillery, while the right was pierced... by heavy shells from the gunboats. Column after column was marched up towards the slope of the hill only to be thrown into complete disorder, and scattered... Whole ranks were mowed down... Still... the columns of the enemy were pressed upon against the left... and sent reeling... back again across the plain. The left having been reinforced during a... lull in the firing, the defenders... became... the assailants, and rushing down with fixed bayonets upon the... enemy... repulsed them... with terrible slaughter.

After the first repulse, the enemy brought out several batteries... and commenced a furious cannonade of Porter's lines, to which the artillery in front of Couch and Heintzelman responded... making the place... untenable.

Just before the sun went down, a final... attempt was made... and simultaneously with... a terrific cannonade, the rebel lines were pushed forward out of the woods once more, and over the fields fronting the hill. They came on, this time a little to the left of their former direction of approach... But... again their lines were rent by... artillery...

...having assaulted the left unsuccessfully, they approached next the centre, and right... For nearly two hours they ran head foremost agains the storm, until our gunners, out of shot, put in stones, and cut the chains off their harnesses for charges to their guns, or knocked down the foremost of them with their rammers, as they rushed on the batteries. Everywhere they were... beaten back.

...the battle raged on until the sun went down, and... the enemy... routed along the entire line... they retired into the woods... leaving to the Union army an undisputed line of march to the James River...

(From the HISTORY OF THE FIRST MASSACHUSETTS INFANTRY)

****

CHAPTER 9
*
HARRISON'S LANDING AND THE MARYLAND CAMPAIGN

July 2

Dear Nellie, I am on James River about 6 miles from Fort Darling[150] am well and in good spirits. Been fighting every day for the last three days.

     Yours Affectionately   Charley

****

July 2, about six miles from Fort Darling

      Harrison's Bend   James River July 14th / 62
        [Dated in error - should be July 4th]
Dear   Nellie,

  I have not received a letter from you for a long time every thing like a regular routine has been out of order. Saturday last,[151] rumors of all kinds were afloat mostly disastrous to us Saturday evening received orders to be prepared to march instantly with only such property as necessary, no officers tents taken. Sunday morning at 3 o'clock we were ordered to get ready immediately to start not taken any company property but carry it into the center of the camp and place it in a pile to be burnt, which was done, my tent I cut slits in, my mess chest was broken into small pieces, tin ware perforated and every thing made useless. After the destruction was completed our Brigade marched to the front, we, not yet knowing only suspecting that we were to retreat, were much surprised at this, I went with forty men on the Williamsburg road in advance of the redoubt to watch and give timely notice of the enemy, after remaining on outpost an hour I was ordered to return as soon as the 1st Mass had left the redoubt in my rear which occurred soon. Now commences one of the finest

---

[150] Part of the Confederate defences on the James River, about 7 miles below Richmond, at Drewry's Bluff.

[151] This letter has been wrongly dated, by a different hand to that of Johnson's. The letter appears to be describing the days leading to, and the action in, the battles of Glendale (June 30), in which Col. Wyman was killed, and Malvern Hill (July 1). It is clear from the narrative following the description of Malvern Hill that it was written on July 4.

retreats in history.[152] Our Brigade covered the retreat on part of the first day. We fell back a mile and a half to some earth works, to await the enemy and to prevent his following too close out our main body. We remained about an hour when the enemy made their appearance in our camp in force and immediately commences shelling to feel where we were and in a little while our batteries responded with effect, and the fire was continued until the rebel batteries cease fire, in the mean time the rebels made an advance but were received with a well directed fire continuing with more or less vigor for an hour in different parts of the line, when the rebels ceased their attacks. One of the rebel shells pass by me and took off an arm and both legs of a poor fellow. The rebels having remained quiet for an hour or so we commenced retiring, leaving a brigade about a mile behind the first position to cover our retreat and the main body, and from that start we kept a quick gate [gait] without halt which told terrible on the men. We arrived at our resting place for the night at about six o'clock, without any incident except hearing heavy firing in our rear showing the enemy were following us close. Laying with a rubber blanket on sticks over my head I passed that night occasionally disturbed by firing on the picket. At eight o'clock the following morning we marched about a mile halting once or twice and last took our position on a hill behind a fence, and waited the approach of the enemy. At noon we heard severe cannonading on our right, also heavy musket firing which gradually approached our position and last it seemed to be confined a little to the right of us. We were on a hill on the left hand side of the road our right resting on the road and extended across it, on the right hand side of the road was a large open undulating field extending into the wood like a peninsula. The rebels commenced shelling a battery placed in front of our right and charged upon it in large force, and the horses came running through the right of our lines without riders, then commenced a fearful musket fight which continued off and on until dark, the enemies shell bursting about us and throwing up dirt right around us; once our regiment broke but it rallied finely, our color bearer had the staff shot off above his hand but seized the flag and waved it bravely. One of my men while laying down to avoid the shells was grazed on the back taking off some skin closer to the back bone, making a very slight wound; I had only four wounded in my company. Colonel Wyman was killed near me while on horse back, his horse was immediately after shot. We had to continue behind the fence all night long on the alert, the rebels being in force in our front. At three o'clock we were ordered to fall back quietly which we did arriving in our new position in about three hours, we had hardly stacked arms before we were carried to the front and on our way the rebel artillery appeared in sight and the battle commenced. Our position was not an agreeable one being in the enemies front, in a valley, concealed from their sight by woods. There was an abrupt hill in our rear, on which was our batteries, which played over us as well as the rebels. On our left towards evening the contest was warm and their was an incessant fire of artillery mostly our[s]; Magher[153] Brigade charged and drove the rebels two miles, the rebels made some magnificent charges on our batteries to be only met by a terrific shower of cannister making horrible havoc among them. We were also this night obliged to do picket duty and to leave at three o'clock in the morning and the last place commenced our severest march. The cloud had looked

---

[152] In view of the fact that McClellan's advance on Richmond had been turned decisively by the Confederates into a signal retreat, it might be speculated whether Johnson was being ironic here. The text contains little to suggest this, although at the end of his letter of July 4th, Johnson notes "a large majority of the officers dissatisfied with the fighting" and, certainly, McClellan's failure was clear to all. At the beginning of his letter of July 7th, too, Johnson refers to his "laconic account of our change of front."

[153] Irish-born Brigadier-General Thomas F. Meagher (1823-1867)

suspicious and a[t] last they emptied themselves in a perfect waterfall which made the roads with the great[est] travel extremely muddy, and the soil being clayey, slippery. We continued our march in the rain thoroughly wet untill noon when we arrived in a large field equally muddy on which we did our best part the night, it raining nearly through the night. The next morning we had a few shells from the rebels and started off again with a cloudy sky, awful roads but no rain, making a halt of an hour, then started again waded across the Chick[ah]ominy, wetting up to the waist, finally arrived in a large field where we were to pass the night, with out any covering, we not supposing we were to leave when we started, as we were being at the time on inspcewting[sic]. I had no overcoats, no blanket, the ground was wet, also my pants up to my waist; I obtained little sleep in the first of the night, but woke up cold. This morning we started off again but came back and I have hopes that we will quietly remain here, two or three days at least. This is the first day I have not had a rebel shell come uncomfortably near me since I started, and also the first night that I have been prepared to have a comfortable sleep. Our artillery has been firing today I suppose a salute but they have sent shells also. I can hear the bands playing at a distance celebrating the fourth of July. The day is fine and our camp is on one of the large Virginia plantation, near the Chickahominy,[154] every thing at this moment is quiet, the sun has disappeared and the moon has commenced to shine, is half way between day and night. I am writing out side of my dog house on an old cracker box. I had a good supper to night, coffee and *[next line illegible]* fry, which is quite luxurious compared with hard tack and cold water which is all we have had on our march. Our regiment is not in a good condition Colonel Lt Col[155] & Adj; the first killed, the other two wounded and a large majority of the officers dissatisfied with fighting and the necessary hard march. Mail closes.

     Yours affectionately   Charley

****

            July 7th /62   James River

Dear Nellie,

  It is about six o'clock in the morning, and I am hurrying this up to send by the seven o'clock mail. Last Saturday I had everything prepared for a long stay, had commenced a letter to you, and was going to hear a band in the evening, when, much to my disgust, we received orders to pack up. We started and marched a mile or more, stacked arms and rested for the night, next day we laid around, and have finally located, where I am writing this. I expect to receive a wall tent to day which will give some more room; now I am in a shelter tent, cosy and comfortable, but not room enough in it to sit erect. I have received since I wrote all the back mail, containing compass, and postage stamps. I believe the farm our army is on belongs to Stonewall Jackson[156] . Farms here, or rather plantations, are as large I should think as Rhode Island, embracing several thousand acres. Magnificent fields of wheat are immediately sacrificed to the comfort of the soldier, and you can see a constant procession of men

---

[154] It is unclear where the campsite was located. The main encampment of the Army of the Potomac after the retreat from Malvern Hill was in the area of Harrison's Landing, encompassing the two major plantations of Berkeley and Westover.

[155] Lt. Col. George A. Meacham, resigned July 22, 1862.

[156] Johnson is mistaken here. "Stonewall" Jackson spent his boyhood at his uncle's establishment at Jackson's Mill, Weston, subsequently in West Virginia, but went from there into a military career.

passing to and from their camp, those returning are generally buried in wheat. I hardly recollect where I left of in my last letter in which I endeavored to give a laconic account of our change of front, some men call it the nine days fight[157] , but may refer to it again. A prisoner captured at Fair Oaks says an officer corresponding to Lieut Rogers[158] description was taken by them to their hospital and there died and was decently buried. I must close or lose the chance to send this. Give my regards to all.

        Yours Affectionately   Charley

"Dear Nellie please excuse me for breaking open this letter I will not do it again but I was anxious to hear if he was well. F.R.J."

****

The Boston Daily Journal of the same day reported the regiment's tribulations of the past fortnight, apparently from a member of the regiment. "THE MASSACHUSETTS SIXTEENTH INFANTRY. This regiment has certainly known enough of hard fighting during the past fortnight to make up for any ease or peaceful comfort enjoyed by us during the early months of our regimental history. Yesterday we received our second baptism of blood, having had two sanguinary conflicts during one short week. Being held as a reserve in the morning, the regiment was in the afternoon sent forward into the woods as a support for an advancing battery. This service being performed, the regiment found itself face to face with the enemy. An attempt was made to outflank us by the foe. Their orders could be distinctly heard, so close were they upon us. The sixteenth regiment, in fact, was confronted by a rebel brigade, and subjected to a murderous cross fire, by which it lost 29 men in killed, wounded and missing... Setting up a shout, the regiment returned the double fire, but at last was complelled to retire from the unequal strife, though in good order. Its officers rallied the men and kept them in position, and being relieved, all the ground occupied by our forces was retained. Thus, twice during one brief week has this regiment suffered heavy loss in face of the foe. It has, too, been almost consistently on picket duty, digging intrenchments or under arms. These things tell on our strength and numbers, but this old Bay State Regiment "bates not one jot of heart or hope", but longs for the order, "forward march to Richmond." When it shall be given by the proper military authorities and not by ignorant civilians, it will be obeyed with enthusiasm and courage. Gens. McClellan, Heintzelman, Hooker, Kearney, Grover, &c. were almost constantly on the field yesterday. The engagement assumed the proportions of a battle; I know not what name it bears, perhaps 'Woodland Battle,' from its location. This context must be 'the beginning of the end'." A list of the casualties follows.

The account is signed "A.B.F." - undoubtedly the Regimental Chaplain, Arthur Buckminster Fuller, whose comment about "ignorant civilians" clearly shows him to be among the many Union officers who were convinced by their popular leader, McClellan, that politicians at Washington were conspiring against him. It is particularly interesting to see an example of these sentiments being published openly in the press.

****

        July 11th /62 Harrison Landing James River

Dear Nellie,

---

[157] The Seven Days' Battles before Richmond (June 25 - July 1, 1862).

[158] See footnote to letter of June 19, 1862.

We have since we settled in this last place, been very quiet. I am or rather the regiment, is camped on the slope of a hill on the top of which we are digging strong entrenchments. We do no picket duty and the "Johnnies" have not made any noise or molested us in the least in this quarter. I have nothing to do day time and it is difficult to pass the time. I wish I had some books to read, perhaps father with his daily papers that he sends, and which I am most glad to receive, might add The Home Journal or some other weekly. I am not particular what. We have had magnificent weather, at noon the sun is very hot, but not having anything to do can live through it. I have not as yet received mother's box but expect it today or tomorrow. This delightful weather is continually carrying me back to Lexington and the pleasant time which we often have had there; if I am alive next summer I hope to occupy it. Do you or have you been up there since it has been occupied by the new family. I envy them the enjoyment of it, which if they are any lovers of the country they must, & I suppose *[line lost]* to attend to business, next September, I shall be at home for that purpose, if I can get there. They say here "it is easier to go to heaven than to get your discharge." Charley sent in his application for a discharge a second time and it was a second time sent back. "Old Abe"[159] paid us a visit day before yesterday as he rode past the lines he was accompanied by all the generals, little Mac among them. Mac has let his whiskers grow all over his face, they are bright yellow and, if you want to know what he dont look like, you can look at his likeness as it is shown at shop windows[160]. I am very hard up for cooking utensils, and in fact for things *[line lost]* if I leave in Sept, it will only be a short time from now to then. Nellie, you must make up your mind that I may not be able to obtain my discharge. I am thinking of putting my application ahead and letting it go on file; I shall have to make out a strong case if I can I am still in a shelter tent, the principal inconvenience is that I find it difficult to dress, not hardly being able to sit upright. I expect to receive a wall tent. Does Berk enjoy good health by the sea shore, I suppose he does being out of doors so much. I hope the 300,000 troops will be along soon and help us fight[161], if the war is not ended soon I cant see through the labyrinth that our poor country might be entangled in, by the interference of foreign power[162]. I wish you would send me some butter by letter. Give my regards to all.   Yours Affectionately   Charley

****

The Boston Daily Journal for July 12 carries yet more news about the 16th; this time the article is unsigned: "Nobly has this regiment borne itself amid the shock of the past week's battles. They have fought often and fought well. Costly is the libation of blood it has offered upon Liberty's altar. Our Colonel, P.T. Wyman, was shot on Monday, June 30, in the heat of the terrific action of that day. He died instantly, without one groan or

---

[159] President Abraham Lincoln.

[160] An interesting, and possibly unique, observation on the appearance of McClellan in the field; as Johnson observes, the published images of him, both photographs and engravings, invariably show him clean shaven, with the exception of a dark-looking moustache and a small goatee beard.

[161] A War Department Order had been issued on July 2, 1862, calling for a further 300,000 volunteers; 421,465 were raised (Lord, 1960).

[162] There was widespread concern that the European powers might recognise the Confederate States of America and enter the war on their side in order to secure supplies of cotton, the cutting off of which to the mills of England and France was causing serious hardship and economic disruption to those countries.

sigh. A great effort was made to carry the body with the regiment, and transmit it to Massachusetts, but this was found impossible, and the body was decently interred about two miles from here. He was a graduate of West Point, a skilled disciplinarian and officer and will be greatly missed by the regiment. Lieut. Col. Meacham was also wounded through the hand, by the accidental discharge of his own pistol, and has been compelled to return to his home. Adjutant Merriam was shot through the neck. He has shown much heroism in action and won honor in the regiment. Sergeant Whiting of Co. B was killed early in Monday's action, and quite a number of others, whose names, doubtless, appear in the Surgeon's lists of mortality. Many too were wounded and some are missing, who yet may appear to gladden our sight again. Many regiments did nobly and well, throughout these long and weary days of hard fighting. From them I take no laurels, when I say that side by side with them for valor and coolness stands the Sixteenth Massachusetts. Our ranks are thinned today, and we are but the shadow of what we were. Yet the regiment is ready again for action, and the moment the trumpet sounds the note to advance or to stand in line to resist attack, be the foe never so numerous these men will stand to their arms and do battle again for humanity and their country. The regiment now under the command of Major Lamson, is encamped about a mile from this house, in the edge of a beautiful grove, seasing [sic] repose and refreshment, of which it stands in sore need."*

****

Harrison's Landing   July 14th /62

Dear Nellie,

My situation has changed for the better, or plainly I have better accommodations than I had when I last wrote. When I first occupied my shelter tent I had it to myself and there was a prospect of my taken some comfort even if I could not sit erect; but when Mr. Tucker rejoin the regiment, although acting adjutant, he came in with me it put a new face on the affair. his bundles exceeded mine in size and when we were both inside, there was only room for us to lay down, consequently every thing that stand in the tent had to go to make up the bed. In pleasant weather we did well enough, but when it rained, we were deprived of the pleasure of sitting in front of the doghouse as also eating our meals out of doors, etc. The first heavy rain demonstrated beyond doubt that the cotton want waterproof, but there was one dry place in the center of the tent, occasionally we shut ourselves up like closing a spy glass, and called our selves comfortable. But now I am to relate the worst defects of the establishment; our camp is situated in a corn field, in newly ploughed land, rain and travel make the going dangerous, and a man can't tell but he may be sot [sic] if you were out only five minute each boot would have at least 3 lb of mud, now as I was obliged to crawl into my house over Mr Tucker, and when in had to place my feet in my overcoat or least my blanket, it would not take long to fill up my house with mud; my method was to enter all but my feet then cry out for my servant to come and rub the mud off, not withstanding which it was not entirely a preventative against bringing mud into my house. Yesterday I receive a fly, which is a covering usually placed over a wall tent to insure against leaks, it has no ends no sides, merely a straight piece of canvass. I went to work yesterday notwithstanding it was Sunday to arrange my fly to make ourselves comfortable. I placed three logs one on top of the other for sides and I aim today closing up the ends with bushes and shall have a low house adjoining the rear of my tent if we stay here another day. I have for my bed, four crucks[?] drove into the ground, two sticks resting on them and long sticks in them, over the latter are thrown bushes on which with my blankets I sleep. The change is so much for the better, being able to stand up, sit erect and lay down at full length and plenty of room, these thing combine with the fine weather of today makes me very cheerful. Charley Mayo was temporarily attached to my company but he take but little interest I suppose he is not well; well or not a man should have spirit enough to meet the occassion, and whatever he is obliged to do, do it cheerfully. We with the exception of two or three days lately have had very fine weather, cool nights; last night the wind blew through my fly "right smart" and it was a cool breeze from James river it has not died away yet and although it is noon I am not uncomfortable. if the "Johnnies" keep quiet as they have done lately and we stay here you can imagine me highly enjoying myself, my new quarters are now so pleasant in comparison with the old. Father wants to know if any of the sixteenth charged with the 1st [Massachusetts] I can ans yes. We were placed on top of a hill behind a rail fence and when the action first commenced[163] the 1st M.V. were to our rear at the foot of the hill on the border or some woods. We had been an half hour firing (Colonel Wyman being killed) when the first came up and formed behind us, and received orders to charge over us and the fence, which they did, some of the men and officers thought we were going with them and went; some few of mine left before I could stop them one returned soon after with a prisoner. The first words he said "take me away from the bombs"; three of our regiment which went with the first were sent back or finding the regiment did not follow come back of their own accord. It would have been the height of folly to have gone with the 1st because if we went, there was no support, nothing in case of a failure for our men to rally behind, and our place was an important one, for, if the rebel had carried it they could have taken possession of the road which our army was to retreat on, and would be in the rear of a large part of our force. There are great many instances or rather adventures occurring all the time both to officers and men, one of my privates got confused and by mistake (this occurred at Fair Oaks) got into another regiment and was exposed to a severe fire and fought considerably more than he would have if he had remained with us. That fight of Malvern hill, was carried away into the evening, I have before described our situation as being in a valley, this valley ran along considerably to our left and the hill on which our artillery or most of it was placed bounded the north side of it. There was a battery of Parrott guns[164] over our heads but they did not say anything after night fall. Part of our batteries were partially hidden, and all we could see was the flash whilst there was a battery in advance, the mouths of the guns seemed to be directed at us the flash being so distinct; it was truely a fine sight for us, it is said to have [been] the heaviest artillery firing which has as yet taken place. Our Brigade was inspected to day and ordered to put ourselves in fighting trim but I imagine it is only a matter of caution. Two weeks more here will invigorate our troops amazingly. There are a great many sick a hundred nearly in every regiment[165]. I am brigade officer of the day, and escaped inspection which is very tedious. I have not received my box as yet understand there lot of boxes being assorted, hope mine is one of them. I have received your lot of postage stamps and am well provided now. Must close as dinner is waiting. Give my regards to all. We are finely located and are strongly now fortified one of our front is defended by a pond quarter of a mile wide in some place, affording excellent chance for bathing which is improved by every body.

       Yours Affectionately   Charley

---

[163] The Battle of Glendale, June 30, 1862

[164] These cast iron, reinforced-breech guns, invented by Robert P. Parrott, were the Union Army's most frequently-used rifled cannon. They were produced in 10, 20, 30, 60, 100 and 300-pounder models.

[165] Disease was by far the greatest killer in the Civil War, accounting for some two-thirds of all deaths.

****

The Boston Daily Journal for the same date gives a further update on the Regiment's experience and present state:- "Major Lamson[166], left in command of this gallant regiment by the death of Col. Wyman and the wound of Lieut. Col. Meacham, has transmitted to Gov. Andrew a report of the casualties of the 16th, in the battle of Charles City Court House on June 30. Major Lamson also mentions as having earned especial distinction in that action, 2d Lieutenant J.B.Thompson, Sergeants Maurice Roche, Charles Huesey, Joseph H. Chase and Jonas F. Cappelle. Sergeant Winn and Corporals Flanders and Glynn are also honorably mentioned for gallant conduct. Sergeant Cappelle bore the Commonwealth's colors on the field, and when the staff was shivered by shell and ball in several places, still held aloft its shattered remains in the face of the overwhelming fire of the enemy. The whole of Co. C, Capt. King, was exposed through the greater part of the action to a heavy fire of grape and canister at an outpost in advance of our position, and when ordered to rally on the regiment, did so with a coolness which called forth the congratulations of Col. Wyman.

"The death of Col. Wyman is announced by Major Lamson in the following terms: 'I regret the necessity I am under of communicating to Your Excellency the death of our much beloved Colonel, Powell T. Wyman, who was instantly shot dead in the battle of Charles City Court House, June 30, while encouraging his regiment to deeds of bravery and glory, which I am happy to say he had so nobly inaugurated by his teachings and glorious example. I trust the records of Massachusetts will find place for the name of one whose distinguished services and untiring energies in this war must certainly entitle him to all honor. It is fitting in this place to mention also the conduct of Adjutant Waldo Merrriam, who was severely wounded at the side of Col. Wyman when he met his death.'

"By reason of the death of the Colonel, and the absence of the Lieut. Colonel, Capt. Gardner Banks[167] is also at this time discharging the duties of a field officer."

****

Harrison's Landing   July 18th /62

Dear Nellie,

I gladly received a letter from you and mother last evening. We have had some very hot days lately and the last three we have had every evening a severe Sunday shower; the lightning is very severe and vivid, the thunder is very heavy   beats all the artillery firing we are able to produce. While our regiment was at Suffolk I made the acquaintance of a pretty girl, and she promised to make me a secesh flag but failing to find any material she obtained this one from a little girl belonging to a strong Secesh family. Lieut Tucker is at present a little under the weather   Charley Mayo is with Co.

---

[166] Daneil Sanderson Lamson, died 1912, at Weston Massachusetts.

[167] Gardner Banks; Capt., Aug. 1, 1861; Major July 23, 1862; Lt. Col., Sept. 30, 1862; Col., Nov. 28, 1862. Discharged for disability, Sept. 2, 1863. Rheumatism contracted during service disabled him for active service; his last battle was Fredericksburg, and he was discharged for disability on Sept. 2, 1863. He was ill at home at Waltham Mass., for several months, after which he went south to Louisiana, where he became a planter. He returned home four days before his death on July 9,1871. One brother was Nathaniel Prentiss Banks, noted pre-war Abolitionist, Governor of Massachusetts, 1858-9, and a Major-General during the Civil War. Another Brother, Lt. Hiram Banks, was killed in action with the 16th at 2nd Bull Run, Aug. 29, 1862.

H and in fair health, Jimmy is first rate and a good soldier, plenty of spirits and pluck; he may be inclined to make his road easy but I don't blame him. I have a horse which was found by some of the men on our retreat, he is very thin but I am trying to fatten him, and have him carry my baggage on a march. You would be surprised to see what muddy water we are obliged to drink especially after a shower, but we are satisfied and put up with what we can get, at home we should think ourselves hard up to be forced to drink such water. I don't think that there will be any move for some time, some even think not until Sept. as the rebels, they reason, are about as strong as they can be, while we at that time will have, I hope, an immense army Send forward your 300,000 men they won't have to wait long for something to do; mother never show her innocence more than when she writes that she should try to send some brandy by Clifford[168], it would go down his throat before he had left Boston, never trust an Irish soldier with liquor, and know your man before you trust any other nation. No privates or non-coms would be allowed to have liquor about there person, it would be taken away from them. It is a wonder Hattie Hull don't enlist, she seems to have the muscle according to your account. If I ever should be sick at a hospital don't you ever come to see me; there are generally thirty or forty in a room and there would not be the least accommodation for you, any way be sure to wait until I write. I wish you would send out as soon as possible, some cheap second hand novels (paper cover) we are terrible hard up for something to read. David Orr is now at Fortress Monroe at hospital how he ever got there is beyond my knowledge[169] . Lieut Tucker says that the box has proved a treasure, he enjoys the tea & sugar. I will close now. Give my regards to all

          Yours aff[ectionately]   Cha[rles]

Father has learnt by paper before this the loss of the regiment so I wont write it as it is difficult to get names[?]. Everything eatable is still frightfully high.

****

                        July 23 /62   Camp Harrison's Landing
Dear Nellie,
    I write this in some haste, have just returned from a review by Genl McClellan of Genl Heintzelman corp d'Armee, which we are in. On returning I found mother box much to my delight; that bounce[170] is just what I want, not having entirely got rid of my diarrhea. The bottle of Cherry brandy was broken as well as one tumbler of preserves; anything in thin glass is apt to leak out by the glass cracking. The weather has been quite fine not so warm as usual. Tell father if he will send in two week in a small box a qt or two of brandy I can put it to use, he can charge it to my account. The Drs say, it is a wonder any of us are well, he says we are working out the malaria which we inhaled at Fair Oaks[171] . There is a great many cases of diarrhea and there

---

[168] Private Daniel Clifford, a 39-year-old currier from Charlestown who enlisted in Co. F on July 12, 1861, was wounded at Fair Oaks on June 18, 1862 and was presumably returning from home leave. He was finally discharged for disability on October 3, 1862.

[169] David Orr, an 18-year-old Boston seaman when he enlisted as a Private in Co. F on July 12, 1861, was reported missing in action at Glendale on June 30 - hence, perhaps, Johnson's puzzlement at how he arrived at Fort Monroe. He deserted at Falmouth, Va., on December 14, 1862.

[170] An alcoholic fruit drink, in this case probably the Cherry Brandy referred to by Johnson in the next sentence.

[171] It was generally believed, at the time, that malaria was contracted from the 'miasmatic vapours' arising at night from swampy ground, the original meaning of the word being from the Italian for "bad air". It was only in 1890 that its nature as a mosquito-borne infection was discovered.

is rarely more than one officer to a company. I am alone with mine. Lieut Tucker is sick in my tent with slow fever, I think he shows some good signs of fast improvement, although he don't think so himself. Lt Mayo is pretty well. Must close on account of mail. Give my regards to all.

Yours aff[ectionately Charles]

****

"Second Malvern Hill"

August was ushered in by a tremendous display of fireworks, on the night of July 31st, the rebels posted about forty pieces of artillery... on the south side of the James, and at midnight opened on the shipping and camps near the river. The gunboats responded, and after an hour of uproar the rebels withdrew...

A few days later, Hooker returned the compliment by a reconnaissance in force to Malvern Hill. Late on the afternoon of August 2, he marched ... with his division, a regiment of cavalry, and two horse batteries; but being misled by an incompetent guide, returned to camp before morning, on the afternoon of the 4th, however, he moved out again... The division followed a circuitous route, by a back road which entered the Quaker road near the scene of the great battle of June 30th at Glendale. The few inhabitants along the line of march were placed under guard to prevent their carrying news to the enemy, and about midnight the division halted within a few hundred yards of the crossroads, which were known to be held by a rebel cavalry picket. Strict orders were issued against lighting matches, loud conversation, or any unusual noise, and the troops lay quietly on their arms until morning, with the first dawn of which the march was resumed.

The rebel pickets fired a few shots and scampered off, when the column, with the cavalry and a battery in the lead, turned into the Quaker road and marched rapidly for Malvern Hill. A section of artillery, posted on the lawn of the quaint old brick mansion on the hill, opened fire on the column approached, and one shell burst in the ranks of the Second [New Hampshire] ... General Hooker, seated on his favorite white horse under a widespread wayside tree, directed the troops to position when they came up. Grover's brigade filed to the right and took position between the road and the battery, which was already replying to the rebel guns. It was a most unequal fight for the rebels as they were also under fire from a gunboat in their rear; the shells from which were, however, as much an annoyance to Hooker's men as to the Johnnies, as many of them passed completely over the hill and exploded near Hooker's lines.

Had General Patterson[172] advanced promptly with the Third Brigade and occupied the river road, the battery and its support of four hundred cavalry would have been bagged. But he failed to do so, and rebels wisely concluded to go while they could...

---

[172] Son of Major-General Robert Patterson, Francis Emgle Patterson was promoted 1st Lieutenant in the pre-war years, and at the outbreak of the Civil War was made Colonel of the 17th Pennsylvania. He served in the east at Williamsburg, Seven Pines, and Second Bull Run, where he commanded the 3rd Brigade of Heintzelman's 3rd Corps. However, he was investigated, questionably, for unauthorized retreat. Shortly thereafter, he was found dead in his tent from a gunshot wound, deemed accidental.

The Cavalry at once set off in pursuit, and pressed the enemy sharply in a running fight in which the lieutenant-colonel in command was mortally wounded. Grover's brigade advanced on the first signs of flight... Lieut. Joe Hubbard, then serving as an aide on General Grover's staff, dashed into a squad of five, and they came in with him on his nonchalant assurance: "It's no use, boys, you can't make it; come along". All in all, about a hundred prisoners were picked up. The following day, August 6th, Hooker was reinforced by Sedgwick and Couch, but the day passed quietly, and during the night the entire force was witdrawn to Harrison's Landing. With the installation of General-in-chief Henry Halleck, it was decided to withdraw McClellan's army from the Peninsula and join it to that of General Pope. The move was earnestly opposed by General McClellan; but as Lee was detaching troops against Pope in such numbers as to threaten to overwhelm him, while McClellan was unwilling to resume offensive operations without large reinforcements which the government was powerless to send him, Halleck adhered to his plan, and spurred McClellan to move quickly...

(From the HISTORY OF THE SECOND NEW HAMPSHIRE INFANTRY)

****

Camp Harrison's Landing Aug. 3 /62

Dear Nellie,

I received your letters of 23, 55 [sic] & 28th with pleasure. I am looking impatiently for that box. Thank Mr Albert for that cherry brandy & no doubt it will be beneficial. Last night our division made a reconnaissance travelling over a very bad road not muddy but full of stumps, I only stumbled once. The firing the other night[173] did not effect us although we were wide awake could see the shell burst and the flash of the guns, the firings were very rapid. In the Naval engagement which according to the papers appears imminent we shall I think be out of the range of the shell unless they succeed in driving our boats. I have heard the music of small shells and am anxious to hear a large shell but only one, that I think would be sufficient. There is not an officer whom I have spoken with but advocate drafting and that immediately, we deserve to feel here that we have a strong and energetic hand to control the movements and manage affairs. We consider that time is valuable and if we persist in being so slow in reinforcing we shall awake, may be some morning and find that the rebels with an overwhelming army threaten some important point. There is an appearance of a lack of appreciation of the situation of affairs somewhere. The officers and men must have confidence in government and Gen'l and must have strong trust or rather faith that every thing is understood in relation to our need, if this confidence is lost the backbone of the army is gone. Tell father that the papers he sent me pertaining to Charles Stearns[174] bear on the face that he has been paid to July 1st and that the mistake in the figure did have no weight with the paymaster he cannot expect any pay till the 1st of August at the earliest. I will caution father about believing all he says as he has plenty of brass with not the best of character. He has been court martial and convicted of stealing a pair of glove while at Camp Hamilton which is not the only offence. He behave bravely though in the fight. I received this

---

[173]The firing on Union forces between Harrison's Landing and Shirley Plantation by Confederate batteries at Coggins' Point, on the south side of the James River opposite Berkeley plantation, sinking two Union army transports.

[174] Charles F. Stearns, a 19-year-old clerk from Roxbury, Mass., enlisted on July 13, 1861 as a Private in Co. F. He was wounded at Fair Oaks on June 18, 1862 and discharged for disability on July 30.

morning Aug. 4th your letter of the 30th. We go on picket this morning and as it promises to be a pleasant day shall have a pleasant time. Lt Tucker is slowly improving it is hard to gain strength in this climate, in fact a well person has but little desire to work. Charley & Jimmy are well. Give my regards to all.
[*Yours Affectionately   Charles*]

****

Aug 7 / 62   Camp near Harrison Landing
Dear Nellie,
Since last Monday I have seen some hard work in the way of travelling. Last Monday at seven o'clock we went on picket it being a fine day; the road leading through the woods made the march out pleasant. The picket station was very pleasantly situated and after the picket were established I made preparation to be comfortable, I went to work by building a protection from the sun from the rails of a fence. As there was a cavalry patrol outside of our picket extending nearly two miles out there was not so much occassion of vigilance as usual I had command of three companys as a reserve and had imagined that I should past the 24 hours of picket duty pleasantly. At noon to my surprised we were relieved with orders to return to camp immediately. Arriving at camp I had order to give every man two days rations and be ready to march. Our march in from picket was in the middle of the day exposed considerably to the sun, which made the perspiration run off of us. It was twilight before we started, our brigade being some ways ahead, in fact we found ourselves to be the 1st regiment. The night was magnificent bright moonlight, the roads in fine condition mostly through the woods, I should like to drive a fast horse over some parts of it as it was admirably adapted to it. The march was continued without much of any interest, we had a green regiment ahead of us which mislead us and rather disheartened the boys; there is nothing that will take the courage from the men so quick as to lose the way, as we are as likely to receive a shot or rather a volley from our men as well as the rebels. I am to tired to write having been marching nearly three nights. I will write more about in my next. This bullet came from a spherical case shot fired by the rebel burst near us and this ball struck at my feet, I picked it up and send it to you. The range of the rebel shells was fine bursting directly over us. Our regiment had eight injured and any quantity of narrow escapes as the ball litterally rained around us. Give my regards to all.
Yours   [*Charles*]

****

Aug 8/ 62   Camp Harrison's Landing
Dear Nellie,
I closed my last letter in a hurry and shall continue the brief description of our three days reconnaissance in this.[175] I believe in my last I had arrived or nearly to the end of the first nights journey. There were no incidents of importance we lost our road once but the mistake was quickly rectified. I enjoyed the first night journey, the first

---

[175] Dyer notes an Expedition from Fredericksburg to Frederick's Hall Station and Spotsylvania Court House on Aug. 5-8, but does not list the 16th as among the participating regiments. However, it does give the 16th as present at an engagement at Malvern Hill on Aug. 5, in which Union forces suffered 14 casualties. In the final sentence of his letter of Aug. 7, Johnson refers to the 16th sustaining 11 casualties, and is presumably referring to this action. It can only be assumd that the three-day reconnaissance to which he refers was the one menioned in Dyer.

part of which was made pleasant by a splendid moon and after the moon had set, we travelled through thick woods which refreshed us by the coolness of the breeze rendered so by the dampness of the ground. At 2 o'clock in the morning we caught up with our brigade, which had halted and was laying on their arms, we being then two miles inside of where the rebel picket were that is we had driven the rebel pickets in two miles. We had order to rest ourselves, being cautioned to keep quiet and to be ready to meet an attack. The rest was not at all satisfactory to me as I was responsible for any noise that the company made, and several seemed to have a very bad cold and would cough to loud. At half past three in the morning we got under arms and commenced the advance, at the first start there was a little firing of small arms which gradually ceased. We soon struck in to the road that we had previously retreated on, on the rear of Glendale Hill passing the buildings used as hospital during the fight of the 30th. We continue our march, having to recall our retreat by the various evidences which thrust themselves on us; especially did we remark the effect of our severe cannonading of Malvern Hill; trees on either side of the road were cut down, and here and there a large one was able to remain standing although having a shell pass through its center. We advanced some ways on the roads when the advance guards came engaged with the enemies pickets and soon the skirmish commenced by the artillery opening on us, our batteries soon replying. As we approach our batteries by the main roads, we could hear the shells bursting, and as the head of our column deployed from the road the rebels directed their whole attention to our brigade. I have not before had shells explode so near to me. The rebel shells were admirably directed, bursting directly over the roads, they were what is called spherical shot; they are shells filled with bullets and when they explode the bullets scatter. Our regiment never behaved better i[n] fact I began to understand the meaning of the word veterans for although when the shells exploded and the bullets and pieces flew all about the regiment did not hesitate in its advance once, although they were continuously meeting wounded men being brought to the rear it seemed to have no effect on there nerves. We soon left the road and formed on the left of the battery engaged, when we laid down to await further instructions. We had a very good view of the rebels battery and of their encampment. The firing did not continue very long after arriving in our new position before we (the Generals) deployed a brigade to charge on the hill, the arrangements made, the brigade advanced, which admonished the rebels that it was time for them to leave, which they did, and by the time our brigade arrived at the top the rebels were down on the other side. It was no doubt the intention to capture the entire rebel force, which could have been done as well as not if we had been certain the force was so small, or in all probability some brigade did not get into its position in time. The rebel ought to have made more resistance It seems that they had sent for reinforcements and expected a division every moment our brigade was obliged to prepare at the same time we were fighting in front for an attack on the rear. We soon followed the advance brigade to the top of the hill, stacked arms and rested. Prisoners were continually being brought in by the cavalry and from whom we gathered considerable information. They acknowledge to have lost severely in their attack on Malvern Hill July 1 completely demoralizing some parts of their army. They give us credit for fighting well. The prisoners on the whole were good looking men aside from their clothing which was shabby and dirty, they were full of hope for their cause. There was a great difference between them since some were quite communicative and others morose and sullen. They were without coffee or tea in the army (Rebel) but otherwise were well fed, the citizen often sending them supplies. We remained with our arms stacked during the greater part of the day, giving some license to the men to roam about in reasonable distance from their regiment. On the summit of Malvern Hill, surrounded by fine trees of every variety is situated a brick house[176] built in shape of a cross having a large wooden ell [sic] attached to it; the situation was lovely, from the grove in the rear or front I dont know which, was as fine a scene as is usually witnessed. As you stood on the hill, which sides here were precipatous [sic] with a cool breeze fanning you and thick foliage of the trees protecting you from the hot rays of the suns, you were prepared to enjoy the scenes before you, in a valley seemingly not a mile off, lay the meandering James river, looking muddy and shallow, two gunboats some distance apart with the star and stripes flying was resting quietly on the river; to the right on the other side of the river the land was again hilly dotted here and there with fine summer residences and one object especially attracted my attention was the snowy tents of a rebel encampment the extent of which I could not conjecture was probably but a small part of it was visible. All I wanted was my family an easy chair and peace to have fully enjoyed the scene. I envy the owner of the place in peace time, but pity him now, his house is riddled with bullets, his grounds disfigured and it would require time besides money to bring it back to its former beauty. At another house in the or rather in an ice house adjoining it was quite a collection of clothes left behind in our retreat which the rebel had gathered for their winters use, these were set fire to and I am sorry to say that the fire spread and at last consumed the farm house a fine building leaving the place desolate such is the horrors of war. We soon had news from the scouts that the rebels were approaching in force and were at Glendale hill; preparations were made to receive them and as the right approached we were got ready to resist a moon-light attack if it should take place. There was all the while skirmishing between the rebel pickets and ours. Our scouts continually bringing news that the rebels were being reinforced, and at twelve o'clock midnight it was not considered judicious to have an engagement; an engagement to be of any benefit to us must be such that we could crush by number and scatter the rebel force; to simply drive them back without completely demoralizing them would have caused us to remained on the hill, perhaps longer than we desired, and consequently would require a large force to keep up communication. We commenced our retreat in silence our regiment being rear guard. The first part of road was awful, muddy and disagreeable. Our regiment continue to march until it arrived at a smaller stream crossed over the bridge which was thrown across it and formed on both sides of the road parellel with the stream where we were to wait until the remainder of the army had crossed over when we were to cut the bridge down and to hold the crossing until the army had a good start. Trees were cut ready to fall on both sides of the stream. This was quite a romantic spot situated in a valley in dense woods; the scene would have made a fine night picture; the moon had gone down leaving every thing dark, we had a small fire to light up the bridge to enable the troops to pass over quickly, the fitful flashes of rays of light, the glistening of arms and the noise caused by preparing to fell the trees and different order given by officers made what would be a novel scene to a civilian or a fine study for a painter. Luckily for us when we had made up our minds to have a hard time of it and after the infantry had all passed, Gen Hooker said there was cavalry enough to protect the bridge and we need not wait. On way to camp we did some double quick, the regiment coming in in good shape but a little warm. We lost by the shelling the first day 8 wounded from the regiment. The rebel had approached on three different roads and were supposed to be 50,000 strong, which will give you an idea of their strength around Richmond, when

---

[176] Possibly the West House, which is approximately in front of the position where Heintzelman's Corps was posted.

you considered that they have a large force watching Pope another force at Petersburg, City Point, Fort Darling &c *[no further pages]*

****

                              Aug. 12 /62   Harrison's Landing

Dear Nellie,

My last letter contained a brief account of the expedition to Malvern Hill. We are now expecting to move every moment and in fact we were to have moved yesterday afternoon at 2 o'clock, but we didn't; everything is packed up and sent to be stored and as we are now it will be impossible for us to stay over two or three days. I don't mean that the enemy are threatening us but to all appearances everything except what is requisite for our support in the commissary line is limited to five days, everything being sent to the landing and placed on board transports. We expect to march somewhere, we imagine the first halt or rather the place of concentration will be Fortress Monroe, but it is merely conjecture. We hope to be conveyed by transports but we dare not set our hearts on it, for fear we shall be disappointed. We are now in the midst of the hot season and we sometimes hear loud stories of the height of the mercury. I was told it was 130° in the shade. It is warm but not having anything of consequence to do in the middle of the day I lay down and face it patiently. I have not suffered from heat yet, I perspire freely and drink great deal but I could not tell from my own feeling that it was very warm. At noon the sun is scorching almost hot enough to draw the temper from steel, anything that will absorb heat when exposed to the sun at midday becomes uncomfortably hot to handle. The government has at last awoke to the vastness of the work before it now begins to show signs of energy of appreciation of rebel determination; the call of 300,000 9 months men,[177] the recommendations that drafting should commence immediately, has delighted the army. If anyone can recall the words which seemed to fill the mouths of the majority of the North before Bull Run and which that battle seemed to obliterate for a time, we must recollect the oft-repeated expression "we have troops enough" and as long as we were successful you could not make the North believe that we hadn't. They could not appreciate a people so desperate as the rebel, or they would not. If this new call is carried out faithfully and if we can in six weeks have an additional force of 600,000 men we have done more to show the South our determination, to make them despondent, to crush the courage of their armies and to show them their helplessness than many a well-fought battle. The knowledge that our reserve, equalling nearly their whole army, is ready to pour down upon them on any advantage gained by us, or is ready to strongly support any defeated, or worsted, or tired army rendering nugatory any advantage they may have gained by a transient success, will placed before their eyes a picture of hopelessness, will to place the time so remote when the Confederacy will be acknowledge, that if we are successful in the several conflicts which appear about to take place, will cause a reaction which will break up the rebellion. We ought to give the South its due, acknowledge its pluck, appreciate its determination, the courage of it army and take off our coat and prepare ourselves for our arduous and severe conflict otherwise we shall be again surprised by the resources of the south. The advantage which the rebels gained by our retreat from before Richmond has cost them all it was worth, if not, why have they not followed it up, why have they not again attacked McClellan, or Washington, have they kept their word or made their boast good, of entering the northern states and demanding peace from Washington,

---

[177] On August 4, 1862, a War Department order called for 300,000 9-month militia .

Baltimore & Philadelphia.[178] Can it be that they feel so strong that they can wait until our army is reinforced with 300,000 men and a reserve of 300,000 more created? If they can so can we, but they don't feel their strength they are still afraid that McClellan['s] power like a hornets lies in his tail and they dislike to tread on it. They never followed us from Malvern Hill although they were supposed to number 50,000 men on our last leave of that place. The rebel prisoner whom we captured on last reconnaissance, acknowledge that the blow we struck them was severe, Magruder accused of being drunk and slaughtering men, two of their Generals accused of not doing their duties Hill and Hugee [Huger][179] an acknowledgement in rebel papers of continued arrivals of large bodies of stragglers at Richmond during the conflict, putting a climax on all previous statements by a partial confession that a whole division turned their backs are strange accounts of a victorious army. There is no doubt that the [loss the] rebel suffered in following us up was nearer than they could afford or dare to acknowledge. Notwithstanding all that I have written, the rebel feel that they must keep the prestige which they earned by that famous retreat, their soldier are not composed of very poor men, those that I have seen were fine, intelligent-looking men all probably have plenty of courage left. Taking every thing into consideration, their belief that the warm weather is unfavourable to us as it is the opposite to them I must confess that I am somewhat astonished that they wait so long before they strike, it is a mistake on their part, and our government is happily taken advantage of it. Draft! Draft! that is the word which places confidence in our government which shows although at the 11th hour that we have one which is awake to the dangers and dares to look them in the face. The North, at last, appears to be aroused, thank heaven, let it once apply is [sic] entire strength to suppression of this unnatural war throw aside every other object and it can be accomplished before another spring. Comfort at home with prosperity rarely brings a person to the right condition to feel what war is nor does it permit one to contemplate the disasters which would follow an unsuccessful ending of the war. I don't believe we shall leave this place at present, our movement depends on somebody's else. Nellie, I received your letters of Aug. 7th & 3rd, every time we march I burn all *[no further pages surviving; perhaps Johnson went on to say that he burnt all his wife's letters when they broke camp, which would explain why none appear to survive]*

****

Second Bull Run

On the day before August 23rd, 1862, the fleet conveying Hooker's division was

---

[178] Lee had, in fact, already commenced his first invasion of the north, which would culminate in the battles of Second Bull Run (Aug. 29-30) and Antietam (Sept. 16-17).

[179] Magruder had successfully delayed McClellan in front of Yorktown by deluding him into believing that Magruder's force outnumbered him, and repeated the tactic during the first part of the Seven Days' Battles; but then strain, exhaustion and a reaction to medicine he was taking brought about a signal deterioration in his performance and at Malvern Hill, on July 1, his demeanor gave rise to concerns of drunkenness. These were taken up by the press, which singled him out as a scapegoat, and he was transferred to the Trans-Mississippi for the remainder of the war. Major-General Benjamin Huger's (1805-77) slow performance in the battles resulted in his being accorded a similar fate. Ambrose Powell Hill (1825-65) suffered several reverses during the battles, which he blamed on "Stonewall" Jackson's failure to support him, but went on to become a Lieutenant-General and one of Lee's Corps Commanders until his death in battle seven days before Appomattox (Current, 1993).

at Aquia Creek, where it remained for several hours while it was being determined whether the division should land there, as had some of McClellan's troops, or proceed to Alexandria and go to Pope by rail from that point. The stop was taken advantage of by many of the men to have a good swim in the Potomac...

The fleet arrived at Alexandria that night, and the following day the troops were disembarked and went into camp about two miles out from the city. Late on the afternoon of the 25th the division was packed upon trains of box cars, every place, inside and out, where a soldier could stick, being occupied and started to reinforce Pope.

It was long after dark when the trains arrived at Manassas Junction, where a short delay was made. There was considerable good-natured chaffing between McClellan's men and the guard holding the station. It was apparent that Stonewall Jackson was the nightmare of the region, and not without reason, as the very next night, he swooped down and drove or carried off the whole crowd.

At midnight the division arrived at Warrenton Junction, and the next day went into camp in a delightful location near Cedar Creek, where the men were assured they would rest several days. But Stonewall Jackson had not been consulted on that matter, and they remained only the one night in the new camp.

Early on the morning of the 27th the troops were routed and ordered to be ready to march at five o'clock. The occasional reports of the cannon at Manassas indicated that there was trouble in the rear... of a very serious nature. Stonewall Jackson... had made a rapid march through Thoroughfare Gap, and captured Manassas Junction... and the great depots of army supplies which had been gathered there.

But if Jackson was rapid in his movements, the counter movements to head off and crush him before Lee could reunite the widely separated wings of the army were also prompt. Hooker's division—the nearest the scene of the action—marched directly for Manassas Junction accompanied by General Pope himself. On arriving at Catlett's Station, about two miles from camp, evidence of the recent presence of the enemy and of his destructive tendencies were found...

The day was intensely hot, and many men suffered from sunstroke; but the march was pushed with all of Hooker's accustomed energy, the troops using both the railroad and the highway, which were... close together... at length, as the head of the column emerged from the woods into a broad farm clearing, a rebel outpost was sighted... A battle line was immediately formed—a front of two regiments on either side of the road. Grover's brigade was upon the right, the New Jersey Brigade on the left, with the Excelsior Brigade marching by the right flank immediately behind the New Jersey line... The rebel battery... disappeared... and the division advanced about two miles farther, unopposed, when at Kettle Run, Ewell's entire division was encountered...

Grover's brigade was at once halted, while the other two pushed forward on the left of the railroad, passed through the skirt of trees, and engaged Ewell, who was found in position, awaiting attack... A rebel battery opened, and burst a number of shells over Grover's brigade, but it soon had enough to attend to... when one of Hooker's batteries trundled along the railroad track... The fight was short, lasting less than an hour...

Ewell was driven back towards... Manassas Junction. The fight had cost Hooker *three hundred men, mostly from the Excelsior Brigade... Grover's brigade advanced rapidly to lead the pursuit. It pushed through the timber belt across a portion of the battle field, and through the rebel camps, strewn with personal possessions of the late occupants.*

Hooker had no cavalry with which to press the enemy, and although Grover's brigade pushed forward rapidly ... it could not get within reach of the retreating force... The pursuit was pressed about two miles, being suspended about nightfall near Bristoe Station, where the division went into bivouac in front of Broad Run. Through the night Hooker's pickets saw upon their front the light of burning trains and stores, which Jackson was destroying preparatory to an evacuation of the junction.

In the morning (the 28th) Reno's division came up, and... continued on to Manassas, which it found abandoned. In the afternoon, Hooker's division also advanced, passing through the devastated junction, and at night went into bivouac at Blackburn's Ford...

The following morning, the division moved toward Centreville Heights, from which there was a comprehensive view of the country clear to the Bull Run Mountains, the smoke of battle was seen, while long lines of dust mapped the routes of marching troops.

Jackson had taken position near the old Bull Run battle-field, there to await the arrival of Longstreet... Hooker's Division followed the Warrenton Road from Centreville, crossing Bull Run at the stone bridge, and at eleven o'clock Grover's arrived on the field... Jackson occupies a strong defensive position, his left near Sudley Ford, and his right on the Warrenton Road, near the little hamlet of Groveton. For most of this distance the line was along the alternative cuts and fills of an unfinished railroad; and his front, except for a little distance near Groveton, was screened by a belt of thick woods from one hundred to six hundred yards in width. His old division, under Starke, held the right of this line, Ewell's the center and A.P. Hill's the left.

Soon after Grover's arrival he was ordered to report to General Sigel, whose troops, since early morning had been engaging the enemy in the centre. The brigade marched down the Warrenton road toward Groveton, past the Stone House and the crossing of the Sudley Road, and at length filed into the fields to the right, when the First Massachusetts was sent forward to support Sigel's line, while the remaining four regiments rested in two lines, sheltered from the enemy's artillery by a roll of the field in front. The position was nearly opposite the southern limit of the woods, and in view of the batteries on Jackson's right, which sent a shell over every little while as a reminder to the Yankees that they were being watched.

From the woods came the sound of an irregular, dropping fire of musketry, occasionally swelling into a business-like volley, then receding to the old monotony. At three o'clock Grover received orders to advance and attack the enemy. The brigade at once moved up the edge of the woods and there formed in order for battle. Grover placed his command in two lines — the Second [New Hampshire] in the center of the first, with the First Massachusetts on its right and Eleventh on the left. The advance was to be over the ground where Milroy's[180] brigade of Sigel's corps had been engaged all day

---

[180] Born in Indiana, Robert Huston Milroy served as a judge for 4 years, and entered the Union Army as Colonel of the 3-month 9th Indiana regiment. He took part in early actions in western Virginia, rising to

against the center of Jackson's position, held by Ewell's division. Milroy rode up to Grover, meeting him just to the rear of the Second, where the two were joined by the regimental commanders. There was an earnest consultation, lasting but a few minutes. They are behind a railroad bank, and the only way you can dislodge them is to charge, some of the men heard Milroy say—and then they know what was coming... Grover rode the length of the line, telling them they were to fire one volley, then rely upon the bayonet. Then he took position in the rear of the left wing of the Second and gave the order to advance.

Slowly and steadily the line went forward... The left of the line approached an open field, and a halt was ordered while Grover went forward to reconnoiter the front. A dozen bullets, either one of which came near costing the service a good general, warned him of the presence of a vigilant enemy...

... after spying out the land to the front, Grover moved the brigade a considerable distance by the right flank before closing with the enemy. There was spirit of grim determination in that line... Every man knew the supreme moment was close at hand...

Hardly had the advance been resumed when there was a crash of rebel musketry... the regiments of the first line were driven in upon the second, a few rods beyond the railroad, and here occurred the most desperate fighting of the day - a hand-to-hand melee with bayonets and clubbed muskets... The second rebel line was routed and scattered to the rear... A third line was encountered, but the charge had spent its force.

But it was soon apparent that the Second's headlong dash had carried it much farther than the rest of the line had advanced; the Eleventh, on its left, had crossed the embankment and pulverised the first line but was thrown back by the second line. The First had been able to carry a portion of the first line and not to hold that long. Grover rushed the Sixteenth [Massachusetts], from the second line, into the gap that the Second had cut, in an effort to flank the enemy; but it was without avail... the brigades of Starke and Bradley T. Johnson were at this critical moment hurled up from the rebel right and thrown upon Grover. The Second held on until it found itself not only overwhelmed in front, but flanked... when the men made a break to escape capture. As they crossed the railroad bank they were exposed to a murderous fire from each flank...

The brigade came straggling back into the field where it had been formed for the charge but here the flight ended, the men rallying on the flags of their respective regiments with a spirit which showed how little daunted they were by the ordeal through which they passed. A line was gathered facing the woods... At this time a brigade of the Ninth Corps came up and advanced into the woods just to the right, and in a short time came pouring back as Grover's men had done... The repulse was followed by an immediate advance of Pender's brigade of Hill's division. The counter

---

Brigadier and then Major General in 1863. He was outfought at Winchester, "virtually gobbled up" by "Sonewall" Jackson. Enroute to Gettysburg, Confederate General Ewell captured 3,400 of Milroy's men, and all his 34 guns. He held no further command. His soldiers were called "Milroy's weary boys." He was brought before a court of inquiry, exonerated ten months later, thence served under Major General George H. Thomas organizing militia units. He became an Indian agent after 1872 and died in 1890 in Olympia, Washington.

attack fell directly on the gathered fragments of Grover's brigade... and at last the brigade fell back.

The remnants of the brigade were now assembled in a little grove by the side of Young's Branch, and the rolls called. Out of about fifteen hundred men the brigade lost four hundred and eighty six killed, wounded, and missing...

Official reports, and history, have done full justice to the charge of Grover's brigade. General Heintzelman says in his report:- "the most gallant and determined bayonet charge of the war. He broke two of the enemy's lines, but was finally repulsed by overwhelming numbers in the enemy's third line. It was a hand to hand conflict, using the bayonet and the butt of the musket... The First, Eleventh, and Sixteenth Massachusetts, and Twenty-Sixth Pennsylvania were engaged."

The following extract from General Milroy's official report of 2nd Bull Run is also interesting as showing how Grover's charge appeared from his standpoint.

"Toward evening General Grover came up with his New England Brigade. I saw him forming a line to attack the Rebel stronghold in the same place I had been all day, and advised him to form his line more to the left, and charge bayonets on arriving at the railroad track, which his brigade executed with such telling effect as to drive the rebels... Meanwhile I had gathered the remnant of my brigade, ready to take advantage of any opportunity to assist him. I soon discovered a large number of rebels fleeing before the left flank of Grover's brigade... My regiment immediately dashed out of the woods... after the retreating foe, but before their arrival at the other side of the meadow the retreating column received a heavy support... and came surging back, driving before their immense columns Grover's brigade and my handful of men.

That night, Hooker's division slept upon the ground where Burnside's brigade had opened the battle in 1861... The forenoon of the 30th passed rather quietly on Hooker's front. Jackson maintained his position of the previous day... A movement of rebel troops in the vicinity of Groveton, early in the afternoon, led to a short-lived belief that the rebels were retreating. At two o'clock in the afternoon the battle was renewed in earnest upon the plateau to the south and west...

Hooker's men were interested spectators of Longstreet's attack on McDowell's corps, nearly the whole of the battle line being visible. At four o'clock the battle had grown to tremendous proportions, and soon after this hour the order suddenly rang out for the division to "Fall in!" There were indications of an advance on Hooker from a point near Groveton...but when the division moved forward, the rebel force went quickly back to the cover of the woods.

The excitement...had hardly quieted down when an aide arrived with orders for the entire division to cross to the other hill immediately. Batteries were limbered up in a hurry, and the troops were off at the double-quick in the direction indicated... Grover's brigade came into position several times, but did not become engaged... In the movements of troops it was now plainly to be seen that the battle was lost; and when Grover's brigade at last marched down the hill and turned into the Warrenton road, it came under a terrific fire from artillery which Longstreet had massed to sweep the valley...

Grover's brigade forded Bull Run Creek a short distance above the stone bridge, thorugh water waist deep, and before midnight was in camp at Centerville, where it remained until the afternoon of September 1st. On that day Jackson attempted to gain a lodgement on Pope's line of communications, and the battle of Chantilly ensued.

Late in the afternoon Kearney's division, followed by Hooker's, was sent to support Stevens' division of the Ninth Corps, which had been attacked. The rebels were driven back, but both Stevens and Kearney were killed.

The battle was fought in a cold, pouring rain. Grover's brigade, with pickets thrown to the front, was posted in line along the Centreville Road, which was crowded with the trains pushing toward Washington. Cold and shivering, the men stood in line in the dense jungle of dripping bushes, while the battle raged upon the right. There was some comfort to be got out of the situation, in nagging the demoralized stragglers who always form the fringe of a fight.

The fighting was kept up long after the darkness of night had come, but Grover's brigade did not become engaged. When the firing had died out, the brigade was moved to the right near the scene of the fighting, where it spent a comfortless night... in... a flooded sweet potato field.

Two days later, on the afternoon of September 3d, Heintzelman's Corps arrived at Fort Lyon, near Alexandria and became a part of General Banks' command, occupying the defences of Washington, while the army engaged in the campaign which culminated at Antietam.

(From the HISTORY OF THE 2ND NEW HAMPSHIRE INFANTRY)

****

                         Aug 23, 1862   Camp near Alexandria

Dear Nellie,
    I am now 3 miles from Alexandria, expecting to march and join Pope[181] . I am well and in good spirits. They talk as if the decisive battle would take place soon. Give my regards to all. You must not expect to hear from me often.
                        Yours Affectionately   Charley

****

                                       Washington Sept. 1st [1862]

Dear Nellie,

---

[181] In June, 1862, Major-General John Pope (1822-92) was given command of all Union forces in the east not under McClellan on the Peninsula, the force being called the Army of Virginia and its remit the protection of Washington D.C. and the creation of diversions to detach enemy troops from McClellan's front. After the Peninsula, McClellan began a slow withdrawal, prompting Lee to attack Pope before McClellan's forces could join him. Heintzelman's Third Corps was among those of McClellan's forces which reached Pope's Army to participate in the 2nd Battle of Bull Run (August 29-30, 1862); Heintzelman was wounded and his Corps driven back by the Confederates. Johnson writes very little about the battle in his letter of September 1. Pope's signal defeat resulted in his transfer to command of the Department of the Northwest and McClellan's return to overall command of Union forces in the east; it also resulted in Lee's decision to carry out his first invasion of the north, culminating in the Battle of Antietam, September 17. Contrary to Johnson's expectations, the 16th did not join Pope to participate in the battle.

I am very comfortably situated in Washington. I have been quite yellow with the jaundice but am improving. I suffered only one day with pain, and with the exception of a little soreness about the liver feel as well as anybody. I am a very shabby looking individual having no change of cloth not even an extra shirt or stocking and without money having only twenty five cts to buy my breakfast with. In ordinary times it would be easy matter to obtain my pay as I have only to have a certificate that I am under medical care from Dr Glymer, but the times has called all his assistant surgeons to the field leaving him almost alone, and every officer sick or wounded is obliged to report himself to him and he is responsible that the officers have medical assistance you can judge how much he has to attend to and what little chance I should have to see him. Being in pressing need I telegraph to father to see if he could not advise some method to obtain funds, then I could if an oppotunity occurred obtain my certificate and money. I suppose every thing which we bought from Alexandria to camp near Warrenton is destroyed. I have yet to learn if my company accounts are safe; the cause of our goods being consumed was that our baggage wagons was not with us and we had no means of transportation. The fighting has been very severe on both side,[182] Wm Davis John Neil[183] of my company are wounded a number whose names I can't recall for certain are. The first day march was so severe that the companies straggled considerably I not being able to keep up and the men failed to come to time[?]. Those men who have once fell behind rarely succeed in finding the regiment until after battle

Sept 2nd I am now going to send and obtain the signature of Dr Glymer which if I can get near him I shall have, when obtained my pay will be easily procured. Give my regards to all.   Yours Affectionately   Charley

Save this for Nellie.

My Dear Mrs Converse I have not heard from Nellie hope to hear tomorrow, and glad that Charles is safe, poor fellow he must have been most exhausted to leave his men, yours in haste,

    affectionately   J.B.Johnson

         ****

          Camp near Fort Lyon[184]   Sept. 7 / 62

Dear Nellie,

I hope you and father arrived home safe. Our camp is finely located on one of the hills about Alexandria. The Capitol is in plain sight from my fly but we are not quite near enough the summit to have a view of the Potomac, but a short walk give you a fine scene. I was agreeably astonished on my arrival to find that most of my clothing had been safed and most of my company books, they were brought on one of the men back. What I had on hand to eat such as pickled salmon and sardines my Lieutenant disposed of. The greatest inconvenience may arise from the loss of my company papers but it can't be helped. After I left you I made my way immediately to the wharf on arriving I found to my chagrin that the last boat 5 o'clock had left and

---

[182] The Second Battle of Bull Run, Aug. 29-30, which Johnson missed owing to his absence on sick leave with jaundice.

[183] Private John O'Neal

[184] One of the Forts south of the Potomac, the largest, and westernmost, of a chain of five forts defending Alexandria, on the heights south of Hunting Creek. Traces of a bomb-proof of the fort still exist on the south side of James Drive (See Cooling & Owen, 60-64).

that it was necessary for me to obtain a past from Provost Marshal; I had given up my room and I was very much opposed to remaining in Washington after you left[185] I wishing a change of scenes. Hearing there was another wharf which the boats sometimes landed, I hired a carriage rode to other wharf to find on arrival Manuel[186] and Lt Chase[187] of our regiment in the same fix as myself; the last boat had gone. Not wishing to give it up we proceeded Lieut Chase and myself to another wharf where we found a tug boat about to proceed with a schooner in tow to Alexandria. The night was perfect and I was in no hurry so I was in condition to enjoy it. After the tug had run into several lighters we got under way   We arrived in Alexandria where we were again stopped to show our pass. Lt Chase shew his I not having any. After arriving at Alexandria I proceeded to City Hotel where I passed the night with some officers from my regt, eat breakfast at seven o'clock the following morning and immediately started for camp a distance of three miles. After leaving the city which was soon done I was impressed with the generally appearance of the country, my road leading through meadows over hills from which tops a magnificent view was obtained, of the Potomac, Alexandria and Washington. The breeze was delightful and there seems even in the immediate presence of a camp in the country to exist a calm meditative quiet. An active campaign like the present affords fine opportunities, though somewhat fettered by fatigue and military discipline, to enjoy fine country scenes.   Tuesday. I meant to have finished this letter yesterday morning, but, at 2 o'clock yesterday morning we were called up and went on picket. If we were to go to Washington again or are there together we must visit the spot where we did picket duty yesterday. The reserve was placed on the summit of a hill which overlooked a magnificent valley. This valley was in the shape of a V and seem to separate or sever two ranges of hills for on the other side of the valley at various distance hills of all magnitude gracefully and gradually raised their heads. Houses dotted the hills looking white and clean giving a generally appearance of civilisation and comfort. Following with your eye the line of the mountains opposite and you suddenly reach a fine view of the Potomac at a distance I should think of twelve miles. You could also see the trees around Mount Vernon[188] being much taller than those about them. I enjoyed the time I was on picket very much, taking dinner at a farm house where every thing was kept very neat and clean although the dinner was very plain consisting of corn cake and butter cold water & pie yet the surrounding were so comfortable that anything would have tasted well. We have enjoyed fine weather, the evenings have been unusually brilliant. As I write this, the wind is blowing, fresh & smart through the tent, forcing me to hold on to the paper, which notwithstanding my precautions has left me several times. I received your letter from N. York and was mad with interest. We receive the papers every morning. It is the impression that Heintslmans [Heintzelman's] Corp d'Armee will remain where it is unless urgent necessity call for it, we defend Alexandria, somebody must, and the men need rest. Give my regards to all.

[*Yours Affectionately   Charles*]

---

[185] Evidently Nellie had visited him, despite his continual admonitions against it.

[186] Presumably Johnson's Black servant; see also letter of Sept. 14th.

[187] Joseph H. Chase; Sergeant, July 12, 1861; 2nd Lt., July 6, 1862; 1st Lt., Aug. 11, 1862; Captain, A.A.G., U.S.V., Feb.29, 1864.

[188] About sixteen miles south of Washington, on the west bank of the Potomac. As the home of George Washington, both sides took care to respect and avoid damaging the property during the war.

****

Sept. 11th /62

Dear Nellie,

I have not received any letters from you but the one from N. York. The mails are regular in their arrivals but I imagine all the mail does not arrive owing to force of business. Every thing is high in Alexandria and the forces seem to increase every day, the reason given is that government monopolizes the cars between Baltimore & Washington leaving but little means for outside transportation and also that schooners with freight from Baltimore cannot land their freight for the government is occupying most of the wharves. I have done some cooking for myself and succeeded finely. I made some quite good fishballs the other day, they relished well. I have succeeded in living well considering the means which I have. I am always able here to have butter and generally nice little rolls, beefsteak, fried potatoes, sauces, boiled potatoes, fishballs, and boiled eggs have been my principle side dishes, tomatoes raw, stewed & fried, poached eggs & [fried?] eggs; you see that I can have quite a variety to choose from I have not as yet had ham & eggs but expect to soon. Peaches, watermelon, mushrooms, apples are generally to be obtained near camp from peddlars wagons. The weather has been showery but it was needed to lay the dust. There is a general impression prevailing in our division that we are not to be called into active service unless absolutely necessary; yet there is a rumor of an expected move some say two or three miles farther from Alexandria others mention Arlington Heights as our destination, the latter would be from what I hear an admirable situation, only six miles from Washington of which it commands a good view but we doubt such good news although we hope it. Jaundice is becoming quite prevalent, some officers and several privates have it. It is hard work to see what was the cause of our defeat unless we lay it to incompetency or treachery; great many officers say McDowell's a traitor and attribute his boldness which he is sometimes said to show to have a complete understanding with the rebels and in order to be known well wear a most peculiar hat, similar to an inverted wash bowl; others say that the artillery were admirably arranged but McDowell caused the infantry to advance beyond it rendering the artillery useless, and that when the infantry fell back, the rebels followed them so close that the artillery was unable to fire so limbered up and left.[189] I had a good, in fact splendid, view of the ground occupied by our troops Saturday morning and I saw three batteries open, one of the rebels and one belonging to us, the third I imagine was ours as I *[rest of letter missing]*

****

Sept. 14 /62   Camp near Fort Worth[190]

---

[189] Another example of the soldiers reflecting McClellan's conviction that his efforts were being deliberately thwarted by those in power. Irvin McDowell, Union commander during the first major battle of the war, First Bull Run, had been appointed, without advising McClellan, to command the forces protecting Washington during the Peninsula Campaign, and was placed in command of the 3rd Corps of Pope's Army of Virginia during the Second Bull Run campaign. McDowell's conduct during the battle was severely criticised, and he was in fact under investigation by a Court-Martial, after the battle, at the same time as Fitz-John Porter, for the same offence of disobedience of orders. He escaped Porter's fate by giving evidence against him and by use of political influence, but saw no further active service for two years and in July 1864 was posted to command of the Department of the Pacific.

[190] One of the forts forming the western defences of Alexandria, it survived in good condition until 1970, when the site was developed.

Dear Nellie,

We have again changed our location and in several senses it is a change for the better, from rear of our camp only a short distance we have a fine view of the Potomac where a small stream enter given it from the direction which we look an appearance of a small lake. We are also near several houses among them is the famous Fairfax Seminary[191] now used as a hospital. I still succeed in living well and enjoying myself. Manuel has left me. He has desire to leave for some time and consequently very careless having lost my revolver, dressing case, and coat cape in three successive nights. I am now without any servant except what I take from my company. 33rd and 34th Mass lay near us. the 33rd have been doing provost guard duty in Alexandria and I hear are going back there again for the same purpose giving them a very pleasant duty to perform. They are also to be quartered in barracks. I think we shall remain where we are some time but anything in regard to how long we stay in a place is mere conjecture that we hardly allow ourselves to think long of remaining. After every meal I generally enjoy a good smoke, sometime sitting on a stump enjoying the view. My box arrived yesterday the lemon or what I suppose to have been lemons were nothing but dust the case was slightly mouldy and the sage cheese sent by Mary was shrunk & dried but claret was fine. I believe everything else arrived I believe safely. Tell father that the box of Lewis' condensed milk was different from what I usually get with his name on it, it would not dissolve. I know you sent it but I supposed father might have bought it for you. I have not tried father .... cherry juice keeping it for the purpose for which he intending it. Jimmy is well so am I. I have received your letters of Sept. 8th & 10th also fathers paper. Give my regards to all There are nothing but rumors about generally without foundation, we are quiet and have been except one change of position we may have another any time.

       Yours Affectionately   Charley

    ****

      Sept. 17, 1862   Camp near Ft. Worth

Dear Nellie,

I received your letters of Sept. 12th last night. In regard to keeping a girl, the only reason in favor of your doing without would be that with your time fully occupied with Berk it would be time would pass swifter to you. In regard to punishing Berk by putting him in a closet, if it render him afraid of being left alone or afraid of the dark I would not use it as a means of punishment. Nothing last so long as early impression a child naturally courageous may be made timid by injudicious bringing up. I am more afraid of his being scared when young and lasting through childhood than I am of his being spoiled. I received a letter from Lt. Tucker today, he is at Hammond General Hospital Point Lookout Md. I shall write him today if I dont go on picket. He describes himself as improving fast, having had an attack of the fever again which on its leaving him left him with chronic diarrhea. Tell Mr. Tucker (the one that sent the box to P.E.T.) that I received the box for Lt. Tucker and confiscated it and he would oblige me by sending the bill of the contents of the box to father and he will pay it. I want you to send the bill to me as I desire to know the prices as I have disposed of some of the bottles. At the time I received the box I had no knowledge of Lt. Tucker whereabouts. I fear that two of my men wounded in skirmish of June 18th /62 must have reenlisted in some new regiment as I should think it was time for their return, they might

---

[191] The Fairfax Theological Seminary, near Alexandria, Va., served as a hospital during the war.

reenlist to secure the bounty. It has been threatening rain for some time but it does not hardly make up its mind to although last night we had a gentle soothing rain, not violent, lasting five or six hours. We have heard and consequently rejoice at the good news from Maryland[192] but I look forward to the magnitude of engagement and although the engagement was not a decisive battle yet I hope it will lead to such. We are very short of officers in our regiment and the number of men for duty is small with an addition of some recruits and had only 500 men to draw rations for that includes a large number sick in quarters. I think 350 men is all the effective men we have this includes non-commissioned officers (sergeants & cor) Col Lamson[193] has not yet returned I understand he is quite low. Cpt. Lawson[194] has gone in an ambulance under a flag of truce for Lt. Banks body[195]. I hope he may be successful in obtaining it. Give my regards to all.

       Yours Affectionately   Charley

****

      Sept. 22 /62   Camp near Alexandria

Dear Nellie,

I have received your favors of Sept. 14th and 16th. You can see by the heading of this letter that I have not moved. We are not as pleased on the whole with the result of the fighting in Maryland as we expected to be from the first accounts. We have driven the rebels from Maryland but that is all. We are no nearer the end of the war as I can see. The loss of Harpers[196] or rather the war material gained by the rebels including the number of prisoners paroled make up loss on the whole against us. We may have enough moral power by the results to balance accounts. The 24 hours that we took to bury the dead are considered by some high military men as giving the enemy every opportunity for recrossing the river, the time we occupied in burying the dead should been spent [sic] in attacking the enemy. McClellan may have been at loss to understand the intentions of the enemy and might have expected as determined resistance on the following day as was unwilling to run any risks that might have endangered the previous results. We are enjoying fine weather now, cool nights. I am somewhat of a hurry, but have no news to write. Boxes come through now but it is hardly safe to send them as we may move any moment, though I think everything looks favorable to our remaining. Give my regards to all.

     Y[ours Affectionately   Charles]

****

---

[192] The Battle of Antietam, Maryland, Sept. 17th. Lee's first invasion of the North was halted here, in what proved to be the bloodiest single day's fighting of the war.

[193] Daniel S. Lamson: Major, Aug. 1, 1861; Lt. Col., July 23, 1862; resigned, Sept. 29, 1862.

[194] Henry T. Lawson: Capt., Aug.1, 1861; Major, 2nd Mass. Heavy Artillery, Aug. 25, 1863; died of disease at New Berne, N.C., Oct. 1, 1864.

[195] 2nd Lieut. Hiram B. Banks, killed in action at the Second Battle of Bull Run, Aug. 29, 1862. He was the brother of Col. Gardner Banks, and also of Maj. Gen. Nathaniel P. Banks.

[196] Harper's Ferry, the scene of John Brown's famous raid in October, 1859, and a Federal garrison commanding the junction of the Potomac and Shenandoah Rivers, captured by "Stonewall " Jackson during Lee's 1862 Maryland campaign on September 15.

Camp near Alexandria   Sept. 26 /62

Dear Nellie,
    I have received your favors of 17th 21st & 25th. There is so little doing that I have nothing to write and it is hard work to commence a letter. I saw Mrs Oldenhauser today she was in our camp; if you had not notified me of her being at Alexandria I should not have spoken to her, she looks well. We go on picket tomorrow at eight o'clock if it is pleasant I shall enjoy it. We now commence to have cold nights and I am almost inclined to send for my other Blanket and frock coat. You might have a thick vest made & sent me at Edmund's tailor. We have just been paid off I have now two more months' pay with me, shall send some of it. since my expenses are larger here than usual owing to my having a chance to satisfy my appetite. There seems to be some prospect of our remaining here as we are to have Sibley tents[197] to issue to the men. If fruit is very cheap now you might send me some as well as a boiled ham which I think would eat well. Give my regards to all. Excuse the shortness of the letter.
                Yours Affectionately   Charley

****

---

[197] Invented in 1857 by Henry Hopkins Sibley, U.S. Regular Army and later a Confederate general, and modelled on the conical Indian teepees which he saw while accompanying Fremont's expedition to the West. Also known as a Bell Tent, it was 18 feet in diameter and 12 feet high and accommodated 12 men. The Federal Army used large numbers, but withdrew them from field service during 1862 (Lord 1963).

CHAPTER 10
*
BURNSIDE AND FREDERICKSBURG

After Antietam, on September 17, 1862, the two armies sat facing each other across the Potomac, and it was not until October 26th that the ever-cautious McClellan finally stirred his army into movement and crossed the Potomac. He suddenly found himself situated between widely-separated sections of Lee's army – an opportunity which an abler, more decisive commander would have seized to defeat Lee in detail, but an opportunity which McClellan had already let slip once before, when he failed to act after the discovery of Lee's "lost order" before Antietam. But the ever-slow McClellan was not the man, and on November 7th, his patience finally exhausted, Lincoln ordered Ambrose E. Burnside, commander of the 9th Corps - whose luxuriant side-whiskers have given us the word "sideburns" – to take command of the Army of the Potomac. Burnside, who had distinguished himself early in the war in command of the successful amphibious operation which resulted in the securing of the Federal base at New Berne, North Carolina, had gained a reputation as a capable and popular corps commander; but even he knew, deep down, that he did not have the necessary ability to be an Army Commander, and only reluctantly accepted what he clearly regarded as a burden, at Lincoln's insistence. In hardly more than a month, his self-doubt was to prove only too well founded.

He reorganised the Army of the Potomac into three "Grand Divisions": the right, under Edwin V. Sumner; the centre under Joseph "Fighting Joe" Hooker; and the left under William B. Franklin. The 16th Massachusetts found itself in the last, in Joseph B. Carr's Brigade of Dan Sickles' 2nd Division of George Stoneman's 3rd Corps. By the 20th, the whole army was near Falmouth, two miles north west of Fredericksburg on the north bank of the Rappahannock.

Burnside's plan was to make a feint towards Culpeper, in an effort to deceive Lee as to his intentions, and then make his way to Falmouth, where he would cross the Rappahannock and march on Richmond. Had he immediately forded the river, while it was fordable, he could have chosen his position and awaited Lee's arrival; but he insisted on waiting for his pontoon trains to arrive from Washington, by which time heavy rains had swollen the river, making it passable only by bridges, by which time Lee's Army of Northern Virginia had crossed the river and entrenched itself in an unassailable position on the heights south and west of Fredericksburg.

The disaster which the impending battle would prove to be for the Federals may be dealt with briefly here, since most of Stoneman's Corps was to spend it in reserve by the pontoon bridges at Franklin's Crossing; had it been called upon by Franklin to support the fierce, and initially successful, assault by the divisions of George G. Meade and John Gibbon on Jackson's position between the Mine Road and the Richmond and Fredericksburg Rail Road, the Confederate right might have been turned and the course of the battle perhaps altered. But other than David B. Birney's 1st Division, no units of the 3rd Corps were ordered forward to support the attack - an inexcusable failure – and Carr's Brigade sat out the battle on the south bank of the Rappahannock, in front of the Left Grand Division's pontoon bridges.

Ironically, one man from the 16th Massachusetts did see action at Fredericksburg, but not with the regiment, and he was killed in action. The tragic story of the regiment's Chaplain, Arthur Buckminster Fuller, one of eleven Union Chaplains to die in battle, is told in several contemporary accounts.

Fuller was born in Boston on August 10, 1822; his older sister was the noted writer, feminist and member of the Transcendentalist movement, Margaret Fuller. After graduating from Harvard in 1843, he went through Cambridge Divinity School and spent the years 1843-5 as a Minister in the west, running a liberal academy, but returning because he missed home, yet much influenced by his experience in the west. He was ordained Pastor of the Unitarian Society in Manchester, New Hampshire in 1848 and of the New North Church, Boston, Mass. in 1853. Tragedy struck repeatedly in the ensuing years; his sister Margaret, her husband and child were lost in a shipwreck in 1850; his wife, Elizabeth, whom he married in 1850, died of cholera in 1856, leaving him with two children, Edith Davenport and Arthur Ossoli; and his mother died in 1859. He married Emma Reeves in 1859; they had two children, Richard Buckminster and Alfred Buckminster.

Fuller was noted as an outspoken evangelical Unitarian, active in the temperance movement and, to the disapproval of many of his parishioners, an outspoken abolitionist. He served on the Boston school board and advocated free public education for all children, but embraced the nativism of the mid-1850s, publishing two sermons attacking the Roman Catholic Church. The influence of his sister led him to support the idea of women pursuing a professional career, and he honored her memory by editing and republishing her works.

On the outbreak of Civil War, Fuller resigned his pastorate at Watertown and enlisted on August 1 as Chaplain of the 16th Massachusetts Infantry. "I am willing to peril life for the welfare of our brave soldiery, and in our country's great cause," he wrote. "If God requires that sacrifice of me, it shall be offered on the altar of freedom, and in the defense of all that is good in American institutions."

At first, the regiment saw little action, and Fuller assisted in the post hospital, holding services, and teaching reading and other subjects to foreign-born soldiers and escaped slaves. He loved his fellow soldiers and they admired him. His services were so well-attended that other chaplains, when going on leave, often asked him to substitute for them.

In March 1862, Fuller, with others of the 16th, witnessed the battle between the *Merrimack* and the *Monitor*, writing an accurate and comprehensive eyewitness account. After the *Merrimack* withdrew, Fuller wrote: "David had conquered Goliath with his smooth stones, or wrought-iron balls, from his little sling, or shot tower."

He was glad when the regiment went into the battle zone on the Peninsula. "I know no holier place, none more solemn, more awful, more glorious, than this battlefield shall be," referring to the 16th's "baptism in blood." Unlike some chaplains, he went onto the battlefield with his men, shouting encouragement, leading prayers, and tending the wounded. By the end of the campaign, he was so seriously unwell that he was obliged to return home to Massachusetts, but in October, his health to some extent restored, he rejoined the regiment, receiving a hearty welcome from the men. "My own family could not be more cordial and more affectionate." However he was still too unwell to accompany the regiment on its march to Fredericksburg, and remained behind, helping the wounded in nearby hospitals. To his dismay, the doctors declared him unfit for duty, and he could now only hope for an appointment as a chaplain in an Army Hospital. "You can hardly realize the pain I felt when I found I could not share the field campaign without throwing away health and life," he wrote his wife.

He appears to have gone forward to rejoin his regiment, however, in order to give them his farewell address, which the men gathered to hear on Sunday, December 7, and on the 9th Fuller wrote to his wife that he was coming home. "If any regret were mine, it would be that I am not able to remain with my regiment longer; but this is, doubtless, in God's providence," and on December 10, he was honorably discharged. Still with the regiment the next morning, he learned that they were likely to be in the attack on Fredericksburg. Engineers building pontoon bridges to cross the Rappahannock came under heavy fire from Confederate sharpshooters, and volunteers were sought for an assault by boat to silence them.

Although officially discharged, and unwell, Fuller promptly offered his services to the attacking force, joining one of the boats. Reaching the opposite shore, he found himself with the 19th Massachusetts Infantry, which was preparing to advance on the city. Captain Morcena Dunn of the 19th wrote an account of what followed for the Boston Herald of Dec. 25th.

"I saw him for the first time in the streets of Fredericksburg. We came over in boats, and were in advance of the others who had crossed. We had been here but a few minutes when Chaplain Fuller accosted me with his usual military salute. He had a musket in his hand and said: 'Captain, I must do something for my country. What shall I do?' I replied that there never was a better time than the present, and that he could take his place on my left. I thought he could render valuable aid, because he was perfectly cool and collected. Had he appeared at all excited, I should have rejected his services, for coolness is of the first importance with skirmishers, and one excited man has an unfavorable influence upon others. I have seldom seen a person on the field so calm and mild in his demeanor... His position was directly in front of a grocery store [on Caroline Street]. He fell in five minutes after he took it, having fired once or twice. He was killed instantly, and did not move after he fell. I saw the flash of the rifle which did the deed."

The *Boston Herald* for December 23rd (page 4, col. 1) gave more details:

"The body of the late Rev. A.B.Fuller... was examined at the house of R.F.Fuller Esq. at Wayland, yesterday, by Dr. Hunt, of Weston, who said that 'he was shot in two places – one bullet entering the left arm on its outer surface (the arm apparently being raised to a right angle with the body) and lodging within the chest; the other entering the body on the left side just above the spine of the ilium, and leaving the body on the opposite side, a little posterior of the same level. Either ball would have been almost instantly fatal....' Gov. Andrew [has written] a letter to a brother of the deceased, in which he pays a feeling tribute...: 'His conduct was worthy his state and his blood. It will be forever remembered. Nor was it too soon for a good man to die, falling, as he did, in splendid devotion to a sublime idea of duty, adventuring his life beyond the necessities of his position or the occasion of his office, but not beyond the dictates of an ardent nature, nor, in my judgement, beyond the highest and best idea of the example and decorum of the occasion."

The funeral was covered in detail in page 4, col. 6 of the Boston Herald for December 25th, 1862:

"FUNERAL OF REV. ARTHUR B. FULLER

"The funeral obsequies over the remains of the late Rev. Arthur B. Fuller were performed this noon, at the Chauncy Street church. The body was brought to the church early this forenoon, enclosed in a rich, ornamented rosewood casket. The latter was decorated with the American flag, and a profusion of elegant flowers wrought in bouquets and wreaths, which encircled a photograph of the deceased, taken several months prior to his death. A plate bore the following inscription: 'Rev. Arthur Buckminster Fuller, Chaplain of the 16 Regiment Massachusetts Volunteers; killed at the battle of Fredericksburg, Va., 11th December, 1862. Aged 40 years. "I must do something for my country" '.

"The church was crowded with a very large audience, and among them were His Excellency Gov. Andrew and Col. Lee, of his Staff, and Maj. P. A. Ames, of the 1st Division, M. V. M. Also a detachment from the Cadets, in uniform, and the Boston Brigade Band.

"The services were unusually interesting, solemn and impressive. They consisted of a voluntary by the choir; chant; reading of Scriptures by Rev. Rufus B. Ellis; Soldier's Funeral Hymn, from the 'Army Melodies', edited by the deceased and Rev. J. W. Dadmun[198]; addresses by Rev. Rollin H. Neale, D. D., Rev. E. O. Haven, D. D., Rev E. A. Sears and Rev. James Freeman Clarke; hymn; prayer and anthem.

"The remarks of the reverend gentlemen were singularly touching in feeling and sentiment. Rev Mr. Neale spoke of his departed brother as a kind, open-hearted, generous, whole-souled man. He was noble in spirit and philanthropic in nature, and his going into battle, where he met his death, was characteristic of him – acting with a noble heroism and a self-sacrificing patriotism.

"Rev. Mr. Clarke had known him from a boy. Many principles which he had cherished had been instilled into his mind by an older sister, while he was but a youth. He received his education at Cambridge, graduating in the divinity school in 1847. Soon after, he went to the west and settled in Northern Illinois, acting both as missionary and teacher. Since his return to New England he has been settled over various parishes. He always attended to duty, was decided in his opinions, and it was his nature to be active, kind and useful.

"In numerous instances the audience were moved to tears, and all were impressed with the conviction that the community had lost a noble and true friend, and a man of exalted character.

"The pall-bearers were Samuel Smith, C. J. F. Sherman, George P. Richardson Jr., Henry S. Dalton, Samuel B. Krogman, and O. T. Taylor.

"The hearse which bore his remains to their last resting-place in Mount Auburn was draped with the national colors, and trimmed with rosettes of black and white, and drawn by four horses wearing heavy black plumes. A large number of mourners followed the remains to the grave, and dropped their tears over the sepulchre of this fallen patriot and philanthropist."

At the funeral, James Freeman Clarke declared that "Arthur Fuller was, like most of us, a lover of peace, but he saw, as we have had to see, that sometimes true peace can only come through war. So he went, with a courage and devotion which all must admire, and fell, adding his blood also to all the precious blood which has been

---

[198] Rev. J.W.Dadmun and Rev. Arthur B. Fuller: ARMY AND NAVY MELODIES: A COLLECTION OF HYMNS AND TUNES, RELIGIOUS AND PATRIOTIC (Boston, 1862, 63pp, 10th edition. This "is now used by the regiments of Generals Sherman, Burnside, and Butler."

shed as an atonement for the sins of the nation. May that blood not be shed in vain."

Inevitably, there was speculation as to why Fuller risked his life to accompany the 19th Massachusetts, which was not his regiment, into battle. The 19th's own chaplain had long since fled. He believed that men deserved a chaplain by their side during a fight, and had many friends in the 19th: it was his Christian duty to go with them. However, time dimmed his memory. Thomas Wentworth Higginson, Colonel of the 1st South Carolina Volunteers, a Black Regiment, wrote in *Harvard Memorial Biographies* that the fallen chaplain had been a self-assertive, intensely earnest man, but who was "less gifted in intellect" and "less devoted to artistic culture" than his famous sister. Fuller related far better to ordinary people than he did to the intellectuals who preserved his sister's memory, and so, unlike hers, the memory of his name and deeds faded, his name only being revived in the twentieth century by dint of the renown of his grandson, Richard Buckminster Fuller (1895-1983), architect, poet, author, and inventor.

****

Monday Oct. 6/62   National Hotel Washington

Dear Nellie,

I obtain a leave of Abscence of twenty four hours to visit Washington in order to see some wounded men in hospital. I return to camp this afternoon. There are not as many officers about the streets as when you were here but still they are not scarce. Shall buy a pair of boots and some military books before I return. Fortunately my appetite is not so strong as when previously here and am perfectly satisfied with hotel fare[199] . There are five men from our regiment at Georgetown College Hospital[200] all suffering from severe wounds they seemed very glad to see me. The Georgetown Hospital is very nicely kept the wounded men appeared clean and every thing had the air of good order & tidiness. There seems to be so general an impression that we shall remain where we are that you can send me my other pair of pants & Dress coats although when they arrive I may have left. General Hooker is in Washington and improving finely he has hosts of admiring friends visit him daily;[201] while the Governor of Indiana[202] was conversing with him, he remarked that he had fought with McClellan long enough and want to go out west, which from rumors I think that the President will gratify him; McClellan would rather lose his right arm than lose Hooker. Hooker & Kearney[203] were almost invincible when fighting together and I always associate both names together although one is dead. There is but little news

---

[199] The leading hotel in Washington D.C. was Willard's, on Fourteenth Street. A popular rendezvous for officers, politicians, reporters and diplomats, extant menus show the availability, even during wartime, of a large and varied choice of dishes.

[200] Georgetown College, Alexandria, Va., was a Catholic College pressed into service as a military hospital between August 1862 and February 1863. A soldier of the 11th Pennsylvania Cavalry, visiting in December 1862, described it as "the cleanest and airyest place for the sick I have seen yet." (Samuel M. Potter letter, University of Virginia collection).

[201] Major-General Joseph Hooker, Johnson's Division Commander, had been wounded in the foot at the battle of Antietam.

[202] Oliver P. Morton, of Indiana, one of the most effective of the Northern war governors.

[203] Philip Kearney, wealthy soldier of fortune and a bold and popular general, called by Lieutenant-General Winfield Scott "the bravest man I ever knew", killed in action at the Battle of Chantilly, Sept. 1, 1862.

outside of our regiment: Col Lamson has resigned & resignation accepted and from what I can learn Adj Merriam will be Major, Major Banks Lt. Col[204] ; the promotion of Adt Merriam to Major[205] will cause some trouble and I think that there is some probability of two or three captains resigning owing to be jumped. I rank very low being six but if there should be any resignations I should perhaps get color company or rather be third in rank. If I had kept the rank which I left Boston with I should probably be senior Captain, but Gov Andrew issued an order which altered the rank of all the Captains. Give my regards to all.　　　　Affectionately,　　　　Charley

****

　　　　　　　　　　　Wednesday Oct 8/62　　　Camp near Alexandria
Dear Nellie,
　　I have received your favor of Oct. 5 giving me notification that a box would be forwarded, with a list of its contents from which list I should judge that the box must be more than ordinary size. Unfortunately we received orders late this afternoon to be prepared to march at a moment's notice which looks as if our stay would be short. I have formed no idea of our destiny or who will take our place to defend Alexandria or hold the fortifications about it. I hope the move will not be made untill the box arrives and I have had time to digest its contents. Today has been intensely hot, on our march in from picket exposed as we were to the sun I believe that I perspired more than any time during summer. After I wrote the letter from Washington I spent the remainder of the day or that part that I was in Washington in the company of Mr & Mrs Copeland & Mrs Copeland (old Lady). Mrs Copeland "born" Walker was a schoolmate of yours at Mr Emerson's and also an acquaintance of mine when I lived in Roxbury; we visited the Capitol, Patent Office & Smithsonian Institute, our brass buttons passed us in without any trouble and I also took dinner with them we are being boarders of the National. They have commenced to deduct three pr cts from the officers pay. I have a new colored man whom I like very much pay him $10.00 pr month which will have to come out of your allowance. I have about settled in my former style of life that is my voracious appetite has abated somewhat and am not so strongly tempted to buy every thing which I see, our men on being paid off behaved like fools not having money for some time and having been through so much deprivation that most of them let themselves lose and very few have at this day any of it left. I must confess that I was a little that way myself. Enclosed you will find two excellent likenesses of Gen'l Hooker & Kearney. One stone from your ring has gone missed it this afternoon. I have received letter from you of Sept 30 and Oct. 3rd. I think it would be safe to have my crate sent by express for if I leave here they will keep it safe, but sprinkle some things over it to keep off the moths. Give my regards to all.
　　Yours Affectionately　　　Charley

****

　　　　　　　　　　　Oct. 13/62　　　Camp near Alexandria
Dear Nellie,
　　I went to Washington Saturday morning & returned last night to camp. On my return your box was awaiting me much to my pleasure. Every thing arrived safely

---

[204] Gardner Banks, Captain Co. H, June 29, 1861; Major, July 23, 1862; Lieut. Col., Sept,.30, 1862; Colonel Nov. 28, 1862. Discharged due to illness Sept. 2, 1863. Brother of Maj.-Gen. Nathaniel P. Banks.

[205] 1st Lieut. Waldo Merriam, promoted Major Sept. 30. Killed in action at Spotsylvania, May 12, 1864.

except that the pickle had leaked from your oysters and a few pears spoilt. I don't know whether your oysters are spoilt or not, the rest arrived safely. In sending my dress coats & pants add to the bundle my other blanket which was strapped on the top of my trunk went when it was sent. Your box perhaps might have been obtained sooner if the Quartermaster had gone to the express office, I obtained it Saturday morning. We belong to the 1st brigade Sickles[206] division instead of Hooker's. There is little news to write we have been expecting to move but still we have no definite knowledge. The nights are very cold and as soon as the officers feel that we are to stay they will prepare for winter. I think the climate is no better here than in N. England; the same week you can be comfortable sleeping with nothing over you and uncomfortably cool with a blanket and heavy overcoat. I have received your letter of Oct. 7. Give my regards to all. I saw Dr Bartlett of Concord in Washington.

        Yours Affectionately   Charley

I received your envelope of stamps

****

        Oct 20 /62   Camp near Alexandria

Dear Nellie,

  I will write a few lines. I have just received notification to go on picket and have but little time to write. The nights have become cold and it is difficult to keep warm but soon whether we are satisfied or not that we are to remain we shall prepare for winter. Tell Father I should like to hear from him about the results of last years labor. Received two novels from Lt. Tucker; I am now reading Victor Hugo's works "Les Mis[e]rables"[207] . They have adopted a new plan of picket & fatigue duty which will give us but little rest. Our sutler was robbed last night of $900.00, probably by some of the soldiers. Give my regards to all.

        Yours Affectionately   Charley

Received yr Letter Oct 14

****

        Oct. 29, 1862   Camp near Alexandria

Dear Nellie,

  There is but little to write about and I do not feel like writing, consequently you will receive a short letter. In case I had no objections to your paying me a visit what would you have to pay Lottie while you were with me a month either with or without Berk. If we should stay here through the winter I might be willing you should pay me a visit, but you would be obliged to undergo great deal of inconvenience more than

---

[206] Daniel E. Sickles, Brig.-Gen. Commanding 2nd Division, 3rd Corps, Sept. 5, 1862 - Jan. 12, 1863. Sickles was one of the most colorful of the Union commanders. An attorney, Corporation Counsel of New York City, a New York State Senator and a Member of Congress, he killed the son of Francis Scott Key in Washington, D.C. before the war, outraged at his wife's infidelity with Key; the sensational trial resulted in Sickles becoming the first person in the U.S. acquitted of homicide by reason of temporary insanity. Sickles later was Minister to Spain, and had an intimate relationship with Queen Isabella. He served in Congress again, died in 1914, and was buried in Arlington National Cemetery.

[207] Victor Hugo's epic novel of the 1830 revolution in France had been published in 1862, and was popular with soldiers on both sides. At a time when supplies, particularly of shoes and clothing, were in short supply, the ragged soldiers in the Confederate Army of Northern Virginia humorously referred to themselves as "Lee's Miserables".

you can imagine. For twenty five dollars I imagine I can prepare a place where you would be warm, equal in size to two wall tents. This is only what I think of it now I may change my mind when the time comes. Qr Master Copeland[208] would have his wife here perhaps at the same time. I bought a few boards today to floor my tent. I hope soon to know whether we shall stay or not three weeks will decide the question. The men are being worked very hard now. I anticiapate a much harder winter than last, we are doing a full regiment's duty with 300 men. Lend me ten dollars without waiting for Lt. Tucker, my expenses are not much but I have been obliged to buy so many little things that my money goes. If the woolen blanket has not been sent, send with it three pair merino wool socks, those I bought in Washington are about useless now. I send you a bullet taken from the last Bull Run Battlefield. We had a storm the other day lasting through night which blew my tent down. To day is very pleasant. Let me know about your decision as soon as possible in regard to coming. Give my regards to all.

                     Yrs aff   Charley

****

Nov 4 /62   Camp near Manassas Junction

Dear Nellie,

We have changed our position since I last wrote. At present we are near Manassas Junction on the railroad against the place where the rebel cavalry run off our locomotive and captured a company of Dutch soldiers last Friday[209]. Sigel[210] whole corp d'armee has moved forward towards Thoroughfare Gap. The enemy are supposed to be in force about twenty miles from here, it being my humble opinion that they will not risk a battle if they can avoid it.[211] Our situation is in a very bleak, wild country there is but one house near us occupied. Old rebel barracks are scattered about here in every direction[212] ; wood that they cut for their own use is

---

[208] 1st Lieut. C. F. Copeland, Regimental Quarter Master. A resident of Boston, he enisted on July 17, 1862 as 1st Lieut. in Co. F, 16th Massachusetts Infantry. He mustered out July 27, 1864, living in Boston after the war.

[209] Action not identifiable from Dyer. Soldiers of German extraction or origin were generally nicknamed "Dutchmen" by the other soldiers.

[210] Maj.-Gen. Franz Sigel, at the time commanding the 11th Corps, Army of the Potomac, was a refugee from Germany following the revolution of 1848, having fled to the United States via Switzerland and England. Though his military abilities were limited, he retained a prominent role in the Army through his ability to enthuse the immigrant German community in the North to enlist in large numbers around the slogan "I fights mit Sigel". He fought in Missouri, and at Elkhorn Tavern in Arkansas, contributing to Union fortunes. He gained the rank of Brigadier and Major General. Coming east to support Union forces there, his fortunes waned in a string of battlefield defeats, most notably at the battle of New Market, Va., where the teenage Virginia Military Instuitute Cadets helped defeat Union troops. He was eventually removed from field duty and resigned in 1865. He became active in Republican politics, then switched to Democratic allegiance, living nearly 40 years after the end of the Civil War. He died in New York City in 1902.

[211] Dyer indicates a large number of minor skirmishes in the Northern Virginia area during the first half of November.

[212] The area around Manassas was occupied by the Confederates as winter quarters during 1861-2.

found in abundance, finely piled for measurement. There seems to be no doubt of our staying here. We are now without tents but expect them today. I am writing this in a shelter tent brought on my back. I hope my stove will come with the tents though I expect to lose the lumber. Our brigade is not all together and probably will not be unless we move. Heavy frost nights. I go on picket in half an hour. In one of the rebel barracks there is a body of a child, 8 or thereabouts years old, they say there are several bodies in other barracks which may be true or not. I have received another letter. Give my regards to all.

        Yours Affectionately   Charley

You will give up thinking of paying me a visit this winter.

****

"On the 8th of November occurred the first snow-storm of the season. The men had at the time nothing but shelter tents and rubber blanket; and many of them suffered severely with the cold. It led to unusual activity in the construction of cabins and huts... On the 8th of November the whole army was startled with tidings that Gen. McClellan had been removed... and that Gen. Ambrose E. Burnside had been appointed to succeed him... Gen. McClellan was still a favorite with many of the troops, and to the [soldiers] his removal, occasioned, as they believed by political hostility, was exceedingly distasteful. The majority, however, did not care who led them, provided he led to victory."

(From the HISTORY OF THE FIRST MASSACHUSETTS INFANTRY)

****

      Sunday Nov. 9 /62   Near Bristow [Bristoe] Station

Dear Nellie,

  I have seized the first opportunity to drop you a few lines. My regiment is at Warrenton Junction about three miles from here. My company is detached from the regiment to guard the railroad about here. We remain where we are as long as the regiment remains at Warrenton Junction. I am comfortably situated in a house. I have a room to myself with a large fire place my men when off duty occupy the remainder of the house. My Lieut will occupy the same room with myself when he returns. I shall be lonesome here if I stay but pretty independent. I make my own details. I have not received any letters for four or five days no mail having arrived. We bivouac during the snow storm at Bristow Station didn't mind it much. Have not seen any fighting and if McClellan is successful don't expect to. Our prospect of being paid is very small for some time to come at least, I shall be obliged to draw on you every little while, my pay rolls are in but other companies are not. I am almost isolated at present, the cars not having commenced to run and the nearest station being a mile at which they will not stop as there is only a company at it. I have no horse and have to send to the regiment every morning a morning report also to obtain the mail as well as other matters. Give my regards to all.

      Yours affectionately   Charley

****

"On Monday, Nov. 10, Gen. McClellan held a parting review of such of the troops as he could... gather in the vicinity of Warrenton... He rode a handsome horse, splendidly caparisoned, was accompanied by an imposing retinue of staff... and was greeted along the lines by demonstrations of unmistakable respect and affection..."

(From the HISTORY OF THE 2nd NEW HAMPSHIRE INFANTRY)

****

Nov. 12, 1862 Walnut Run

Dear Nellie,

I am still at the same place from which I last wrote. McClellan and staff pass over this railroad yesterday At Warrenton Junction the troops there were drawn up in line to receive him when McClellan step on to the platform they gave him 9 rousing cheers. Colonel Blasdel[213] introduced him saying "here the general, boys we have fought under I hear he is to leave us". McClellan made a few remarks, "Boys, you have fought with me on the peninsula and I know your worth all I can ask of you is to fight as well with Gen'l Burnside as you have done with me", he was deeply affected so much that it was difficult for him to speak tears rolling down his cheeks. As the cars left he stood on the rear platform with his hat off and the soldiers broke ranks giving vent to the wildest enthusiasm, running after cars cheering as long as they could keep up with them[214]. Genl Hooker went down to take command of our Corp d'Armee, he also stop at Warrenton Junction, great many of our officers accompanying him to Warrenton He says he is bound to have his red division with him and says all that is left of them after the war may go home and lay about until ten o'clock in the morning. He is an active, go ahead, bound to fight sought of a General, he will satisfy the north as far as fighting goes. I still occupy a house. The Doctor calls it the country seat. We are enjoying fine weather now; the days mild the nights chilly roads in excellent order. Have heard considerable cannonading the last day or two, today every thing is quiet. I wish you would send me photographs of the place in Lexington. How is Winnie & Austin & the rest of them. Give my regards to all. Enclosed you will find a new kind of bullet the three pieces separate and in close quarters are like Buck & Ball, the heaviest piece having the original force of a minie Bullet[215] .

Yrs afftly Charley

****

Nov. 16, 1862

Dear Nellie,

---

[213] William Blaisdell, as a Lieut Colonel in the 11th Massachusetts Infantry, brigaded with the 16th. He was wounded at 2nd Bull Run, and also during the Overland Campaign in 1864 He was killed at Petersburg, VA on June 23, 1864, and was posthumously brevetted Brigadier General as of that date. Blaisdell had prior service in the 4th U.S. Infantry from January 19, 1841 to April 22, 1853.

[214] McClellan was a brilliant organiser and motivator, and was idolised by his men, a sentiment Johnson clearly shared. However he took his his fatherly love for his men to an extent which made him reluctant to risk their lives in battle. He habitually greatly exaggerated the strength of his enemy in the belief that he was always outnumbered, when the opposite was almost always the case, always blaming the Government for deliberately withholding troops from him. In the face of his inaction after Antietam, Lincoln finally replaced him on Nov. 7, 1862 with Maj.-Gen. Ambrose E. Burnside.

[215] The .58 calibre 3-piece Shaler bullet, patented Aug. 12, 1862 and, according to Lord, issued in limited quantities during 1863. Johnson's letter clearly shows that it had in fact been issued by early November, 1862. It did not fulfil its anticipated purpose; firing it from a rifled musket did not achieve the close-range separation of the three elements achieved with Buck and Ball (a cartridge containing one .69 calibre ball and three small lead pellets) fired from a smoothbore musket.

I am in the same situation from which I last wrote, but if rumors are true expect to leave in a day or two, and join the grand army in its forward march. We are in Carr's[216] Brigade, Sickles' Division, Heintzleman[sic] Corp[s] d'Armee. The weather has been fine equal to our October weather but there are at present indications of a rain. On the first announcement of the promotion of Lt. Merriam to Major. there was some talk of resigning by the three senior captains but I have not heard much about it since; it was generally expected that he would be major some time ago so it was no surprise. I have been told the future plans of the army, part of which plans have commenced to be executed. The line of the Orange and Alexandria Railroad will be abandoned as a means of supplies, the frequent raids on it and the necessary force it would take to effectually guard it, are some of the reasons, the others you will soon see by following the plans. Our army or parts of it are on the way to Fred[er]icksburg and the advance guard must occupy it now as it has been on it way for two days.[217] The advance was followed by the main part of the army on different roads in supporting distance of each other, I suppose we shall form part of the rear guard and consequently expect to leave this place. We are still threatening the front of the rebel army along the Rappahannock at Waterloo and thereabouts; (but that it only a ruse) we also have Sigel Corps d'Armee about Thoroughfare Gap to protect Washington as well as the rear of our army. The advantage of occupying Fred[er]icksburg is that we can obtain our supplies by a railroad easier to protect viz the Aqu[i]a Creek R. Road and at the same time being further into the enemies country and threatening various important places in different directions. After the army has arrived at Fredericksburg it is to keep that as its base of operations and take junction of railroad which in our possession will cut of all communication with Richmond and the Northern Part of Virginia, it is near that junction that we may have a big battle. The fault of this plan is that in my very humble opinion that it would seem to tempt the rebel to enter in small force Maryland or even with some 40,000 or more men threaten Washington, but they will probably keep to their former policy of massing their troops, they need every man to meet our large army to check its advance and they will not weaken their strength by dividing their army. They are desperate people and Richmond being strongly fortified they may throw in a part of their army sufficient in their opinion to hold it and with the remainder threaten both Maryland and the rear of our army. We shall not leave Washington deserted nor Maryland without some protection. Now our army approaching Richmond in this direction is not the only one working for its downfall. At the same time that we strike at the junction Richmond will be threatened by two other large armies one I imagine will strike near Petersburg starting from Suffolk the other on the Peninsula will strike at some important place; both of these last armies are formidable in number and either alone are of sufficient strength to alarm the rebels. If these three armies can co-operate together the surrounding of Richmond looks

---

[216] Brig.Gen. Joseph B. Carr, commanding the 1st Brigade, 2nd Division, 3rd Corps from Sept. 16, 1862 to Jan. 12, 1863 when he assumed command of the Division. Born in New York City, Carr was a Colonel of militia at the outbreak of the war. He commanded a brigade in the 3rd Corps, fought at Big Bethel and was promoted to Brigadier General following the Peninsula Campaign and 2nd Bull Run. He fought well at Fredericksburg and Chancellorsville, and was commended by his superior, Major General Andrew A. Humphreys, at Gettysburg; however, the U.S. Senate failed to act upon his nomination as Major General and he was junior to his brigade commanders. He commanded a Black division in the Army of the James, and at war's end was Brevetted Major General of Volunteers. He entered manufacturing, and was New York Secretary of State from 1879 to 1885. He died in Troy, New York in February 1895.

[217] Dyer shows the 16th as engaged in Operations on the Orange & Alexandria Rail Road on Nov. 10-12. This was the commencement of the movements which would culminate in the disastrous Union defeat at Fredericksburg on Dec. 12-13.

probable, it is no doubt the biggest effort yet. Our regiment receives those new bullets and patent cartridges. You will find another sample of bullet but which I believe will not be adopted. Genl Hooker says he is afraid without his old division and rumor says he is to have us under his command. Give my regards to all.

[*Yours Affectionately Charles*]

****

Nov. 23 /62   Wolfe Ford Occoquan R.

Dear Nellie,

I have received your favors of Nov. 13 and 16th. I have before acknowledge the receipt of two letters containing ten dollars each, have you send another ten? We yesterday forded the Occoquan River, the water being over my boots or rather the tops of them. We have been marching in very disagreeable weather, having 4 successive wet days, making the roads awful and the men uncomfortable. Where we are now encamped there are two forts quite strong and some rifle pits built by the rebels last winter. Stephen D. Devine[218] descriptive list was sent to Newark to the hospital at which he was staying, it may be there now. I am sitting on the ground writing the weather is clear and chilly. Have regimental inspection at 9 o'clock this morning. If I was to stay during my three years enlistment I should make strong exertions to join a battery, a Lieut in battery has twice the convenience that any line officer can have. I would rather have a junior 1st Lt. berth in a battery than to be Captain of infantry, on march they ride, in fact have two horses and they can manage to live well. In this regiment there is no chance of promotion whatever and I almost rather have any berth that would keep me out of the mud. All my postage stamps are stuck together although they were in an inner pocket and in a pocket book

[*Yours Affectionately   Charles*]

****

Near Falmouth Va.   Nov. 29 /62

Dear Nellie,

Hear we are again in the front as we call it, but to my surprise everything indicate anything but a rapid advance. We are a mile and half from the Rappahannock river. Lt Hills[219] and myself visited Falmouth yesterday which is half a mile up the river above Fredericksburg. As we walked along the bank of the river we had a good view of the enemies pickets on the opposite side within easy gun shot from ours, their pickets were in groups of fours about three rods apart each group having a fire and most of them having their blankets on, their reserve was behind a brick mill seemingly about 200 strong. The enemy pickets and ours often hold conversation with each other. Fredericksburg is quite a large place for the south but its streets are apparently deserted, giving it, to me, a sad and gloomy appearance enhanced by having a church bell striking the hour of four rather slowly, I at first thought that it was tolling for somebodies deaths. There has been no endeavour on our part to build the bridges

---

[218] Private, Co. F, discharged for disability Nov. 23, 1862.

[219] 1st Lt. Joseph Hills. Hills, a 20-year-old clerk from Boston, Massachusetts, enlisted on July 12, 1861 as a 1st Sergeant in Co. F, of the 16th Massachusetts Infantry, rising through the ranks of 1st Lieutenant, 2nd Lieutenant, and Captain. He was wouned on May 3, 1863 at Chancellorsville and almost to the day a year later was killed on May 6, 1864 during the Wilderness Campaign. See illustration 18, which shows a personally addressed cover Hills had printed for himself.

across the Rappahannock, which are badly damaged. The commissary apartment [sic] here owing to lack of transportation has been unable to fully supply the wants of the men, and the army as a whole is rather poorly provided for both in clothing and food. I have men in my company with toes out of shoes and soleless shoe, without stocking and ragged pants and my company as a whole is as well provided for as any. We have been marching in this poor condition for the last fortnight over the worse roads that a man would risks his neck on, exposed to cold rain and even frosty freezing nights, yet the men stand it well, better than the horses which generally are looking poor and spiritless. I am continually making our requisitions, but they are met slowly, the government must be short in her supplies in several articles especially shoes and blankets. Rumors are afloat that Louis Napoleon[220] is endeavouring to arrange an armistice between the rebels and ourselves for six months. There is evidence of something unusual transpiring, rumors say General Burnside has left for Washington probably to consult concerning this armistice. We are drawing tents for the men and there are other indications that the army is to remain where it is awhile, perhaps the whole winter. I bought two loaves of bread at Falmouth of the baker for twenty five cts the loaves were smaller than our five cts loaves. About my resigning; there are several difficulties in the way, there would be but small chance of my resignation being accepted when the army is in the field, and there is great doubt whether it would be accepted any time before the war ends whenever I should see fit to send it in. I was much pleased when seeing the pickets of the two armies so near each other without the usual demonstration of hostilities; there was a feeling of security which I cannot account for as I walk besides the river bank, usually the presence of any officer in sight of the enemies pickets was followed by a shower of bullets. I have received your letter of Nov. 20th. Give my regards to all.

Yours Afftly   Charles

****

Dec. 10 /62   Camp near Falmouth Va.

Dear Nellie,

I have received your letters of Dec. 1st & 4th also the letter from father containing $10.00. There is a great scarcity of money among the officers the majority are completely dry. I heard rather a profane story the other day and as I have seen the clergyman there may be some truth in it; I will relate. In a certain N. York regiment composed of German Turners[221] was an old German surgeon unable to speak a word of English, although in reality a surgeon, nominally he was a chaplain; this was brought about on account of the Turners appreciating the benefit of a surgeon and not of a chaplain, consequently this surgeon was elected chaplain and accepted the office, making three surgeon in the regiment. There happened to be a private of the regiment

---

[220] Emperor Napoleon III of France, who was lobbied by Confederate envoys in Europe to join with England in negotiating a ceasefire between the contending sides; the aim was to secure recognition of the South and, eventually, Southern independence. The South also held out promises of advantageous trade terms from a grateful independent Confederacy. Although Napoleon was favourably disposed towards the South, he would not act unless England took the first step. This never happened; although England officially took a neutral stance, and sold munitions of war to both sides, it always evaded the question of recognition, realising that it would mean war with the United States. This would have not been in England's interests, dependent as it was on imports of Northern wheat almost as much as on on Southern cotton. It would also have risked the Northern seizure of Canada in retaliation.

[221] Possibly the 20th New York Infantry (see footnote 17)

die and of course it was the duty of the worthy surgeon to do the funeral honors, he rehearsed his part before the funeral. The funeral took place and as the coffin was placed into the grave, with the most solemn air said in broken English "This is the first time that this man was buried in Virginia, and D--n me (throwing in dirt) if I ever bury him again["]. V which in former times stood for volunteer now is made to stand for victim M V means Mass. Victims &c. We are off to day, start this afternoon for the other side of the river, (that is my belief) we may have some quarrel in getting across and we may not. The general opinion is the Peninsula is where we are bound, there are several ways of going and we shall know to night what way we take. There is nothing to write about. The officers have a new game of cards the person beaten has his nose rapped. Give my regards to all. Yours affy

Charley

****

Monday, Dec. 15, 1862   Rappahannock River

Dear Nellie,

I am all right[222]. Major Merriam & Lt. Hills are in good spirits and health. Please inform their friends. Had a little skirmish with the enemies pickets yesterday loss small. Corporal Dennis C. Murphy was wounded in the hand, the only one of my company wounded. Total loss 2 killed 15 wounded. No comm. officers hurt. The rebels occupy a very strong position having forts erected on hills concealed by woods. Their troops (Reb) are concealed from view while ours are exposed to view to them, being on plain. There was a short armistice yesterday a great deal of good feeling was exhibited. Their plan of sentiment was for the two armies to meet without any generals take a drink then go about their work. Pleasant weather.

****

The Boston Daily Herald for December 20th advised its readers of the death and funeral of Chaplain Fuller: "The body of the late Rev. A.B.Fuller, Chaplain of the 16th Regiment, was examined at the house of R.F.Fuller, Esq., at Wayland, yesterday, by Dr. Hunt, of Weston, who said that he was 'shot in two places - one bullet entering the left arm on the outer surface (the arm apparently being raised to a right angle with the body) and lodging within the chest; the other entering the body on left side just above spine of ilium, and leaving body on opposite side, a little posterior of the same level. Either ball would have been almost instantly fatal.'

"The funeral will probably take place on Tuesday next, with religious services in some Boston Church, attended by the State Government, and the Cadets acting as escort. Gov. Andrew has written a letter in regard to Chaplain Fuller's death, to a brother of the deceased, in which he pays a feeling tribute to his memory, and says: 'His conduct was worthy his State and his blood. It will be forever remembered. Nor was it too soon for a good man to die, falling, as he did, in splendid devotion to a sublime idea of duty, adventuring his life beyomnd the necessities of his position or the

---

[222] Johnson's only reference to the disastrous Battle of Fredericksburg, in which Burnside's ill-advised frontal attacks on well-defended Confederate positions led to the defeat of Union forces with heavy casualties. The 1863 Adjutant-General's report states that "The only part we took in this engagement was as a reserve to the picket line below the town, sending out two companies at a time to relieve the skirmishers. Our loss was - enlisted men killed, 3; wounded, 10." One of the 16th's losses was its Chaplain, Arthur Buckminster Fuller (see footnote 2 and pp.134ff).

occasion of his office, but not beyond the dictates of an ardent nature, nor, in my judgement, beyond the highest and best idea of the example and decorum of the occasion.'"

****

Sunday Dec 21 /62   Camp near Falmouth Va.

Dear Nellie,
Having nothing especial to do I will drop you a few lines. Dr Whiston called this afternoon and brought with him a request from Langdon Sheriff of the 1st Mass Vol[223], that when I wrote home I would inform his friends that he was doing well. Langdon Sheriff is related to Mrs W. Soule, he was wounded in the arm, has had four inches of bone taken out, the doctor says he is doing well; he will have the use of his arm. If I have time tomorrow I will try to visit him before I send this letter. I forgot to mention that Jimmy is fat and well. It has been growing colder every day, I hope tomorrow that the scale will turn and commence to grow warmer. It is so cold to day that at midday there was no signs of a thaw. While I was on the move about Fredericksburg I had to subsist of raw pork & hard tack, now although without butter I am doing very well. What the next move is to be I can't conjecture. It is reported here that we were ordered to cross where we did against the opinion of all the leading Generals including Burnside. Rumor says that on the receipt at Washington of the information that we had recrossed the Rappahannock a telegram was sent to Gen Burnside inquiring on what authority he had recrossed. Burnside replied "by the dictates of my judgement and common sense". Rumor also says that he has gone to Washington to obtain his resignation. If you have read Gen Lee's official report you will see that he refused to dispute our passage across the river more vigorously on account as he says of the complete command that our batteries on Stafford hills[224] had of the plains on his side of the river. Now when we were on the same plains on the other side of the river he had us in a worse position as the hills on which the rebel batteries were, formed an indented line to the plain enabling the rebels to pour a fire in front and flank mostly from heavy guns placed behind earth works. If we had been successful I think the effort would have cost us so dear both in men and material that we should have been unable to profit by it. The rebels if they had suspected the movement would have shelled us handsomely. The army is not at all dispirited and except with the loss of men we are as well able to advance as ever. Monday. I have seen Langdon Sheriff he seemed in good spirits and looked well. Please send me by mail another 3.00. Sutlers[225] prices are as follow[s] sausages 40 cts per lb, Pork steak ditto, butter sixty cts per lbs cheese 40 you see as I am paying the mess bill that

---

[223] Wounded at Fredericksburg, Dec. 14, and discharged Feb. 9, 1863. Died 1910.

[224] Stafford Heights, on the opposite side of the Rappahannock River from Fredericksburg, occupied by the Federal Artillery during the battle. This observation of Johnson's was, sadly, little more than wishful thinking; Lee no doubt declined to contest the crossing in the full knowledge that any attack against his lines would be suicidal, as indeed, it proved, prompting Lee to utter his well-known statement, "It is well that war is so terrible; we should grow too fond of it."

[225] Civilian traders who accompanied most regiments and and were authorised to sell the soldiers a wide range of goods, both necessaries and luxuries. Although subject to military law and obliged by the regulations to sell their goods at a reasonable price, they gained a reputation for charging high prices, sometimes justified and sometimes not. They did, however, frequently have to work under difficult conditions.

10.00 can't last long. Give my regards to all.   Yrs aff
    Charley

****

                           Decr 29 /62   Camp near Falmouth Va
Dear Nellie,
    I have received your favors of the 16th, 18th, 21st & 23rd Also the kind letter from your father the spirit of which I truly appreciate. Tell him I will do all in my power to obtain my resignation but my power is very limited, a business man can hardly judge what absolute power in that respect superior officers have. The rumors afloat do not seem to indicate active movements at present at least. We expect to move our camp but not very far unless it is to be nearer wood I can not see the utility of the move Every thing is quiet no news nor excitement. Our part of the army is in excellent condition in every respect ready to move either way. We passed a pleasant Christmas, the officers having a game of base ball in the afternoon. To day Colonel Tannatt[226] took formal leave making a few appropriate remarks and introducing our new Colonel Gardner Banks. Major Merriam will probably be Lt. Col. and Capt. Richardson Major[227] . We have lately been enjoying fine mild weather how long it may continue I can't say, but we have every reason to expect soon a long spell of rain which will make the roads impassable. Give my regards to all. Yrs aff   Charley

****

[undated, probably early January 1863]   Camp near Falmouth Va.
Dear Nellie,
    I have received your favors of 25th, 28th & 30th, one of which contained ten dollars. There has been but little doing with the exception of drill which occurs daily. Gen. Sickles kept an open house the officers of our regiment went in a body to pay their compliment to him. The entrance to his tent was through a wide clean street on either side of which were the tents of his aids, at the entrance were two small flags with an evergreen archway, which archway was covered with wreaths and emblems; and street and officers tents were tastefully adorned and presented a lovely and pleasing coup d'oeil. After drinking to the general's health and passing a few compliments we passed to a house adjoining where was spread what appeared to my salt pork and hard-tack eyes a miraculus[sic] and enchanting sight; on both ends of the table were two large finely roasted turkeys, in the middle was a large bowl of punch, the remainder of the table was filled up with cranberry sauce & fries and on a side table was a large pail of fine eggnog being topped with foam & nutmeg giving it a very tempting mouth-watering appearance. After taking [a] little taste we left to make room for others. Standing outside we had a good opportunity to see the leading Generals of the army, occassionally 4 or 5 together. Gen Hooker was there, with his usual smiling face and shaking hands with every one. I suspect a slight limp in his gait. The entertainment lasted until late at night but few officers showing their bad breeding by either drunkenness or noise. New Years afternoon we had a good game of

---

[226] Thomas R. Tannatt, Col. July 14 - Dec. 28, 1862, when transferred to be Col., 1st Mass. Heavy Artillery.

[227] Samuel Richardson, from East Cambridge, Mass. He was a 36-year-old Deputy Sheriff when he enlisted on July 2, 1861 as a Captain in the 16th Massachusetts, and was promoted to Major on November 28, 1864. He was mustered out on July 28, 1864.

base ball. Last Saturday we moved our camp about two miles in the midst of thick woods and we are all now working to make ourselves comfortable. Our camp is now very romanticly situated it being enhanced by the undulating character of the land which rises and fall in the most irregular way. The splendid moon light nights and the numerous camp fires surrounding by men in every posture have made scenes which you would highly appreciate. Yesterday our corp d'armee was reviewed by Genl Burnside. The day was perfect mild & warm hardly any freeze and the field in which the review took place was in admirable condition for marching. Each regiment was in column at half distance on the center and in that order we marched in review. It was one of the finest review I have witnessed, the marching was admirable and Genl Burnside could not but have been pleased with it. Our brigade was bothered by the band which has been recently organised out of wretched material and the tune they played was good enough but one part was performed quick time and another at slow time which put the men out, but notwithstanding we did well. I have just received your New Years letter and am glad to learn that you do not dislike error as much as you use to[228] . It is threatening rain now and as we have had a long spell of mild pleasant weather I am afraid that we shall as long a spell of unpleasant weather. I think that it will be next to an impossibility for me to obtain my discharge, yet when ever I think there is a good opportunity I shall endeavor to get it. Give my regards to all.

                Yours aff   Charley

****

                                    Camp near Falmouth Va.   Jan. 10 /62 [sic]
Dear Nellie,
I have received your letter of Jan. 4 also one of Jan. 1st. In your letter of Jan 4th you express joy because I stated I should try to obtain my resignation. It is easy to make the attempt but very hard to gain the prize. At the time I wrote that letter my application for a discharge had been in a week; the other day I received it back disapproved, I send the paper to you so you can judge for yourself how difficult it is to obtain a discharge. You will see that Col. Tannatt gave it a fine endorsement and it was also approved by Gen. Carr as commander of the brigade and division. Genl Sickles being absent, and disapproved by Genl Stoneman & Hooker for the reason that "No obligation of a private character can be considered in connection with those of the service." I can't help but think that Col. Bank[s] & Major Merriam exerted themselves to defeat my application although I may be very wrong in thinking so, I have not yet heard of a discharge being given otherwise than on a surgeon certificate of disability. Lt Woodbury[229] made an application for discharge and went with it in person and says that Genl Hooker promised him he should have it yet it came back disapproved. In the 2nd Delaware regiment a 1st Lt. applied for a leave of Absence for twenty days on account of the dangerous illness of his wife it came back not granted endorsed somewhat similar to this, "A discharge would be granted sooner than a leave of absence", he applied for a discharge and got much to his surprise a dishonorable one. I wish you would send by mail a meachum [meerschaum] pipe small thick bowl with a case not to cost over five dollars, I find great comfort in a pipe and would like one valuable enough to make me careful not to lose it. When the firm wishes me to

---

[228] Perhaps a humorous reference to his erratic writing style, and Nellie's evident habit of pointing it out.

[229] The only Massachusetts Line Officer with this name was 1st Lieut. Henry T. Woodbury of the 23rd Mass. Infantry.

resign I shall expect a strong letter from them. At present it is of no use trying as Col. Bank[s] does not favor it and would not probably approve it. The only right a soldier has is to obey orders. I don't feel bad you should not. Send me another ten dollar the sutler has come, orange and lemons etc. I paid .75 cts for a small jar of preserves which when I eat them I found to be sweetened with molasses. I am a little afraid of the jaundice so I shall go into fruit strong. You can find out at the express office if they bring boxes to Belle Plain[230] . I know they do not now but they may, when they do you can send a box. Rumor says there will be a move soon across the river am glad of it. I see father has got back by the direction of my papers, Give my regards to all.

                    [Yours Affectionately   Charles]

****

                  Camp near Fal. Va   Jan. 17 Eve 9 o'cl

Dear Nellie,

I shall just drop you a few lines to let you know that tomorrow we start either in advance or retreat I don't know which some say we are to return to our camp again and consequently will leave our tents behind but there are as usual so many rumor afloat that I can't tell which one is true. You probably will not hear from me for a week perhaps more perhaps less. Sunday 11 o'clock movement postponed for twenty four hours. Cold weather but pleasant. I am occupying my spare time in making laurel root pipes. There is nothing to write about camp life being very monotonous. Give my regards to all. yours

                                              aff   Charley

****

                  Jan 24 63   Near Falmouth Va

Dear Nellie,

I will drop you a line to let you know that we are back to our old camp with probability of remaining some time. The weather having rendered the roads impassible we have returned to our old position. The army were in fact fast in the mud and only five mile from their supplies yet were liable to suffer for want of food owing to the extreme I might say impossibility of transporting anything[231]   have received pipe & X dollars. Give my regards to all   Yrs aff   Charley

****

---

[230] The army supply base on Potomac Creek, about 10 miles east of Fredericksburg.

[231] Following the disaster of Fredericksburg, Burnside attempted a further operation against Lee north of Fredericksburg on Jan. 20-24, 1863. This movement of the whole Army of the Potomac, halted by torrential rains, became known by the derisory nickname the soldiers gave it - "The Mud March".

138a

 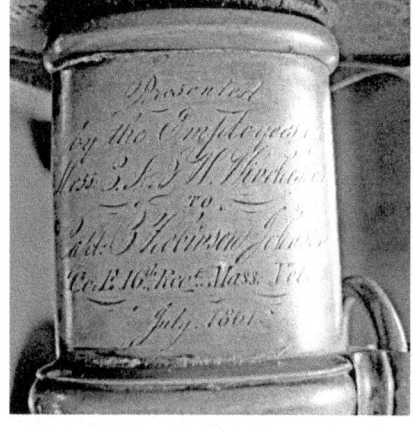

2. Captain Charles Robinson Johnson

4. Inscription on the throat of Johnson's sword: "Presented by the Employees of Mess: E. A. & W. Winchester to Capt. C. Robinson Johnson, Co. E, 16th. Regt., Mass. Vols., July 1861"

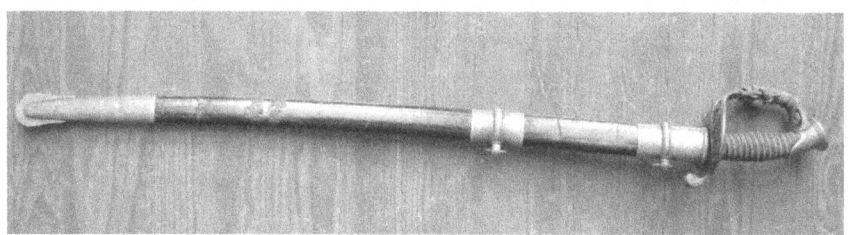

3. Johnson's U.S. model 1850 officer's sword

138b

5. Johnson's dress epaulettes and japanned tin box

7. Johnson's grave, Mount Auburn Cemetery, Cambridge, Mass.

6. Johnson's Commission

8. Col. Gardner Banks,
16th Massachusetts Infantry

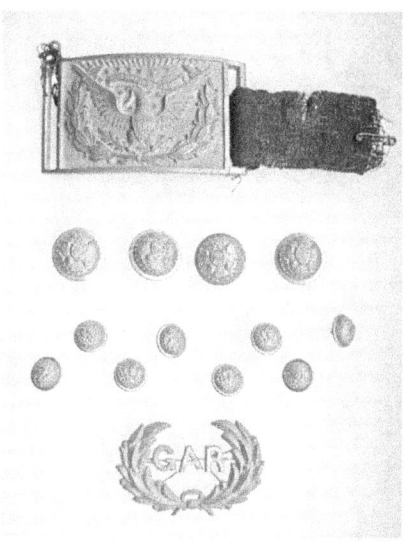

9. Belt plate, buttons and G.A.R. hat wreath of Col. Gardner Banks, 16th Massachusetts Infantry

10. Lt. Col. William Blaisdell,
16th Massachusetts Infantry

11. 1st Lieut. John B. Brown,
16th Massachusetts Infantry,
c. 1880s

12. Charles Frederick Copeland,
1st Lieutenant and Quartermaster,
16th Massachusetts Infantry
(c. 1880s)

13. 2nd Lieutenant Ward
Frothingham, 16th Massachusetts
Infantry

14. Chaplain Arthur Buckminster
Fuller, 16th Massachusetts Infantry

15. Grave of Chaplain Arthur
Buckminster Fuller, Mount Auburn
Cemetery, Cambridge, Mass.

138e

16. Corporal Henry Scales Harrington, 16th Massachusetts Infantry

17. Captain Joseph S. Hills, 16th Massachusetts Infantry

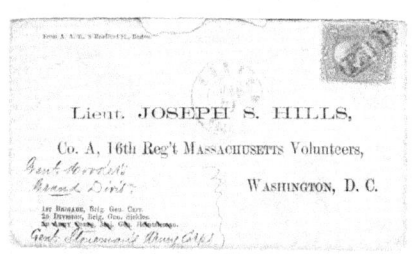
18. Printed cover for Capt. Joseph S. Hills, Jan. 1863

19. Surgeon Charles C. Jewett, 16th Massachusetts Infantry

20. Captain John Pittman King,
16th Massachusetts Infantry

21. Major Daniel Sanderson Lamson,
16th Massachusetts Infantry
(post-war)

22. Captain Richard J. Lombard,
16th Massachusetts Infantry

23. Waldo Merriam,
Adjutant and later Colonel,
16th Massachusetts Infantry

138g

24. Captain John Chandler Putnam,
16th Massachusetts Infantry

25. Major Samuel Richardson,
16th Massachusetts Infantry

26. Lieutenant Henry M. Sturgis,
20th Massachusetts Infantry & Staff
of Maj. Gen. Hiram G. Berry

27. Colonel Thomas Redding
Tannatt, 16th Massachusetts Infantry
(post-war)

28. 2nd Lieutenant Payson Tucker, 16th Massachusetts Infantry

29. Assistant Surgeon Edward A. Whiston, 16th Massachusetts Infantry

30. 1st Lieutenant John U. Woodfin, 16th Massachusetts Infantry

31. Colonel Powell Tremlett Wyman, 16th Massachusetts infantry

32. Grave of
Colonel Powell Tremlett Wyman,
Mount Auburn Cemetery

33. Major-General Hiram G. Berry,
commanding 2nd Div., 3rd Corps,
Feb. 8 – May 3, 1863

34. Major General David Bell Birney,
commanding 3rd Corps,
May 29 – June 3, 1863

35. Brigadier General Joseph B. Carr,
commanding 1st Brig., 2nd Div.,
3rd Corps, 10 Sept. 1862–12 Jan.
1863 and 23 May–Oct. 5, 1863,
and 2nd Div., 3rd Corps,
12 Jan.–8 Feb. and May 3–23, 1863

36. Brigadier General Cuvier Grover, commandng 1st Brig., 2nd Div., 3rd Corps, July 24–Sept. 16, 1862

37. Maj. General Samuel P. Heintzelman, commanding 3rd Corps, Mar. 13–Oct. 30, 1862

38. Major General Joseph Hooker, commanding 2nd Div., 3rd Corps, Mar. 13–Sept. 5, 1862

39. Maj. General Andrew A. Humphreys (as Brigadier General), commanding 2nd Div., 3rd Corps, May 23–July 9, 1863

40. Brigadier General Henry M. Naglee, commanding 1st Brig., 2nd Div., 3rd Corps, Mar. 13–July 24, 1862

41. Major General Daniel E. Sickles (as Colonel, 70th New York Infantry), commanding 2nd Div., 3rd Corps, Sept. 5, 1862–Jan. 12, 1863, and 3rd Corps, 8 Feb.–29 May and 3 June–July 2, 1863

42. Major General Daniel E. Sickles with Union and Confederate veterans at the 1913 Gettysburg Reunion

43. First National Colors of the 16th Massachusetts Infantry, July-Aug. 1861–Feb. 1863

44. First State Colors of the 16th Massachusetts infantry, July-Aug. 1861–June, 1862

45. Second National Colors of the 16th Massachusetts Infantry, c. June 1862–Dec. 1865

46. Second State Colors of the 16th Massachusetts Infantry, c. June 1862–Dec. 1865

138m

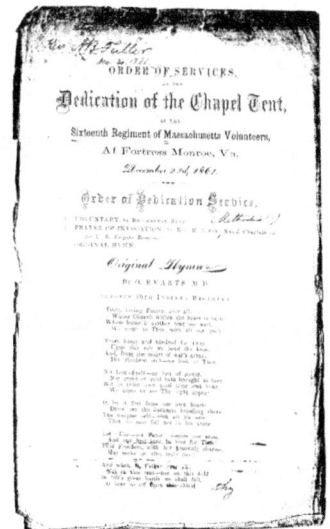 

47 / 48. Programme for dedication of the Chapel Tent of the 16th Massachusetts Infantry, Fortress Monroe, Dec. 22, 1861

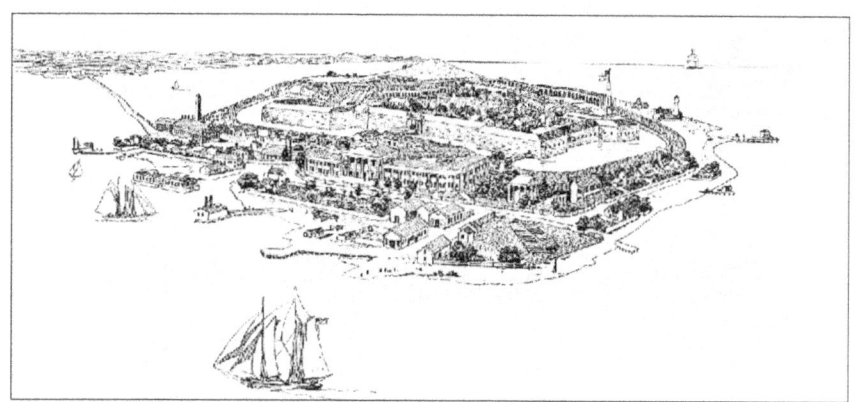

49 Birds-eye view of Fortress Monroe, Virginia

50. The army passing the Hygeia Hotel, Old Point Comfort, Virginia

51. The burning of Hampton by the Rebel Forces

52. The ruins of Hampton, Virginia

53. Federal troops at Hampton, Virginia

54. Rebel batteries on Sewall's Point, opposite Fortress Monroe

55. Battle between the U.S.S. *Monitor* and C.S.S. *Virginia*

138q

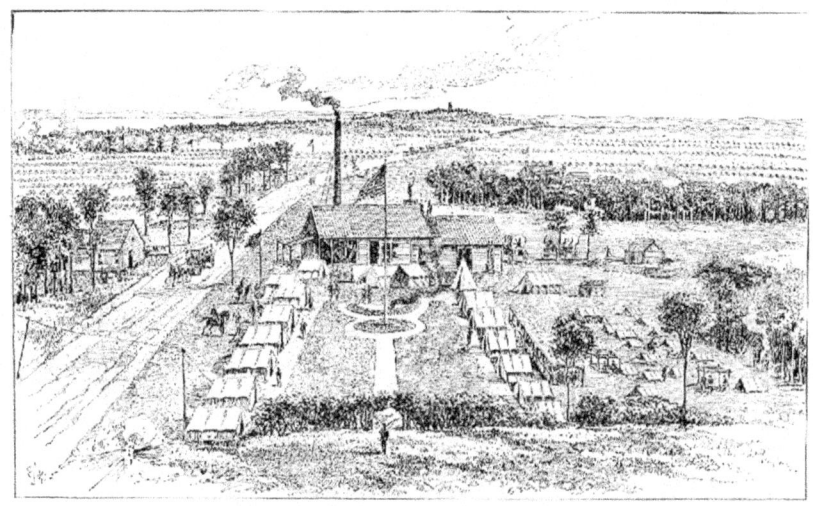

56. Headquarters of General Heintzelman, commanding the Third Army Corps, at Howe's Saw-Mill, before Yorktown

57. The City of Norfolk, Virginia

58. The reoccupation of Norfolk by Union forces under General Wool, May 10, 1862

59. Gen. McClellan's Army on the march through the woods from Williamsburg towards Richmond

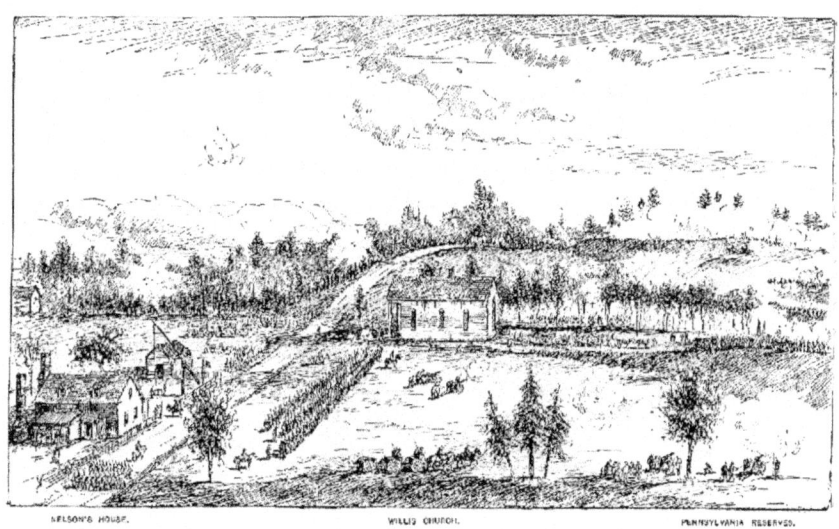
60. Heintzelman's Headquarters at the Nelson House, Battle of Glendale

61. The Battle of Charles City Cross Roads, June 30 1862

62. Heintzelman's Headquarters at Malvern Hill, by the river

63. Harrison's Landing, on the James River, the new base of the Army of the Potomac

64. General view of the encampment of the Army of the Potomac at Harrison's Landing

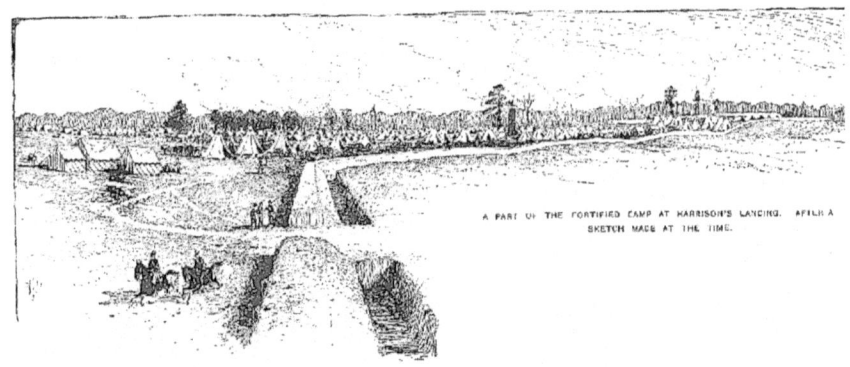

65. Part of the fortified camp at Harrison's Landing

66. Left defense of the camp at Harrison's Landing, Kimmeridge's Creek

138w

67. The U.S.S. *Vanderbilt*, on which the 16th Massachusetts sailed from Harrison's Landing to Washington, D.C.

68. Heintzelman's Headquarters, Fort Lyon, defences of Washington, D.C.

69. Heintzelman's Headquarters at Alexandria, Va., September 3, 1862

70. Reconnaissance balloon, James River, mentioned by Johnson in his letter of April 3, 1862

71. Warrenton, Virginia

72. General McClellan surrendering the command of the
Army of the Potomac to General Burnside

73. McClellan's adieux to his officers at Warrenton, Virginia

74. Fredericksburg, Virginia, viewed from Falmouth

75. Fredericksburg: Union troops crossing the river during the bombardment

76. Chaplain Arthur B. Fuller was killed during fighting such as this in the streets of Fredericksburg

77. "The Mud March", Jan. 20-24, 1863

78. Suffolk, Virginia

79. President Lincoln reviewing the troops at Falmouth, Va.

80. Camp of the 12th Massachusetts Regiment at Falmouth, Va.

81. Abandoning the winter camp at Falmouth

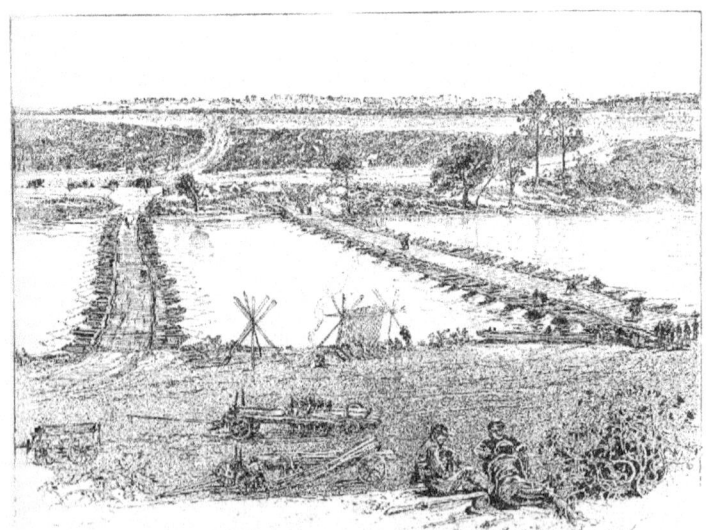

82. Franklin's Crossing, where the 16th Massachusetts was posted during the battle of Fredericksburg

83. Union troops crossing the Rapidan at Ely's Ford

84. The 2nd and 3rd Corps repelling
Jackson's assault at Chancellorsville

138ff

85. Gettysburg: view to the rear of the 16th Massachusetts' position on July 2, 1863, looking towards Cemetery Ridge. Emmitsburg Road behind viewer; memorial to Willard's Brigade in distance.
Taken 2008

86. Gettysburg: view to the left (south) of the 16th Massachusetts' position on July 2, 1863, from the regiment's memorial, Emmitsburg Road at right.
Taken 2008

138gg

87. Gettysburg: view to the immediate front of the 16th Massachusetts' position on July 2, 1863; the dead ground to the front meant that they would not have seen Wilcox's Brigade until it appeared 20 yards away!
Taken 2008

88. Gettysburg: view to the right (north) of the 16th Massachusetts' position on July 2, 1863, in the direction of Gettysburg; Emmitsburg Road at left.
Taken 2008

89. Gettysburg: right hand flank marker of the 16th Massachusetts. Taken 2008

90. Gettysburg: view (south) along the front of the 16th Massachusetts' position on July 2, 1863, from the right flank marker towards the regimental memorial on the rise, in the centre of their position. The distance from the right flank marker of the 16th to the left flank marker of the 11th Massachusetts Infantry (the next unit in the line) is approximately fifty-five yards. The monument between the guns is for Lt. John G. Turnbull's Batteries F & K, 3rd US Artillery. The memorial at right is to the 5th New Jersey Infantry.

Taken 2008

91. Gettysburg: memorial for the 16th Massachusetts Infantry. Taken 2008

CHAPTER 11
*
1863, TO CHANCELLORSVILLE

All Johnson's letters between the "Mud March" and his return from leave of absence after his wound at Chancellorsville on May 26 – namely, those dated from January 25 to April 28, 1863 – are addressed from Camp at Falmouth, Va. They tell, often in some detail, of camp life, military operations and expeditions, and the usual talk of people at home and supplies and home comforts Johnson wanted Nellie to send.

Since Johnson went home to recover from his wound, there are unfortunately no letters covering this battle in which the 16th Massachusetts played a pivotal role, and it was therefore considered important, for the narrative and for the purpose of providing a history of the regiment during Johnson's time with it, that an account be researched, focusing particularly on the experience of the 3rd Corps and the 16th Massachusetts. It has been assembled from three sources: the History of the 1st Massachusetts Infantry; John Bigelow's magisterial 1910 account of the campaign; and Bruce Palmer's short but clear narrative of the battle published in 1967. The narrative and the excellent and detailed maps in Bigelow's volume enable us to develop a reasonably good idea of the whereabouts of Johnson and his regiment during the battle.

h

"General; I have placed you at the head of the Army of the Potomac... I believe you to be a brave and skilful soldier...What I now ask of you is military success... Beware of rashness, with energy, and sleepless vigilance, go forward and give us victories." With these words – and an admonition that it was despite his reputation as a ruthlessly ambitious political general - President Lincoln notified Major General "Fighting Joe" Joseph Hooker on January 26th, 1863 that he was to succeed Burnside. Hooker also had a reputation as a drinker; "when whiskey had loosened his tongue," commented Brigade commander Regis de Trobriand, "he indulged in boastings that one hearing could not accept as gospel truth, or reckon modesty [among] his virtues."

However, Hooker had a talent for organization. The Army was properly fed and housed, sanitation improved, and the men's training taken in hand. He also discontinued the three Grand Divisions of the Army of the Potomac as an impediment to efficiency, and reorganised it on a Corps basis. The army soon forgot Fredericksburg, leading corps commander Darius Couch to remark that the men had changed "from a condition of the lowest depression [according to historian Stephen Sears, 25,363 men – possibly as much as 20% of the Army - were listed as absent without leave or deserted] to a healthy fighting state." To a newspaper correspondent Hooker boasted: "If the enemy does not run, God help him".

All was not well at high command level, though. Sickles' assignment to command of the III Corps, though temporary, upset Howard, commanding the 2nd Div., 2nd Corps, who asked Hooker that he be assigned to the command, citing rank. Though Sickles and Howard were both commissioned Major-Generals on 29th Nov. 1862, Howard accepted, ranking from that date, but Sickles did not, thus ranking only from March 29, 1863. Not wishing to relieve Sickles, Hooker assigned Howard to the 11th Corps, from which command Sigel had been removed. However, Howard's appointment was not welcomed by the many German soldiers of the 11th Corps, since he had replaced their countryman, Sigel. They felt this as a slight against Germans, knowing and caring little for Howard's good fighting record.

Facing Hooker was the Army of Northern Virginia under Lee, supported by his brilliant colleague, Lieutenant-General Thomas Jonathan "Stonewall" Jackson. Still, despite a string of defeats, punctuated only by the repulse of Lee's invasion of the North at Antietam in September, the North did not give up and, unlike the South, it could replace the 70,000 casualties of the 1862 campaigns – larger than Lee's whole army – much more easily.

From February 7th to May 25th, the Second New Hampshire Infantry were absent on duty in their home state, and the regimental history has nothing relevant for this period. The history of the 1st Massachusetts relates that "Great reviews were held... in April... at one of which, on the 9th, President Lincoln and wife, Secretary Seward... and all the general officers of the army were present.... An immense number of infantry and artillery were present, the cavalry having been reviewed previously." The president sat his small black horse with ease, his long legs hanging straight down, the feet nearly reaching to the ground. He was dressed in a plain black suit and a worn black hat. His pale, sad face contrasted strongly with the florid countenance of General Hooker, who rode by his side. The ceremony was followed by a display of drill by the 5th New York Zouaves. "I have under my command the finest army on the planet," Hooker remarked to Lincoln. "I recall with sadness", says reporter Noah Brooks, "the easy confidence and nonchalance which Hooker showed in all his conversations with the President... One of his most frequent expressions.... was 'When I get to Richmond' or 'After we have taken Richmond'. The President, noting this, said to me with a sigh, 'This is the most depressing thing about Hooker... he is overconfident.' "

The armies faced each other that winter across the Rappahannock River in the vicinity of Frdericksburg. Learning from Burnside's disastrous piecemeal attacks at Fredericksburg, Hooker proposed crossing the river in the face of Lee's army and observing Lincoln's advice to "put in all your men". He would send General George Stoneman's 10,000 cavalry to cut Lee's rear and destroy his supplies, while six corps would cross upriver from Fredericksburg, in two succeeding movements, forcing Lee to retreat and destroying him. Hooker boasted to his fellow officers, "My plans are perfect."

Stoneman set out on April 16, slowed by rainstorms, and Hooker left Sedgwick's 24,000 men to hold Lee at Fredericksburg, while the main force under Meade, Slocum and Howard marched 30 miles westward up the Rappahannock around Lee, forcing him to retreat so that Sedgwick could cross. Lee's 62,000 men would be caught in a pincer movement by Hooker's 130,000.

Hooker issued his orders for his "great turning movement" on the 27th: the 1st Corps to cross the river at Fitzhugh's Crossing, the 6th Corps at Franklin's Crossing, at or before 3.30 a.m. The 3rd Corps was to cross, as a support, at or before 4.30 a.m.

on the 29th, at either crossing. The troops, as far as possible, were to be concealed until they executed the demonstration. Before 3.30 a.m. on the 29th a demonstration in full force was to be made with a view to securing the Telegraph Road and barring that route to Richmond. In the event of the enemy detaching any considerable part of his force against the troops operating towards Chancellorsville, Sedgwick was to attack and carry the works in his front at all hazards, and establish his force on the Telegraph Road to prevent the enemy's turning his position on that road and gaining the route to Richmond.

"On Monday morning, April 27", continues the history of the 1st Massachusetts, "the Fifth, Eleventh and Twelfth Corps broke camp [and on the night of April 30 were massed] at the junction of the Orange Court House road with the road to Culpeper, about five miles from United States Ford... The Second Corps... took position at Banks' Ford, five miles above Fredericksburg, on Wednesday [29th] while the First, Third and Sixth proceeded down the river to a little above Port Royal.

At 10 a.m. on April 28th, the 3rd Corps was reviewed by a number of distinguished visitors, including Secretary Seward, the Swedish and Prussian Ministers, the Governors of Maine and New Jersey, and Hooker and Staff. The infantry line alone was a mile and half long, the regimental colours and the designating flags of brigades and divisions adding colour; the troops, in heavy marching order, took an hour to parade by.

Sickles was to prepare to support the 2nd Corps: "The commanding general directs that you have your command in readiness to move early tomorrow [28th] with subsistence (eight days) and ammunition... Further instructions will be sent to you later in the day". However, no "further instructions" arrived, and the Corps remained with the left wing under Sedgwick. The left wing (1st, 3rd, 6th Corps) was to break camp on the morning of the 28th, but rain prevented movement until noon, when the 1st Corps took up the march. The 6th followed about 3 p.m., and the 3rd about 5 p.m, the roads lined at every stop with discarded equipment. The 1st Corps halted at Fitzhugh's Crossing about 5.30 p.m., the 6th at Franklin's crossing about 9 p.m, and the 3rd Corps between these two corps and somewhat in rear of them, approximately two miles downriver from Fredericksburg, also about 9 p.m, with its train still parked near Falmouth.

"The First regiment received the order to move on Monday, April 27. Each man was to have three days' cooked rations in his haversack, five days' small supplies – such as sugar, coffee, salt and hard bread – in his knapsack, and sixty rounds of ammunition... The men were greatly troubled at being loaded down so heavily; and large numbers threw away the bulk of their rations during the next three days, finding it utterly impossible to keep up... Tuesday afternoon, April 28, the whole division left camp and took the road leading down the river to the point where Gen. Franklin crossed during the preceding December. It was six o'clock before the regiment started; and, owing to the darkness of the night and the crowded condition of the roads, progress was so slow that it took four hours to progress three miles."

On April 29 the Union advance crossed upriver, still in the same position near Franklin's Crossing. Sickles, under orders to hold his command "well in hand and in all readiness to march at a moment's notice", was still in the same position near Franklin's Crossing, with a view to reinforcing the right wing. The right was to advance from Chancellorsville to a point giving it command of Banks' Ford. Once there, it could be reinforced by Gibbon's 2nd Div., 2nd Corps, and soon afterward by the 3rd Corps, assuming that the latter started from below Fredericksburg about the same time as the right wing from Chancellorsville. "Early the next morning" [1st Massachusetts] "another start was made, to a position where the division could act as a support to a portion of the Sixth Corps, in crossing the river. Before daybreak the

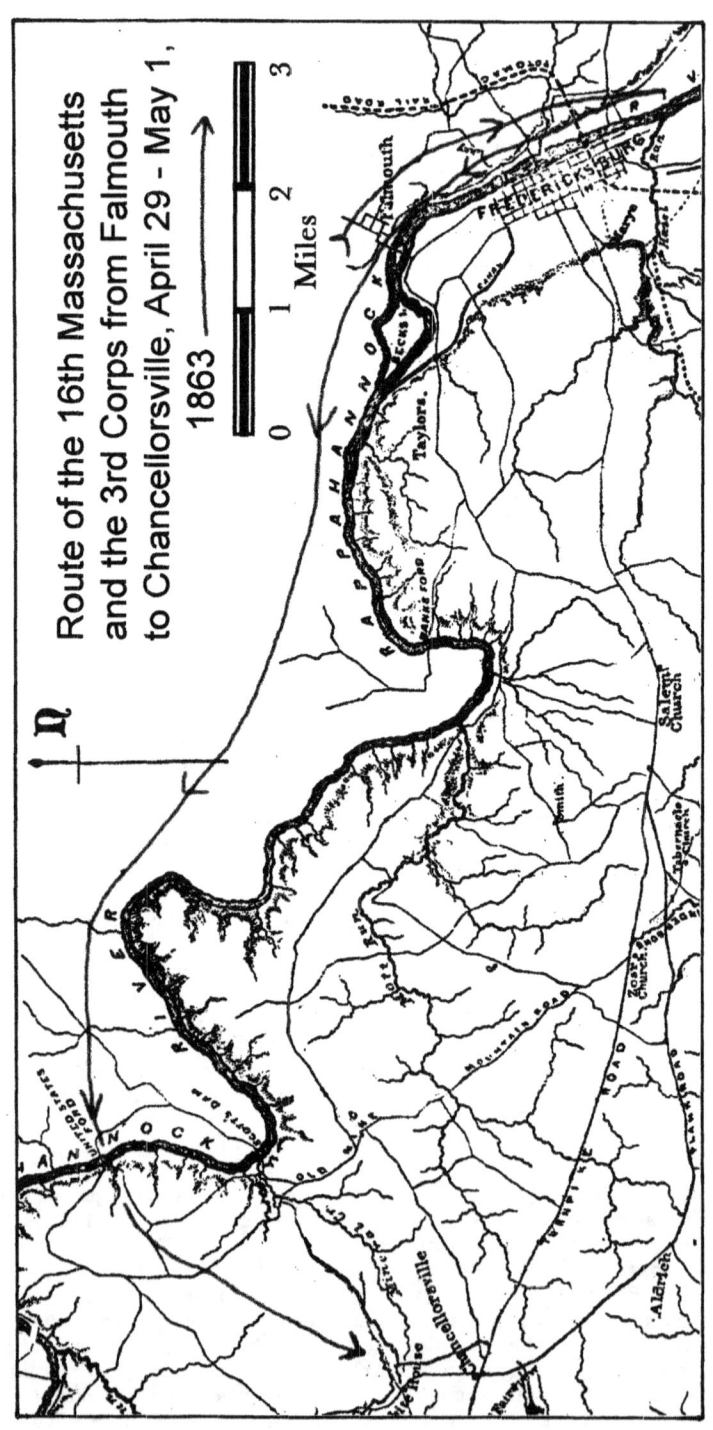

pontoon-boats... were in the water... A part of Gen. Russell's brigade was detailed for this service... at half past four a.m., every boat left the bank, and made for the opposite side. A thick mist hung over the river, which obscured objects... and favoured the... voyagers. As rapidly as they could force the clumsy vessels through the water, they approached the rebel side, and were soon lost to view. In a few minutes more a volley was heard from the rebel rifle pits, showing that... they had effected a landing... The boats, coming back empty, were... filled again with reinforcement, upon whose arrival a line was formed... and a charge ordered upon the rebel entrenchments. They were captured... Both sides of the river being now in our possession, the pontoons were... laid, and our troops began to cross over. Simultaneously... Gen. Stoneman started with his cavalry to gain the rear of Gen. Lee's army..."

"The First remained in the woods below Falmouth, in column of regiments with the rest of the brigade, all day on the 29th. Towards evening it became cloudy, and the rain fell all night. The next day, at noon, marching was resumed through the valleys and byways, so as to be concealed from the enemy, and continued until after dark. The command then went into bivouac, not far from United States Ford, and remained until nearly twelve o'clock the next day. The rest of the division preceded them at seven o'clock, leaving them a rear guard to a long train of wagons, loaded with ammunition and supplies. These frequently got mired on the way to United States Ford... The ford was crossed at one o'clock, and after a short halt in an abandoned rebel camp, the regiment joined the brigade within a short distance of the Chancellorsville House, then occupied by Gen. Hooker as his headquarters..."

Then, on the 30th, it was decided that the right wing should wait at Chancellorsville for the enemy to attack it and, as indicated in the narrative of the 1st Massachusetts Infantry, orders were sent to Sickles at 12.30 p.m. "to march to United States Ford and cross by 7 a.m. tomorrow" – a march of approximately 12 miles to the ford some ten miles upriver from Fredericksburg. The order was received at 1p.m. and by 1.30 the Corps was under way. Orders had been issued to replace rations which had been consumed, but some of the troops refused to burden themselves with the new rations and left them lying on the ground. The brigade commissaries returned them to the supply wagons. The corps marched in three parallel columns, well concealed from the enemy, to Hamet[232] on the Falmouth-Hartwood road, where it went into bivouac about 11.30 p.m. The train, left below Fredericksburg, broke camp about 5 p.m., and when it reached Falmouth, the officer in charge was ordered to push forward the ammunition section at all hazards and park the baggage and supply sections, which did not leave Falmouth during the campaign.

Lee gave no orders to oppose the crossing; Stoneman might be only a diversion from the main attack. Meeting no resistance, orders were issued for the main Union force to cross, Hooker boasting "The Rebel army is now the legitimate property of the Army of the Potomac." By mid-afternoon, Lee had established that the main Union advance was towards Ely's Ford, and ordered R.H.Anderson's division, already at Chancellorsville covering United States Ford, to move to meet it. At twilight the Army of the Potomac was halted by a rainstorm.

Early on the 30th Jackson offered to attack immediately, but Lee preferred to wait, ordering Anderson to dig field fortifications. Lee even considered a retreat; the only alternative was a pointless assault by Anderson against three Union corps. Reinforcements could only come from men opposing Sedgwick at Fredericksburg, which would weaken the Confederate right and be noticed by Federal observation

---

[232] Bigelow, p.231, though Park Historian Donald Pfanz advises that he does not know of this village and questions whether this is a misprint.

balloons. However, Lee saw that the move might be made under cover of darkness, and ordered McLaws' division to join Anderson at midnight, followed at dawn by Jackson and the II Corps. Only 12,000 men under Jubal Early faced the Federals at Fredericksburg.

In the meantime, Stoneman had vanished, and Hooker, feeling that he was groping blindly, grew nervous. All he had to do was uncover the ford and bring across Sedgwick. Instead, he slowed the advance and ordered rifle pits and gun emplacements to be dug. Worrying over maps, he is said to have cried to chief of staff Warren: "My God!... I know nothing of this ground!" and went on the defensive, merely telling his staff to place the centre where the Orange Plank Road and the Orange Turnpike met – a small group of buildings known as Chancellorsville. Meanwhile, unknown to Hooker, Lee had broken a cardinal rule of war and divided his army in the face of a vastly superior enemy; Early would hold Sedgwick at Fredericksburg, while the rest of the army would hit Hooker, relying on surprise.

The morning of May 1, Bigelow tells us, was a beautiful day. A fresh soft breeze stole through the forest, rustling the banners uncased to dry. Warren had gone towards Fredericksburg on a reconnaissance. Hooker was waiting to hear from him and from the 3rd Corps. A calm like that of an old-time Sabbath rested upon the camps. The corps commanders, impelled by impatience and curiosity, drifted over to Chancellorsville, and were encouraged by the complete confidence which Hooker showed. At 7.30 a.m. the 3rd Corps commenced crossing at United States Ford and massed on the south bank.

About 11 a.m. Sickles' Corps gathered at the junction of Ely's and United States Ford Roads, about half a mile north of Chancellorsville. On the south bank of United States Ford, it left Mott's brigade (3rd, 2nd Div.) and Jastram's and Seeley's batteries, to guard the bridge, the ambulances remaining on the north bank. By midday, Hooker feared that a force of Confederate cavalry was demonstrating against his right and rear, and ordered Graham (1st Brig., 1st Div., 3rd Corps) to picket well out to the right and rear, connecting on his right with Whipple (3rd Div, 3rd Corps), who was to connect his right with Berry (2nd Div., 3rd Corps). Graham halted at Dowdall's Tavern to await further orders; Whipple and Berry established a line of outposts extending from the Plank Road to the United States Ford, a line of over two miles, the position of the 16th on which is not clear.

The 1st Massachusetts history tells us that "At noon, Friday, May 1, portions of the fifth and twelfth corps were advanced... in the direction of Fredericksburg. Before two o'clock they came across the enemy... the rebels opened a heavy fire... the union troops then fell back... The enemy soon followed... They were received with a point-blank [volley] which... arrested their progress. But those in the rear, who had not felt the Union lead, were not to be kept back... so onward they pressed, until a second volley [halted them]... They were just on the point of falling back when they were re-enforced, and... again came forward... For nearly half an hour both sides stood facing each other... equally determined not to yield... [until the] rebels... retreated back into the woods..."

"Just as they were retiring, the Massachusetts First was double-quicked up to the left, on the line of the Banks' Ford Road, in light marching order. Knapsacks had been unslung at the rear...; but, just as the right company reached the battle-field, the order was given... "Prepare to stack arms!... Stack arms!.. Rest!". The companies were then sent back, one at a time, for their knapsacks; and the men prepared to bivouac, for the night, behind their stacks. They remained undisturbed till the next afternoon."

As McLaws and Anderson made contact with Union pickets on May 1, Lee and Jackson rode towards the action which had started in the tangled second-growth woods known as the Wilderness, where the Federal 5th Corps skirmishers were slowly giving ground.

Hooker now considered two alternatives: to select a line of defence and entrench it, or to select a point of attack and advance upon it. The former was adopted. The line chosen was the one actually held, with the right thrown back to a better position. At 4 p.m. Sickles was directed to bring up his whole Corps except Mott's Brigade (3rd, 2nd Div.) and Seeley's battery, still guarding United States Ford, and get rapidly into position parallel to the Plank Road at Chancellorsville. The Corps arrived in the vicinity of Chancellorsville while the Confederates were pressing Slocum in his front and on his right. Graham's Brigade took up position in rear of Best's batteries at Fairview Cemetery, ready to support them or to support Williams' 1st Division, 5th Corps, engaged in repelling Wright's attack.

About sunset Birney's Division (1st), minus Graham's Brigade (1st, 1st Div.) moved up the Plank Road to the right of the 12th Corps, and bivouacked near the interval between the 11th and 12th Corps. Shells and bullets reached the troops as they came into position. To discover the enemy's movements five or six men had climbed to the tops of the highest trees, which gave a view over the surrounding woods, but also exposed them to the rebel sharpshooters. Jastram's Battery [2nd Brig., 1st Div., 3rd Corps) moved up from United States Ford, and about midnight bivouacked near Chandler's. Whipple's Division (3rd) bivouacked in reserve at Chancellorsville, as did Berry's 2nd Division (less Mott's 3rd Brigade, still at United States Ford); Johnson and the 16th seem, therefore, to have spent the night of May 1st about three-quarters of a mile north-west of Chancellorsville. During the night, Sickles ordered Birney to occupy at daybreak the line between the 11th and 12th Corps, to give those units some relief.

Hooker had decided that it would not be prudent to put the mainly German-speaking troops of Howard's 11th Corps at the centre, not least for fear of orders being not understood, or misunderstood, at a critical moment, and had taken the precaution of placing them on the far right of the line, far from what Hooker presumed would be the centre of the battle.

After sunset, heavy cannonading from the Fairview cemetery and rifle fire from Slocum's 12th Corps told Lee the enemy's approximate position. Jackson was confident that he could drive the enemy back across the river the next day; Lee was less so, but ordered a reconnaissance to locate the Union right, where Howard's 11th Corps lay, to the west of Sickles' 3rd Corps, ending in woods where an assault could be launched unseen. Stuart found this weak point, and Lee now knew the approximate positions of the whole Union army. A man on Jackson's staff who knew the area, sent to find a route by which the Confederates could attack the Union right, returned early the next morning, May 2nd, with the news that a track had been found leading to a road running beyond and behind the enemy right flank.

Jackson immediately proposed to take his whole Corps and attack the Union right with his 26,000 men with such suddenness that the enemy would be driven back to the Rappahannock. Lee realised that this meant splitting the army yet again, leaving him with only McLaws' and Anderson's divisions to hold the 70,000 Union troops facing him; but it need only hold until Jackson hit the exposed Union right. "Well," he said, "go on." At 7 a.m. on May 2, Jackson headed southwest, and Lee's army was now split into three parts: Early's 12,000-13,000 at Fredericksburg, Lee with Anderson's and McLaws' 14,000 facing the Union center, and Jackson's 26,000. Early had instructions to hold as long as Sedgwick remained, to send reinforcements if any Union troops were detached, and to join Lee immediately if Sedgwick withdrew.

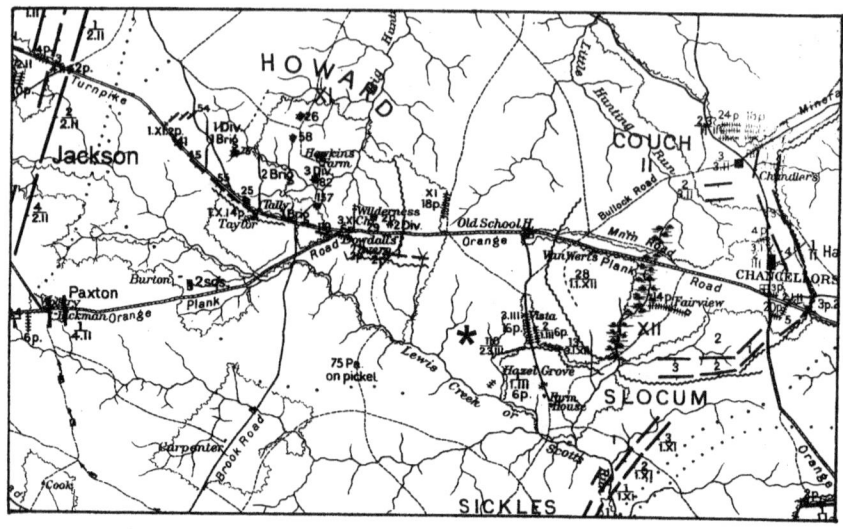

Chancellorsville - positions at 5 p.m., May 2, 1863: * marks 2nd Division, 3rd Corps *(from Bigelow, 1910, Map 18)*

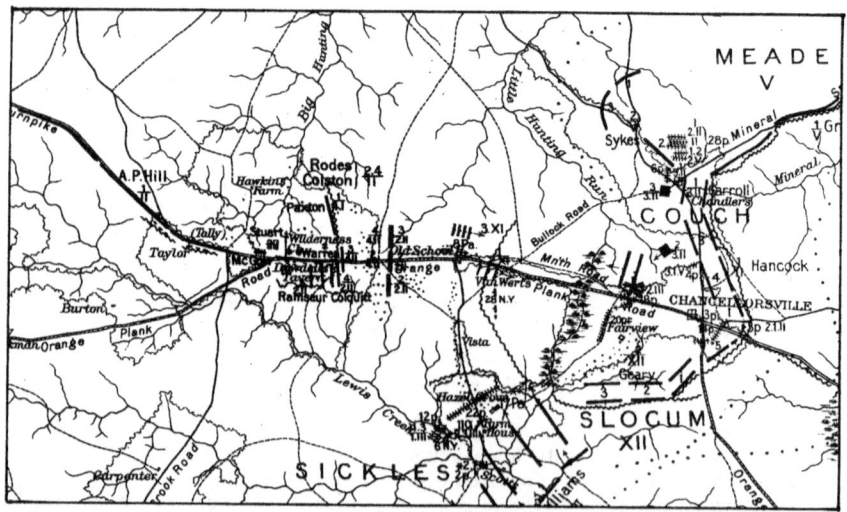

Chancellorsville - positions at 7.15 p.m., May 2, 1863: * marks 2nd Division, 3rd Corps *(from Bigelow, 1910, Map 21)*

Anderson and Laws held a line about two miles long, the men six feet apart. The risk Lee was taking was enormous.

The Union line on Howard's left (east) was held by Sickles' 3rd Corps, in a line something over a mile long extending in an arc westward from the north to the south of, and between half a mile and a mile from, Chancellorsville; the front was held by Birney, with Berry and Whipple in reserve in the Chancellor clearing. Hooker ordered him to make a reconnaissance in front and to the left of Chancellorsville. The 11th Massachusetts and the 26th Pennsylvania, both of Carr's Brigade, were sent out, the former in front of Hancock, on the Turnpike, the latter on the Plank Road, each with a detachment of Berdan's Sharpshooters. About 1 o'clock Sickles received reports from Birney indicating that a column of the enemy was moving towards the Federal right. This indicated to Sickles either a retreat on Gordonsville or an attack on the Federal right flank – perhaps both, for if the attack failed, the retreat might be necessary. Sickles quickly sent staff officers to Hooker with the report, proposing that he use his whole corps to attack the enemy. He also warned Howard on his right and Slocum on his left, suggesting that, if necessary, they co-operate. About noon Hooker sent him orders to "advance cautiously towards the road... and harass the [enemy] as much as possible" with Birney's (1st) and Whipple's (3rd) Divisions, but Berry's 2nd Division was held back, remaining in its overnight position at the junction of the Plank and Ely's Ford Roads..

Sickles acted immediately, moving a division forward, but at the same time opening a gap in the line between himself and Howard. Probing the woods, his men ran into the 23rd Georgia of Rodes' division, but aside from some Federal artillery fire and skirmishing, no further action developed, and by mid-afternoon Jackson's lead elements were forming up for an assault. The 1st Massachusetts History relates this activity: "A movement had been observed in the woods by our pickets, which indicated that the rebels were falling back... or intending to attack the Union right. To ascertain their intentions, a reconnaissance was ordered, under Gen. Sickles," but errs in asserting that this "developed the fact that the whole of Stonewall Jackson's division [sic] was massing upon the right... for an assault..." and in suggesting that Jackson's flank attack followed immediately.

About 2.45 p.m. Sickles told Hooker that he could reach the road on which the enemy was marching and break his column, adding that, as he expected stubborn resistance, and bearing in mind Hooker's instruction to move cautiously, he would not advance until support from the 11th and 12th Corps closed up on Birney's right and left. At the same time he informed Howard and Slocum: 'I am advancing a strong line of two brigades to ascertain whether the enemy is retreating. General Birney reports that he has reached a brigade of the enemy in rifle-pits, posted, as I think, to cover the retreating columns. I will attack if the enemy is not stronger than the reports so far represent him... Please support my advance." The message was received at 3 p.m. by Howard, who replied that he had no troops to spare, and at 3.30 by Slocum, who referred the matter to Hooker.

Cavalry scouts reported to Hooker that the enemy column had disappeared, but Hooker's believed that it was still being harassed by Sickles, whose artillery, too, was briefly heard; when it ceased, it was considered that Sickles' operation had been checked or given up, but Howard continued to believe that it was progressing well.

At 4.10 p.m., Hooker ordered Sedgwick to "cross the river as soon as indications will permit; capture Fredericksburg with everything in it; and vigorously pursue the enemy. We know that the enemy is fleeing, trying to save his trains. Two of Sickles' divisions are among them." Sickles, however, was not "among them", though Hooker presumably believed that the movement observed and reported by Sickles indicated the retreat of a portion of Lee's army, and hoped that by the time his orders reached Sedgwick the retreat would be a rout. At this time, according to Warren's subsequent testimony, "there was a general feeling that Lee's army was running away."

Meanwhile there was disturbing news for Lee. Misunderstanding instructions sent verbally as a precaution against the risk of despatches being captured (though there were, in fact, no Union forces between Lee and Early), Early had left Fredericksburg and was marching to join Lee, exposing the whole Confederate rear to Sedgwick. Lee ordered him to return immediately, hoping that the mistake had not been noticed.

In the meantime, Jackson had formed his troops in three lines perpendicular to the Turnpike and extending about a mile on each side of it. His men took their positions silently, orders were transmitted in a low voice, the bugles were quiet, and Jackson's soldiers even refrained from cheering him. Jackson expected to come upon positions at right angles to Hooker's main line and to overlap them on both flanks; his intention was that, when he had advanced far enough to connect with Lee, part of his force would be directed upon Chandler's to take Chancellorsville well in rear, severing Hooker's communications with the Rapidan and Rappahannock fords and driving his routed army upon the latter river. About 5 p.m. Sickles received orders from Hooker to attack the enemy on his right flank and check his advance, but advising that he must rely upon the forces he had, as no others could be spared.

Then came a rumble of battle from the west; Jackson's attack had begun.

Unaware of Jackson's movement, Howard's 11th Corps were at rest, their rifles stacked and food and coffee cooking. At 5.15 p.m., Jackson ordered his men to fix bayonets and go forward. As the bugles rang out through the woods, the line rose and rushed forward. Terrified deer and rabbits were the first the Union troops knew as the Confederates came through the tangled woods towards them, shrieking the "rebel yell", smashing through the camp, overwhelming any small groups who resisted and sweeping over the light earthworks at Talley's Farm and up the slopes of the low ridge beyond.

The Union troops reeled; most of them put up a gallant, if short, fight before being shot down or retreating in disorder into the gap left by Sickles. The situation of Carr's Brigade at this point is shown in the 1st Massachusetts' account: "The German regiments... shortly began to waver and, upon receiving a charge from the enemy... they fell back... The shattered columns streamed back to the rear... The fugitives were panic-stricken and... [ran] away as fast as possible. The rebels were close upon their heels... Gen. Sickles, who was on the spot with two divisions of his corps, immediately sent for the other, and, forming his men across the line of retreat pursued by the panic-stricken Germans, told them they must retrieve the day... He had barely time to make his dispositions... when the rebels came on. They received a series of... volleys... which at once checked their advance... Those who were behind, however, still pressed forward... but found it impossible to advance further... Darkness had also approached... and... they finally retired... [but] one of our lines was broken, and our advance checked..."

While Jackson was rolling up the Federal right, Hooker sat on the veranda of the Chancellor House, enjoying the summer evening. Now and then a shot came from the south and east, where Lee was keeping up a show of force, but nothing occurred to give him anxiety. Not a sound of the attack on the far right had reached them. No message had come for aid, and it was not until between 6.15 and 6.30 that the sound of distant cannonading came to Hooker's ears. The shells flying toward Chancellorsville from the west were thought to be fired by pursuing Federals. Hooker and his staff were listening intently when his aide, Captain Russell, looked through

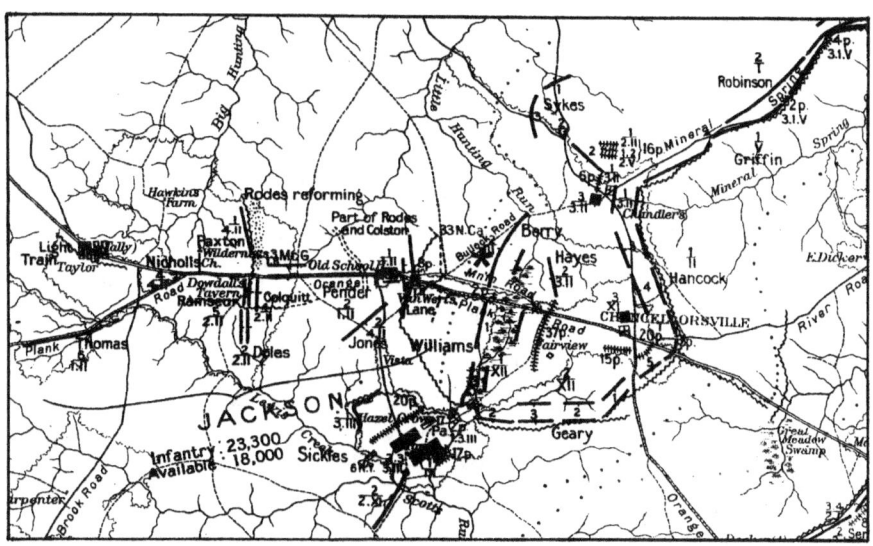

Chancellorsville - positions at 9 p.m., May 2, 1863: * marks 2nd Division, 3rd Corps *(from Bigelow, 1910, Map 22)*

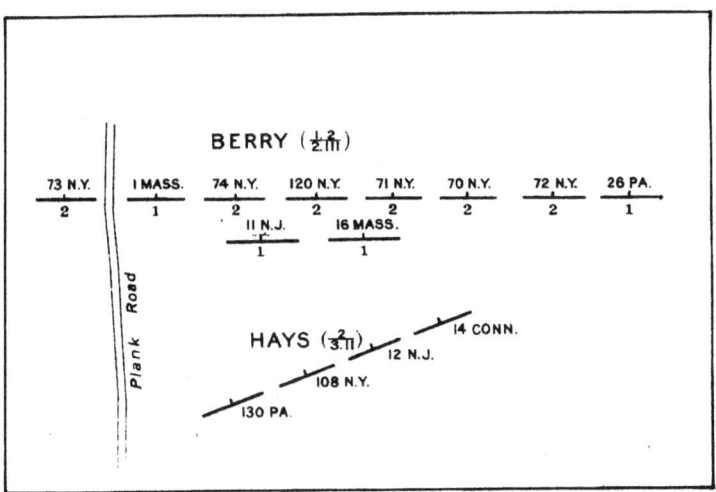

Chancellorsville - formation of Berry's 1st & 2nd Brigades, 2nd Division, 3rd Corps, between 9.30 p.m. and midnight, May 2, 1863
(from Bigelow, 1910, Plan 2)

his glass with some trepidation in the direction of Dowdall's Tavern. A moment later

his glass with some trepidation in the direction of Dowdall's Tavern. A moment later he shouted "My God, here they come!" - meaning Howard's men. Hooker and his staff sprang to their horses and rode some way down the Plank Road before they reached the fugitives and learned that the whole rebel army had struck their right flank and rear.

At 7 p.m. Berry was still near the Chancellor House with two of his brigades – the 1st and 2nd. The noise of the rout and of Jackson's pursuing troops came to the ears of Johnson, the 16th and the remainder of the Brigade, first indistinctly, increasing in volume until it seemed as though pandemonium had broken loose. Then came the panic-stricken fugitives, blindly pushing their way through their ranks. In the midst of the tumult Hooker rushed up. "General!" he shouted, "throw your men into the breach – receive the enemy on your bayonets – don't fire a shot – they can't see you!"

Berry at once advanced at double-time with his 1st (Carr's) and 2nd (Revere's) Brigades; Lt. Col. Waldo Merriam of the 16th Massachusetts later gave the time as 6.30 p.m. Captain Charles R. Johnson may have been close enough to hear Hooker, sitting on his white horse - a familiar sight to his old division - call to them: "Receive them on your bayonets, boys!" Hays' 2nd Brigade (3rd Division, 2nd Corps), ordered to support Berry's division - the largest and one of the best in the Army of the Potomac – followed Johnson and the men of the 16th Massachusetts and forced their way through the retreating men of the 11th Corps toward the oncoming Rebels. Berry was ordered to "cover the rear of the 11th Corps, and if possible to seize and hold at all hazards the high ground which had been abandoned by that corps". A 3rd Corps officer later recalled: "The officers made themselves speechless by striving to rally the 'Flying Dutchmen.'"

By 8 p.m the Federal positions in the Chancellorsville "salient" were as follows: Pleasonton with the 6th New York, 17th Pennsylvania and Martin's Battery were at Hazel Grove. Behind Pleasonton was Whipple's division (3rd, 3rd Corps), and behind him, south of Hazel Grove, Birney's (1st, 3rd Corps), with Jastram's Battery. About a mile south of the unfinished railroad was Barlow's Brigade, and the southern face of the position was held by Slocums' 12th Corps. Berry with his 1st and 2nd Brigades was intrenching between the Plank Road and the Bullock Road; so critical was their role in holding Jackson that it is almost the only occasion in Bigelow's superbly detailed account of the battle where a detailed map (Plan 2) is given showing the positions of the individual regiments involved.

Sickles was undecided whether he should conform to the retreat of the Federal right or maintain his position. His last order from Hooker, about 5 p.m., was to attack. He sent for new orders, which he received, probably about 9, ordering him to hold Hazel Grove. He replied that he would make a night attack, if supported by Williams' and Berry's divisions (1st, 12th Corps and 2nd, 3rd Corps).

About 8.30 Hooker learned that the enemy was in possession of the high ground that Berry was to have seized, and that Berry had consequently established his line "in the valley on the Chancellorsville side of that high ground." This was a ridge which in the enemy's hands would command open ground that extended back to Fairview. As soon as Hooker learned of Berry's position, his division holding a line between the Orange Plank Road and the Bullock Road, about a quarter of a mile west of Chancellorsville, he directed a new line of defence to be laid out, that night, to the rear of the one which he then held, as he would not be able to attack in the morning. The line extended from Chandler's along the Mineral Spring Road, and along the

Ely's Ford Road and the Little Hunting Run.

Albright's Brigade (3rd, 3rd Div., 2nd Corps) was withdrawn, leaving Berry's right flank in the air. Berry despatched patrols to the right in search of troops who were supposed to protect that flank or connect with it, but none were found. He reported this to Hooker, who advised that the 2nd Corps would connect with his right, and at 9 p.m. Hays' brigade arrived and was placed obliquely about 300 yards in rear of the second line, facing southwest. Jackson was unaware of this line and of Sykes' line on the Ely's Ford Road, or of Reynolds' two divisions (2nd and 3rd, Ist Corps) approaching from the United States Ford.

Dusk fell, leaving the Confederate attackers now as disordered as the fleeing Federals in the growing darkness, and the attack deteriorated into confused fighting. Sickles' men re-formed sufficiently to allow Howard's survivors to move to safety; then they fell back to new fortifications at Hazel Grove, just west of Chancellorsville, where Hooker's artillery commander, Henry J. Hunt, had placed twenty heavy cannon. As a mob of retreating Yankees rushed past, the guns blazed into the darkness, hitting Southern and Union men alike. As night fell, the Union troops stood and fought in small units, and reached the trenches at Hazel Grove. The Rebels halted to dig shallow holes as some protection from Union shells. Following the rout of the 11th Corps, there was something of a lull in the fighting, Pleasonton ordering some cannon at Hazel Grove to fire at small parties of Confederates who appeared in the woods west of that clearing. Johnson and the 16th spent the night in Berry's second line, behind his center.

Jackson, determined to finish off the enemy before the night was over, tried to throw his men forward once more, this time northeast, cutting off the Union retreat to the river; when morning came, the fight would be pushed to the finish and Hooker destroyed. He rode forward, a few staff officers accompanying him. "The danger is over!" he snapped to one of his staff. "The enemy is routed. Go back and tell A.P.Hill to press right on!" Then he turned – he had been no more than a quarter of a mile in front of Berry's Division - and rode back the way he had come, towards his lines. The time was about 9.15 p.m.

Suddenly shots rang out. Jackson and his party had ridden into the 33rd North Carolina Infantry who, mistaking them in the dark for attacking enemy cavalry, immediately opened fire. Lieutenant Morrison of Jackson's staff cried out "Cease firing! You are firing into your own men!" "It's a lie!" a voice in the darkness shouted back and another volley rang out. Several of Jackson's staff were killed or wounded, and Jackson himself was hit three times and struck in the face by a branch as he tried to control his horse. He collapsed into the arms of Captain Wilbourn, a Signal officer. After issuing a final order – "You must hold your ground" – Jackson was taken to a field hospital, where his left arm was amputated. Lieutenant Wynn of Jackson's staff rode to Ambrose P. Hill, Jackson's second-in-command, to advise him of Jackson's wounding, but shortly afterwards, in a second disaster for the Confederates, Hill was seriously wounded by shrapnel. Lee received the news with dismay, and placed his chief of cavalry, Stuart, in command of Jackson's Corps.

About 10 p.m. Mott's 3rd Brigade of Berry's Division started from United States Ford for Chancellorsville, and Sickles received permission to make his proposed attack. An aide was sent to communicate with Williams and Berry, returning at 11 p.m. with the report – apparently erroneous - that they were ready. Berry, who was killed next day, left no report of what he had understood; the report of Captain Poland, his chief of staff, contains no mention of it, not is there any reference to it in the report of Carr, who succeeded Berry, or in that of either Brigade commander present.

At about 11 p.m., Sickles, with authority for his night attack and, as he understood, promise of cooperation from Williams and Berry, ordered Birney to advance. Receiving the cross-fire of friend and foe, the troops, despite orders to the contrary, opened fire, and dashed through the darkness at whatever might be in front of them. Those on the right charged a battery of the 12th Corps before they discovered that they were attacking friends. The two foremost regiments attacked Lane's Brigade but were repulsed. The troops in the center reached the Plank Road, but could not hold it. Knipe's Brigade, on Ruger's right, repulsed two advances of the enemy, and Berry, with the 16th Massachusetts, one. As two of Sickles' brigades fell back from the Plank Road, portions ran to the rear, apparently as much panic-stricken as any of Howard's men had been, and having to be rallied at the point of the bayonet.

Though the support Sickles expected from Berry and Williams did not materialise, Berry does not seem to have been at all responsible for the failure, though Williams, in the absence of his Corps commander, should have made arrangements for action by his division. Sickles' night attack nevertheless justified itself, as he held a more advanced position. Best's artillery and Berry's infantry dug hasty intrenchments. About midnight the 7th New Jersey started from Humphreys' left and the 11th Massachusetts from Hancock's front to rejoin their brigades in Berry's Division.

Had Jackson not been wounded, he might well have achieved his aim of resuming the advance and moving against Hooker's line of retreat. But he would not have gone far; a good part of his force would have been checked by the artillery at Fairview Cemetery or the infantry in front of it and at Hazel Grove, and the rest would have come up against Berry and Williams and been repulsed. What was perhaps possible at 7.15 p.m., when Rodes brought the line to a halt, was no longer feasible at 9 p.m., when Jackson was ready to resume the advance.

Had Sickles been properly supported in his movement beyond the Furnace, he may well have repulsed Jackson's troops. He has been criticised for causing a gap in Hooker's line, which left the 11th Corps without support, but the blame appears to lie with Howard's orders; he had been ordered to support Sickles' advance, and did so with Barlow's brigade, but he had no orders to advance his whole corps. That Sickles was not cut off from Hazel Grove was due to a Confederate blunder.

When Lee wrote his despatch at 3.30 a.m. on May 3, urging Stuart to press the Federal right, the situation was now very different from that in which Jackson had been able to "press on... turning the positions of the enemy". Instead of overlapping the enemy, Stuart's lines were now overlapped themselves. At Hazel Grove, on Stuart's right, Sickles had Birney's and Whipple's divisions, Barlow's 11th Corps Brigade, and 38 guns. On Stuart's left and front the Federal lines had been materially strengthened and extended. On the east (Fredericksburg) side, Chancellorsville was covered by troops including Berry's 2nd Division with the 16th Massachusetts.

Before dawn, the 11th New Jersey, on the left of Berry's second line, was moved to the left, where it rested on the Plank Road. The 11th Massachusetts was placed on its right, and the 16th Massachusetts was moved to the right in support of the 26th Pennsylvania.

During the night Sickles reported the situation at Hazel Grove to Hooker and requested instructions. When the message arrived, Hooker was asleep, but he seems to have gone to meet Sickles in person at daylight to order him to evacuate Hazel Grove and march his command to Fairview, and occupy the new line of entrenchments along the skirt of the woods across the Plank Road, in order to reinforce the line occupied by part of the 12th corps, Berry's Division, and Hays' Brigade (2nd, 3rd Div., 3rd Corps).

If I am alive next Summer

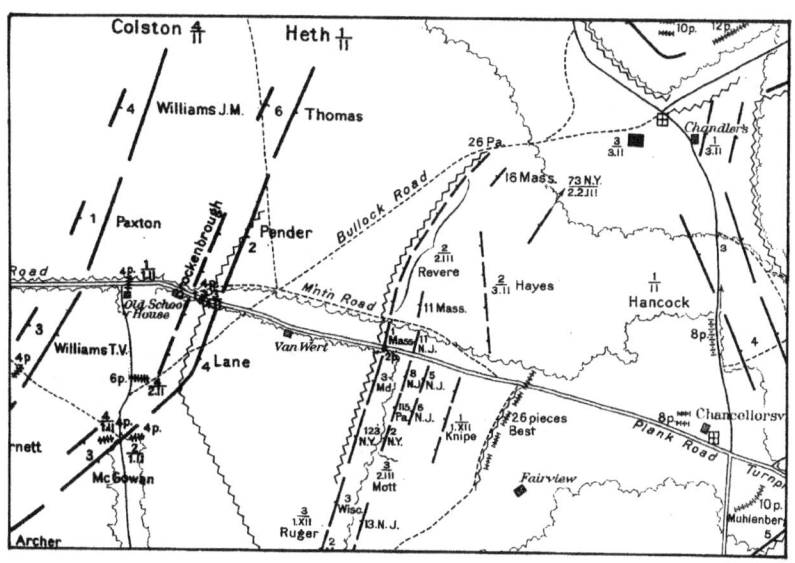

Chancellorsville - showing position of 2nd Division, 3rd Corps, at 5 a.m., May 3, 1863: *(from Bigelow, 1910, Plan 3)*

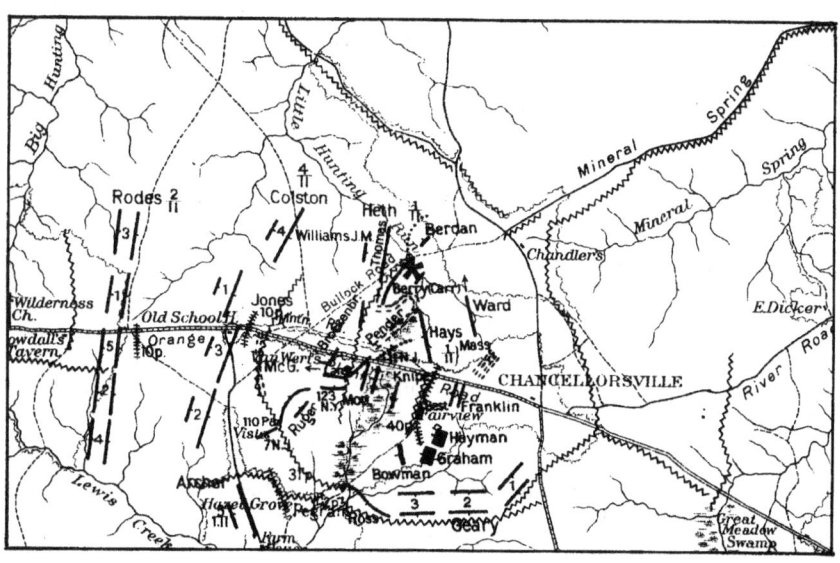

Chancellorsville - positions at 7.30 a.m., May 3, 1863: * marks 2nd Division, 3rd Corps *(from Bigelow, 1910, Map 26)*

At 5 a.m. Sickles proceeded to withdraw his troops. Pender's right now moved upon the exposed flank of Berry's division, the extreme left of which was held by the 1st Massachusetts, resting on the Plank Road. Sickles placed his infantry in support of the artillery at Fairview. The 16th Massachusetts now occupied the unprotected northern end of his line, in the second line behind the 26th Pennsylvania.

At about 7 a.m., Berry directed Capt. Greenhalgh, his senior aide, to ride to Hooker's Headquarters and ascertain whether he should hold his position; but Berry never knew the answer. Berry, unusually, was accustomed to give his orders in person when possible. He told his staff to remain where they were, while he crossed the Plank Road to communicate with Mott. The staff protested and offered to go, pointing out that the enemy's sharpshooters were posted in the trees and sweeping the Plank Road. Berry replied that he preferred to give the order in person, and crossed the road in safety. On reaching Mott, he spoke with him a short time, and started to return. He had gained the Plank Road, and was recrossing it, having nearly reached where his staff officers were standing when, from the trees in which the North Carolina sharpshooters were posted, came a wreath of smoke, followed by the sharp crack of a rifle. A bullet struck him in the arm close to the shoulder, passed downward through his body, and lodged in his hip. He fell in the center of the road, and at 7.26 a.m., with a group of staff officers by his side, and the battles lines of his division about him, he died, at the age of 38, one of the most promising young generals of the war.

Captain Poland, on seeing Berry fall, sent an aide to Carr, lately commanding the 1st Brigade, to advise that he commanded the division. Carr at once ordered the 11th New Jersey on the left of his second line to support Dimick's artillery. The 1st and 11th Massachusetts fell back, both more or less shaken or broken. They reformed half a mile from the front line, probably in rear of Hays' brigade. The remainder of Carr's line, consisting of the 2nd Brigade and the 26th Pennsylvania and 16th Massachusetts of the 1st Brigade, broke off regiment by regiment from the left as Pender and Thomas in succession threatened to crush its flank, and fell back to the north. Ward's 2nd Brig., 1st Div., 3rd Corps, was sent to support Carr's right but, not finding Carr, he reported to French, who placed him near Chandler's. Carr had gone to the left of the Plank Road, where he found Mott advancing upon the enemy in two lines. Lane's brigade had suffered from the artillery at Fairview; struck now by Mott in front and Ruger in flank and rear, it wavered and broke. A Confederate writer says: "The onslaught of the enemy was daring and obstinate. They pushed upon the very works, and one color-bearer even planted his flag upon them."

Carr had assumed command of the Division at 7.30, but Revere, commanding the 2nd Brigade, thought that he had succeeded to the command, and before 8 o'clock he marched his own troops – the "Excelsior" Brigade and part of the 1st Brigade, some nine regiments - off the field to the area of United States Ford, on the grounds that the division needed to be reorganised and supplied with ammunition and rations, and to intercept stragglers. The remainder of his division reformed about 8 a.m. in rear of Franklin's brigade.

While Ramseur threatened Graham's right, Graham advance his left against Ramseur's right. Ramseur reported to Rodes that, unless the enemy was driven from his right, he would have to fall back. About this time Stuart rode up and in his usual happy manner ordered a charge. This attack, at about 9.15 a.m., sent Graham's Brigade in retreat to Chancellorsville. Hayman's brigade (3rd, 1st Div., 3rd Corps), led by Birney himself, covered the retreat with a charge, and Carr's Brigade withdrew to Chandler's.

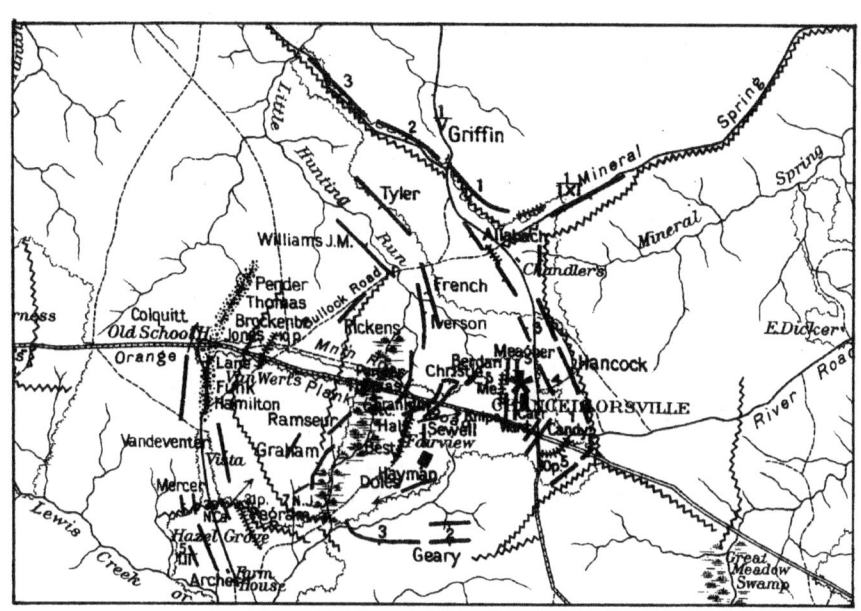

Chancellorsville - positions at 9 a.m., May 3, 1863: * marks 2nd Division, 3rd Corps *(from Bigelow, 1910, Map 30)*

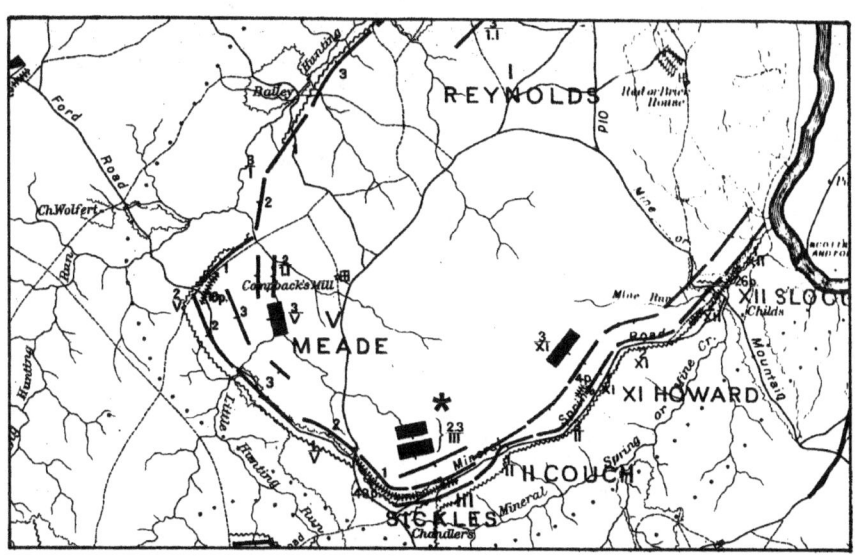

Chancellorsville - positions at 12 p.m., May 3, 1863: * marks 2nd Division, 3rd Corps *(from Bigelow, 1910, Map 36)*

Sickles sent an aide to Hooker with an urgent appeal for support. Hooker, on the porch of the Chancellor House, saw him coming, and bent over the rail in his eagerness to hear his report, when a solid shot struck the pillar against which he had been leaning, splitting it from end to end, and throwing one half of it violently against him. He fell senseless, and was briefly thought to be dying, but he soon revived and showed himself to his troops. By force of will he mounted his horse and started to the rear. In the meantime a rumor that he was killed had spread through the ranks. Couch, the senior corps commander, had heard it, and hastened to the Chancellor House; he was much relieved to see Hooker mounted and returned to the front. However Hooker was unfit to exercise command again during the campaign. Nearly all the rest of the day he suffered pain and his right side was partially paralyzed; but as he rode away, he said nothing to Couch about relinquishing command, nor did he give him any orders. "This", says Couch, "was the last I saw of my commanding officer." On riding to Chandler's, Hooker had a violent return of pain, became faint, and would have fallen from his horse had not his staff helped him to the ground. He was laid upon a blanket, but revived, and was hardly on his feet when a solid shot from Hazel Grove struck the blanket where he had been lying.

Back at Fredericksburg, Sedgwick was ordered to occupy the town, defended by Early, and join the main army, and on the morning of May 3 it seemed that Hooker still held the superior position. The situation could still be saved by a counterattack; Sickles, still aggressive, wanted to counter-attack, but Couch refused to permit it. "It would not have been difficult", says Sickles, "to regain the lost ground with the bayonet, as I proposed to do, but the attack was not deemed expedient (for the want of supports to hold it) by the senior officer present."

Hooker, too, hesitated. Instead of hitting at Lee, he called Sickles back from Hazel Grove, abandoning it without a fight, to the fury and astonishment of Federal officers, just before the morning assaults commenced. The day's action for Carr's Brigade is summarised briefly by the 1st Massachusetts historian:- "Soon after daylight on the 3d, which was Sunday, the rebels came on in overwhelming numbers against the position held by Gens. Sedgwick and Slocum... The conflict that ensued was terrible... Perceiving that any... advance would be impossible, without a repetition of the process which had cost them so dearly earlier in the day, at twelve o'clock the infantry retired..." back, according to the maps in Bigelow, towards the Chancellorsville crossroads and thence northward where Sickles' Corps formed the southern tip of a new Federal salient some three-quarters of a mile north of Chancellorsville.

Hooker was lying in a tent. Raising himself a little as Couch entered, he said: "Couch, I turn the command of the army over to you. You will withdraw it." As Couch came out of the tent, he met Meade, who looked at him inquiring as if at last to receive the long-wished for order to "go in." But a messenger dashed off with orders for Sickles to retire to the new line.

Lee remained determined to smash the Federal salient. Stuart was to continue the assault, and the two sections of the army would join behind Chancellorsville and drive the Federals into the river. Anderson and McLaws moved to support Stuart, who seized Hazel Grove, one mile west of Chancellorsville, and placed 31 guns there, from which he commanded the crossroads at Chancellorsville and Best's position at Fairview Cemetery. Couch ordered a general withdrawal to the Mineral Spring Road. Griffin took charge of a line of cannon to cover the retreat, growling "I'll make 'em think hell isn't half a mile off!" Jackson's Corps stormed the Union lines, but were driven back repeatedly by the defenders and by a furious bombardment from Griffin at Fairview Cemetery, which now became the focus of the Rebel assault. Stuart's cannon at Hazel Grove opened on Fairview, and the Federals started to fall back. The Union line, breached at the Cemetery, gave way, and the two parts of the Confederate army joined up.

The Federal commanders discussed whether a withdrawal could be safely effected. Hooker stated his belief that he could withdraw the army without loss. When the vote was taken Meade, Reynolds and Howard voted for an advance, and Sickles and Couch for a withdrawal. Hooker announced that he would take upon himself the responsibility of withdrawing. As the officers left the tent, Reynolds exclaimed: "What was the use of calling us together at this time of night when he intended to retreat anyhow?"

At Fredericksburg, the Federals finally drove Early from the town. Beyond Chancellorsville, Hooker's men braced themselves along the Mineral Spring Road for Lee's final attack. It never came; Lee's troops were exhausted. McLaws was sent to join Early, but it was not until 6 p.m. on May 4th that the Confederate artillery opened fire on Sedgwick's horseshoe-shaped position between Fredericksburg and Salem Church, and it achieved nothing, Sedgwick, under cover of darkness, falling back across Banks' Ford. On the 5th, a still-dazed Hooker ordered a general withdrawal; Lee's exhausted army could only pursue weakly, and Stuart's artillery had exhausted its ammunition.

Johnson and the 16th recrossed the river with the army at United States Ford. Hooker was almost the first man to cross the river. At midnight (5th-6th) Meade sent word to Couch that the river was over the bridges, that Hooker was on the other side, and that communication with him was cut off. Couch immediately rode over to Hooker's late Headquarters, and satisfied himself that he was in command of the army. He proceeded with Sickles and Reynolds to Meade's Headquarters to confer as to what should be done, and told Meade that the crossing was suspended. "We will stay where we are", he said, "and fight it out." Meade was not satisfied with the situation in which Couch had placed him and sent to Hooker for orders, to be told that the order for a retreat was imperative, and at 2 a.m. Couch received a sharp message from Hooker about crossing the army as he had directed.

The battle was over, the 1st Massachusetts history merely observing: "At daylight Tuesday [the 5th] ... all was quiet again... and... about noon, preparations were made by Gen. Hooker to abandon his position, and fall back across the river. Pioneers... were at once set to work, repairing the old roads... A furious thunderstorm, which broke forth at four in the afternoon, was of material advantage in these operations... Before three o'clock the next morning, all the guns, wagons and mule trains were across; and the passage of the infantry began... As the rain continued falling nearly all night, it rendered the passage of the river unusually hazardous, and reduced the roads to such a condition, that the troops were splashed with mud from head to foot. In this condition, they plodded wearily along to their old camping-grounds, a fourth time foiled and disappointed in their advance upon Richmond..."

It had been a brilliant victory for Lee, but he had lost some 13,000 men, and on May 10th came crushing news; Stonewall Jackson was dead, from pneumonia. As President Jefferson Davis put it at his funeral, "A great national calamity has befallen us."

h

There is no indication of exactly when Charles Johnson was wounded, other than a medical note specifying that it was on the 3rd. The 16th was clearly in the heat of battle from late on May 2nd, when Sickles' 3rd Corps found itself the main obstacle to disaster for the Army of the Potomac following the collapse of Howard's 11th Corps, through the subsequent two days' fighting in the dangerous salient which developed

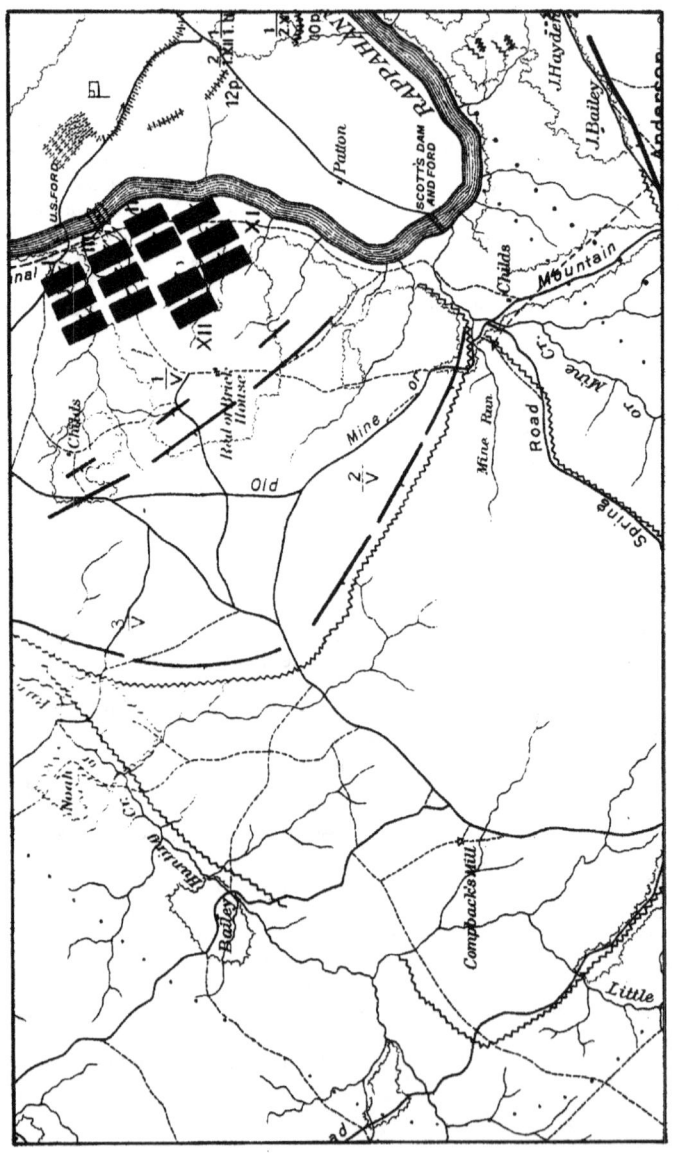

Chancellorsville - position of Army of the Potomac at 5 a.m., May 6, 1863
(from Bigelow, 1910, Map 39)

between the two main parts of the Confederate army. Johnson could have been wounded at any time during the 3rd. Since, too, Johnson went home to recover after his wound, there are no letters describing Chancellorsville, as he would have been able to relate whatever he wished directly to his friends and family at home. In view of the 16th's critical role in holding Jackson's attack, the absence of a letter covering this part of the battle is particularly regrettable.

All we have covering this period, therefore, are two documents; the first is the brief description of his wounding and journey back to Washington contained in the anonymous manuscript, probably written by his wife on the basis of what Johnson told her, now in the collections of the Massachusetts Historical Society:-

"At the battle of Chancellorsville Capt. Johnson was wounded there he could not obtain an ambulance, altho there was several standing entirely unemployed. in fact he said he had rather walk the fifteen miles to get a conveyance to Washington than to ride in an ambulance, So he and others footed that distance and arrived in Washington good while in advance of those that waited for ambulances. Another officer in the same Regt wounded in the same battle said the thought of going into battle, or getting wounded, or the suffering he experienced in loosing his arm were nothing at all compared with his riding in the ambulance off the battle field after having his arm amputated. The poor fellow said it would be the death of him. It was, for he finally died of exhaustion. If he had had proper conveyance after his arm was amputated his life would have been spared so said the Surgeon and other officers."

The second is the Medical Certificate from Johnson's service record, dated Washington, D.C., May 6, 1863, by Surgeon Charles Mayo, certifying that "he is suffering from a Gun Shot Wound of right side of face, received in action near Chancellorsville Va. May 3, 1863. The jaw is not injured" and approving Johnson's application for leave of absence that he will not be able to resume his duties in a less period than "twenty days without risk of permanent disability"[233] . He must have received twenty days' leave, to which period he apparently adhered dutifully, since his next letter to Nellie is from Camp near Falmouth, dated May 27th.

****

Sunday Jan. 25 / 63   Camp near Falmouth
Dear Nellie,
I have just finished perusing the proceedings of Gen'l Porter's Court Martial[234] . He deserves richly his sentence although the Government loses a good officer. He forgot his duty as a soldier the object for which he was fighting everything was forgotten except his animosity towards Gen'l Pope. The proceedings of the court reviewed by the Judge Advicate [sic] is well worth reading and it will be one of the principle items in the history of the war. If the conclusion of the court, that, if Genl

---

[233] Document in National Archives

[234] Maj.-Gen. Fitz John Porter, charged by Pope with disobedience of orders at 2nd Bull Run. Although the incident arose from Pope's failure to grasp the circumstances on the field, Porter's intense dislike of Pope - well known in the army, as Johnson's comment confirms - and his unswerving loyalty to McClellan, was taken at the time to confirm that the disobedience was deliberate, in order to bring about Pope's ruin on the battlefield, and Porter was found guilty. It was not until 1879 that Porter finally obtained a Board of Inquiry, which exonerated him on all charges, and not until 1881 that he was reinstated in the army. In 1885 Lincoln's former Secretary John Hay described Porter as "the most magnificent soldier in the Army of the Potomac, ruined by his devotion to McClellan." The transcript of the court martial is the subject of a full volume of the Official Records: Series I, Vol. XII, supplementary volume.

Porter had followed out faithfully his orders that the rebel army would have suffered a severe defeat, has good foundation and I believe it has, the faithlessness of Genl Porter has not been sufficiently punished. There is no use in recurring to past mistakes unless it be for experience sake and I hope the government will profit by it. I have received your letters of 19th, 19th [sic] 21st Also Adams Express bill. I intended to have written a long letter today but several little things have prevented me. Send me the price of the pipe father sent me it is not exactly what I wanted and I have sold it to an officer, what I wanted of a meerschaum pipe was to watch it coloring. Give my regards to all. I am glad you have such good prospects and think you will have a pleasant time at father's. Berk is doing well I am glad of it.
    Yours affectionately   Charles

****

                              Camp near Falmouth   Jan 26 /63

Dear Nellie,
    We have been under marching orders for three days, but now I think we shall start. It is now 10 o'clock, tents struck blankets rolled up. I am pretty confident that we shall see the enemy and God grant us success. I hope in my next to be able to congratulate our selves on a victory. I have received your letters of the 6th 9th 13th & 15th. I send you a pipe made by my self from laurel root, it is very uncouth and is not finished as well as I should have it on account of the move. Give my regards to all. aff
    Charley

****

                         Jan 31st / 62 [63]   Camp near Falmouth, Va.

Dear Nellie,
    It is now late in the evening and I thought I would commence a letter to you and send it tomorrow. When I sent my last letter it was snowing and when I awoke the next morning (Thursday) I found everything clothed in white the woods looked elegantly and I doubt if a lover of nature could come to a conclusion which impressed him the most, the quite, white sparkling dress of winter or the rustling green or various hues of which summer clothes the forests. The forests in summer although they abstract enchant and appeal to all the best sentiments of the abitue yet there is about us working quietly natures vast production power of recreating and assimilating which fills us with wonder. If I was to form an analogy, it would be of busy life with all its vicissitude; large trees firmly rooted overlooking the landscape looking as if they would last for ever the solid oak and the various kinds of that class walnut and the like claims the resources of the earth beneath them, while the saplings, twigs and bushes tribute their small mite for the privilege of picking the crumbs of these sovereigns of the forest, these young upstarts may have the germ of a sovereign in them the goal is so distance that they bend to every wind and bow to every animal and husband their resources for a long journey, whilst there are others who start up bound to become great in moments, to exhaust their nerves drain their resources and die. Under the pine and lower class of wood grow but little healthy brush unless it is the humble berries, the pines who force nature and are gay through the year seem to be unable to share with anything their living, they grow stately & tall but never command the respect like the first class. Here in the forests you see what is expected of each tree according to his talents and each one works to accomplish its end, whether it be grand or humble, each meets its reverses and has its enemy to contend with the worm and the insect claiming to use the proceeds of their labor and draw

often so heavy as to eat out the heart of their supporters. In the forest in summers you perceive the distant gifts nature has bestowed and the striking distinction in the paths which each has to follow this is in summer when the woods are clothed with verdure; but in winter when snow embraces the forest, covers it in linen of whitest fabrics there is no analogy with busy life their is nothing worldly about it unless it be nuns in white in their cloisters, it would rather reminds us of some stage in the future world where the purifying of the soul commenced, there is no distinction of kind or variety except in the size and posture, some are erect others are humbly bowed down often in groups, while there are others perhaps unworthy uprooted to rise no more. The soft snow flake like the bosom feather of the dove drops noiselessly like a modest tribute to some departed. But the striking contrasts is the light as the ray of the sun shines & pierces the snow at every angle, light is analysed and the rainbow of promise is seen. There is a desire to withdraw from a vision so dazzling which seems to be beyond the threshold of death and as you turn your back, impressed solemnly with the brilliant yet pure scenery from the sun the cool damp air strikes you in the face as if you were passing through the tomb into life and were about to shut out scenes of another world. What is the matter with Charley! What has got into him? Nothing, Nellie, only I think I must have lately ended a stage of seven years when some people say there is a change in feelings and us[?]. The fact is that a camp life is so monotonous and having grown tired of depending on euchre and other games of cards and there being such a scarcity of reading that I took to writing but the writing fever will be short. Thursday & Friday nights were sufficiently cold to freeze the ground solid but not deep enough to better the condition of the roads which you can judge are in an awful condition the sun of Thursday and Friday having melted the snow and the wagon mixing it with the soil have render what boys would call hasty pudding of the roads. The roads Friday morning could be distinctly traced as far as the eye could view resembling a black ink line winding here & there in striking contrasts with the snow on either side of it. How the trees disappear; when we arrived in this place the woods were difficulty entered so thick were they now a wagon can drive most any where. To the rear of our camp every tree has disappeared clearing a large tract of land giving quite a pleasant view, informing us that we were on quite high land.[235] The view resembles <u>our</u> view from Lexington only we do not seem to look down on it as we do there it seems to be more on our level yet displays a remarkably hilly country. In a clear day Bull Run Ridge rises to the sky, in the rear of the landscape, forming as you might say a background. I have received your favors of the 22nd, 25 & 27 also a short one from Austin, tell him it is the best letter I have received from him both in composition and writing and shows marked improvement over any of the first ones. Devine Descriptive list[236] will be sent as soon as I can satisfy myself of the whereabouts of the old one; I have written to the hospital concerning it, Sunday morning. Last night had a game of chess the chess board was made from the end of a cracker box and the men made from the red and white cedar wood they are roughly made but answer every purpose. My opponents were as green as myself and I rather gained an advantage. Father is to sell the Lexington place, pecuniary I suppose it is for the best, besides it was an additional expense to us when we lived there only for the summer though perhaps we felt enough better for it. When I come home for good I can settle in some place where we can make up our minds to remain stationary for awhile. The weather today if it were not for the snow on the ground would be mild. I

---

[235] The armies' insatiable demand for timber, for fuel, shelter, defence, etc., inevitably resulted in the mass felling of trees wherever they were.

[236] See letter of Nov. 23, 1862

have often thought in riding pass woods when seeing large trees uprooted and evidently protected enough from the wind to render it impossible for that element to do it, the cause, and this last snow storm explained it to me; a tree with an inclination to it or not firmly rooted succumbs to the immense weight that nature in the shape of snow piles on it. There is no talk of a move although there are indications that the going may be better. I received from you two illustrated papers. Father's papers come regularly and are much enjoyed. If there could be any means for obtaining a supply of books one might improve himself greatly but as it is ones mind goes to weeds. The army will be the father of a great many sins. I am well and in excellent spirits and enjoying myself. Give my regards to all.　　　　Yours afftly　　　　Charles

****

Sunday Feb. 8th [1863] Camp near Falmouth Va.

Dear Nellie,

Yesterday afternoon we returned from a three days tramp[237] , and it is to it you owe the loss of your letter in the middle of the week. Wednesday evening I played euchre[238] with the doctor & Col & major of the regiment until ten o'clock, then retired with the knowledge that at an early hour of the next morning there was to be a disagreeable brigade inspection, inspections have become quite common lately too often to be enjoyed. I had fairly resigned myself to sleep when somebody called Capt. Johnson awakening me, on my answering informed me that I was to have cooked immediately three days rations and be ready to march at six o'clock tomorrow morning leaving shelter tents & tents standing; this order was unexpected and for a moment caused some bustling in camp but it soon subsided or rather I soon went to sleep. Thursday morning approach and before I was up I was told that it was trying to snow and good prospects of an old fashioned snow storm, weather cold and foundation good. After a hasty breakfast and the usual standing around we formed line and to appearances was the only line formed; after we had become quite cold we stacked arms broke ranks with orders to fall in promptly when notified. Instantly made for my tent where there was a good fire, warmed myself and laid down and soon fell fast asleep. I was awoken when the order came to fall in and this time after some delay we made a start. By this time the snow in small flakes was falling fast and the ground was already covered with white, but the men were in good spirits, the walking being good and the snow so dry that it could be easily shaken off and not melting and wetting their coats. We proceeded at a quick pace our brigade leading the division, which by the way was the entire infantry force ~~with us~~ of the expedition, until we arrived at Gen'l Stoneman's Headquarters where there was a long halt. Whilst we are marching the activity of the body overcomes the effect of the cold by the animal heat it creates and when we halt in the road for a little while the men soon commence to complain of the cold. We stopped at Gen'l Stoneman's so long that some thought that our whatever it was was to be abandoned. Now we could not tell but what we were going on picket few thought we were but the majority thought that we were to make a reconnaissance for some object. After a while we started and marched in the direction we took on our previous grand move but soon inclined to the right. The weather which the soldier watches with as much solicitude as a mariner began to indicate a change, the flakes of snow increased in size and dampness and occasionally we felt a drop we

---

[237] Johnson is here probably describing what Dyer refers to as "Operations at Rappahannock Bridge and Grove Church," Feb. 5-7, in which the 16th took part.

[238] A card game widely popular in 19th century America.

feared of rain. Now if anyone could have been transported from a comfortable fireside and confronted with our army they would have thought us soldiers of Gen'l Jack Frost; men's hair and whiskers were plastered with snow icicles hanging wherever their breath coagulated, in fact we corresponded so well with nature around in appearance that there was but little contrast. We continued our march until we arrived at the outer picket (infantry) where we met a large force of cavalry consisting of detachments of different regiments among them was some part of the Mass 1st cavalry. Here we were some little time before we again took up the march. The cavalry trotted past us accompanied by a battery of flying artillery which rumbled along after the cavalry quite lively (the difference between a flying battery and others is that the cannoneers are mounted instead of walking or riding on the ammunition chests). The object of our scout was for the first time conjectured; we learned that a small force of Stuart cavalry[239] had been hovering about, the 1st Mass cavalry having had a *slap* at them losing one man[240], and we were to cut off their retreat if possible. The road we took led us through forests most of the way occasionally passing a brick house made in the northern manner (the chimney in the house and not outside) showing comfort and prosperity; the road was evidently an old stage road, the telegraph wires were parallel with it and here and there was what once was a country store perhaps post-office near which was generally a church. We went but little farther, the cavalry going ahead and we filing into the woods to make ourselves comfortable for the night. The snow had now turned into rain the men's clothes were damp and the prospects were cheerless, but we soon had a large fire under way gathered cedar boughs to keep us from the ground as we slept; pitched our shelter tents (the men using their rubber blankets for protection, their shelter tents being left behind) the opening towards the fire, stopped the opposite end with a rubber blanket; our house for the night was thus soon built. Coffee was made and supper eat and we were ready to try to sleep. Lt Hills had on the march slept together with me but tonight there were to be three of us and then there was sufficient room. I slept in the middle, directly over my face there was an opening caused by the rubber blanket not joining well the ends of the tents, I was immediately made aware of it by a large drop of rain falling on my face strange to say it annoyed me but happened to think of placing my towel over the hole which stopped it. The men which Lt Hills & myself have to wait on us felt so uncomfortable that they concluded to keep a good fire and not go to sleep and they did keep up such a fire that I was uncomfortably warm. I always make a practice of sleeping in bare feet having my stocking dried by the fire before I go to sleep and keeping them dry until I put them on, and soaping my heel & instep on the inside of my boots to enable me to get them on, and it is only by doing so have I been able to keep my feet sound. At four o'clock Friday morning whisky was given the men but the sergeant to whom was intrusted the distribution of it was himself corned[?] and consequently the men took advantage of it some of them getting over a qt, getting themselves drunk, and depriving one third of the regiment of their proportion. At the hour of sunrise we started, it still raining, the rain converting the snow into slosh and snow water, covering the ice also which deceived many a soldier causing them to go in over boots. We marched pretty rapidly over the continuance of the same road as yesterday, I learnt it was called the Ridge road, until we arrived near the Rappahannock Gold mines, where the roads forked, here our army divided, part going one way to the Rappahannock Station I imagine and we the other to the United States Ford opposite which we encamped. On our way to it

---

[239] The Cavalry of the Army of Northern Virginia, under the overall command of Maj.-Gen. James. E.B. Stuart.

[240] i.e. in the action at Rappahannock Bridge, Feb. 5.

we passed several houses & work shops steam boilers and crushing and grinding machines for pulverising quartz, this placid[241], called the Rappahannock Gold Mines, once yielded 15 to twenty dollars worth of gold dust per diem even then it could not have paid, whether it was worked recently or not I didn't find out. I saw a piece of quartz having small pieces of gold embedded in it but the labor of extraction must cost more than the yield. When we arrived opposite the ford we filed into the woods to encamp for the night about 3/4 of a mile from the river. The weather which had been showing sign of change actually did change for the better, the rain ceased and soon we had the pleasure of seeing the sun, the wind changed around to the north and gradually grew colder. I now found out the object of the exhibition [expedition] which was to destroy the bridge at Rappahannock Station, we were here to prevent and counter raid of the rebel in our rear by the way of this ford. While here we kept ourselves in readiness to repel any attack caused by the enemies curiosity. After I had prepaird for the night, I left the woods and went onto a hill overlooking the ford where I obtained a good view of the earthworks & rifle pits thrown up by the enemy on Burnsides last move it being reported that he was to cross by this ford. I can't believe that 8 simple earth works for light field pieces and a long rifle pit all of which commanded by the hill on which I was could prevent or change his plans, there was more to fear from the woods on the top of the hill, which gradually ascended from the river, covering masked batteries and their making use of house and the fences around it for protection than from these simple earthworks. The rebels had two picket post at the ford of 4 men each and on observing our pickets asked them "to come over" the[y] belonged to the 4th Va & - Georgia regiment. The rebel camp fires could be seen in the woods to the rear of the river in all directions in some places the smoke indicated a large force. I must close and send by todays mail. Our object was accomplished the bridge was burnt with the loss as far as I can ascertain of 4 men whether wounded or killed I know not. In my next I will write about our return to camp. I have received your letters of Jan 29th & Feb'y 1st. Today Gen'l Sickles takes command of Corp D'Armee and I understand that he has a spread and believe has invited the field officers of the Corp. Lt. Hills has a sore heel, otherwise well. Mrs Turner in her letter to Lt Hills tell of her seeing Berk and what he said, corresponds to what you wrote. Wheather pleasant. Give my regards to all

    Yours affly   Charley

****

[address indistinct; no date, but must come between letters of 8 and 17 February, 1863[242]]

Dear Nellie,

In my last I promised to write you how we arrived home. Friday evening passed quietly and the next morning we awoke before daylight with a bright moon shining on us. The morning was fine for marching, cold the roads frozen solid in some

---

[241] Johnson here means "placer", the deposit from which the gold is washed in the separation process.

[242] In view of the first sentence, this letter must follow the letter dated Feb. 8th. However, one-third of the way through the letter, Johnson makes reference ot being paid "last Sunday", which he specifies as being Feb. 1st, indicating that no more than a week had passed since the 1st. This letter must therefore also have been written on the 8th; the end of the letter dated 8th indicates that he finished it in order to catch the day's post; Johnson must therefore have finished detailing his experiences in this second letter on the same day.

places uneven yet mostly smooth & icy in fact the first part of our march might have been done with skates. We passed the Rappahannock Gold Mines[243] at a smart gate the invigorating weather making the men gay. But as the day passed and the sun arose higher the effects of the heat became evident and the marching became more difficult, the pace was too rapid to last without telling on the men, in fact we were to do in one day what we had been two days about. After we had march until noon we discovered that we were near the woods that we encamped on the recent move of Gen'l Burnside.[244] The road now increased in the depth of mud and the travelling was becoming bad fast. Dinner is not in the programme of a soldier on the march no matter how tedious and there was but few rests and those short. We took up new road over fields and hills through vallies, jumping creeks and climbing hills until we arrived nearly home. At last our camp was in sight which help us along and about three o'clock in the afternoon I was resting my weary limbs on my bed in my home. This march although twice the length of the march on the return of the grand army from the unsuccessful move of Gen'l Burnside yet it did not fatigue me as much, though I was an exception; there was more officer and men fell out on this last day march than in the previous march of Gen'l Burnside. I saw one so exhausted that when he fell over he was perfectly helpless and was carried in an ambulance. In our first days march to indicate to you how cold it was I have only to relate that the mens canteens containing water were so frozen they they were obliged to force their bayonet into the mouth of their canteens to enabling them to obtain a small supply of partially congealed water yet we all preferred cold weather with good roads than warm with poor travelling. How important our success I know not but the paper will soon inform me. There are rumors that the ninth army corp is to go out west, another rumors says they are to go to Newbern, another yet say that they they have already started for the latter place. Last Sunday late in the afternoon (Feb. 1st) our paymaster arrived and immediately commenced paying off the regiment, Sunday you see is but little respected in the army as far as work is considered, and succeed in completely finishing his work that night so as to leave at about 11 o'clock. He paid us only up to Nov. 1st The officers having deducted from their pay the three per cent tax and also a reduction of two dollars per month in servants wages. Monday morning Dr Jewett commence to stir about Col. Wyman's monument which you know has been long talked off and some action taking in the manner [matter], the family at the regiment suggestion buying a lot at Mt Auburn and selecting two models for a monument.[245] My company being of a class that does not take much interest in these things I was oblige to subscribe twenty dollars; at twelve o'clock the same day the regiment had nearly raised 500.00 dollars which is doing well considering that the men were only paid for one half the time the government owed them and the numerous debts especially with the sutler contracted during the last five months. I shall send $100.00 home at the first opportunity, you must let me know the state of your treasury once in a while so I can see you do not get short. There is not enough healthy competition between the sutlers they all I imagine make money enough to satisfy the most greedy, all else the government places so many obstacles in their way that the trouble is great

---

[243] Gold was not only found in the far West. Gold deposits have been found in Virginia from Fairfax County southwest to the Lynchburg area. There was a particular concentration of mines in the Fredericksburg area along the Rapidan and Rappahannock Rivers. Mining continued there from the early 19th century until the 1940s.

[244] i.e. the notorious "Mud March", Jan. 20-24.

[245] See illustration 32.

and the cost in proportion it does seem to men as a perfect swindle between somebody which forces the soldier to obtain comfort, generally poor at such enormass prices, the men if they have the means will buy what they desire at any cost, and who can blame them; confine any one to the same diet for eighteen months with but little change and they would feel as the soldier does. I received whilst on the march three days papers they were welcome. There would be an universal joy among us if we could move away from this tremendous mud hole an[d] the idea of going out west or down south would content the men anything but being mired here any longer. Col Blaisdale [Blaisdell] has had command of our brigade for some time owing to the absence of Gen'l Carr; the men have laid the blame of the severity of the march on his shoulders and have nick-named him "Old Cruelty", they say he stopped a man on the last march and asked him to what regiment do you belong? he answered 5th N. Jersey, Col Blaisdell says "Why don't you wash your face and hands they look as if they had not been washed since they were *issued* to you". We have now settled into our usual monotonous routine of camp life and there will be but little to write. The weather has been since our return to camp quite mild, in fact little birds resembling ground sparrows can frequently seen and heard, I saw on our march home a solitary old bird probably lost. Enclosed in this letter you will find $100.00 which will be brought you by my 1st Sergt, a well educated gentlemanly fellow and who will soon received his promotion, a Lieutenancy[246] . Enclosed also you will find a star from our old flag which had been torn out it has been in every battle with the regiment and is now on the retired list. I wish you would have it framed nicely for memories sake. Enclosed or rather accompanying this letter there will be a cigar holder and perhaps a pipe the latter I have not yet received made from laurel root made by Sergt Harrington of Co F. I have given a list of articles which I would like to have sent out to me by Sergt R.J.Lombard and you might include some reading matter if you have any around. The list I believe is two thin flannel drawers, 3 prs merino wool socks, a piece of rhubard[sic] root and a lb of mild fine cut smoking tobacco. I have received your letter of Feb. 3rd also pictorial. Capt Wiley[247] & Capt Donovan start for home tomorrow on ten days leave of Absence after they get back two other officers will apply and my turn may come (doubtful very) in a months. Capt Wiley carries the old flag with him. The "Johnnies" are awaking on naval affairs, I am glad to see that the affair off Charleston harbor[248] was considerably exaggerated it will be a good lesson for them, the blockading fleet. Give my regards to all. Yrs aff Charley

****

Feb. 17 /63   Camp near Fal. Va.
Dear Nellie,
    I have received yours of Feb. 1st, 3rd, 8th & 10th also one from Mother of Feb.

---

[246] Richard J. Lombard, born Truro, Mass., in 1839, was a 22-year-old student from Waltham, Mass., when he enlisted on June 29, 1861 as a Private. He received promotions through 2nd Lt., Dec. 1, 1862; 1st Lt. April 4, 1863; Capt., Dec. 12, 1863. On July 11, 1864 he transferred to the 11th Mass. Inf., and mustered out on October 20, 1864, having fought in most of the major battles of the eastern theatre. After the war he was a member of GAR post 29, Waltham., Mass.

[247] John Wiley, resigned Aug. 26, 1863.

[248] On January 31, 1863, the Confederate Rams *Chicora* and *Palmetto State* attacked the Federal blockading fleet off Charleston, sinking and damaging several ships. Confederate claims that the Blockade had been broken were, however, over-optimistic.

5th. Last evening we returned from picket duty of four days we not receiving any notification that we were to go on picket until late in the evening when we were informed that we were to start with three days cooked rations at seven the next morning. It is now snowing with an inch or two of snow on the ground which will make the roads impassable. I see that our brigade are building bake houses and from that in connection with the weather I think that there will be no move at present. I have been disappointed about my box twice, the regiment has received one lot of boxes from Adams express but mine was not in it, and the regiment has another invoice of one box which was not mine. The boxes sent by Mr Stewart of Roxbury have arrived, Lt. Hills has received his. Enclosed a letter which I received from England in reference to one of my men shot June 18[249] , keep it. I shall close now as I have something to do. Give my regards to all.   aff   Charley

****

Feb. 19 /63   Camp near Falmouth

Dear Nellie,

Since I last wrote we have had very severe weather, having in the first place quite a heavy snow storm which finally turned into rain. I wish you would ask father if he knows the direction of John Flynn the man that lost his arm[250] , if he could see him ask him by whose order he was discharged, to enable me to write and obtain official information of it. I have nineteen men absent sick and I am not advised of the whereabouts of but few of them. I have not received the box yet. Sent Patrick Flarty's[251] descriptive list to father he will see that the man receives it. "All quiet on the Potomac"[252] . Give my regards to all.

Yours aff   Charley

****

Feb. 23rd /63   Camp near Falmouth Va.

Dear Nellie,

I never felt less like writing than now. I have received your letters of 15th & 16th. Lt. Lombard was assigned to my company and is now in the tent with me. That pipe from father is a splendid one, I shall endeavor to take good care of it. I suppose you must have had a severe snow storm as here in Virginia there is no contempable

---

[249] The 16th suffered considerable casualties in the two actions of June 18, 1862 and this soldier, presumably an Englishman, is as yet unidentified. Five men of Co. F were killed, but the birthplace of only one has so far been identified - John Allen, born in Canada.

[250] John Flynn, an 18-year old labourer from Lowell, enlisted as Private, Co. F, July 12, 1861. He received a severe wound in the arm at Glendale, June 30, 1862, as a result of which the arm was amputated. Atfer the war he was a member of GAR Posts 19 (Fitchburg) and 80 (Westborough) and died on Nov. 15, 1931.

[251] Sergeant Patrick Flatery, discharged for disability Aug. 18, 1863

[252] A popular catch-phrase in the North, originating in cynical newspaper comments about McClellan's inactivity between his taking command of the Army of the Potomac in mid-1861 and his first major movement in the Spring of 1862. The phrase became the title of a melancholy song telling of a picket, patrolling at night, thinking of his family at home and close to tears; he sees a a distant flash, hears something rustling the leaves in the trees – and falls, killed by an enemy bullet. The irony of the media focus on the deaths of officers over that of mere privates is made clear in the line: "Not an officer lost –only one of the men". As he is described neither as north or south, the song became popular on both sides.

[sic] amount of snow, in fact it would make sleighing for a week. It has cleared up and a bright sun will shrink up the snow fast. Last night was very cold but severe cold weather does not last long here. I expect to have rain soon. Salutes were fired yesterday in honor of Washington's birth day. I enjoy my evenings very much now there are plenty of books about. I am much oblige for those which you sent. That tobacco was what I wanted thank John for it. Lt. Lombard say he had a very pleasant call. Every thing remarkably quiet here. Drawers fit like a drum head. Excuse the shortness of this and give my regards to all.

        Yours aff   Charley

****

       Feb. 26th /63   Camp near Falmouth Va.

Dear Nellie,

  I learn from Lt. Lombard you expect me home on leave of absence which there is no chance of my obtaining. I have applied and it was forwarded and approved as far as it went but was sent back to the adjutants office to comply with an order issued after it was forwarded, that was its death. Col Banks give the preference to all officers who have never been home, he came so tardily to that conclusion that I had hopes but now they are dispelled. You must not entertain any idea that I shall be able to come home. Today is has [sic] rained very hard and the snow has disappeared accordingly, the prospects are that, tomorrow will be a fine day and you can now obtain an occasional glimpse of the moon. We have now large details from our brigade to work on corduroy roads to enable us to bring supplies to the army. I have received your letter of Feb. 19 also one from Austin which shows great improvement. I send you a photograph of Capt. Wiley one of the 16th Captains. Our cavalry videttes were driven in lately, relying on the high state of the river as protection, they became careless and the rebels swam across, captured 25 horses and wounded several men.[253] Such raids dampen the ardor of our men and increases the desire of the rebels for more of the same. Received your letter of Feb. 22nd today. Give my regards to all.

        Yours aff   Charley

****

       Mch. 1st, 63 Camp near Fal[mouth], Va.

Dear Nellie,

  Today is the first day of spring and from today I hoped the government will be able to report nothing but favorable news until the war has ended. We are having a mild day with gentle rain which gives evidence that spring in reality is approaching and we shall soon have warm weather. Birds are warbling and hopping about lively during the day and in the night stow themselves away how and where I know not, but when the morning put an end to cold night they are alive and playful. You are disappointed at my not coming home on a leave, but you must consider it all for the best and imagine me as comfortably situated, so comfortably in fact that I desire no better. Reading matter has become so plenty and my time so little taken up evening that when I combine the time killing game of chest [sic] with interesting reading I find but little difficulty in contenting myself. I will send my gold pencil point so that you can send me some leads and I wish you would buy a bottle of red ink and send with

---

[253] The only cavalry action mentioned by Dyer at this period in which Union forces suffered casualties was a skirmish at Ashby's Gap on Feb. 19. In this action, the casualties were, however, more than "several men" - according to Dyer, 6 killed, 19 wounded and 64 missing.

my watch by one of the returning officers. I hear that there are some express boxes at division H'd Q'rs being roughly handled by Provost Marshal[254] . The news from N. Carolina is not of a cheering nature neither is that from N. Orleans and vicinity[255] but they only delay and do not expect the results it is to be hoped. I should like a new photograph of yourself & Berk; send it. I have received your letter of Feb. 22nd. Tell father if the result at the factory was not as favorable as wished last year, what will they be unless the price of soap increases in proportion with the raw material we shall have another; that is the mercantile world, another 1857 before long[256] . Send, if you have the opportunity, two color hankerchiefs. Give my regards to all.

 Yours Afftly   Charles

****

             Mch. 5 /63 Camp near Fal. Va.

Dear Nellie,

I received your letter of Feb. 27th and was surprised to learn that you had been a week without hearing from me, some letters must have been miscarried. I would like take tea with you, Capt. Dallas & Lt. Tucker but it will be impossible while the war last I am afraid. Don't forget to send me a photograph of yourself & Berk, won't it do as well as coming home. Tell father to write what they are doing to meet the present high price of tallow here and the small profit with [which] must be the result of shipping to England tallow oil it burns quite dull there. I have given up looking for that box so has Mr. Hills for his barrel that was sent him. We have nearly completed a corduroy road to Belle Plain it passes through our camp it is not as well made as might be but it may answer the purpose for which it was made. I wrote a letter to Lt. Tucker yesterday. I send my pencil point in this letter, it should have gone by the last. There is nothing transpiring & nothing that appears like a move. We have drills to day and nothing comes harder to me than to be obliged to drill my company the men take but little interest. We have had some genuine March weather, squall accompanied with rain and snow lasting perhaps 20 minutes, then it would be pleasant again. Mrs Richardson & Mrs Banks are still here. I imagine they will soon return with Major Richardson. There is nothing to write about. Excuse the shortness of my letter. A private of my company James Cairnes couldn't obtain his discharge has now gone home on furlough of 10 days I am afraid he will not arrive home he was so reduced by Diarrhea, he lives in Cottage Place, Tremont St, Roxbury[257] . Give my regards to all.

      Yours aff   Charley

---

[254] The Provost Marshal was responsible for army police duties. It is unclear why they would be handling soldiers' parcels, which would normally have been distributed through the army postal service or, more commonly, by the Adams Express Company.

[255] It is uncertain to what Johnson is referring here; there appears to be little news coming out of either areas in the press of the day. The news coming out of New Orleans may perhaps relate to the slow progress of the Yazoo Pass expedition in the Vicksburg area.

[256] The "Panic of 1857" was a major financial crisis which would have still been fresh in the memories of businessmen of the day.

[257] James Carnes [not Cairnes], a 19-year-old papermaker, enlisted July 12, 1861. His discharge for disability came through on March 17, 1863.

****

Mch. 8th /63   Camp near Fal. Va

Dear Nellie,

I was pleasantly surprised to find the long looked for box day before yesterday. It seemed me [sic] to hold more than any box of that size could; every thing was in good condition and I am now enjoying it. I think you & I better make up our minds that Capt. Johnson remains in the service during the war as I don't see how he can get out of it. I am very sorry I did not write to Gov. Andrew to obtain a Lieutency [sic] in one of the new batteries as their is no situation so uncomfortable as infantry captain or who has so few conveniences compared with his rank in other services. I suppose there are no more chances now. A mounted 2nd Lt. or private in cavalry dont know the hardships of a campaign compared with a foot officers. Thank Mrs Billings for her gift it was appreciated. I have received your favors of Feb. 24 & Mch. 1st Our weather is mild & showery keeping the roads about so. Every thing is quiet here and their is no reason to expect any active movements for some time. Those walnuts went like hot cakes and are with raisins very much liked about nine o'clock of an evening.

Every thing is so quiet here that unless I take interests in politics I can't find anything to write about. That report about Vicksburg was a cruel hoax an editors should be more careful in spreading rumors without foundation[258] . You must not wait for me to come home before you have Lieut. Dallas[259] to tea if you do it will be indefinitely postponed. My pipe is coloring handsome. Give my regards to all.

               Yours aff   Charley

****

Mch. 11 /63   Camp near Falmouth Va.

Dear Nellie,

I have received your letters of Mch 3rd & 5th. I have received your photographs and am much pleased with them, should better like to see the original. Every thing quiet about here and it is impossible to write any news or even anything. Capt Amory[260] & Capt Lamson have returned my watch & red ink I shall obtain tomorrow, they being in his valise. Thank John for that tobacco. Sergt King of my company will probably be at home soon so will also Lt Hills. I think you had better send by either Sergt or Lt. Hills two lbs of mild tobacco. I should like pair of boots size 8 with broad heels & soles, with steel nails on the outside of the heel to prevent them running over; I think that there will be but little chance to send them as there will be but little convenience for any one returning to bring a large bundle, but if you should have a chance send a pair. Berk has change[d] some and I desire to see him very much, he doesn't look like you he seem homely enough to be a Johnson. The weather is very changeable rarely having over twenty four hours pleasant. Mch 12 '63 6 A.M. going on picket now. Give my regards to all.   Yrs Aff   Charley

****

---

[258] Possibly this relates to Grant's unsuccessful attempt to dig a canal across a neck of the Mississippi river below Vicksburg to enable the U.S. river fleet to by-pass the guns of the city's defences. This was reported at the time in the Boston newspapers, but was not a hoax.

[259] Alexander J. Dallas, killed at Chancellorsville, May 3, 1863.

[260] William A. Amory became Major, 2nd Mass. Heavy Artillery, July 31, 1863.

Mch. 16 /63   Camp near Fal. Va.
Dear Nellie,
I have received your letters of Feb. 12, Mch. 8 & 10th, the one dated Feb. 12th was stamped Mch. 3rd at Boston P.O. Sergt. King, now orderly sergt. of my company, left this morning for home, also Capt Roche[261] & Lt. Hills. Serg't King says he will bring out to me any small bundle, perhaps you had better send the boots by him & tobacco by Mr. Hills, the boot want to be of the best make as I have found by experience that a good boot (of good material) wears a great deal longer than a cheap one enough longer to more than pay the difference in price; I don't want anything but a plain top and do not wish it more than ordinary height, the top of the boot not to be sewed on to the foot, the front of the foot & top being of the same leather, do not want double uppers if you can get single. Serg't King[262] proposes to be married whilst in Boston, he is to be married at the old brick Church near your aunt Freeman's and on the same St.; he is to marry a Miss Fanny March who lives on Snow Hill St, no. 23, she has no father living and lives with her mother a Mrs Childs. Rev. Mr Algers marries them but I can't tell on what day the deed will be done. You had better buy a small present, say $5.00 or thereabouts, and send it to him from me[263] . You had better have my buggy put in good condition and sold. We returned from picket yesterday having the good luck to have pleasant weather, before we arrived at camp it commenced raining which turned into hail and before the night was over we had several storms with hail and thunder. We can obtain plenty of baker's bread the 1st Mass. has a bakery and our brigade bakery commenced operation last Saturday. 1/15 of the line officers, 1/3 of the field officers & surgeons, 1/2 of the regimental Staff can go home at a time, you can perceive that my chance is small, there is no branch of the service that an officer of the rank of Capt. has so few favors as in Infantry. There is a little snow on the ground but it will soon disappear. Give my regards to all
     Yrs Aff   Charley

****

Mch. 19 /63   Camp near Fal. Va.
Dear Nellie,
I have received your favor of the 13th of Mch. St. Patrick day was celebrated in Meagher Brigade in a most satisfactory manner to all concerned but unfortunately the programme was interrupted by a fight on our right which caused that brigade to be under arms, the cause of this firing, which could be heard at our camp, of the results I have not been able to hear two stories alike and consequently don't know, you will have learnt by the papers before this reaches you of the results as well as the cause of the fight[264] . At Meagher Brigade there were three platforms built one occupied by Gen Hooker and the judge with other Genl etc., the 2nd by ladies and the 3rd by officers.

---

[261] David W. Roche, killed at Gettysburg, July 2, 1863.

[262] John P. King, promoted 1st Lieut., Feb. 14, 1864.

[263] Why Johnson should buy Sgt. King a wedding present is not known; perhaps he was an employee of Johnson's manufacturing company.

[264] Johnson explains in the P.S. to this letter that the engagement to which he refers was the battle of Kelly's Ford, March 17. Meagher's Brigade (2nd Brigade, 1st Division, 2nd Corps) may have been under arms but were not involved in the action.

They say that champagne was circulated pretty freely but not being there could not vouch for it being true. These three platforms were situated on a two mile track laid out for steeple chases which were to commence at ten o'clock St. Patrick morning, there were several fences 4 ft high also ditches 8 ft wide by 4 ft deep partially filled with water; Gen'l Meagher[265] was dressed in complete jockey uniform white hip boots little cap and riding whip. There was fine horsemanship displayed but with some accidents two horses were killed and a Q[uarte]r M[aste]r injured. A grease pole containing a furlough on top caused great deal of amusement but I believe no one obtained it, greased pigs and footraces in bags were to have taken place if the brigade had not been called under arms; this brigade is about 5 miles from us, I not having a horse did not go to witness the fun. Gen'l Hooker & Sickles rode through our camp yesterday & Gen'l Hooker & another Gen'l who I did not know today. A corduroy road recently built runs through our camp and we have army wagons without cessation rumbling pass us. It is the general opinion, more imaginary, there we shall move about the first of April. Col Banks has a lame leg and is trying to get home on sick leave his success is doubtful. Capt Amory's name is among those officers who are to be dismiss unless they appear before a certain board and satisfactorily explain etc; now Capt Amory was not absent without leave and he can give satisfactory reason & proof that he was not absent more than ten days; but there are some officers in our regiment who could not do it & have been reported at brigade Hd Qrs as absent without leave but their names does not appear among the proscribed. Give my regards to all.

   [Yours Afftly Charles]

P.S. I have just heard concerning the raid of the 17th.[266] Our cavalry 2,500 strong crossed the river and attacked the rebel outpost drove them in and engaged the rebel cavalry commanded by Gen'l Stuart in person & forced them back three miles towards Culpepper, capturing a rebel Col and Major besides a number of rebel privates and horses. Lt Bowditch of 1st Mass Calvary [sic][267] was killed & Major Chamberlain was wounded, total loss in 1st Mass Cal. does not exceed 40 killed, wounded & missing. It is consider a great success. Mrs Richardson & Mrs Banks called to see Mr Lombard & myself this afternoon; they say the war will end in forty days having their information from a Col just returned from Washington. I give it no thought it is absurd.

****

         Mch. 22 / 63 Camp near Falmouth Va

Dear Nellie,

  I have received your favors of Mch 15th & 17th also one from Austin of Mch 15th, tell him to write often I am always happy to hear either from him or Winnie. Tell father I was happy in receiving his long letter of Mch. 16th. I appreciate the situation. Yesterday morning there was continued fire of musketry but have not heard even a

---

[265] Irish-born Thomas F. Meagher, an activist in the Irish independence movement, escaped in 1860 from Tasmania, where he had been sentenced by the British government, and came to America. In winter 1861 he organised what was to become the renowned "Irish Brigade". After the war he was acting Governor of Montana in 1866. He was drowned in the Missouri River following a fall from a riverboat during a drunken spree on July 1, 1876.

[266] i.e. the battle of Kelly's Ford - see footnote above.

[267] 1st Lieut. Nathaniel Bowditch, mortally wounded, died March 20.

rumor; probably it may have been practising but it did not sound like it[268]. There are some movements taking place that seem to point to an early removal of a part at least of our forces but as we can't expect favorable weather at present I think it only means the transfer perhaps of a Corp d'Armee somewhere, or as reporter would say when he did not know, "not at liberty to tell." It cleared off beautifully this afternoon, after a storm of two days, it being as mild as summer, the birds singing lively, it being now evening the music of the frogs taking the place of the birds and the new moon would make it very pleasant out of tents if the footing corresponded anyway with the weather which he does not, being aweful. I enclose your photograph together with one of Lt. Lombards. Tell Carnes that he need not accept of a discharge unless he wishes as the Government is obliged to take care of him but he better consult his own wishes; tell him Wilson & McDonald have been discharged. Tell Winnie if he was in the army I should think he was a paying of it with his cold, the medicine given here would be a dose of salt. That puts me in mind as Abe would say[269] of a soldier to whom the Dr. gave an emetic, running to the Dr. saying he could not keep it on his stomach, can't say the Dr., I will give you another one then. Give my regards to all.   Yr aff   Charles

****

Mch. 26 /63   Camp near Falmouth Va.

Dear Nellie,

I will write you a few hurried lines. Indications seem to point to an early move, officers are to have an opportunity to send all baggage over twenty lbs for storage. There is also a rumor that they will stop granting leaves of Absence after the 1st of April, which will prevent my coming. Lt Hills & Serg't King have arrived, Mr. Hills is very desirous of the war ending. Serg't King was married after he obtained the boots from father, he was prevented from marrying on his arrival on account of shortness of funds, the person with whom he kept his accounts had gone to Portland; he brought me out a fine cap with bugle & cord knot on it made by his wife[270]. The boots will do very well if they do not shrink they were at first a little low in the instep going on rather hard but they are very comfortable and the second time trying went on very easily. That tobacco of Father's is mild but don't send father for tobacco unless he will smoke it first on trial, if Brewer sold it for tobacco & a prime article he fibbed. I have received your letter of Mch. 19. I am wondering where my pencil point is. Give my regards to all.

Yours Respectfully   CRJ

****

---

[268] Dyer records no action for March 21; therefore it may, indeed, have been musketry practice.

[269] Abraham Lincoln's penchant for illustrating his points by a story or joke was well known at the time, and disapproved of by many who considered such a practice tasteless and did not appreciate his purpose in illustrating in this way the points he wished to make.

[270] The "bugle" was the insignia used to denote infantry; home made examples such as this were often very ornate, particularly when made for officers. Officers' headgear was further decorated by hat cords - blue for infantry, red for artillery and yellow for cavalry. However, to hold a cord, Johnson's hat must have been a felt hat with a brim, rather than, as he states, a cap; the army forage cap had no brim and could not hold a loose cord, which rested on the brim and around the crown.

Camp near Falmouth Va.   Mch. 30 /63

Dear Nellie,

I have received your favors of the 19th, 22nd & 24th. There is no doubt but what I shall not come home as no furloughs will be granted after the 1st of April. We are preparing to move, to commence the summer campaign; officers baggage is to be reduced Line officers to 20 lbs & Field & Staff to thirty including mess kit, the mes[s] kit is imaginatory it can't exist under those regulations. Mr Hills new valise which he bought while at home. aside from it being large weighs itself alone 16 lbs leaving four lbs of clothing for him to carry; he will send the box home and take a carpet bag. I shall send in it two old company books and my belt plate which recently broke, it has been every where with me since I left Camp Hamilton at Fortress Monroe, I thought you might have it repaired and use it for a similar purpose. The weather here is still unsettled but the roads are fair. I shall have nothing to eat but soldier fare on the march namely hard tack & salt pork but shall enjoy it as probably I shall be hungry, only think if I can learn to love it how cheap we can keep house on salt pork & Hard Tack. We don't know which direction we shall move and I am glad of it. Hooker is popular he is our old brigade old division & our old Corp commanders and we hope he will succeed, their is no braver, cooler general in the service than he and being an old army of the Potomac officer he has the confidence of that army[271] . I was surprised to see how well Winnie writes, he will be a fine penman. I am afraid I shall not see that box unless it comes through in a hurry. Capt. Dallas has arrived and delivered me the handkerchiefs and leads. Give my regards to all   Resp Ch
Send postage stamps

****

April 2nd /63   Camp near Falmouth Va.

Dear Nellie,

The box arrived safely Mch. 31st every article in excellent condition; thank Mrs. Leel[?] for the gingerbread & other articles also every one that contributed to it. Instead of keeping it for my own use I invited the line officers in and bought apples, more nuts & raisin and oranges also cigars to make a small lunch on my birthday, only I was rather early in doing so, three days beforehand. My wall tent a hardly able to contain them all, but nevertheless it did very well and they all seemed to enjoy themselves, appreciated the pickles especially also that hogshead cheese or whatever it is called. I made a discovery today which I wish I had know the evening before, I had an idea that the tin box contained nothing but ginger bread but was surprised by Mr. Hills exclaiming "I have found something here" & on examination it proved to be some pies, they were in excellent preservation. The rumors yesterday were that the enemy were approaching, and are in some force at Culpepper & Warrenton, the rumor today is that Gen'l Hooker himself has gone on a reconnaissance with all the cavalry; also that we were not to move for fifteen days and were to cooperate with the Western army. The nights lately have been quite cold and lately have had quite a snow storm but it does not stay long on the ground. I have received your favor of Mch. 26. I had the pleasure of conversing with Miss Gilson You have perhaps heard of her as being with Major Fay[272] when he visits the hospitals. she is quite pretty & Mr Hills is well

---

[271] Major-General Joseph Hooker assumed command of the Army of the Potomac from Burnside on January 16, 1863.

[272] Not identified. There were several officers named Fay from Massachusetts, none of them of higher rank than Captain, and none of them medical officers. There was a John W. Foye, 11th Mass. Inf., promoted Major and Surgeon on April 23, 1862 and a Surgeon of U.S. Volunteers from March 26, 1863.

acquainted with her, she formerly being his schoolmistress. I may call on her with him. Give my regards to all,   Yours affty   Charles

****

April 5 /63   Camp near Falmouth, Va.
Dear Nellie,

I was disappointed today in not receiving a letter from you; I have not received one since last Wednesday. Last night we were visited by a severe snow storm accompanied with a violent gust of wind which continued until late this afternoon since when the weather has moderated and there is but little snow on the ground. Tomorrow we are to be reviewed by Genl Hooker, our Corp[s], the 3rd, unless it be postponed on account of the weather. I do not know when we shall move, indications do not point to an early start at least, not immediately but every thing is being prepared to that end. We have not been favored with warm weather but we have with wind and dust, the wind drying up the mud with astonishing rapidity. I have received your letter of Mch. 29, 1863. Mr Lombard wishes to be remembered to you & Capt. Dallas to the whole family and expresses his regrets at not being present at the evening party. We are having brigade drills every pleasant afternoon by Gen'l Carr and are of three hours duration. Sergt. King wife will soon open a new room somewhere on Washington St. I will send you the address as soon as I obtain it. There are no rumors afloat of any consequence, although there is one that Gen'l Sickles[273] may be sent to Texas, but I don't believe it. You some times write as if you were afraid your letter would be too long, the longer the better it suits me. I called with Lt. Hills at the division hospital to see Miss Gibson & had a very pleasant call & had the pleasure of hearing some fine music by the 33rd Mass. band who were serenading Gen'l Carr at the time. All the officers of the brigade have bid Gen'l good bye as it was supposed by himself that he was to leave on account of not being confirmed by the senate. In fact I believe he had orders to turn over his command, but I think Gen'l Hooker is interceding on his behalf to have the president reappoint him; he is not generally popular[274]. Give my regards to all.

Yrs Affectionately   Charles

Send some postage stamps.

****

April 23 /63   Camp near Falmouth Va.
Dear Nellie,

I am safe in camp having had a pleasant journey here[275] excepting perhaps

---

Johnson's handwriting does, however, appear to say Fay rather than Foy.

[273] Maj.-Gen. Daniel E. Sickles, Commanding the 3rd Corps. He was not sent to Texas, but remained with the Army of the Potomac. His highly controversial movement at Gettysburg several weeks later imperilled the whole Federal army and resulted in the loss of his leg and, of course, Johnson's own death. Sickles nevertheless went to his grave, in 1914, convinced that he had saved the day at Gettysburg.

[274] Carr remained with the Brigade, temporarily assuming command of the Division at Chancellorsville on the death in action of its commander, Maj.-Gen. Hiram Berry.

[275] From where is not known. His comment in the last paragraph, "I arrived back", suggests that he may have been home on leave.

the latter part of it which was dampened by the rain which fell in torrents. The regiment has returned to it old & usual routine and we dont know when we are to move. The soldier will have to endure more fatigue this summer than heretofore the orders limiting the men to fewer articles of apparel and increasing the amount of rations. The men are allowed to carry only an overcoat rubber 1/2 shelter tent[276] ; their woolen blankets are to be turned in they not being allowed to carry them, they are obliged to carry five days rations in their knapsacks, the rations alone weighing $17^{1/2}$ lbs & three more rations in their haversack. I am fearful that in warm weather the men will be unable to stand this system and if the army has severe marches it will cause a serious depreciation of the army owing to men being used up and unable to follow. All the wall tents have been turned in and I have changed my tent now occupying an A tent, Mr Lombard & myself, but it is better arranged & more cheerful than my old wall tent[277]. During my absence the men were all ordered to turn in their woolen blankets and every body expected to move but since then the blanket have been restored to the men.

 I arrived back in excellent season having plenty of time to make the connections and got on board of the steamer without provost marshal's pass. Wednesday was a splendid day and the country corresponded and I never enjoyed a ride more or saw a finer country than I then passed through, every place seemed to have an appearance of comfort & ease which forms a great contrast with what we see here. I have received the keg of tongues. Weather stormy and the ground in bad condition the rain storm of today being severe. No news. Give my regards to all and a hug for all pretty girls.

      [Yours Affectionately   Charles]

          ****

        April 26th /63   Camp near Falmouth Va.
Dear Nellie,

 I looked anxiously today for a letter but none arrived shall expect to receive one tomorrow. The roads are now dusty in this high locality but they may be muddy in lower land. Last Sunday Genl Hooker met Genl Halleck[278] , Secretary Stanton[279] & President Lincoln at Acquia Creek[280] . They were together about 3/4 of an hour their

---

[276] The most commonly used form of tent, particularly on active service. Made of cotton, they measured about 5'6" square. Each soldier carried a half-sized sheet which, when buttoned to a comrade's half, and draped over a stick or bar supported by two further sticks, or by two muskets with fixed bayonets stuck in the ground, formed a rough-and-ready shelter for sleeping. The soldiers nicknamed them dog tents or pup tents, since they considered that they would only comfortably accommodate a dog (Lord 1963).

[277] The Wall, or Hospital tent, had four upright sides 4'6" high; it measured 14'6" x 14' and was 11' high at the center. The 'A' tent, named because of the resemblance of its end to the letter A, was one of the commonest types. It was of canvas stretched over a 6' horizontal bar supported on two 6' high posts. It usually held 4 men, but sometimes had to take 5 or 6 (Lord 1963).

[278] Maj.-Gen. Henry W. Halleck, second senior army officer at the outbreak of war. On the strength of his pre-war reputation, he was appointed general-in-chief in 1862, based at Washington, D.C., but in this role he hindered rather than helped the war effort. When Grant was apppointed Lieut.-Gen. in March 1864, Halleck was made Chief of Staff, but his duties were mainly administrative and he had little impact on strategy and the outcome of the war.

[279] Edwin M. Stanton, Federal Secretary of War.

[280] The Federal supply base on the Potomac, about ten miles from Fredericksburg.

business is unknown their results unknown, but to that meeting was laid the cause of our not moving. Today I heard a startling rumor which accounts for the rebels being so well informed as to our movements and checkmating all our moves. One of the telegraph operators at Genl Hooker's Hd Qrs has been proved to be a traitor, he had a wire, very small, extending across the river which he could connect or disconnect at his pleasure with the operating instruments and hold direct communication with the rebels, all telegraphs from & to Genl Hooker were sent & received by two operators one of them being a spy. If this should prove true and the source can hardly be doubted, being told me by an office clerk of Gen'l Sickles, whom he heard relate it, it is indeed startling. Directly about me there is no appearance of a move but rumors from a distant say that a corps move tonight another tomorrow morning, we live on these rumors and calculate our chance of starting. Everything stand as they were at the last anticipated move the hospitals being removed to Acquia Creek or vicinity and very sick men sent to Washington; five days rations are still being kept in the men knapsacks and we need but a short preparation to be on the road. The men of the 1st having challenged the men of the 16th Regt. to a game of base ball and the 1st being worsted, the officers of the 1st Regt thought they would try, the challenge was accepted and the game was played yesterday with satisfactory success to us, the 16th coming off victor in 13 innings, there being twelve officers of each Regiment on a side. Genl Sickles had a review of the 1st Division this afternoon it was complimentary to Gov Parker of N. Jersey[281] it was a fine review and must have been gratifying to Gov Parker that the N. Jersey troops comprise such a large part of it, there being one entire Jersey Brigade and one large regiment in another Brigade. The roads & the weather are favorable to move, the rumor which I previously mention may be true and the advance of the Army may be tomorrow morning be on the move but every thing is so still that I cannot believe that it is anything more than a large reconnaissance. I sent my old valize to Adams Express to forward home but they would not take it, they said they had no transportation to Washington, I have left it to the tender mercy of our sutler you may see [it] some time. Capt Dallas sent his regards to you he has just entered the tent. Our officers beat the 1st officers badly; I was not in the game they scored 50 for the game to the 1st 6 and they feel mighty elated about it. We have a very short service by our new Chaplain[282] every dress parade, he has a fine voice and reads well. Our army will decrease rapidly about the 1st of May great many of the N. York regiments time expires about that time some have already been mustered out. Lt Hills is in good spirits I have not seen Jimmy since my return. Give my regards to all my friends & love to Berk.

      Yours Afftly   Charles

       ****

     April 28 /63 Camp near Falmouth Va

Dear Nellie,

It is now three o'clock and after we move at four, I don't know in what direction. I do not anticipate any fighting immediately. Some of our troops they say are at Warrenton but we may fall back to Stafford Court House not far. Stratagy[sic] for

---

[281] Joel Parker (1816-88), Governor of New Jersey 1862-66. A "War Democrat", he was critical of Lincoln's policies but supported the war effort.

[282] Charles W. Homer; he was appointed on April 13 but, as Johnson notes in his letter of May 27, resigned soon after, on May 19.

the present, it will end in a fight sometime I suppose. I am in good spirits and well. Give my regards to all. Yours

Aff   Ch

****

If I am alive next Summer

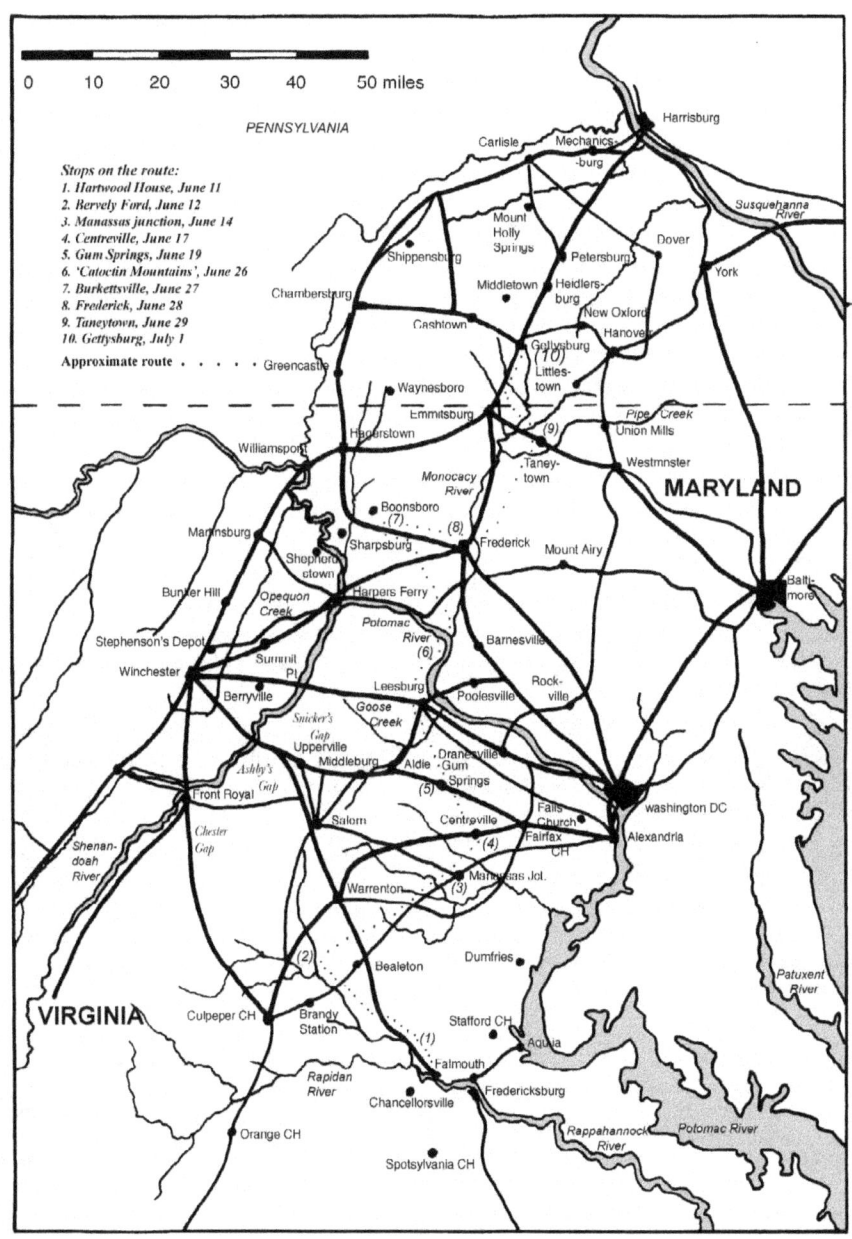

The route of the 16th Massachusetts Infantry from Fredericksburg to Gettysburg.
June 11 - July 1, 1863

CHAPTER 12
*
GETTYSBURG

Johnson's letters resume immediately after his return from leave of absence. They give detailed vignettes of the march to Gettysburg. The History of the 1st Massachusetts Infantry picks up the narrative after Chancellorsville:

"After a long and tedious march, the First Regiment reached its old camping ground, near Falmouth, at five o'clock on the afternoon of the 6th of May. The men were drenched to the skin, bespattered all over with mire; and many of them, having lost their knapsacks, containing overcoats, blankets, and a change of apparel, were in... a sorry plight... The weather continued gloomy and cold for several days...

"Until the 19th of May, the regiment remained at hill-side camp... The old routine, of guard-duty, drill and picket, was resumed;... new clothing, blankets, accoutrements, etc. were distributed... and every thing... put into good working order...

"As the hot weather was approaching, and shade indispensable, many bowers were erected in front of the officers' quarters and elsewhere which gave to the camp an extremely gay and picturesque appearance... From the middle to the last of May, the heat... was very oppressive... all day long the sun poured down... The... consequence was considerable sickness...

"In the first week in June, Union scouts reported rebel cavalry movements along the Rapidan... which created the suspicion that Gen. Lee was about to invade Pennsylvania or Maryland again....

"On the 5th, Gen. Hooker ordered Gen. Howe's division of the sixth corps to cross the river below Fredericksburg and develop the enemy's strength... several batteries were brought down to the river-bank... Under cover of the artillery, the pontoon-boats were carried down the bank and launched... and the 26th New Jersey carried the works...

"On Tuesday the 9th of June, while the rest of the army was at rest, two brigades of Cavalry under Gen. Buford... crossed the Rappahannock at Beverly Ford to make a reconnaissance in the direction of Culpeper...

"Reliable information [was obtained] of a movement... [by] Gen Lee, combining the invasion of Pennsylvania [and] a blow at Maryland... One hundred thousand militia were called out... and Gen. Hooker put the whole of his troops in rapid motion...

"Thursday, June 11, the [division] broke camp at twelve o'clock, and proceeded... to Hartwood Church. They arrived at seven o'clock, and bivouacked in the open field for the night. The march was resumed the next morning, and continued until nearly ten o'clock, p.m., to Beverly Ford. Nearly thirty miles were traversed at a rapid pace, through clouds of dust in some places so dense, that vision was impossible beyond a few yards; and a large number of the men fell out by the wayside, utterly overcome by heat and fatigue....

"On the night of Sunday, June 14, the First Regiment... commenced moving in the direction of Warrenton Junction. The men were kept marching all night, by a circuitous route, and arrived at their destination at eight o'clock the next morning. After a short halt, they proceeded in the direction of Bristoe Station, and finally bivouacked in the vicinity of the Junction. The weather... was oppressively warm, the roads as dry as ashes, and water scarce... The daily marches were unusually long, and made at an unusually rapid pace; so that the roads were lined with stragglers – representing almost every regiment – some of whom had been sun-struck, and were completely broken down. To add to the discomforts... the woods and fields had been set on fire... which filled the atmosphere with smoke and cinders, compelling the soldiers to bivouac upon the open plains."

The History of the 2nd New Hampshire Infantry adds a surreal dimension to the journey:

"This night march from Rappahannock Station to Warrenton Junction is memorable for one of the most ridiculous stampedes on record, when the bulk of Joe. Hooker's old fighting division was routed by one runaway team. The troops marched upon the rairoad, while the wagons and artillery followed the turnpike, which in its general course was parallel with the railroad, crossing and recrossing it at various points. At one of these crossings a team got into a flurry and bolted into the column... The men in the immediate vicinity at once gave it the right of way, and the bolt swept in both directions like the tumble of a row of bricks. The plodding men could hear the coming storm from afar off, and when peering through the gloom, they saw everybody stampeding for the bush, they no longer stood upon the order of their going, but went. The average momentary impression probably was that the rebels had set a car running wild down the track to break up the procession. Officers, from mere force of habit, shouted 'Halt! Halt!' at the top of their voices, at the same time their legs were carrying them along as fast as any of the men. The ditches were filled with sprawling men, while those who escaped that trap met their fate on stumps and other obstructions to rapid travel in the dark. The panic subsided as rapidly as it arose, and after a short time spent in gathering and sorting the debris... the column was again pushing on for Warrenton."

The account of the 1st Massachusetts Infantry resumes:

"June 16, Bull Run was reached and crossed; the next day Centreville was occupied, where the command halted a day; and, on the 19th, Gum Spring, a dilapidated village on the Leesburg Turnpike, was entered.

"Here the command remained six days, in a pleasant grove by the roadside, acting as support to the pickets. The whole country was infested with guerrillas... it became necessary... to keep a closer watch than usual...

"A march followed, by the way of Edward's Ferry, to the mouth of the Monocacy River, which, for length, severity and discomfort, exceeded anything the army had ever been through before. The Potomac was crossed at the Ferry, on a bridge twelve hundred feet in length... It was nearly five o'clock in the afternoon when the Maryland side of the Potomac was reached; and a heavy rain had set in, accompanied by a raw, cold wind. The tow-path of the Ohio and Chesapeake Canal proved to be the only available route to the Monocacy; and, as this was very narrow, progress was necessarily slow. The rain, which fell in torrents, raised the canal so that in some places its waters poured over the embankment into the Potomac River; and the flood led many soldiers to mistake the path, and plunge head first into the canal. There was no place to rest, with any comfort; and therefore the march was kept up, at a quick pace, until one o'clock a.m. The consequence was, that whole regiments fell out of line, and staid until morning on the narrow strip of land between the river and the canal; while, of other regiments, not more than one man in ten attempted to push through with the head of the column..."

The difficulties of the "towpath march" are confirmed in the history of the 2nd New Hampshire Infantry:

"The official report of General A.A.Humphreys, commanding the division, speaks as follows of this day's march: 'At 10 a.m. the division marched to Edwards Ferry, through Fairfarm and Franklinville, and crossing the Potomac on the pontoon bridge about 5 p.m., marched on the towpath of the canal to the mouth of the Moncacy, reaching that point about midnight, after a march of about 25 miles, that portion of the towpath being rendered very fatiguing and exhausting by a heavy rain that set in at nightfall... The whole command, officers and men, were more exhausted by this march than by that of the 14th and 15th.'

"This "towpath march", unprecedented in some of the circumstances attending it, ruined for the time being General Humphreys' popularity with the men of the division. This was doubtless unjust, as the difficulties of the march could hardly have been anticipated, and when they were appreciated it was so late that the only course was to go ahead, regardless of consequences. Night came on, dark and rainy, and the men jogged along the narrow pathway, which soon took on a treacherous coat of slimy mud. The frequent splashings, sputterings, and volleys of "cuss words" which told of a "man overboard", were the only cheerful feature of the occasion. The men grumbled at being trailed along that treacherous "hogback", while a good turnpike, though inaccessible to them, lay just the other side of the canal. No halt, no rest, but they plodded along, hour after hour, hoping to reach a lock or a bridge by which they might get out of the trap; but no such avenue of escape opened up. One by one, squad by squad, the exhausted men sank upon the ground and refused to go farther, until the little cut-offs of land on the river side were covered with stragglers. Commanders of regiments were left without the colors, and almost without men, and when General Humphreys arrived at his goal he had hardly enough of his division with him to form his headquarters guard. In the morning a stream of men poured from the towpath across the Monocacy acqueduct, and it was late in the forenoon before the division was assembled and the march resumed."

Once more, the narrative of the 1st Massachusetts serves to describe the progress of the 16th:

"On the 22nd of June, Gen. Hooker's army held the line of the Potomac, from Leesburg up, and had possession of all the gaps in the Bull Run Mountains. The enemy had advanced into Pennsylvania, in separate columns...

"By Saturday the 27th, Gen. Hooker's forces lay in the vicinity of Frederick, Md... Greatly to the amazement of the Union army, Gen. Hooker was relieved of his command on the 27th, and Major-Gen. George Meade, the commander of the fifth army corps, was appointed in his place. The change was totally unexpected... and created considerable disaffection among the soldiers. Gen. Meade himself was no less surprised... Nevertheless he entered at once upon his... duties; moved... to cover Baltimore, keep between the enemy and Washington, and threaten the crossing of the Susquehanna, below Harrisburg, endangering Lee's line of retreat.

"Friday, June 26, the regiment started at ten a.m... and moved towards the high land formed by the Catoctin and South Mountain ranges, near Point of Rocks, Maryland...

"After passing the night... between the hills... the march was resumed in the morning, and continued first to Jefferson, a small village at the base of the Catoctin Mountains, and then to Burkettsville, on the road to Crampton's Gap, which led over South Mountain... The next day, a rapid march was made through Middletown... at the foot of South Mountain and not far from Frederick City, where the Stars and

Stripes fluttered from nearly every building,... and at ten p.m., a halt was made three miles beyond.

"At five o'clock on the following morning, marching was resumed in the direction of Taneytown, where the column was greeted in a most friendly manner by the people, and tarried all night. On the 30th, ...the march was resumed in the direction of Emmitsburg... most of the people [seemed to be] staunch supporters of the Union. They waved handkerchiefs and flags as the troops went by, and supplied the hungry with bread, pies, milk, and poultry, for a reasonable compensation. One little girl in the neighbourhood of Bridgeport seemed never weary of shouting, in her shrill, childlike way, 'Hurrah for the Union!' and when one of the soldiers responded, 'Three cheers for you, little girl!', she answered quickly, 'Three cheers for you too, sir!'

"The command arrived at Emmitsburg, a post village on the Pennsylvania line, at two o'clock, Wednesday, July 1... Considerable disloyalty had prevailed among the people; and their manners towards the soldiers were stiff and frigid.

"Hardly had the men pitched their shelter-tents on a knoll of ground beyond the town, when rapid and heavy firing was heard to the front and right... caused by the advance of Gen. Reynolds corps beyond the town of Gettysburg, against a division of Gen. Hill's... corps posted across the road to Chambersburg. ... The [rebel] advance compelled Buford to retire, to whose support Gen. Reynolds came hastily forward, when he was fiercely assaulted in the streets of the town... A brisk engagement immediately ensued... Gen. Reynolds incautiously rode forward to reconnoitre, when his staff were greeted with a shower of bullets; and, during the confusion which followed, a rifle-ball struck him... causing instant death.

"The eleventh corps now arrived, and Gen. Howard immediately disposed the divisions of both corps to dispute the enemy's advance... Both parties desired to hold Cemetery Ridge, which was the most important military position in the vicinity...the enemy charged upon the town... Lapping over both flanks of the Union corps, their numerical superiority made the endeavour successful. Gen. Howard gradually drew his men off from the town, and concentrated them upon Cemetery Ridge... while the enemy pressed on, occupied the town, and swept in a semi-circular line to the north and east of the ridge...

"Meanwhile, the First Regiment rapidly approached the scene of conflict. Large numbers of Dutch farmers were passed on the road, sitting with their families on the fences fronting their estates, gaping at the troops moving by..."

Unknown to the troops, the action about to be taken by Sickles would irrevocably fix the course of the battle on July 2.

Meade had intended to post the 3rd Corps at the southern end of Cemetery Ridge, with Little Round Top to its left. Sickles, however, was becoming aware of Confederate activity to the west of the Emmitsburg Road, and had two worries: his left was unsecured, and the ground to his front along the Emmitsburg Road was about 40 feet higher than his own position – not unlike his Corps' position at Chancellorsville only two months before, where the Confederate artillery, in a similar commandng position, was able to inflict heavy losses on his troops. Unable to communicate with Meade because of Staff problems at Headquarters, Sickles went in person to Meade to seek permission to occupy the line of the Emmitsburg Road and - Sickles later claimed - received permission to post his corps as he saw fit "within the limits of the general instructions" already given. Sickles immediately moved his Corps forward to a new line running 1,500 yards along the Emmitsburg Road and then turning southeast for 1,700 yards to the Devil's Den.

The 1st and 2nd Brigades of the 2nd Division – the 16th Massachusetts among the former - arrived before dawn and occupied the west slope of Cemetery Ridge east of the Trostle Farm; by 10 a.m. the 3rd Brigade had joined them. With the 16th in the First Brigade, commanded by Brigadier General Joseph B. Carr, were the 1st, 11th and 16th Massachusetts Infantry; the 12th New Hampshire Infantry; the 11th New

Jersey Infantry; and the 26th and 84th Pennsylvania Infantry, though the last was absent, detailed to guard the corps supply trains. At about 11 a.m. the 1st Massachusetts Infantry was deployed as skirmishers along the Emmitsburg Road and, shortly after noon, the division was ordered to advance to the road to extend Birney's line northward and to link with the 2nd Corps, the 3rd Brigade in reserve. An officer on Cemetery Hill, observing the 1st Brigade advancing to take up position, noted "how splendidly they march. It looks like a dress parade, a review." The 26th Pennsylvania occupied the right flank, about 300 yards south of the Codori Barn. To its left was the 11th Massachusetts, near the Rogers buildings. The 16th Massachusetts lay to the right of the Klingel buildings with about 100 men occupying the area of the house itself. The 12th New Hampshire and 11th New Jersey occupied the Brigade's left. The Brigade's right was unprotected and its front was over-extended.

Throughout late morning and the afternoon the troops lay on their arms, awaiting events. It was not until about 3.30 p.m. that Meade finally came to inspect the position on his left. To his dismay, the 3rd Corps' one-and-a-half mile long line was not only heavily over-extended and its flanks unprotected, but had been pushed forward to form a dangerous salient jutting forward from his main line and vulnerable to a likely flank and frontal attack; and its reserve was minimal. Sickles offered to fall back to the main line, but Meade realised that it was too late: "You cannot hold this position, but the enemy will not let you get away without a fight." With the enemy already advancing, Meade could only try to ensure that he gave what support he could.

At 4 p.m. the Confederate artillery on Seminary Ridge commenced bombarding Sickles' line, and Longstreet launched his attack on the Union position, starting at the opposite (left) flank of the 3rd Corps while, on its right, 1,500 yards to the north, the men of Carr's Brigade could only wait, listening as the battle gradually and relentlessly approached them from the left, at the same time anticipating the inevitable frontal attack from the rest of McLaws' still inactive line. The fighting first focussed on the Round Tops, culminating in the successful defence of Little Round Top against Hood's Division by Strong Vincent's Brigade. At the same time, attacks on the Wheatfield, Peach Orchard and Devil's Den immediately west of Little Round Top were met by a determined Union defence. Inevitably, however, by about 6.00 p.m., the salient appeared ready to collapse and, in the midst of this, Sickles himself was seriously wounded.

There is abundant literature on the second day's fighting at Gettysburg; our narrative, however, must now focus on the fate of Johnson and the 16th. With the start of the collapse of Sickles' Salient, the long-awaited attack on Humphreys' Second Division was coming, with the added uncertainty of whether it would be frontal, from the west only, or whether the collapsing Union line to the south would expose its left flank too. McLaws' Division started its advance towards the Emmitsburg Road, the Confederate line marching at an angle to the road so that its southern end would hit the road before its northern end.

Barksdale's Brigade was the first to reach the Emmitsburg Road line, hitting Humphreys' left and causing its almost immediate collapse. On Humphreys' right, Carr's Brigade was about to be engaged, though the men along the Emmitsburg Road, including the 16th, were unlikely to to be able to see the Brigades of Wilcox and Perry as they advanced, hidden by the slope of the low ridge to the west. Ironically, Sickles' initial worry that his position would be dominated by Confederate artillery because it was too low was now offset by the fact that the dead ground in Humphreys' immediate front was invisible to the Union defenders.

Carr's Brigade received the full force of Wilcox's and Perry's attack, the 16th

Massachusetts, at the centre, facing Wilcox's 9th Alabama. With no supports, Carr followed the units on the left in an almost immediate withdrawal to the main line

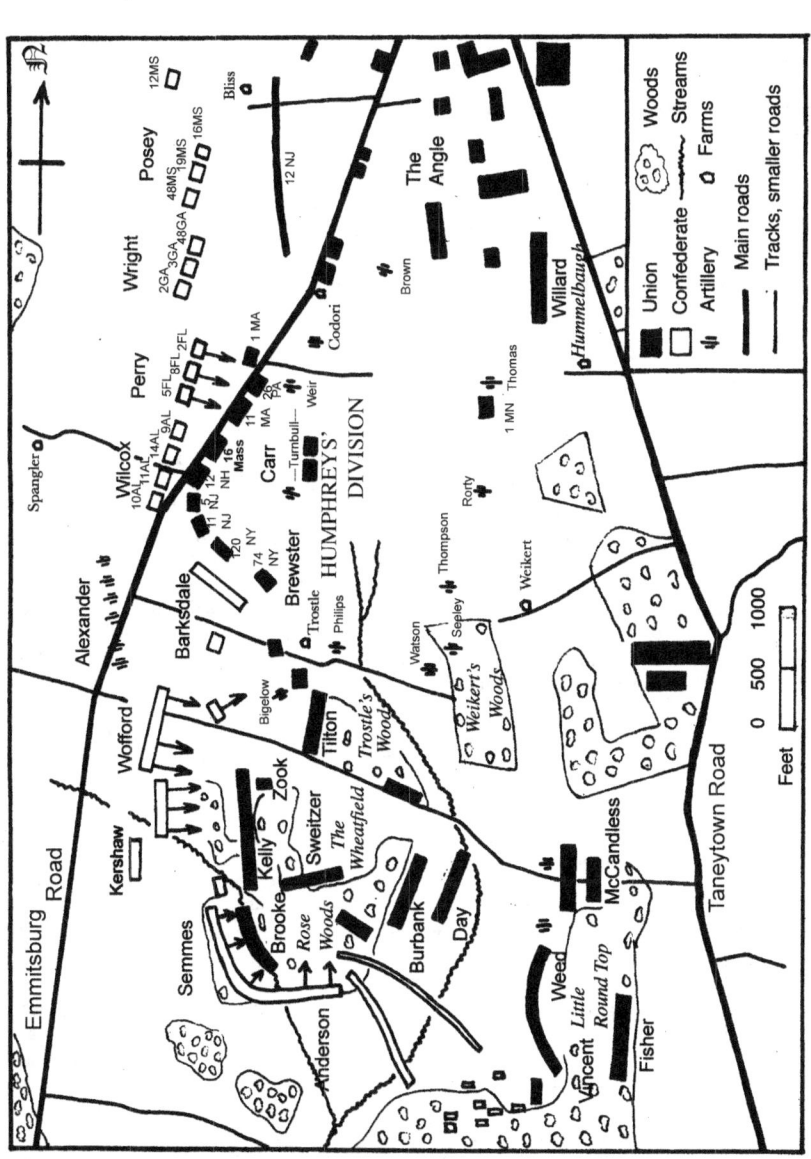

Gettysburg, July 2, 1863: The attack on Humphreys' Division

along Cemetery Ridge; to the right, Wright's and Posey's Brigades continued to advance towards the Emmitsburg Road. Humphreys' right did not, however, turn and run as the left had done, though they were still being forced back, suffering heavy losses in the process. It was presumably at around this time, or shortly after, that Johnson was wounded. As Humphreys' men withdrew, they gave ground only grudgingly – the Iron Sixteenth now surely living up to its nickname.

Humphreys now pulled his line back faster, to avoid being surrounded – a movement which became recognised as one of the best-conducted retreats of the war, under extreme pressure, saving a portion of the command to fight again. Unfortunately we cannot know whether Johnson participated in this movement, or whether he had already received his fatal wound.

Wright's, and part of Posey's, Brigades, continued their advance against the determined but vain resistance of the small Union force now opposing them, though at the Bliss Farm the rest of Posey's Brigade had been halted by Union skirmishers along the Emmitsburg Road. Perry and Wilcox, however, continued in pursuit of the now disorganised mass of Humphreys' troops, some of whom nevertheless slowed down their retreat in the hope of making a stand. Events, however, were about to take a surprising turn.

Wright's Brigade had penetrated as far east as the Second Corps Line on Cemetery Ridge near "The Angle", a spot to become legendary the next day as the key position in the Union repulse of Pickett's Charge. At this point, he was met by reinforcements from Doubleday's Third Division of the First Corps, while Humphreys, who had managed to rally some of his men on Cemetery Ridge, poured a fire into Wilcox's and Perry's regiments. Perry's Florida Brigade was now halted by the 19th Maine and other regiments of the Second Corps as well as the 13th Vermont Infantry from Doubleday's command; to the north Second Corps troops, augmented by reinforcements, began to drive Wright back, while further Union reinforcements now pouring in from the Taneytown Road began to fill the disastrous gap in the Union line to the south. The heavy Union counterattack obliged Wright to order a retreat, made more imperative by the fact that Posey was still being held at bay by the remarkable defence of the Union skirmish line east of the Bliss Farm; if any Union troops had played a disproportionate role in defeating Longstreet, it was these skirmishers.

By now, Humphreys had managed to rally the remains of his Division to the extent that he could once more advance his line towards its old position along the Emmitsburg Road, hastening Perry's withdrawal. The Confederate force was spent, and a retreat to Seminary Ridge was the only option.

As regards the retreat from the Emmitsburg Road and the fate of the 16th during the remainder of the day, the exact details of this extremely confused phase of the battle remain obscure. John Heiser, Gettysburg Battlefield Park Historian, kindly gave the following very helpful account, which gives some indication of the events during and after Johnson's wounding:-

"The events which took place on July 2 with Humphreys' Division (Carr's and Brewster's Brigades) have been somewhat glossed over; even the participants are unclear in their reports of the fighting retreat which took place that afternoon. Brewster's New Yorkers were scattered to the left of Carr's line and when Humphreys ordered the fighting withdrawal from the Emmitsburg Road, it was mostly Carr's Brigade which took the brunt of the Confederate onslaught from Barksdale's Mississippians and then Wilcox's Alabamians. The only regiment of Brewster's which was able to hold some semblance of order was the 120th New York, which fell in on the left of Carr with an assortment of companies from Brewster's other regiments mixed into a line to their left. Carr's regiments, including the 16th Massachusetts, fell

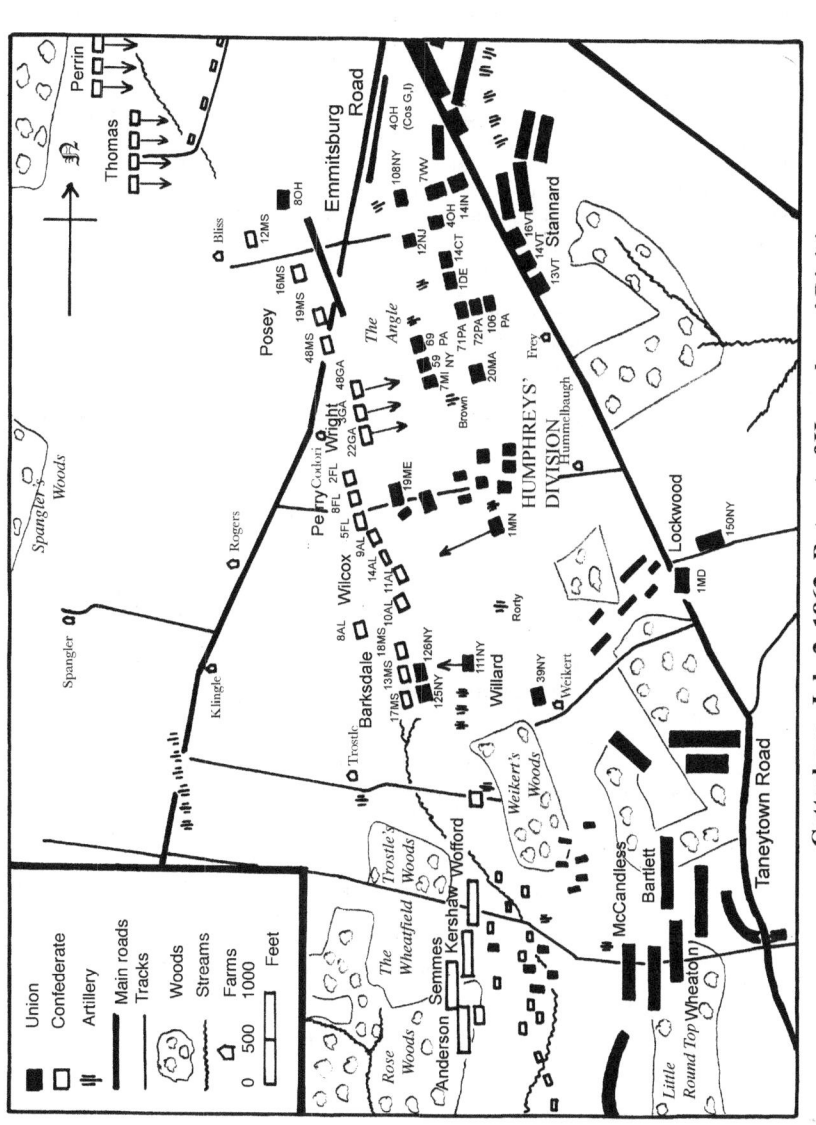

Gettysburg, July 2, 1863: Retreat of Humphreys' Division

back deliberately, stopping every few yards to fire into the pursuing Confederates. The direction they took was to the northeast, roughly in the direction of the northern area of Cemetery Ridge.

"Though Humphreys later stated that it was a heroic defence – which it was, it was also a disastrous withdrawal filled with confusion. Halfway back to Cemetery Ridge, part of Carr's Brigade broke off. The 12th New Hampshire followed and rallied around Seeley's Battery (K, 4th United States) near the banks of Plum Run, the slow-moving creek between the Emmitsburg Road and Cemetery Ridge, attempting to defend two of the guns which were withdrawing by prolong (being pulled back by the gunners instead of towed attached to the limber). Part of the 11th New Jersey and 105th Pennsylvania (from Graham's 1st Brigade, 1st Division, 3rd Corps) were also around this group. The remainder of Carr's dwindling force, including the 16th Massachusetts, moved northeast towards a small knoll where General Hancock had his field headquarters, and evidence shows that it was near this knoll that most of the regiments finally gave way under the heavy fire delivered on them from Wilcox and Perry, who had crossed the Emmitsburg Road and were sweeping down the slope into their flank. The 1st Minnesota Infantry and 19th Maine Infantry, placed just east of the knoll to support the Union battery just in front of the knoll, both had men from Carr's and Brewster's commands pass through their lines, some wounded, others unwounded but showing 'the effects of being driven like cattle', as one soldier put it. By the time Humphreys was able to rally what was left of his force, it was close to the end of the fight and after the arrival of the Vermont units from Stannard's Brigade, sent there by Doubleday from his Division. A brief counterattack was made by Carr's Brigade at the end of the fighting; they recaptured several Union artillery pieces which had been left on the field, but nightfall brought an end to the fighting and a final withdrawal to Cemetery Ridge.

"It is thought that Humphreys rallied what was left of his Division on the Hummelbaugh and Patterson farms at the central area of Cemetery Ridge. He was later joined by the remnants of the First Division (Birney) and the corps formed in mass behind (east of) Cemetery Ridge near the present location of the Pennsylvania Monument. They remained here throughout the third day, except for a brief foray by Birney's regiments to the center of the Union line after the close of Pickett's charge."

Three other features of the 16th's day of action at Gettyburg should be noted. Firstly, the 16th's Colonel, Waldo Merriam, was wounded during the course of the action, but there are no letters or reports which indicate where or when this happened. Secondly, it was Captain Matthew Donovan (Major, June 1864) who rallied the shattered regiment that evening and led it through the rest of the campaign; hence the fact that official report of the regiment's activities in the Gettysburg campaign was submitted by him (see Appendix 4(3)). Thirdly, the losses of the 16th during the battle must be noted; according to Busey, of 245 officers and men engaged, 15 were killed, 53 wounded and 13 missing: total 81, a third of the regiment's already much reduced strength.

As at Chancellorsville, the exact time and place of Charles R. Johnson's wounding is not known. As described earlier, a manuscript in the collection of the Massachusetts Historical Society summarises Johnson's army career and the circumstances of his wounding and death. The document is unsigned, but appears to be contemporary and may have been written by his wife from Johnson's own verbal account. The section covering Gettysburg and Johnson's death follows; the time given for his wounding – "about 5 p.m." – and the note that the Union front was retreating, suggests that it occurred at the beginning of of Humphreys' retreat from his Division's position along the Emmitsburg Road:-

"Capt. Johnson was wounded about 5 o'clock P.M. on the 2nd July at

Gettysburg. He received his first wound on the head, which laid him insensible on the ground a few moments, when he recovered his conscientiousness [sic] he felt that he must do all in his power to get from off the battlefield, as our front was retreating and the enemies advancing close upon our front, and as he was between our own and the enemies batteries firing grape and cannister. He was about raising himself from the ground when he received another wound in the thigh (supposed by a sharpshooter) which prostrated him again, supposing his leg was broke, found however he could use it, tied a handkerchief around it, got up and was about to limp to our front when a cannoneer came along he urged him to put him on his limber, said he could not he must go on with his cannon, so left Capt. Johnson to get off the battle field best way he could. In making another effort he found our men aiming directly where he was, he immediately waived his handkerchief not to fire, they obeyed his sign, held fire. He succeeded in reaching our front, limped alone to the rear three quarters of a mile to a resting place for the night. On the bare ground cold and damp, without any covering or protection whatever from the heavy dews of the night, there he laid alone all night with chills and shakes, wounded bleeding and painful, an agonizing mind, no succor, no soothing words or kind acts to cheer him through those dark and lonely hours of that long dreary night. Morning finally brightened upon his lonely situation saw four soldiers passing by, he hailed them, they came to him - got them to spread a shelter tent which they had, upon four guns to form a kind of litter, they placed him upon it, conveyed him nearly to the Corps hospital, when they met a stretcher he was transferred to it, then to the Hospital which is two miles from the place where he rested all night. At the hospital had his wounds dressed for the first time. He slept three nights in the Corps Hospital on straw spread where mud was ankle deep. The Hospital was nothing more than a fly tent, just holding one or two person lying full length.

"While at the Hospital their food was hard tack - once they did have a pint of beef tea divided among three men. The supplies however came up just as he was leaving the Hospital for home. [Editors' note: On July 5, 1863, three days after his wounding, Johnson wrote to his commanding officer asking for a leave of absence to convalesce from his wound. The request was approved by the administering surgeon, and as noted above, he made his way home. On July 10th, he wrote again to his commanding officer, giving information about his address].

"Said he could not describe the wretched days and nights which he passed in this flytent hospital - A current of water running within his reach in his fly tent which he occasionally used in bathing his heated wounds. Previous to the battle a heavy rain had occurred which had swollen the streams.

"Waited four days for a conveyance to Littleton [Littlestown]. Lt. Col. kindly offered him one of his horses - could not accept he was unable to ride. Finally Capt. Johnson & Lt. Harris[283] hired a farmer to take them to Littleton a distance of eight miles. This noble hearted farmer charged the poor fellows five dolls. apiece. They rode lying full length on the bottom of the wagon covered with straw. Arrived at Littleton in the evening, drove the team into the barn, the two laid there all night on bottom of the wagon.

"Took the cars for Balt. arrived there in due time conveyed to Hotel there on a stretcher and back to the cars for Phila. on mattresses. Lieut. Harris was left here to go to a hospital being unable to proceed any further. Capt. J. proceeded on his

---

[283] Henry A. Harris, a 21-year-old clerk from Holliston, Mass., enlisted July 2, 1861 as a Private in Co. B, 16th Massachusetts Infantry. He was promoted to Quarter Master Sergeant on April 4, 1862; 2nd Lieut. on Nov. 30, 1862; and 1st Lieut. on May 4, 1863. He was wounded in the left leg at Gettysburg on July 2nd, was discharged for wounds on December 19 1863, but died, presumably from complications arising from the wound, on June 24, 1865.

journey alone, arrived home Friday morning. So overjoyed was he to get home that he forgot the sad short past time which he had been through to get home.

"When coming off the battle field at Gettysburg, there were but few ambulances and those belonged to other Corps, and would not take any only those what belonged to that Corps.

"After much suffering and neglect on the battle field he by extraordinary effort and indomitable will to get home he reach the goal of his happiness, home, the 10th of July, eight days after receiving the severe wounds. He only had three bright days after reaching home. The wound in the head began to develop its fatality on the fourth day, insanity, paralysis, convulsions and then follows death. Noble brave and accomplished officer, sacrificed all the comforts of home and a bright future, solely for the love of doing his duty to his beloved country. A noble and elevated sacrifice. As the Rev. Mr. Hague said 'he died for all of us' for what would have become of our beloved country but for the noble army of the Potomac at the battle of Gettysburg. He died July 17th, 1863, aged 27 years."

****

Camp near Fal[mouth]. Va.   May 27 / 63

Dear Nellie,
On arrival at camp[284] I was agreeable surprised to find the camp most romantic in its situation and as pleasant as a man could wish. I had a companion, a pleasant one, from Washington to the camp, Dr. Jewett['s] wife, who has come on to make a short visit. The officers are of the impression that we shall not move from here until September. I heard at Washington Beauregard had reinforced Lee with 30,000; if so, the rebel army will attempt something. Gen'l Hooker was at Washington yesterday and spent 3 or four hours with Senator Wade[285]. The officers talk about having their wifes out here and I should not wonder if there were a great many ladies about. I cannot believe that it is a good place for them so many inconveniences and the liability to start at a moment's notice and the few accommodations for transit are weighty reasons against them being here. You must not think of it. I hope this will find you & Berk well. Give my regards to all. our Chaplain has resigned.
Yours Afftly   Charles

****

Camp near Falmouth   May 31 /63

Dear Nellie,
I have received your letter in which you conclude to board at Lexington. I am pleased with your choice for I think the town is very healthy and is an excellent place

---

[284] After returning from leave following his wounding at Chancellorsville.

[285] Benjamin F. Wade, Ohio Senator 1851-69. He was Chairman of the powerful Joint Committee on the Conduct of the War. A Radical Republican in favour of vigorous prosecution of the war, he opposed Lincoln's moderate reconstructions plans and, after Lincoln's death, opposed President Johnson's unsuccessful efforts to implement Lincoln's aims. The ambitious Hooker had appeared before the Joint Committee after the Seven Days' Battles, and his testimony was highly critical of McClellan, whom Wade also wished to see replaced. This visit was presumably connected with the Committee's investigation into the disaster of Chancellorsville; because of their support for Hooker, the Committee exonerated him of blame for the defeat.

for Berk. I have also received those letters of Lombard & Miss Toomey. The weather is & has been perfection itself and our camp is prettily located being surrounded by wood, and although really on a hill with ravine around it yet in comparison with the higher hills which are about us we are in the valley. Our camp is said to be the best in the army. The men have raised their shelter tents two or three feet from the ground, and their beds made from poles resting on crockets driven into the ground are the same distance from the ground. The front of the men's tents have an arbor of pine boughs which increases the room which they have. The streets are laid out with sidewalks and are graded. The entrance to two of the streets is under two handsome bough arches these are extremely poor draught of them which you can see.

The officers at the entrance of their tents have built bough houses which are cool & cheerful. The only fault we can find is that when the wind blows strong it is dusty, but nothing like the old camp. I sent you home a poem delivered by Dr. Reynolds on St. Patrick's day, the sentiments you will find are strong for Mac[286]. He is a strong Chartist and talks confidently about Ireland being free and in fact they have their meetings here in the army and are gathering many members. Dr Reynolds is a genuine specimen of an Irish man, full of fun and funny sayings, he has heavy gray whiskers all over his face & notwithstanding his aged appearance he is as lively as a schoolboy[287]. Tell Mr Hills if you see him that I don't expect him back here June 10th. It has been a splendid day and at twilight I only want you and an open buggy to have fully enjoyed the weather. There are a great many rumors about, all of them may be

---

[286] i.e. Maj.-Gen. George B. McClellan, to whom many soldiers still remained loyal, particularly after the major Union defeats of Fredericksburg and Chancellorsville; a song of the period was titled "Give us Back Our Old Commander".

[287] Chartism was a powerful but short-lived movement in England to secure equal rights and universal (male) suffrage, before fading after the economic boom of the 1840s and the failure of the 1848 popular revolutions in Europe. At the end it was associated with the Irish fight for freedom, and many Irish Chartists emigrated to America. The Chartists looked to America as the land of the free, and a number used their military experience in the Civil War to support the Fenian movement. Dr. Reynolds was probably George W.M. Reynolds, author, editor and a leading member of the Chartist movement in Britain in the 1840s who spoke at the great Chartist meeting on Kennington Common, London in 1848, of which a daguerreotype exists. Although he called for a Chartist Parliament in opposition to the established one, he was opposed to those Chartists who advocated physical violence. In 1856 he founded the newspaper Reynolds' News, which continued in publication until 1967. Ray Boston's 1971 book, "British Chartists in America", does not give Reynolds as one of those who went to America; he must therefore have been on a visit.

untrue, but I think there is no doubt that Gen'l Hooker expects the army to move northward before long. I have been acting field officer during Major Richardson visit to Washington, Lt Col Merriam being on Gen'l Court Martial. I have been trying some mild cases of depravity. To night I was in command at dress parade. I am the senior Capt. present for duty. Give a kiss to Berk for me. Write as often as you can. Give my regards to all. Yr affec Charles

****

June 2 /63   Camp near Falmouth Va

Dear Nellie,

Feeling the truth of your remark, that you may be lonely at Lexington for a while, being the first time away from your friends, I thought I would drop you a few lines often instead of writing a long letter occasionally. The weather has continued to be as I last described it, beautiful. The great drawback being the dust which in localities exposed to the wind is so thick as to blind anyone. In fact you cannot see a rod ahead. Yesterday afternoon while the major was absent a brigade review was ordered and I had command of the regiment. Marched the regiment to the review ground and on arrival was greeted with clouds of dust hiding everything from sight; we were not there long before we returned to camp, the review being postponed on account of the dust. It is now twelve oclock having just left Capt. Donovan's tent, he having entertained the officers of the 37th New York who leave tomorrow morning for home, the 38 N. York are accompanying them.[288] Major Richardson returned late yesterday not accomplishing the object he went for which was to bring his wife to camp, she not having left Boston. Having heard army rumors lately that indicate a move and if he remain .... Ask Mr Hills to bring me some paper collars a little larger than the last, and they must be stand ups, say 25. It cost more to live in this camp than in the old. It has been costing Mr. Lombard $1.00 a day our calculation has always been fifty cts, he cant explain the difference in cost unless we buy more things from the sutlers than usual. My wound is not yet well but doing well. Now Nellie dont give up to the blues if you have them as I fear you will. Stir around go into town doing something to drive them off, they will go with a little perseverance. A whip-poor-will is crying within my hearing, it has an old familiar sound like Lexington. This will be difficult for you to read and so it will take up some of your time. I must close and go to bed. Give a kiss to Berk for me, as well as the girls you meet also give my regards to all. Tell mother she hasnt written yet. Did father have any money refunded on those tickets which I left for him for N. York.

****

June 4 / 63   Camp near Falmouth, Va.

Dear Nellie,

I have received your letter of May 30, and I am glad to see by the tone of it that you are in good spirits; Mrs Richardson is in camp with her two children. The ladies must have been somewhat alarmed early this morning as at four oclock we were awakened and told to fall in and stack arms and be ready to march at a moment's notice. I packed up everything and laid down with my boots on; but soon we were relieved from that order and went about our usual days duty. The weather has been

---

[288] The 37th (in the 3rd Brigade, 1st Division, 3rd Corps) and the 38th (in the 2nd Brigade, 1st Division, 3rd Corps) both mustered out in June.

perfection itself; one evening we had a little rain, but it was hardly sufficient to lay the dust. Tomorrow morning at five o'clock we start on a picket duty of three days and shall arrive back in camp sometime Monday morning. I shall try to write you once on picket if it don't rain; there is no indication of rain now but we may expect it any time. There are rumors that indicate activity on the part of the rebels. One rumor says there has been fighting about twenty five miles up the river (Rappahannock). My wound is nearly well it has not bothered me any. I am much pleased with that picture and you might send me one occasionally; if you can find one with a large Newfoundland dog watching over his master you might send it. I am glad Berk is so well and happy hope he may continue so through the summer. I enjoyed the society for a little while of Mrs Jewett & Richardson, now don't be jealous, Mrs Jewett is very pleasant. I will not mention the ladies in camp any more for fear you may desire to come out but I think the weather is not settled yet not will it keep settled till September. I think we shall have some squalls before that. I believe I have one more envelope directed to E.A. & W. and after that I shall send my letters to Lexington. John O'Neal has joined the invalid detachment but is still a member of my company and his name stays on my rolls. The end of this month will bring any quantity of work for me, I may commence to do it soon. I went to division hospital Dr. Crozier of our regiment is there[289]; Miss Gilson is also there, but there happened to be a funeral at the 1st Mass. of the assistant Surgeon, who died of typhus fever[290], and a Sergeant, the Doctors and nurses had gone to it. I saw a wounded man of my company, there he was doing well & now I must bid you good night. Give my love to all especially Berk.

      [Yours Affectionately   Charles]

****

          June 6 /63 On Picket near Pot[omac] Creek

Dear Nellie,

It is now about five o'clock in the morning, crows are noisy and small birds are active and the weather pleasant. Yesterday afternoon we have somethings that rather stirred us up. The first was in shape of an order requiring three days rations to be cooked and kept on hand all extra baggage to be sent to the rear, this order had hardly been read by us when rapid cannonading was heard in the direction of Fredericksburg which was continued for an hour or more. We had been expecting the rebel[s] on our left and so I laid the cause of the firing to them, but I since learnt that it was our troops, the poor 6th Corp[s] who had for the third time crossed the river and were firing in what was supposed to be the rear guard of the rebel army. This morning everything is quiet no firing heard in any direction, the movements of Genl Lee are strategic, intending to deceive; but I think his end is Maryland and that his force must be around Culpepper. In fact I think his army or a part of it is on the move, northward now, but this is only conjecture on my part[291], and this move of Hooker's would seem to be an attempt to trouble Lee's rear, in fact to cut off his communications with Richmond. I shall have to await the future to unravel the plans of both armies. Capt King, the senior captain, will soon be back which will prevent my

---

[289] Assistant Surgeon Thomas Crozier, Jr. joined the regiment April 23, 1863; transferred to 11th Massachusetts Infantry July 12, 1864.

[290] Neil K. Gunn, died at Falmouth, June 3, 1863.

[291] Johnson was nevertheless correct. The advance of Lee's army had moved out of Fredericksburg on June 3, though it was June 12 before Hooker had definite information of the direction of Lee's march.

having the pleasure of occasionally having temporary command of the regiment. Capt Wiley who is now on the sick list has taken general command in the absence of full officers and Capt King but he is now sick. Capt O'Hare[292] is also my senior but since the battle of Bull Run where he was wounded he has been absent on detached service, but he has been ordered to report to his regiment by the Secretary of War but he has not yet reported, he will try hard to remain where he is. The ladies have made arrangements to go to the division hospital; the surgeon in charge having his wife there offer[ed] to accommodate the ladies in a hospital tent when the army moves. I find I have two envelopes, instead of one, directed to care of E & S.M.W. which I shall send, so you will receive one more letter with the old address. Milk is worth on picket 30 cts per quart but notwithstanding the price it is so rare a chance to obtain that I shall have some bread & milk for supper. The 5th Corp is supposed in the neighbourhood of Bealton[293], waiting, perhaps, and watching for something to turn up. I only wish I was where I could take advantage of this fine weather, I do enjoy it here and my spirits are buoyant as possible. Have just finished eating. What luxury do you suppose, strawberries and milk, the strawberries are 40 cts per quart. Occasional firing has been heard on a North[er]ly direction, seem to me to be this side of Warrenton Junction[294]. Give my regards to all.

      Yrs aff   Charles

****

      [undated, c. June 8th, 1863]   Camp near Falmouth, Va.

Dear Nellie,

The tone of your last letter pleases me, that you enjoy and like your new boarding place well at the commencement of the trial argues that you will continue to like it. I hope the boarders will be pleasant people and agreeable to you. I have today returned from picket and am in camp comfortably situated with no thoughts of a move, notwithstanding the rumors of a move and the bearing of the orders issued. But I think Hooker is only endeavouring to bother Genl Lee in his supposed anticipated movement. No one, thank fortune, has any certain knowledge what is up, even the staff officers of [the] Corp Genl are enquiring what [is] the news everyone is in doubt and have their own theory. The whole of the 2nd Division and part of the 3rd Division of the 6th Corp Gen'l Sedgwick's have laid across the river a mile below Fredericksburg for two days, but today they are again on this side of the river. I was obliged to stop writing to attend to retreat parade and before I renewed writing I met a clerk from Corp head quarters and he told me that the 6th Corp had advanced 2 or 300 yds farther into the enemies country instead of retiring, you can judge from the two different rumors in this letter how reliable we must think they are. The whole army is supposed to be ready to march at a short notice, we keep on hand 3 days cooked rations as six days ration are supposed to be loaded in the teams; all extra baggage is sent to the rear, but notwithstanding these orders, the ladies still arrive and are expected to arrive. Mrs Major is still here, Gen'l Carr wife is here also, and the Gen'l agree to send them with their baggage, if we should move in a hurry, in an ambulance to Acquia Creek. Dr Jewett sent his wife away perhaps he was a little nervous about the move. The 5th Corp is way up the Rappahannock river, either

---

[292] Thomas O'Hare, mustered Aug. 1, 1861; mustered out July 27, 1864.

[293] Bealeton, a station on the Orange & Alexandria Railroad about 25 miles north-west of Falmouth.

[294] Also on the Orange & Alexandria R.R., about 5 miles closer to Washington than Bealeton.

contemplating a reconnaissance or a move by Lee which they intend to checkmate. Altogether the stratergy [sic] is blinding us in the army and if it can do the rebel it is all right. I can not imagine a forward movement by Hooker, yet it may be so, our army having been reduced by regiment leaving whose time has expired, by wounded from the last battle being away and the number sick from the fatigue of the last fight. The sick have all been sent away from regimental hospital to the general hospital and I was told that the number that reported was 13,000 an immense number if true. owing to the absence of the Captain senior to me I was detailed as field officer of the day and had the opportunity to enjoy three miles of the country on horseback. I visit[ed] the lines of picket early in the morning starting at three o'clock, I enjoyed the ride much as the country was very hilly and woody; our picket line ran across Potomac Creek which I had to ford. I consider my wound is entirely healed, I wear nothing over it. The weather for two days has been very cold I was told that there was a frost this morning. I am now writing with my coat on and am not any too warm. I have received two photographs of myself. Give my regards to all as well as love. Direct your letters as usual.

[Yours Affectionately   Charles]

I have a piece of petrified hickory wood found near Potomac Creek, but don't know whether to send it home or not. The keg of pickles have arrived in good condition.

****

Camp near Fal Va   June 10 / 63

Dear Nellie,

I looked for a letter to night from you but was disappointed; none came. You have not answered one question which I have asked, whether father ever received any money for those tickets to N. York? Capt. Donovan's wife is at Williard's[295] Hotel Washington but find it hard work to obtain a pass to the army; Capt. King & his wife is also there, he is due at his regiment tomorrow, I believe Capt Donovan & Capt King have made arrangement whereby they may arrive safely. Capt King by his acquaintance with some quartermasters can get transportation to Aquia Creek on a government transport where no pass will be required and they are to meet an ambulance there which will bring them to the 16th regiment. I rode with the Quartermaster to the river side where our ponton's bridges are thrown across, to see what was up. I found a small force across who had thrown up earthworks like a half moon, encircling our troops, both flanks of the fort or rather line of earthwork rest on the river. We have batteries on this side of the river in position to assist those on the other side. As I was down by the river I heard several shots on picket, which sounded uncomfortably natural but every thing else was quiet as camp life, the soldiers having their shelter tents up and laying under them. Every day the appearance of a movement disappears, yet yesterday there was a heavy cavalry fight, the results unknown, but there is a rumor that we had our usual poor luck. Gen'l Stoneman was not in command, he being away, but since he has joined his command I hope we shall have good news, I have great confidence in him.

Those pickles the men have enjoyed, notify father I have forgotten whether I wrote you about the changes in our regiment, caused by promotions, or not. Mr Lombard is now 1st Lt. and has been transferred to company I, 1st Serg't Woodfin of Co E has been promoted a 2nd Lt and assigned to my company[296]. Lt. J. Brown who

---

[295] Willard's Hotel (see footnote for letter of Oct. 6, 1862).
[296] John U. Woodfin, a 27-year-old Cordwainer from South Reading, Mass., enlisted on July 12, 1861 as 1st Sergeant. He was promoted 2nd Lt. May 11 and 1st Lt. Aug. 30, 1863, and was killed at the Battle of the Wilderness, May 6, 1864.

is on Gen'l Grover's Staff has also been transferred to my company but little good he will do it at N. Orleans[297] . Give a kiss to Berk and love to all. The weather still hold fine there must be a dry time soon if we don't have rain.

Yrs aff   Ch

****

Near Beverly Ford   June 14 /63
[Letter actually written over a series of days between the 14th and 19th]

Dear Nellie,

    I am writing this letter not knowing when I shall have chance to send it. I received a letter from you & mother yesterday. We left camp so suddenly that I had no chance to drop a line. I hardly at the time believed we were to move; but we did, June 11. We started from camp at 2 and one half o'clock and marched to Hartwood Church where we camped during the night. At half past three we were awoken, prepared breakfast and about six o'clock started on our 2nd days journey, which proved to be memorable as the greatest achievement in marching which our regiment has done. We have never prided ourself on the forced marches we have made, so this day's journey made [may] not appear as great compared with other regiments doings. The country which we passed through was green and pleasant to look at, the footing excellent and if it had not been for the dust there would have been no draw back, unless some people would have found fault with the heat which would have been extreme if the wind had not fanned us and kept us comfortable. The dust on some parts of the road was so thick as to hinder from view every thing a yard from us I breathed through my *[line missing]* was filled with dust, my ears and every part of my person that the air could reached was dusty, the heat caused perspiration which with the dust formed mud making horrible looking fellows of us. About eight o'clock we arrived at Rappahannock Station and filed off into an open field where we stacked arms and got ready to remain for the night but we soon got notice that we were to fall in, and fall in we did, the men mad & cross at the fooling, as they called it, most of the men irritated by sore feet and chaffing, and marched at a rapid rate a distance of little over two miles although in the condition of the men it seemed three times as long; we filed off into some woods within 200 yds of Beverly's ford, the place where part of the cavalry fight took place[298] , there being dead horses here & there as evidence of the fight. We turned in without washing ourself or pitching shelter tents. But I had hardly settled for the night when I was sent for & told that 36 privates would report to me with the proper number of non-coms for picketing the river, The serg't major made the attempt to raise the 36 men and was obliged to report with 26, that being all that had kept up with the regiment during the last two miles marching for when we arrived at Rappahannock Station we had but very few men who had straggled, we succeeded in

---

[297] 1st Lt. John B. Brown was a 24-year-old dry goods salesman from Ipswich, Mass., when he enlisted on July 1, 1861 as 1st Lieut. in Co. I. Cuvier Grover, formerly commanding Johnson's Brigade, was assigned to various commands in the Department of the Gulf from Dec. 1862 to July 1864. Brown had presumably been assigned to Grover's staff during the latter's time with the Army of the Potomac, but evidently remained on the 16th's rolls; he resigned Oct. 31, 1863.

[298] Brandy Station, June 9, 1863, the largest cavalry battle of the war. Although technically defeated, the Union cavalry for the first time showed that it could match the heretofore invariably superior Confederate horsemen. The boost to its morale was invaluable and foreshadowed the growing Federal cavalry superiority as the war progressed.

getting enough corporals to take the place of privates to nearly fill up the number, so you see I had not 36 men with me yet had all the regiment. My [*top of next page headed* "at Manassas Plain going to move all well"] duty was rather a hard one considering the used up condition of the men being up since half past three in the morning the majority of the time on their feet, foot sore, weary and sleepy, they were called upon to be wakeful, vigilant and observing, My duties were to form a line of pickets along the bank of the river, which is not a mile wide, making no noise, from the left of the first Mass, who were all at the ford untill I arrived with pickets from the Rap[pahannock] station. the men were not allowed to even whisper, the first part of my picketing was comparatively easy, there being a path. I have forgotten to tell you of the country. Along the road side run a canal but the banks of the river was considerably higher, the banks on either side were lined with trees and bordered on our side with level land over grown with rank weeds some three or four feet high. The men walked along this path in single file myself at the head, a sergeant in the rear who was to leave three men at every place that I stopped, but the men moved so slowly at the rear that he had more than three post where I only intended to have one. The path began to grow indistinct and I soon found myself in rank weed grass covered with dew and under my feet were dry corn stalks which cracked and made the noise I tried most to avoid. I soon found myself in a corner, the river making a turn of nearly right angles, was directly in my front on my left was a narrow canal hid by bushes on either side which extends into the river, probably used as a drain for the land, at first light I thought that I should be obliged to retrace my steps, but on examining the drain for a little distance I found a path by which I crossed it. When I arrived thus far I found I had only two men left and I posted them at this path so as to find it easily again, by this time I was pretty well wet from my knees downwards, my overcoat protecting me higher up. We had not as yet seen anything of the picket whom we should have connected with on my left, so a corporal was sent to find them and see what distance there was between us. After the corporal had been gone an hour and no signs of his returning, and knowing that distance in the night is so deceptive especially when you follow a meandering river, and the noise from the water fall which was at the principal ford sounded to distinct to be very far off, I sent a sergeant to bring in 12 men and extend the others to cover the ground, he did not return for some time. The sergeant came at last back and reported that the three left posts he could not find and the fourth were so close to the rebel cavalry picket that they could hear the orders given them by the officer of the guard and he (the sergeant) did not like to take them away. The corporal at last came back with anything but a satisfactory report, he had kept on until he had come to a ditch which he did not like to cross as the mud was so deep; he had not seen any of our pickets and described the road as one very hard to travel. My orders were to withdraw the pickets before day light and I had made up my mind to commence to withdraw the picket about three o'clock in the morning and as it only lacked about 1½ hours from that time I concluded that it was best to have things remain as they were as the enemies & our pickets were so close that I did not want to hazard a shot as it would have awaken the reserves and caused them to stand under arms unnecessarily, and I knew they were pretty well use up. The Cavalry had told me between the Beverly ford & Rappahannock station there was no place that could be easily forded and they hardly thought it necessary to picket where I was, under the circumstances I felt justified in doing as I did. As my mind was made up to leave as they were the pickets, and as I was to form a new picket line before day light, the corporal and myself started to make a small observation of the locality of surrounding land as it was ordered to post the picket out of sight yet where the lookout could have a good view of the river. I found the country well adapted for the object desired; the plain bordering on the river run back only from 500 to 1000 yds where the land ascending to high hills with woods here & there, fine places to conceal men and an excellent situation to obtain a view of the river. Having learnt what I could of the country I return to my stand and awaited for three o'clock to come around. I could hardly tell the time, in fact had to guess until I caught a ~~fly glow~~ *[line missing but probably* glow worm by the light of which I could] plainly see the time. Three o'clock at last arrived and I sent a Sargeant and corporal to withdraw our line the Sargeant was to take three posts from the right of the line and take them directly to the rear and conceal them; the corporal was to bring the remainder to me. Mannassas Junction June 17. This morning whilst we were packing up, the sergeant major said there was a chance to send a letter and I immediately enclosed what I had written without signature or remarks as there was so much hurry, part of it was written lying on my back and I dont know how intelligible it will be. Continued: The men came in single file and one of them raised my anger as he had thrown over his shoulders a rubber blanket with the white lining out making him self very conspicuous, but I think he was not noticed by the rebels as there was a mist hanging over the river obscuring object beyond, besides it was not bright enough to discern objects, except close to. I found three admirable hills where I posted those men with me, keeping one man on lookout at each post, and my view embraced every thing desired. Those men whom the Sargeant took with him from the right I visited and altered their position. The hills were separated from each other by valleys, and to the rear of the hills, the country was little undulated intersected by running brooks, the hills acting as curtains concealing those in the plain from view of the enemy. The place at which I stayed was near a beautiful spring, which belonged to an unoccupied house, having about it the usual number of outhouses, one of which contained a colored family from whom I obtained some fresh milk which tasted finely. The house itself had been used as a hospital during the late cavalry fight,[299] being surrounded with bayonet sheath, the cavalry during the fight having infantry supports, pistol cartridge boxes, clothes, rags & litter saturated with blood. The rooms, inside, had plenty of evidence of the use which they had been put. I only saw one grave which seemed to have an occupant although there was another dug yet it was empty. Around the house there was the remains of a once pretty flower garden, honeysuckles and several varieties of roses were in bloom besides other flowers which names I didn't know. The furniture inside the house was in every state of destruction and some I should judge had been carried away. I spent the greater part of the time until I was relieved reclining on a settee under the shade of some of the fine trees in the gardens, I could overlook the other side where the Johnnies were whilst at my ease. General Birney[300] and staff came to top of the hill, where I was, to obtain a view of the opposite side, there being an old ford, the road to which passed by this house, the rebels with their usual caution having a strong fort in the woods commanding this ford. Gen'l order twenty sharpshooters to be stationed here in case the rebel should endeavor to come across, they *[inserted at top of page:* Capt Bixbee 1st Rhode Island Cavalry had a narrow escape[301] . Saw him to day. most of his regiment had been

---

[299] Brandy Station, June 9.

[300] Maj.-Gen. David B. Birney Commanded the 3rd Corps at Gettyburg on July 2-7. Born in Alabama, he practised business and law in Philadelphia from 1856 to the outbreak of the war. He was Colonel of the 23rd Pennsylvania Infantry, then became a Brigadier General under Philip Kearney during the Peninsula Campaign, and was charged with disobedience and immediately acquitted. He fought at Chantilly and 2nd Bull Run. He was again charged and acquitted at Fredericksburg, and achieved Major General rank. He served at Chancellorsville and Gettysburg, but died of typhoid fever on October 18, 1864.

[301] Capt. Augustus H. Bixby. In his battle report, Col. Alfred Duffie' of the 1st Rhode Island Cavalry, and

captured he has a slight wound, his horse wounded and his pistol "missed"] arrived in the afternoon. I had no opportunity to obtain any sleep until six and I only laid down for one hour during which I was interrupted or rather awaken twice. The walking which I had to do after daylight with my feet wet with the heavy dew made them sore so that by noon after every thing was all right I pulled off my boots and washed my feet with cold water. Our situation was interesting watching the rebel, they seemed busy in repairing a redoubt to the right of the main ford; their force as far as we could see was cavalry and but little of that was see[n], groups of seven or eight could often be seen but never larger numbers, but what were seen seem to be busy about something. The country around give evidence of more cultivation and very large farms well cleared were not rare. About noon I felt somewhat provoked that we want [weren't] relieved. At four o'clock the relief came from another regiment and I joined my regiment where I made arrangements to pass a comfortable night. Before night a detail was made from our brigade to throw up earth works during the night at daybreak we had a very good redoubt for four guns facing the main ford. June 14 we did nothing during the day but lay around the enemy were quiet. Little while before sunset we received orders to be in readiness to march as soon as it became dark, using great precaution against making noise. As soon as it was dark we started and made the first night journey we have as yet made. The march was tedious owing to many halts or rather, checks owing to the road being blockaded, the men not knowing whether to sit down or not and if they did to be obliged to get up in a second. Our marched continued until seven o'clock next morning bring us near Cedar Run near Catletts Station, halting in a valley where the sun came down hot enough to take your breathe away. This place was near where my company guarded the railroad last fall, and I made a call on Mrs Catlett taking everything with me. I had dinner at Mrs Catlett, which was enjoyed on account of the cool air rather than the eatables, which were cold corn cake & butter, coffee without milk, she being nearly eat out; we obtained excellent water at this place and while we, Lt Capelle[302] being with me, were smoking, sitting in easy chairs with a cool breeze fanning us we discovered that our division was again on the move after seven hour rest and in a direction to be easily joined by us. The day was extremely hot and many a poor man suffered the effects of the heat, in fact one or two died it was so reported. We marched until 1/4 of one the next morning arriving at Manassas Junction. June 19 At Centreville. Our cavalry has been fighting away in our front at intervals, heard distance firing this morning. I think we shall not go to Leesburg at present, don't send those collars. I am well.

Charley

Had an opportunity to send this to Centreville, near which we are on our way to Leesburg, by a 9th Mass Battery man. It now about seven o'clock and I anticipate the hot[t]est day yet we have had but one small shower and the heat combined with the dust has already knocked over many men. several death they say has occurred. Direct

---

commanding the 2nd Division, Cavalry Corps, Army of the Potomac, describes Bixby's role in the Division's withdrawal from the battle: "I at once ordered Captain Bixby, the officer commanding the advance, to charge any force in his front, and follow the Aldie Road to the point where it connects with the road to White Plains. This order was executed most admirably. Captain Bixby's horse was shot and he himself wounded."

[302] Jonas F. Capelle, a 19-year-old mariner from Lexington, enlisted as Sergeant, Co. K, July 2, 1861. He was promoted 2nd Lt. June 26, 1862, 1st Lt. Aug. 29, 1862, and Captain on July 3,1863. Mustered out with the regiment, he was Brevetted Major on March 13, 1865. After the war he was a member of G.A.R. Post 57 (P. Stearns Davis), East Cambridge, Mass.

letters the same as usual, I have only received one letter from you since you have been at Lexington, we have had but one mail since we started. I have forgotten all about that week you spoke of, in fact never thought anything about it. Give my love to all.
     C.R.J.
You had been send me [sic] a five $ occasionally

****

                       Gum Spring   June 20, 1863
Dear Nellie,
     Where I left you in my last was at Manassas Junction, having arrived at 1/4 of one in the morning. We remained in that camp until eight oclock then changed our camp one half mile nearer Centr[e]ville and made ourself comfortable for the coming night and at nine oclock June 17 we were again under way crossed Bull Run where we halted until 2 oclock beside of the Run, eat dinner & took a nap. I learnt there that the government had destroyed articles at Manassas Junction for want of transportation, not of much value I suppose, but among them was a large quantity of soft bread which would have been eagerly disposed of by our men. Near Bull Run, Run and river are synonymous, are trees of great diameter, and under their shade I laid for protection against the sun. At 2 o'clock we were again on the march and at 5 o'clock arrived near Centerville where we remained all night. I have often written whilst in camp near Falmouth of the dry weather, and I believe have mentioned the dust on the road. The last night at Beverly's ford we had a small shower, but the ground was so hot & dry that the dust seemed to be as thick as ever. When I awoke next morning at Centerville we expected to start immediately for Leesburg, but we had no such orders and our mess sent out scouts to Centrville to buy up all the Sutlers they could find, as hard tack and tea had wet our appetites for some thing better, we obtained some boxes of fish said to be sardines and ham, pickles & soft bread and laid ourself out to dispose of them. In the afternoon there came up a shower which was a powerful one and it was only the commencement of a series. We had a ditch dug around our tent yet came near being overflowed, the majority of the men were driven out of their tents & sat in the water. The shower held up and we were ordered to pack up and fall in; it was only to move our camp to some higher locality, but it did not benefit me any as it was dark when we arrived at our new camp. It rained whilst we were on the move and we had no convenience when we did halt for pitching tents, but we managed to spend the night pretty well although everything was damp in the morning. June 19 we had orders to change our line and lay our camp but whilst we were about it received orders to be in readiness to move at 2 oclock started and after one of the pleasantest marches we have as yet had and the sun being partially obscured by the clouds the roads are hard and the country beautiful and woody we did ten miles with the greatest ease and I arrived at Gum House as it commenced to rain, and by great hurry got under cover before we were wet and passed a fine night. Here we are now expecting to start for Leesburg soon. Thought we heard [a] little firing, but may have been mistaken, last night. Gum Spring has about [a] dozen small houses here & there and is course right smart place. I am well. Give my love to all but we have not had mail since we started. We think it will bring good results. The rebels are in Penn[sylvania][303] .... *[no further pages]*

****

---

[303] The first elements of the Army of Northern Virginia entered Pennsylvania on June 15.

June 22 /63   Gum Springs Va.

Dear Nellie,

Yesterday I received three letters from you as well as a large number of papers from father. You can see by the heading of this that we have not moved from Gum Springs, we have changed our locality only one quarter of a mile. The government is doing all in its power to make hard work for the officers. The line officers of a regiment were allowed one public horse to carry their blankets, two or three days ago ours were turned in leaving our blankets to be carried by ourselves. It has been the custom in the army for the company officers to employ one of the soldiers as a servant and draw pay for a servant also but now a very strict order has been published requiring a report of soldiers so used, this report being sent I suppose to the paymaster Gen'l, intending to deduct from the officers pay the price which a soldier cost the government, by $25.00 per month, also lossing the pay allowed for a private servant by 25.00 per month making a loss in an officer's pay of $50.00 per month. The line officers generally employ one servant, while each field officer has two or more it will be hard on them, except they have so much power to conceal what they have. Uncle Sam won't make much, the officers understand their position[304]. My Lt and myself have a tall guant [sic] darkey that will help us along considerably. Charles H. Cooke whilst away from the company is beyond my control and I can do nothing for him[305]. I doubt if an opportunity should occur of a majority of a regiment whether I should take it, an officer promoted is mustered into his new rank for three years, and if it be their intention to fill up old regiments with conscripts these officers will have to remain after the men who originally formed the regiment are discharged and by this means old officers will be kept in the service. There was cannonading yesterday and we were ready to move at a moment's notice it was not very heavy but lasted all afternoon[306]. I am glad you are enjoying your self so much and am much pleased with the pictures. Today is a beautiful day, the rain has lasted long enough to lay the dust and the air is cool and delightful. We have fine view of the Rictoctan [Catoctin] ridge an extension of Bull Run Ridge being quite near them. I was obliged to throw away the petrified wood as their was no means to send it home. Give my love to all and a kiss to Berk. I have received a letter from mother and shall try to reply.

[Yours afftly   Charles]

****

---

[304] A Captain of Infantry received $60 per month. Officers were allowed to use soldiers as servants, but General Order No. 91 of July 29, 1862 required them to deduct from their monthly pay the full amount paid by the Government on account of their servants. Officers frequently complained that this made the pay scale insufficient, particularly in the face of high wartime inflation and, for many, the need to maintain a family at home (Lord, 1960). Clearly, however, there were ways around this problem; as Johnson writes, "Uncle Sam won't make much, the officers understand their position". It is not clear to what "recent" order Johnson is referring; none of the General Orders emanating from the War Department during May and June make any reference to the subject.

[305] Cooke, a 23-year-old Clerk from Roxbury, transferred on Aug. 15, 1863 to Co. E, 9th Veteran Reserve Corps - perhaps wounded at Gettysburg? The Massachusetts Adjutant-General's report for 1864, however, shows him as being transferred on Sept. 10, 1862, possibly a misprint. It is not known why Johnson was so anxious about him; he may have been an employee of Johnson's E.A. & W. Winchester Company.

[306] Possibly the engagement at Upperville, Va., June 21.

June 24 /63   Gum Spring Va.

Dear Nellie,

Here we are in the same place and but little signs of a march. We have had most beautiful weather since the rain storm, a cool breeze blowing always and and no severe heat even at noonday and the nights are almost chilly. Their has been rumors of guerillas being about in plenty immediately outside of our picket line, all the damage they have as yet done is burning three wagons and capturing two officers. Our position as far as I can learn is behind the Bull Run and Kittoctan [Catoctin] mountains, our right at Pt of Rocks and Leesburg and our left at Thorofare Gap we holding all the passes in the mountains. The rebels are in Shenandoah valley the most of them about Snicker's Gap, they have a small force this side of the Blue Ridge but their main body is about Snicker's Gap, in the Blue Ridge, they hold I suppose all the passes in the Blue Ridge. There has not been a gun for the last two days every thing seems quiet, the armies appear to be watching each other, and looking for the first signs of an offensive movement. Gen'l Lee I suppose is working out some plan of his, but he shows great caution, his quietness may be the result of circumstances or part of his policy, he must be well posted as to our situation by the farmers who in our opinion are all guerillas. The advance into Pennsylvania was only a raid and a very small part of Lee's army and it was intended as a diversion, but failed to deceive this army[307] . Our cavalry has shown so much dash and fighting qualities lately as to rather check the confidence of that arm of the enemy, beside giving us great advantage in checking the enemies advance and in uncovering their plans. This pleasant weather combined with our lying idle has a bad effect on my feelings making me very tired of my situation, and I wish myself anything but a line officer of infantry. They may soon consolidate but we shall have to wait and see what is to be done with the conscripts, whether they shall form new regiments or fill up old ones. I prefer that they form new regiments and consolidate the old, that is to take an old regiment of ten companies and make five of it, have it commanded by a Col, it would be as effective as a regiment and more like the French organisation I believe, their regiments consisting of three batal[l]ions. We comenced drilling to day. This is the most forlorn place for obtaining anything to eat, we sometimes can lay hold of a small peice of mutton and pig, but for getting soft bread, milk or butter it is almost an impossibility except for those who have horses. Butter I always consider the best part of a meal but we have been without it sometime, and have had to work hard to get pork to eat with our hard tack[308] in fact we have been without it several meals eating only hard tack (plain) and tea. Vegetables we don't know any thing about although we really require them. But I dont find any fault with what we eat but I must confess that the inactivity and fine weather has depress my spirits, making me long for a change of situation. I shall write to mother when I can find an envelope, those I have with me are all directed. Give my love to all and a kiss to Berkeley. I have received but two mails since June 11th they may fear to send them.

    Yrs aff   Ch

---

[307] Pennsylvania, and the State capital, Harrisburg, were indeed the target of Lee's invasion, which perhaps emphasises the success of Lee's initial strategy of keeping his precise aims from the enemy.

[308] A staple, and much maligned, item of army diet. Officially called Hard Bread, it was a biscuit 3 1/8 x 2 7/8 inches and c. half an inch thick. Though nutritious enough, it could be very hard - soldiers wrote of being unable to bite through it, or of having to pound it with their rifle butts to break it - and it was not infrequently infested with maggots or weevils. It is perhaps strange that Johnson has only now mentioned it for the first time.

****

Taneytown Maryland   June 30 /63

Dear Nellie,

I will drop you a few lines to let you know I am well. We arrived here at five o'clock last night marching 22 miles yesterday, coming from Frederick. We are 4 miles from Pennsylvania and are liable to start at any moment. We received a mail last night the first one since June 23. We are having long marches but they are over good roads and through a delightful country, with sympathizing people around us. I will send this and then commence a longer one.

                   Yrs Aff   Ch

****

July 5 / 63
In Hospital 3rd Corp near Gettysburg Pa.

Col,

I have the honor to apply for a Leave of Absence for twenty days, on Surgeon certificate of disability.

           I am Sir   Yours Respectfully
           C. Robinson Johnson   Capt. 16th Mass. Vol.

To:
O. F. Hart   Col. & AssistAdjt Gen'l   3rd Corp Army Potomac

I certify on honor that I am not indebted to any commissary of the U. States[309]

The circumstances of Johnson's wounding, journey home and death are described in the introductory section of this chapter. Let the last word be from Johnson's own comrades, as articulated in the Report of the Adjutant-General of Massachusetts for 1864: "The name of Captain C. Robinson Johnson will awake in the heart of every soldier of the Sixteenth a feeling of respect and love, which can only die when the last patriot of the Sixteenth is no more. His life was so full of noble deeds and heroic acts, that his peaceful death adds to his brilliant record. In camp, on the march, on the field of battle, he was the same. His heroic fortitude, his gallantry, his kindness of heart, reared for him a living monument in the hearts of all soldiers of the command."

h

---

[309] Document in National Archives, Library of Congress, Washington, D.C., accompanied by certificate from C.C. Jewett, "Surgeon in Chief, 1st brig., 2d. Div. 3 Corps and in charge of Division Hospital, Hospital near Gettysburg, Pa. July 5th, 1863"

CHAPTER 13
*
AFTER GETTYSBURG

Appendix 3 sets out the Reports of the Adjutant-General of the State of Massachusetts for 1863 and part of 1864. These detail the full history of the regiment, from muster-in to muster-out. However, for the sake of continuity of the narrative of the History of the 16th, it was decided to put that part of the 1864 report relating to its career after Gettysburg here, as a Chapter on its own.

"...Wapping Heights, Locust Grove, and Mine Run end the list of battles for 1862 and 1863.

Two years and six months of the three years had passed. The record is a proud one. The rough road had been travelled, paved with the sacred remains of our comrades, and fraught with sorrow to many New England Hearts. All could say in truth, 'We have done what we could to sustain the noble record of the old Commonwealth.'

I now commence that part of our history fraught with the most important results, and by far the most severe and hardest year's service - 1864.

The new year found the regiment encamped near Brandy Station, Va., where the men by Yankee ingenuity had erected crude, yet comfortable huts in which to pass the winter, with somewhat if possible of the comforts of home.

Although we remained in camp until May 3d, it was not a period of inactivity. Frequent drills and inspections, a large amount of picket duty and frequent reconnaissances made up the duties of winter and early spring.

In December, 1863, January and February, 1864, ninety-six men re-enlisted for three years, (more than any other regiment in the brigade, three of which were from Massachusetts) thus proving by acts their love of country. All honor to such men, who after enduring the hardships and privations of so many campaigns again voluntarily entered upon a new term of service. The regiment was attached to the Second Brigade, Fourth Division, Second Army Corps.

May 3d was a day of labor. The old huts were levelled, grounds cleared and tents pitched. At dark received orders to move at midnight. Rations were issued and all things were ready. Prompt to the hour we marched, and bade adieu to our old camps, and 'mid the shades of night we cast the last lingering look on the ruins where we had passed so many happy hours, and called by the endeared name of home.

May 4th, at 11 A.M., Crossed the Rapidan. At 3 P.M., encamped on the same grounds where one year previous we fought the battle of Chancellorsville. Indeed, we were sadly reminded of that event. The bones of our fallen companions, whitened by the frosts of winter, were scatted over the field and through the woods, about which were blooming in innocent beauty the violets and other spring flowers. While passing along the familiar paths, I seemed to see the forms and faces which from that day hence were seen on earth no more.

May 5th. Marched near Barker's Store, on the Brock Road, in the Wilderness, where we arrived at 2 P.M. Threw up a line of works of fallen trees and earth, advanced through a thick wood intermingled with underbrush about half a mile, where we engaged the enemy's skirmishers. The entire corps was hotly engaged until 8 P.M., without material change of lines.

May 6th. The sun rose to a cloudless sky, but the smoke of battle soon obscured its brilliant rays. At 6 A.M., the entire line was advanced about one mile, the battle raging fiercely until 11 A.M., when the heavy reinforcements of the enemy were thrown in masses upon our lines. At this time the Sixteenth showed its real pluck, and held the ground until the entire line both to the right and left had fallen back. We retired slowly, contesting each foot of ground until we reached the works, when we were assigned the right of the brigade along the second line of works. At 5 P.M. General Longstreet's Corps (rebel) made its famous charge upon our line. The advance line of battle fought the masses of the enemy until their ammunition was expended, when they were obliged to evacuate the works and seek shelter at our rear. While so doing, the enemy occupied the advance line. In a moment, as if by magic, the Sixteenth leaped the works and charged the enemy, forcing him back, and captured a large number of prisoners. The brave and impetuous Lieutenant William Ross was the first to reach the captured works. The flag of the Sixteenth first waved over them after the recapture.

Colonel McAllister, commanding brigade, particularly mentioned the Sixteenth in his official report for its good conduct.

In this day's fighting, Captain Jos. S. Hills and Lieut. John H. Woodfin, were killed.

Captain Hills was a young man of great promise. He entered the service as a sergeant, and was the first promoted from the ranks. No officer in the regiment had a more enviable record. In battle he knew not fear, and obeyed and executed orders with that alacrity which distinguishes a good soldier. Firmness, strict temperance, and morality, were traits in his character which stood forth so prominent that none failed to observe. Lieut. J.H.Woodfin was a good officer, and, like Capt. Hills, was promoted from the ranks.

From May 7th to May 10th, marched from the Wilderness to Spottsylvania, moving by the left flank, each day erecting from one to three lines of earthworks.

May 10th, at 8 A.M., the regiment was ordered out as skirmishers, and were immediately engaged. Remained on the line and under fire all day. Twice, in the afternoon, a portion of the line was "assembled", and advanced and took possession of a house, situated on elevated grounds, about one-fourth of a mile in advance. We were unable to hold the position, as the enemy concentrated the fire of twelve pieces of artillery, and made the place quite untenable. Our loss was heavy.

I heard Major Willian, of Gen. Mott's Staff, remark: "The sixteenth Massachusetts won the admiration of all who saw it on the 10th of May,"

At this time, the Fourth Division was consolidated with the Third Division, and the brigade to which the Sixteenth was attached was designated the Third Brigade.

May 12th was a memorable day to the Army of the Potomac and the country. The morning was foggy. At 10 A.M., a drenching rain set in, and continued all day.

Before daylight, the Second Army Corps was formed in line of battle, and advanced (over the grounds on which the Sixteenth skirmished two days previous) taking the enemy by surprise - were in their camps while they were yet sleeping. The result of that day's action, in captures of guns and prisoners, are well known. The Sixteenth is entitled to a share of the glory.

After the aforesaid line was captured, the enemy rallied and were reinforced. Soon after, the almost bloodless victory of the morning was turned to a most severe battle. At 12 M., the Sixteenth was ordered to the right, along the crest of a hill, where the enemy had regained a few rods of the works lost in the morning. Along the entire line, this seemed the only contested spot. Our object was, that the enemy should capture no more of the works, and that a steady fire be kept up, so that no reinforcements could reach those already there.

The musketry fire was terrific. It was at this point a tree, some fourteen inches in diameter, was actually fallen - being cut down with bullets - it being between the fire of the contending parties. Regiment after regiment was thrown in this deadly position, and were cut down before the terrific fire like grass. Indeed, the blood flowing from so many killed and wounded, mixing with the rain then falling, gave the running water the appearance of streams of blood.

The men fired upward of three hundred rounds of ammunition of various calibre; after which, they were relieved to clean their pieces.

In this action our loss was heavy, including Lieut. Col. Waldo Merriam, then commanding the regiment, killed.

Perhaps there is no one but have wished [sic] he could forget some deep sorrow which has fallen to his lot. With me, when I learned Merriam was dead, I wished I had, or could not have, known it. I was filled with grief. I saw tears in many a soldier's eye when we last gazed upon his lifeless form. He was a brave and good officer - forgetting self while serving his country, and ever willing to sacrifice personal comforts for his country's good.

From May 10th to the 20th, was under fire each day, within one mile of the Spottsylvania battle-field.

Marched at midnight, May 21st, passing through Bowling Green; encamped, at 5 P.M., two miles beyond Milford - making a march of twenty-five miles. This was the first night of undisturbed repose since May 3d.

May 22d, threw up a line of earthworks.

May 23d. Marched from Milford to the North Anna River. The regiment was immediately placed on the skirmish line, under a sharp fire from the enemy's sharpshooters. One officer (whose name I will not mention) [footnote added - "The officer was Captain Lombard"] had eight shots fired at him while crossing a field, each throwing the earth upon him - yet he escaped uninjured. Were relieved at dark, joined the brigade, and took position about two miles to the left in an open field, where we were directly under a severe artillery fire for several hours on the morning of the 24th. At 9 A.M., was one of the first regiments to cross the river under a terrific fire from the enemy's artillery. Took position on a ridge of hills, from which position the enemy fled at our approach.

May 26th, at 10 P.M., recrossed the North Anna, marched a few miles to the left, and bivouacked. May 27th, at 12.30 P.M., continued the march in a southeasterly direction, crossing the Pamunk[e]y River at 3 P.M., on the 28th, and took up position thirteen miles from Richmond. On this march the command was short of rations, the men eating parched corn in lieu of bread.

May 29th. Advanced our lines about three miles, and erected very strong earthworks. 30th, were under fire while erecting a new line of entrenchments.

May 31st. At 10 A.M., moved forward, crossing a miry swamp, with frequent ditches; yet, by the aid of the artillery, we drove the enemy from their works, continued the advance across an open field, under a severe fire of grape and canister, which seemed to plough the very ground under our feet. Yet the men advanced without flinching for a moment, and gained a road of some importance, along which we took position. I never saw the regiment acquit itself more honorably, under such exceedingly trying circumstances. At dark the regiment was relieved. During the night the enemy regained the position which the Sixteenth took and held during the day. Our loss in officers was Captain John Rowe, mortally wounded; Lieutenants Ross and King, quite severely wounded. Captain Rowe entered the service a sergeant; was promoted for good conduct and faithful service. From a long and intimate acquaintance, I learned to prize him for his sterling traits of character and kindness of heart. In his death the country lost a good soldier, his widowed mother a noble son, and his comrades an associate whose life is worthy of emulation.

June 1st, marched at midnight, and arrived at Cold Harbor late on the afternoon of the 2d. 3d. Supported the First and Second Divisions of Second Army Corps in an advance, with slight loss. At 1 P.M., marched to the right, and formed a junction between the Fifth and Eighteenth Army Corps, and threw up a strong line of earthworks under a heavy artillery fire.

June 4th was relieved, and marched to the left, and bivouacked for the night. 5th. At 3, P.M. marched to the front and remained until 8, P.M., under a severe fire from artillery; then marched to Barker's Hill, the extreme left of the army, and took position and fortified. The regiment held this position until the night of the 12th, when we marched towards Long Bridge.

June 13th, crossed the Chickahominy, and bivouacked on the banks of the James River, at 8 P.M. Owing to the extreme heat, this march was a severe one, although the distance was only twenty miles.

June 14th, crossed the James at 4 P.M., at Wilcox Landing, and bivouacked for the night at Windmill Point, south of the James. The 15th was an intensely hot day. At 11 1/2, A.M., were on the road for Petersburg; reached the outer works at 12, midnight. These works were captured by the colored troops. It should, however be stated that the works were only garrisoned with the citizens of Petersburg. All who saw, admired the honest pride with which the colored troops viewed their captures from the enemy.

June 16th. The fore part of the day was occupied in turning the captured works. At 6 P.M., formed in line of battle and advanced on the enemy's second line of works, which encircled the city. The enemy's skirmishers were soon driven in, and we advanced for half a mile, through a wild and rugged wood, under a desultory fire, until we gained the crest of a ridge of hills, where the fire of the enemy was most deadly. At this time many of our bravest and best men were killed or wounded. After gaining this advantageous position, we were ordered to intrench, - which, however, could not be done until darkness obscured our movements. By daylight the works were completed, under the continued fire of the enemy. Quite a number were wounded, with spade in hand. It is quite surprising what an amount of work can be done in a few hours by willing hands and faithful hearts. Fortifications the most formidable sprang up in the short space of a few hours, erected, and, I might say, in many instances engineered, by the enlisted men. In many cases, the officers only need look on and see the work progress.

June 17th. Was under fire all day, losing a number of men. At 7 P.M., moved to the right and took position in a cultivated field in rear of a half-completed line of works, which were finished during the night under a severe musket fire.

June 18th. At daylight, advanced over an open field in our front to the enemy's works, which they evacuated on our approach. The advance was continued through a thick wood, under a desultory fire, until we gained a position known as the 'Hare House'. On the afternoon of the same day, the First Maine Heavy Artillery charged the enemy's works. Nobler and braver men I never saw. Other regiments have probably done as well, - but none better. The Sixteenth lost a number in killed and wounded during the day.

June 19th; was on the skirmish line; relieved at midnight on the 20th, - slight loss. 21st. Marched to the left near what is called the Strong House, and threw up a line of works.

June 22d. Advanced about a mile, took position, and commenced to fortify. General Barlow's First Division had made connection with Birney's Third Division, and Barlow was further prolonging his line, when it was found that the enemy had flanked Barlow, owing to the Sixth Corps not making the connection in time. The enemy was then "gobbling" up the men quite rapidly. the word "flanked" was passed from one regiment to another, and in a few moments the line swept back from left to right, and all efforts on the part of officers to stop the panic was fruitless. I speak from experience when I assert there is no word which so much demoralize men as, "We are flanked." I have seen it all through the army. In different regiments, brigades, divisions and corps, the same feelings exist. It was of this that the rebel General Early complained to his army, and issued an Order upon it.

June 23d. Took up position in rear of the works erected June 21st, near the Strong House, and remained in this position until the night of July 11th, when it left the front and proceeded to this State to be mustered out, having served the full term of three years.

Five officers and one hundred and ninety six men remained at the front - the men either recruits or veterans. They were formed into a battalion and attached to the Eleventh Massachusetts, and were afterwards made a part of that organization by the act of consolidation.

Assistant Surgeon Thomas Crozier, Captains R. T. Lombard and Henry S. Nutting, Lieutenants James F. Mansfield and F. McQuade were the retained officers. All had served three years, except Dr. Crozier. It matters not whether these officers remained voluntarily or by compulsion - they are entitled to much credit for the faithful manner in which they discharged their duties after the regiment had departed, - they previously expecting to return to their homes and friends after three years' service.

The regiment arrived in Massachusetts July 22, 1864, and was mustered out on the 27th of July, 1864.

I find it quite impossible to give the losses in each engagement, the regimental reports having been lost. The consolidated report for 1864 is as follows:

Killed and died of wounds received in action - officers,	4
Enlisted men,	19
Wounded - officers,	4
Enlisted men	74
Missing - enlisted men,	9
Discharged - officers,	5
Enlisted men,	38
Died of disease - enlisted men,	3
Deserted - enlisted men,	50
Joined from desertion - enlisted men,	13

Losses, &c, since the organization of the regiment:	Officers	Enlisted men
Killed,	12	62
Wounded,	22	357
Missing,	2	107
Died of wounds,	3	72
Died of disease and other causes,	2	60
Discharged,	31	311
Deserted,	-	165
Joined from missing,	2	18
Joined from desertion,	-	13

I have thus briefly endeavored to give a true and unbiased account of the operations, losses and conduct of the regiment during the three years' service. Whether the regiment has done well or ill, it is not for me here to say; but I feel assured that a grateful people will in after years honor the men, whether living or numbered with the countless dead, who fought to crush a rebellion against a government which our fathers reared - the government of equal rights, justice and liberty."

****

CHAPTER 14
*
JOHNSON'S CIVIL WAR SOUVENIRS

The Civil War soldier was conscious that he was participating in a momentous historical event, and was therefore assiduous in collecting souvenirs of his wartime experiences and military achievements. As a result, a vast quantity of relics, of every imaginable variety, survives to this day, in museums, collections and, of course, in the possession of many of the solders' families, cherished by their descendants.

Johnson was clearly no exception. Although we are fortunate that his letters, sword, epaulettes, commission and photographs still remain to us, the letters also record that he sent home a quantity other relics gathered during his travels, which have not survived.

Since Johnson was so careful to record that he was sending these relics home, it was considered that a schedule of them, as examples of what might be accumulated randomly by a soldier during the course of his service, would be of interest to both social historians and collectors, and this is therefore set out here:-

Letter date: Details

Sept. 8, 1861 - "I should have sent you by last letters two small pieces of the secesh flag which waved over Fort Hatteras and also some threads out of a Lieut. Col. Sash who was captured there..."

Dec. 23, 1861 - "Yesterday was the dedication of the Chaplain's tent and the line officers also had Hon. Chas. Train to lunch. Enclosed you will find two programmes of the dedication."

Jan. 9, 1862 - "There has been a drawing of Camp Hamilton by one of our regiment sent to be put into one of the pictorial [newspapers] and I was obliged to agree to take 20 copies... shall send the copies to you."

Mar. 16, 1862 - "I meant to have mentioned the pleasant evening I spent at the Delaware regiment at their theatre... I send you one of the programmes which was reduced to the present state by being in my vest pocket while marching to Newport News."

Mar. 26, 1862 - "I did not save anything for a relic except two little pieces of paper which I found on the shore which I enclose..."

"...I send you two engravings of Camp Hamilton. This two pieces of papers were from the Congress."

April 7, 1862 - "I send you home two confederate bills, saw some for five cts, these that I send come from Richmond and are of the best quality."

May 11, 1862 - "I send you some rebel papers and some peanuts".
May 16, 1862 - "I send you a sword found in the rebel storehouse at Portsmouth, I have been told that some of the cavalry are armed with similar swords, there is also a sample of the balls used by the crew of the Merrimac in their boarding pistols." Johnson's letter of May 29 suggests that the sword did not reach its destination.
July 18, 1862 - "While our regiment was at Suffolk I made the acquaintance of a pretty girl, and she promised to make me a secesh flag but failing to find any material she obtained this one from a little girl belonging to a strong Secesh family."
Aug. 7, 1862 - "This bullet came from a spherical case shot fired by the rebel burst near us and this ball struck at my feet, I picked it up and send it to you."
Oct. 8, 1862 - "Enclosed you will find two excellent likenesses of Gen'l Hooker & Kearney."
Oct. 29, 1862 - "I send you a bullet taken from the last Bull Run Battlefield."
Nov. 12, 1862 - "Enclosed you will find a new kind of bullet the three pieces separate and in close quarters are like Buck & Ball, the heaviest piece having the original force of a minie Bullet."
Nov. 16, 1862 - "You will find another sample of bullet but which I believe will not be - adopted".
Jan. 10, 1863 - "I send the paper [application for discharge] to you so you can judge for yourself how difficult it is to obtain a discharge."
Jan. 26, 1863 - "I send you a pipe made by my self from laurel root, it is very uncouth and is not finished as well as I should have it on account of the move."
Undated, early February 1863 - "Enclosed also you will find a star from our old flag which had been torn out it has been in every battle with the regiment and is now on the retired list. Enclosed or rather accompanying this letter there will be a cigar holder and perhaps a pipe... made from laurel root made by Serg't Harrington of Co F."
Feb. 26, 1863 - "I send you a photograph of Capt. Wiley one of the 16th Captains."
March 22, 1863 - "I enclose your photograph together with one of Lt. Lombards."
March 30, 1863 - "I shall send in [Mr. Hills' valise] two old company books and my belt plate which recently broke, it has been every where with me since I left Camp Hamilton at Fortress Monroe, I thought you might have it repaired and use it for a similar purpose."
c. June 8, 1863 - "I have a piece of petrified hickory wood found near Potomac Creek, but don't know whether to send it home or not." [June 22, 1863: "I was obliged to throw away the petrified wood as their was no means to send it home."]

****

APPENDIX 1
*
ITINERARIES OF CHARLES R. JOHNSON AND THE 16TH MASSACHUSETTS

There is no regimental history of the 16th, this volume substituting until such time as one is written. The detailed evidence for the movements of the regiment has been worked out from three sources – (i) Dyer's *Compendium of the War of the Rebellion*, (ii) Johnson's own letters, and (iii) the itinerary published in the 1865 regimental history of the 1st Massachusetts Infantry, which was Brigaded with the 16th for a considerable part of its service.

It is not always clear from Johnson's letters exactly where he and/or the regiment were located. This has been partly addressed by the use of footnotes to explain references in the letters, but it was felt that a clearer and more comprehensive schedule would help the reader to locate the regiment at any time of its service. This is shown below, and has been compiled from the above three sources. It gives, as far as can be determined, the location of Johnson, and of the 16th, throughout their service, although there are certainly discrepancies between the sources. For example, a note from the 1st Massachusetts itinerary covering the Gettysburg campaign stating "To mouth of Monocacy River, June 30" must be an error as it precedes the arrival at Gum Springs; likewise that stating "To Bridgeport, June 30" since, of the seven Bridgeports in Pennsylvania, the nearest, in Adams County, is still several miles north of Gettysburg. Where there are such discrepancies, the inclination must be to follow Johnson's account. The listing is chronological, and the source for each reference is given by a letter before each entry, as follows:

D = *Dyer's Compendium of the War of the Rebellion*
1 = *History of the 1st Mass. Infantry (where it generally agrees with that of the 16th)*
A = *Address on letter written by Johnson*
J = *Place/campaign/movement noted by Johnson in letter which expands on the above data.*

(a) Up to date of Johnson's death

D-Organised at Camp Cameron, Cambridge, June 29, 1861.
D-Left state for Old Point Comfort, Va., Aug. 17
A-Camp McClellan, Baltimore, Aug. 25
A-Camp McClellan, Baltimore, Aug. 29
D-Garrison duty at Fortress Monroe, Va., Sept. 1, 1861 to May 6, 1862
A-Camp McClellan, Baltimore, Sept. 1
J-Left Camp McClellan, boarded steamboat Louisiana, arrived Fort Monroe, Sept. 2

(Letter Sept. 3)
A-Old Point Comfort, Sept. 3
A-Old Point Comfort, Sept. 8
A-Old Point Comfort, Sept. 15
A-"Outside Fortress Monroe", Sept. 15
A-probably outside Fortress Monroe, Sept. 22
A-Camp Hamilton, Oct. 2
A-Old Point Comfort, Oct. 5
A-Old Point Comfort, Oct. 9
A-Camp Hamilton, Oct. 13
A-Camp Hamilton, Oct. 14
A-Camp Hamilton. Oct. 20
A-probably Camp Hamilton, Oct. 23
A-Camp Hamilton, Oct. 27
A-Camp Hamilton, Nov. 1
A-Camp Hamilton, Nov. 4
A-probably Camp Hamilton, Nov. 10
A-Camp Hamilton, Nov. 13
A-Camp Hamilton, Dec. 1
A-Camp Hamilton, Dec. 4
A-Camp Hamilton, Dec. 8
A-Camp Hamilton, Dec. 12
A-Camp Hamilton, Dec. 15
A-Camp Hamilton, Dec. 18
A-Camp Hamilton, Dec. 23
A-Camp Hamilton, Dec. 25
A-Camp Hamilton, Dec. 29
A-Camp Hamilton, Jan. 2, 1862
A-Camp Hamilton, Jan. 3
A-Camp Hamilton, Jan. 9
A-Camp Hamilton, Jan. 12
A-probably Camp Hamilton, Jan. 16
A-Camp Hamilton, Jan. 19
A-Camp Hamilton, Jan. 22
A-Camp Hamilton, Jan. 26
A-Camp Hamilton, Feb. 2
A-Camp Hamilton, Feb. 6
A-Camp Hamilton, Feb. 21
A-Fortress Monroe, Feb. 24
A-Camp Hamilton, March 2
A-Camp Hamilton, March 5
A-Camp Hamilton, March 9
A-Camp Hamilton, March 12
A-Camp Hamilton, March 13
A-Camp Hamilton, March 16
A-Camp Hamilton, March 22
A-Camp Hamilton, March 25
A-Camp Hamilton, March 26
A-Camp Hamilton, March 30
A-Camp Hamilton, April 3
1-Transport to Landing on Peninsula, April 6-10
A-Camp Hamilton, April 7 [letter describes Johnson's visit to the Yorktown siege

works]
A-Camp Hamilton, April 9
1-To near York Point, April 12
A-Camp Hamilton, April 13
1-To near Yorktown, Camp Winfield Scott, April 16
A-Camp Hamilton, April 21
A-Camp Hamilton, April 23
A-Camp Hamilton, April 30
A-Camp Hamilton, May 4
A-Camp Hamilton, May 8
A-probably Norfolk, May 9
D-Occupation of Norfolk, May 10
A-Norfolk, May 11 [Letter describes journey from Fortress Monroe to Norfolk]
A-Portsmouth, May 13
A-Portsmouth Navy Yard, May 16
D-Moved to Suffolk May 17, and joined Army of the Potomac at Fair Oaks, June 13.
A-Suffolk, May 19[?] [Letter decribes journey from Norfolk to Suffolk]
A-Suffolk, May 21
A-Suffolk, May 29
A-Suffolk, June 2
A-Suffolk, June 6
A-White House, June 11
A-Fair Oaks Battle Ground, June 15 [Letter describes journey from Suffolk to Fair Oaks]
D-Nine Mile Road, near Richmond, June 18
A-Fair Oaks, June 19
A-Fair Oaks, June 21
D-Seven Days before Richmond, June 25 - July 1 (Oak Grove, near Fair Oaks, June 25; White Oak Swamp & Glendale, June 30; Malvern Hill July 1 & August 5)
A-Fair Oaks, June 26
A-Fair Oaks, June 27 ["I am on James River about 6 miles from Fort Darling"]
A-Camp near the James River, June 28
1-To near Glendale, June 29
1-To Battlefield of Glendale, June 30
1-To Malvern Hill, July 1
1-To near Harrison's Bar, July 2
1-To Camping ground, July 4
1-To Camping ground, July 5
D-Duty at Harrison's Landing until August 15
A-About six miles from Fort Darling, Harrison's Bend, James River, July 4 [Letter describes movements from Fair Oaks to Malvern Hill and the retreat from Malvern Hill]
A-probably Harrison's Landing, James River, July 7
A-Harrison's Landing, July 11
A-Harrison's Landing, July 14
A-Harrison's Landing, July 18
A-Camp, Harrison's Landing, July 23
A-Camp, Harrison's Landing, Aug. 3
A-Camp near Harrison's Landing, Aug. 7 [Letter, and the following, describes a three-day reconnaissance, Aug. 4-6]
A-Camp, Harrison's Landing, Aug. 8
A-Harrison's Landing, Aug. 12

D-Movement to Fortress Monroe, thence to Centerville August 15-26.
1-To near Charles City Court House, Aug. 15
1-To near Chickahominy, Aug. 16
1-To near Barhamsville, Aug. 17
1-To near Williamsburg, Aug. 18
1-To near Yorktown, Aug. 19
1-Aboard the Vanderbilt, Aug. 21
1-Transport to Alexandria, Aug. 21-24
A-Camp near Alexandria, Aug. 23
1-Through Alexandria, Aug. 24
1-To Warrenton Junction, Aug. 25
1-To Camp near the Junction, Aug. 26
D-Bristoe Station, Kettle Run, Aug. 27
1-To Battlefield of Bristow, Aug. 27
1-To Blackburn's Ford, Aug. 28
D-Battle of Groveton, Aug. 29
1-Second Bull Run fight, Aug. 29
D-Battle of Bull Run, Aug. 30
1-Manoeuvring and retreat to Centerville, Aug. 30-31
A-Washington, Sept. 1
D-Battle of Chantilly, Sept. 1
1-To Chantilly, Sept. 1
1-To near Fairfax Station, Sept. 1[sic]
D-Duty at Fort Lyon and at Fairfax Station, Defences of Washington. till Oct. 30, and at Munson's Hill till Nov 2.
1-To near Fort Lyons[sic], Sept. 3
1-Changed position, Sept. 4
A-Camp near Fort Lyon, Sept. 7
A-Camp, Washington area, place not specified
1-To near Fairfax Seminary, Sept. 12
A-Camp near Fort Worth, Sept. 14
A-Camp near Fort Worth, Sept. 17
A-Camp near Alexandria, Sept. 22
A-Camp near Alexandria, Sept. 26
A-National Hotel, Washington, Oct. 6
A-Camp near Alexandria, Oct. 8
A-Camp near Alexandria, Oct. 13
A-Camp near Alexandria, Oct. 20
1-To Munson's Hill, Oct. 20
A-Camp near Alexandria, Oct. 29
D-Duty at Munson's Hill, Oct. 30-Nov. 2
1-From Munson's Hill to Camp, Nov. 1
1-From Camp at Fairfax Seminary to Bivouac, Nov. 1 [sic]
D-Duty at Fairfax Station, Nov. 2-25
1-From camp at Fairfax Court House and back to Village, Nov. 2
A-Camp near Manassas Junction
1-From the village to Station in railroad, Nov. 6
A-near Bristow [Bristoe] Station, Nov. 9
D-Operations on Orange & Alexandria RR, Nov. 10-12
A-Walnut Run, Nov. 12
A-Walnut Run, Nov. 16
A-Wolfe Ford, Occoquan River, Nov. 23
1-To Wolfe's Run Shoals, Nov. 25

A-near Falmouth, Nov. 29 ["a mile and a half from the Rappahannock River"]
1-To Dumfries, Dec. 1
1-To Stafford Court House, Dec. 2
1-To Camp Smoke, near Falmouth, Dec. 3
A-Camp near Falmouth, Dec. 10
1-To bivouac, Dec. 11
1-To bivouac, Dec. 12
D-Rappahannock Campaign, Dec. 1862 to June 1863.
D-Battle of Fredericksburg, Va., Dec. 12-15, 1862.
1-Across River to battle-ground of Fredericksburg, Dec. 13
A-Rappahannock River, Dec. 15
1-Back to Smoke Camp, Dec. 16
A-Camp near Falmouth, Dec. 21
A-Camp near Falmouth, Dec. 29
A-Camp near Falmouth, undated early Jan. 1863
1-Changed camp to near Fitz Hugh House, Jan. 3
A-Camp near Falmouth, Jan 10
A-Camp near Falmouth, Jan. 17
D-"Mud March", Jan. 20-24, 1863
1-To near Banks' Ford, Jan. 21
1-Back to Camp near Fitzhugh House, Jan. 23
D-At Falmouth till April 27
A-Camp near Falmouth, Jan. 24
A-Camp near Falmouth, Jan. 25
A-Camp near Falmouth, Jan. 26
A-Camp near Falmouth, Jan. 31
A-Camp near Falmouth, Feb. 8 [Describes 3-day expedition to destroy bridge at Rappahannock Station, Feb. 5-7]
A-Camp near Falmouth, Feb. 17
A-Camp near Falmouth, Feb. 19
A-Camp near Falmouth, Feb. 23
A-Camp near Falmouth, Feb. 26
A-Camp near Falmouth, March 1
A-Camp near Falmouth, March 5
A-Camp near Falmouth, March 8
A-Camp near Falmouth, March 11
A-Camp near Falmouth, March 16
A-Camp near Falmouth, March 19
A-Camp near Falmouth, March 22
A-Camp near Falmouth, March 26
A-Camp near Falmouth, March 30
A-Camp near Falmouth, April 2
A-Camp near Falmouth, April 5
A-Camp near Falmouth, April 23
A-Camp near Falmouth, April 26
A-Camp near Falmouth, April 28
D-Chancellorsville Campaign, April 27-May 6
1-To down the river, April 28
1-Changed position, April 29
1-To Hartwood Church, April 30
1-To Chancellorsville, May 1
D-Battle of Chancellorsville, May 1-5

1-To north bank of river, May 5
1-To Camp near Fitz Hugh Court House, May 6
1-Changed camp, May 19
A-Camp near Falmouth, May 27
A-Camp near Falmouth, May 31
A-Camp near Falmouth, June 2
A-Camp near Falmouth, June 4
A-On Picket near Potomac Creek, June 6
A-Camp near Falmouth, c. June 8
A-Camp near Falmouth, June 10
D-Gettysburg Campaign, Pa., June 11-July 24.
1-To near Hartwood House, June 11
1-To Beverly Ford, June 12
A-near Beverly Ford, June 14 [letter written over several days from June 14-19, describing journey from Beverly Ford to Manassas Junction]
1-To Manassas Junction, June 14-15
1-Changed position, June 16
1-To Centreville, June 17
1-Changed position, June 18
1-To Gum Spring, June 19
A-Gum Spring, June 20 [Letter describes journey from Manassas Junction to Gum Spring]
1-Changed position, June 20
1-To mouth of Monocacy River, June 20[sic]
A-Gum Spring, June 22
A-Gum Spring, June 24
1-To Catoctin Mountains, June 26
1-To Burkettsville, June 27
1-To Frederick City through Middleton
1-To Taneytown, June 29
A-Taneytown, June 30
1-To Bridgeport, June 30
D-Battle of Gettysburg, July 1-3
1-Gettysburg Battlefield, July 1

(b) From Johnson's death till muster-out

D-Wapping Heights, Va., July 23
D-Bristoe Campaign, October 9-22
1-To Union Mills, Oct. 16
1-To Bristow Station, Oct. 19
1-Through Greenwich to Bivouac
1-To Catlett's Station, Oct. 21
1-Changed camp, Oct. 26
1-To near Warrenton Junction, Oct. 30
D-Advance to the Rappahannock, Nov. 7-8
D-Kelly's Ford, Nov.7
1-Through Bealton to bivouac, Nov. 7
1-To Kelly's Ford, Nov. 8
1-To Brandy Station, Nov. 10
1-Changed camp, Nov. 11
1-Brandy Station to other side of Rapidan, Nov. 26

D-Mine Run Campaign Nov. 26-Dec. 2
D-Payne's Farm, Nov. 27
1-Bivouac to fight near Locust Grove, Nov. 27
1-Through Locust Grove to near Mine Run, Nov. 28
1-Manoueuvring, Nov. 29
1-To Mine Run, Nov. 30
1-Down Plank Road to Wilderness, Dec. 1
1-Across River (Rapidan) to bivouac, Dec. 2
1-To old camp at Brandy Station, Dec. 3
D-Demonstration on the Rapidan, Feb. 6-7, 1864
1-Brandy [sic] to beyond Stevensburg, Feb. 6
1-Back to Brandy, Feb. 7
D-Duty near Brandy Station till May, 1864
D-Rapidan Campaign, May-June (Battles of the Wilderness, May 5-7; Spotsylvania May 8-12; Spotsylvania Court House, May 12-21; Assault on the Salient, Spotsylvania Court House, May 12; Harris' Farm, Fredericksburg Road, May 19; North Anna River, May 23-26; Ox Ford, May 23-24; On line of the Pamunkey May 26-28; Totopotomoy May 28-3; Cold Harbor June 1-12; Before Petersburg June 16-18; Jerusalem Plank Road, June 22-23)
1-To Chancellorsville Battleground of 1863, May 4
1-To Battle of the Wilderness, May 5
1-To near Spotsylvania Court House, May 5
1-Manoeuvring on the battlefield, May 10
D-Po River, May 10
D-Spotsylvania Court House, May 12-21
D-North Anna River, May 23-26
D-Line of the Pamunkey, Msy 26-28
D-Totopotomoy, May 28-31
D-Cold Harbor, June 1-12
D-Siege of Petersburg, June 16-July 12
D-Jerusalem Plank Road, June 22-23
D-Left front for muster out, July 12. Veterans & recruits transferred to the 20th Massachusetts Infantry.
D-Mustered out July 28, 1864
D-Regiment lost during service 14 officers & 227 enlisted men killed and mortally wounded, and 1 officer and 121 enlisted men by disease.

The following table uses the itinerary in the History of the 1st Massachusetts Infantry to give some indication of the number of miles marched each day by the 16th. Plain figures indicate miles marched; those in round brackets ( ) indicate railroad; those in square brackets [ ] indicate other forms of transport (i.e. boat or wagon). (Note – a small number of entries in Dyer appear to be at variance with the account of the 1st Massachusetts).

1861

June 1 Boston to Camp Ellsworth	6
June 13 Camp Ellsworth to Camp Cameron	2
June 15 Camp Cameron to Boston	8
June 15-17 Boston to Washington	(365) + [130] 495
June 19 Washington to Georgetown, Camp Banks	5
July 8 Camp Banks to Great Falls (Cos. I,K)	15
July 14-15 Great Falls to Camp Banks (Cos. I,K)	15
July 16 Camp Banks to Vienna	15
July 17 Vienna to Centerville	13

July 18 Centerville to Blackburn's Ford and back	6
July 19 Centerville to near Blackburn's Ford and back	3
July 21 Returned to Centerville	3
July 22 Centerville to Camp Banks	30
July 23 Camp Banks across the Potomac	2
July 24 To Arlington heights, Fort Albany	1/2
Aug. 13 Fort Albany to Bladensburg, Md., Camp Union	10
Sept. 9 Camp Union to Upper Marlborough	12
Sept. 10 Through the town & returned to Camp	4
Sept. 11 Upper Marlborough to near Nottingham	10
Sept. 12 Near Nottingham to Lower Marlborough	9
Sept. 13 Lower Marlborough to Friendship	9
Sept. 14 Friendship to Upper Marlborough	15
Sept. 15 Upper Marlborough to Hill's Landing	[5]
Hill's Landing to Lower Marlborough	9
Sept. 16 Lower Marlborough to Prince Frederick	12
Sept. 19-20 Prince Frederick to Lower Marlborough	12
Oct. 5 Lower Marlborough to Upper Marlborough	17
Oct. 6-7 Upper Marlborough to Camp Union	12
Oct. 24 Camp Union to opposite Alexandria	13
Oct. 25 Opposite Alexandria to Piscataway	9
Oct. 25 Piscataway to Camp Hooker	25
1862	
April 5 Camp Hooker to Budd's House	1
April 6-10 Transport to Landing on Pensinsula	[160]
April 12 To near York Point	5
April 16 To near Yorktown, Camp Winfield Scott	4 1/2
May 4 To bivouac in the woods	15
May 5 To battlefield of Wiliamsburg	3
May 6 To camp near Fort Magruder	1
May 9 To north side of town	3
May 15 To Burnt Ordinary	9
May 16 Through Barhamsville	15
May 18 To New Kent Court House	6
May 19 To Baltimore Cross-Roads	90
May 23 To Bottom's Bridge	6
May 24 Over Chickahominy and back	6
May 25 To Poplar Hill	4
June 4 To Seven Pines, near Fair Oaks	7
(Dyer gives the 1st at Oak Grove, June 25]	
June 29 To near Glendale	9
June 30 To battlefield of Glendale	1
July 1 To Malvern Hill	3
July 2 To near Harrison's Bar	10
July 4 To camping-ground	1
July 5 To camping-ground	1
Aug. 15 To near Charles City Court House	8
Aug. 16 To near Chickahominy	3
Aug. 17 To near Barhamsville	13
Aug. 18 To near Williamsburg	19
Aug. 19 To near Yorktown	10
Aug. 21 Aboard the 'Vanderbilt"	2
Aug. 21-24 Transport to Alexandria	[175]
Aug. 24 Through Alexandria	3
Aug. 25 To Warrenton Junction	(40)
Aug. 26 To camp near the Junction	1 1/2
Aug. 27 To battlefield of Bristow	12

Aug. 28 To Blackburn's Ford	9
Aug. 29 Second Bull Run fight	12
Aug. 30-31 Manoeuvring and retreat to Centerville	12
Sept. 1 To Chantilly	6
Sept. 2 To near Fairfax Station	10
Sept. 3 To near Fort Lyons	20
Sept. 4 Changed position	1/2
Sept. 12 To near Fairfax Seminary	3
Oct. 20 To Munson's Hill	6
Nov. 1 From Munson's Hill to Camp	6
Nov. 1 From Camp at Fairfax Seminary to bivouac	8
Nov. 2 From Camp at Fairfax C.H. and back to village	6
Nov. 6 From the village to station on railroad	4
Nov. 25 To Wolfe's Run Shoals	8
Dec. 1 To Dumfries	12
Dec. 2 To Stafford Court House	11
Dec. 3 To Camp Smoke, near Falmouth	8
Dec. 11 To bivouac	2
Dec. 12 To bivouac	5
Dec. 13 Across river to battle-ground of Fredericksburg	1
Dec. 16 Back to Smoke Camp	8

1863

Jan. 3 Changed camp to near Fitz Hugh House	1 1/2
Jan. 21 To near Banks's Ford	8
Jan. 23 Back to camp near Fitz Hugh House	8
April 28 To down the river	5
April 29 Changed position	3/4
April 30 To Hartwood Church	12
May 1 To Chancellorsville	9
May 5 To north bank of river	14
May 6 To camp near Fitz Hugh House	14
May 19 Changed camp	1
June 11 To near Hartwood Church	11
June 12 To Beverly Ford	27
June 14-15 To Manassaas Junction	26
June 16 Changed position	1/2
June 17 To Centerville	5
June 18 Changed position	1
June 19 To Gum Spring	10
June 20 Changed position	1/2
June 20 To mouth of Monocacy River	22
June 26 To Catoctan[sic] Mountains	7
June 27 To Burkettsville	11
June 28 To Frederick City through Middleton	17
June 29 To Taneytown	22
June 30 To Bridgeport(?)	4
July 1 Gettysburg Battlefield	13
July 7 To Mechanicstown	17
July 8 To Frederick City	17
July 9 To South Mountain Pass	12
July 10 To Keedysville (manoeuvring)	9
July 11 Changed position	5
July 12 Changed position	1
July 14 Changed position	2
July 15 To near Sharpsburg	11
July 16 To near Sandy Hook	10
July 17 To near Lovettsville	6

July 18 To Hullsborough	6
July 20 To Upperville	16
July 22 To near Piedmont Station, Manassas Gap RR	7
July 23 Through Manassas Gap	9
July 24 Returned to near Markham Station	3
July 25 To near Salem	11
July 26 To near Warrenton	10
July 31 To Warrenton Junction and Alexandria	12 (50) . 62
Aug. 1 To Philadelphia, marched in Baltimore & Philada	2 (150) .152
Aug. 2 To Governor's Island	(85) [3] . 88
Aug. 17 To Riker's	[10]
Oct. 14 To Alexandria, Va.	(285) [12] .297
Oct. 16 To Union Mills	1 (20) . 21
Oct. 19 To Bristow Station	12
Oct. 20 Through Greenwich to Bivouac	14
Oct. 21 To Catlett's Station	8
Oct. 26 Changed camp	1/2
Oct. 30 To near Warrenton junction	4
Nov. 7 Through Bealeton to bivouac	17
Nov. 8 To near Kelly's Ford	6
Nov. 10 To Brandy Station	7
Nov. 11 Changed camp	1/2
Nov. 26 Brandy Station to other side of Rapidan	15
Nov. 27 Bivouac to fight near Locust Grove	3
Nov. 28 Through Locust Grove to near Mine Run	11
Nov. 29 Manoeuvring	4
Nov. 30 To Mine Run	3 1/2
Dec. 1 Down plank-road to Wilderness	6
Dec. 2 Across river (Rapidan) to bivouac	14
Dec. 3 To old camp at Brandy [Station]	12
1864	
Feb. 6 Brandy to beyond Stevensburg	5
Feb. 7 Back to Brandy	5
May 4 To Chancellorsville battleground of 1863	20
May 5 To Battle of the Wilderness	10
May 8 To near Spottsylvania Court House	8
May 10 Manoeuvring on the battle-field	5
May 11 Along the line to the west	1
May 14 Manoeuvring	3
May 15 Manouevring	5
May 17 Manoeuvring	2
May 18 Manouevring	2
May 19 Manoeuvring	10
May 20 Manoeuvring	5
May 21 To Fredericksburg, thence to Belle Plain	20
May 21-22 By steamer up River Potomac	[40]
May 22 Through Washington	2
May 22-23 To New York over the railroad	[280]
May 24-25 On boat to Fall River	[185]
May 25 From Fall River to Boston	(50)
Total distance traveled:	3,311 3/4 miles

The following two items may also be helpful for tracking the service of the 16th Massachusetts infantry:

(i) Departments, Brigades, etc., in which the 16th served:-

Dept. of Virginia, to May 1862, at Fortress Monroe, Aug. 1861 - May 1862
Viele's Brigade, May 1862 - June 1862
1st Brig., 2nd Div., 3rd Corps, Army of the Potomac, June 1862 - March 1864
1st Brig., 4th Div., 2nd Corps, March to May 1864
3rd Brig., 3rd Div., 2nd Corps, May 1864 to muster-out, July 1864

(ii) Commanders of the 3rd Corps, and of its 2nd Division and 1st Brigade, during Johnson's term of service

1st Brigade	2nd Division	3rd Corps
Naglee (Mar.13-Apr. 27,1862)	Hooker (Mar.13-Sep.5, 1862)	Heintzelman (Mar.13-Oct.30, 1862)
Grover (April 27-Sep. 16, 1862)		
|	Sickles (Sep.5, 1862-Jan.12, 1863)	|
|	|	Stoneman (Oct.30, 1862-Feb.5, 1863)
|	|	|
Carr (Sep.16, 1862-Jan.12, 1863)		|
Blaisdell (Jan.12-Feb.8, 1863)	Carr (Jan.12-Feb.8, 1863)	|
Carr (Feb.8-May 3, 1863)	Berry (Feb.8-May 3, 1863)	Sickles (Feb.8-May 29, 1863)
Blaisdell (May 3-23, 1863)	Carr (May 3-23, 1863)	|
Carr (May 23-Oct.5, 1863)	Humphreys (May 23-July 9,1863)	Birney (May 29-Jun.3, 1863)
|	|	Sickles (June 3-July 2, 1863)

****

Appendix 2
*
ROSTER OF COMPANY F, 16TH MASSACHUSETTS INFANTRY

Charles Robinson Johnson: Res. Boston; merchant. Enlisted July 12, 1861, aged 25, as Captain. Wounded Chancellorsville, Va., May 3, 1863, and Gettysburg, Pa., July 2, 1863 (died of wounds July 17, 1863 at Lexington, Mass.).

Charles Henry Mayo: Res. Roxbury; merchant. Enlisted July 1, 1861, aged 29, as 1st Lieut. Transferred March 9, 1862 to Co. H, 16th Mass. Inf. Also had service in Co. D, 3rd Mass. Heavy Artillery.

Payson Eliot Tucker: Res. Cambridge; lawyer. Enlisted July 12, 1861, aged 27, as 1st Lieut.; transferred Dec. 31, 1861 to Co. H. Resigned Sept. 21, 1862. Lived in Boston after the war. Member of GAR Post 68 (Benjamin Stone Jr.), Dorchester, Mass.

Joseph S. Hills: Res. Boston; clerk. Enlisted July 12, 1861, aged 20, as 1st Sgt.; 2nd Lieut. Nov. 10, 1861; 1st Lt., Aug. 11, 1862; Capt. May 4, 1863. Wounded Chancellorsville, Va., May 3, 1863. Killed Wilderness, Va., May 6, 1864.

Isaac F. Kennaston: Res. Lexington; laborer. Enlisted July 12, 1861, aged 22 as Sergeant. Mustered out July 27, 1864.

Thomas W. Coombs: Res. South Reading; bootmaker. Enlisted July 12, 1861, aged 40, as Sergeant. Wounded Fair Oaks, Va., June 18, 1862. Discharged for wounds Feb. 25, 1863. Later service in 59th Mass. Inf. (Dec. 5, 1863 – June 1, 1865) and 57th Mass. Inf. to muster-out at Washington, DC, July 30, 1865.

Henry Scales Harrington: Res. Stoneham; painter. Enlisted July 12, 1861, aged 30, as Corporal. Re-enlisted Dec. 23, 1863. Transferred July 11, 1864 to Co. E, 11th Mass. Inf. Missing March 31, 1865 at Hatcher's Run, Va.; returned. Mustered out May 15, 1865.

Francis Morris: Res. Burlington; farmer. Enlisted July 12, 1863, aged 33, as Sergeant. Discharged for disability at Providence, RI, March 5, 1863.

Nathan Nourse Jr: Born Arlington, Mass. Res. Burlington; farmer. Enlisted July 12, 1861, aged 32, as Sergeant. Discharged for disability at Falmouth, Va., March 11, 1863. Member of GAR Post 36 (Francis Gould,), Arlington, Mass. Died Oct. 20, 1895.

Reuben B. Facemyre: Res. Boston; sailor. Enlisted July 12, 1861, aged 24, as Corporal Wounded Gettysburg, Pa., July 2 or 3, 1863, and Mine Run, Va., Nov. 27, 1863. Transferred July 11, 1864 to Co. F, 11th Mass. Inf.

Jacob F. Jackson: Res. Paris, Me.; carpenter. Enlisted July 12, 1861, aged 27, as Corporal. Discharged for disability Nov. 18, 1861.

William Jones: Res. Cambridge; carpenter. Enlisted July 12, 1861, aged 31, as Corporal. Promoted Sergeant. Mustered out July 27, 1864. Post-war, member of GAR Post 19 (Edwin V. Sumner), Fitchburg, Mass.

George H. Kimball: Res. Charlestown; blacksmith. Enlisted July 12, 1861, aged 23, as Corporal. Transferred July 11, 1864 to Co. F, 11th Mass. Inf.; Sergeant, Oct. 1, 1864. Mustered out July 14, 1865 at Readville, Mass.

Michael O'Loan: Res. Charlestown; teamster. Enlisted July 12, 1861, aged 21, as Wagoner. Promoted Corporal. Killed Chancellorsville, Va., May 3, 1863.

Edward Adams: res. Great Barrington; printer. Enlisted July 15, 18653, aged 28, as a Private. Wounded Wilderness, May 6, 1864. Transferred July 11, 1864 to Co. F, 11th Mass. inf. Mustered out at Readville, Mass., July 14, 1865. State pension No. 522,891, Sept. 23, 1884.

John F. Adams: Res. Philadephia, Pa.; printer. Enlisted Aug 18, 1863, aged 33, as Private and drafted into Co. F. Transferred July 11, 1864 into Co. F, 11th Mass. Inf. Mustered out July 14, 1865 at Readville, Mass.

Barnard W. Alby: Res. Marblehead; mariner. Enlisted Dec. 8, 1863, aged 18, as Private. Transferred July 11, 1864 into Co. F, 11th Mass. Inf. Mustered out July 14, 1865 at Readville, Mass.

John Allen: Res. Pittsburgh, Pa; laborer. Enlisted July 12, 1861, aged 26, as Private. Promoted Corporal. Killed Fair Oaks, Va., June 18, 1862.

John Anderson: Res. Roxbury; machinist. Enlisted July 12, 1861, aged 33, as Private. Discharged for disability, Washington DC, Dec. 11, 1862.

Henry L. Bates: Born Newton, Mass. Res. Bedford; box or boot maker. Enlisted July 12, 1861, aged 25, as Corporal. Re-enlisted Dec. 23, 1863. Transferred July 11, 1864 to Co. F, 11th Mass. Inf. Member and Post Commander of GAR Post 63 (General Wadsworth), Natick, Mass. Died July 29, 1919.

Michael Bohannon: Res. Lawrence; currier. Enlisted July 12, 1861, aged 28, as Private. Discharged for disability, Newark, NJ, Jan. 1, 1863. and transferred to Veteran Reserve Corps

James Bond: Res. South Reading; laborer. Enlisted Dec. 20, 1861, aged 19, as Private. Killed Gettysburg, Pa., July 2, 1863 (as of Co. E).

Patrick Buckley: Res. Charlestown; laborer. Enlisted July 12, 1861 as Private. Promoted Corporal, Sergeant. Wounded Aug. 30, 1862 at 2nd Bull Run, Va. Mustered out July 27, 1864.

James Carnes: Res. Roxbury; paper maker. Enlisted July 12, 1861, aged 19, as Private. Discharged for disability, Boston, Mass., Mar. 17, 1863.

Lyman Center: Res. Somerville; teamster. Enlisted July 12, 1861, aged 23, as private. Mustered out July 27, 1864.

George N. Chase: Born Greensboro, Vt. Res. Wilmington; shoemaker. Enlisted July

12, 1861, aged 19, as Private. Transferred April 6, 1864 to Co. I, 6th Inf., Veteran Reserve Corps, as Musician. Mustered Dec. 29, 1864 as Bugler, 1st Mass. Bn. Cav. Member of GAR Post 5 (General Frederick West Lander), Lynn, Mass. Died Aug. 23, 1903.

George Clark: Res. New York City, NY; tailor. Enlisted Aug 17, 1863, aged 23, as a Private and drafted into Co. F. Died of disease on July 30, 1864, as prisoner-of-war at Andersonville, Ga. Buried in Grave 4295, Andersonville National Cemetery.

Daniel Clifford: Res. Charlestown; currier. Enlisted July 12, 1861, aged 39, as private. Wounded June 18, 1862 at Fair Oaks, Va. Discharged for disability, Boston, Mass., Oct. 3, 1862.

James Collins: Res. South Reading; shoemaker. Enlisted July 12, 1861, aged 28, as Private. Discharged for disability nr. Falmouth, Va., Dec. 27, 1862. Mustered Dec. 5, 1863 into Co. A, 59th Mass. Inf. Transferred June 1, 1865 to Co. A, 57th Mass. Inf. Mustered out July 30, 1865, at Washington, DC.

Leander Collins: Res. Dartmouth; laborer. Enlisted July 12, 1861, aged 35, as Private. Mustered out July 27, 1864.

Hugh Connolly: Res. Milford; shoemaker. Enlisted July 12, 1861, aged 33, as Private. Re-enlisted Dec. 23, 1863. Transferred July 11, 1864 to Co. F, 11th Mass. Inf.

James Connolly: Res. Biddeford, Me.; laborer. Enlisted July 12, 1861, aged 24, as Private. Mustered out July 27, 1864.

John F. Connor: Res. Randolph; shoemaker. Enlisted July 12, 1861, aged 27, as Private. Transferred Feb. 15, 1864 to Co. H, 1st Inf., Veteran Reserve Corps. Mustered out July 22, 1864.

Charles Henry Cooke: Born Brewer, Me. Res. Roxbury; clerk. Enlisted July 12, 1861, aged 23, as Private. Transferred Aug. 15, 1863 to Co. E, 9th Inf., Veteran Reserve Corps. Re-enlisted May 31, 1864; mustered out Nov. 29, 1865. Post-war, member of GAR Post 89 (J.H.Chipman Jr.), Beverly, Mass.

Charles Culver: Res. Canada; laborer. Enlisted July 14, 1863, aged 21, as a Private, and drafted into Co. F. Deserted Oct. 14, 1863 near Union Mills, Va.

James Dagnall: Res. Fall River, Mass.; machinist. Enlisted Aug. 1, 1863, aged 21, as a Private. Transferred July 11, 1864 into Co. F, 11th Mass. Inf. Date of discharge not given.

William Davis: Born and res. Burlington; farmer. Enlisted July 12, 1861, aged 20, as private. Wounded 2nd Bull Run, Va., Aug. 29, 1862; wounded and prisoner-of-war, Chancellorsville, Va., May 2, 1863. Re-enlisted Dec. 23, 1863. Transferred July 11, 1864 to Co. F, 11 Mass. Inf. Mustered out July 14, 1865, at Readville, Mass. Post-war, member of GAR Post 64 (E.D.Baker), Clinton, Mass. Died Nov. 22, 1930.

Charles F. Denton: Res. Charlestown; sailor. Enlisted July 12, 1861, aged 37, as Private. Discharged at Fortress Monroe, Mar. 14, 1862.

Stephen D. Devine: Res. Charlestown; teamster. Enlisted July 12, 1861, aged 40, as private. Discharged for disability Oct. 13, 1862.

John Doherty: Res. Boston; bootmaker. Enlisted July 12, 1861, aged 26, as Private. Wounded Wilderness, Va., May 5, 1864; died of wounds at Washington, DC, June 17,

1864.

John Donovan: Res. Boston; tailor. Enlisted July 12, 1861, aged 28, as Private. Mustered out July 27, 1864. Transferred to Veteran Reserve Corps.

Patrick Doyle: Res. Boston; marble worker. Enlisted July 12, 1861, aged 25, as Private. Mustered out July 27, 1864. Transferred to Veteran Reserve Corps.

Stephen Driscoll: Res. Boston; laborer. Enlisted July 12, 1861, aged 28, as Private. Wounded Chancellorsville, Va., May 3, 1863; discharged for wounds at Washington DC, Aug. 29, 1863.

William Duffy: Res. Roxbury; farmer. Enlisted July 12, 1861, aged 20, as Private. Wounded Chancellorsville, Va., May 3, 1863. Re-enlisted Dec. 23, 1863. Missing in action, Wilderness, Va., May 6, 1864.

Edward Dusenberry: Res. Sheffield, Mass.; painter. Enlisted July 16. 1863, aged 24, as a Private and drafted into Co. F. Wounded May 6, 1864, Wilderness, Va. Transferred July 11, 1864 into Co. F, 11th Mass. Date of discharge not given.

Michael Dyer: Res. Boston; laborer. Enlisted July 12, 1861, aged 24, as Private. Killed Gettysburg, Pa., July 2, 1863.

John Farrell: Res. Lynn; shoemaker. Enlisted July 12, 1861, aged 22, as private. Discharged for disability Oct. 22, 1862.

Leonard Felder: Res. North Egremont, Mass; laborer. Enlisted Aug. 15, 1863, aged 22, as a Private, and drafted into Co. F. Wounded June 16, 1864, Petersburg, Va. Transferred July 111, 1864 into Co. F, 11th Mass. Inf. Date of discharge not given.

Abram Ferguson: Res. Great Barrington, Mass.; laborer. Enlisted on July 15, 1863, aged 25, as a Private. Transferred July 11, 1864 into Co. F, 11th Mass. Inf. Date of discharge not given.

Patrick Flanagan: Res. Newton; spinner. Enlisted Dec. 14, 1861, aged 28, as private. Discharged for disability, Washington DC, Aug. 12, 1863. Transferred to Veteran Reserve Corps. Also had service in Co. I, 10th Mass. Inf.

Patrick Flatery: Res. Somerville; laborer. Enlisted July 12, 1861, aged 30, as Private. Missing in action, Glendale, Va., June 30, 1862; Discharged for disability Washington DC, Aug. 18, 1863.

John Flynn: Born and res. Lowell; laborer. Enlisted July 12, 1861, aged 18, as Private. Wounded Glendale, Va., June 30, 1862; right arm amputated. Discharged for wounds, Newark NJ, Oct. 20, 1862. Post-war, lived in Lowell. Member of GAR posts 19 (Edwin V. Sumner, Fitchburg, Mass) and 80 (Arthur G. Biscoe, Westborough, Mass.). Died Nov. 15, 1931.

Thomas Flynn: Res. Boston; plumber. Enlisted July 12, 1861, aged 34, as Private. Died of disease, Camp Hamilton, Va., April 1, 1862.

Michael Foley Jr.: Res. Woburn, Mass.; hostler. Enlisted Feb. 27, 1864 aged 37, as a private. Killed on May 6, 1864 at Wilderness, Va.

Thomas Foley: Res. Woburn; butcher. Enlisted July 12, 1861, aged 23, as Private. Re-enlisted Dec. 23, 1864. Transferred July 11, 1864 to Co. F, 11th Mass. Inf.

James R. Ford: Res. Detroit, Mich; sailor. Enlisted Aug. 16, 1863, aged 22, as a Private. Deserted Sept. 15, 1864, near Beverly Ford, Va.

Isaac S.D. Freeman: Res. Lowell; merchant. Enlisted July 12, 1861, aged 34, as Private. Killed at Fair Oaks, Va., June 18, 1862.

James Glynn: Res. Roxbury' moulder. Enlisted July 12, 1861, aged 22, as Corporal. Discharged for disability, Newark, N.J., Dec. 4, 1862. Also had service in Co. C, 3rd Mass. Heavy Artillery.

William Greenlough: Res. Boston; carpenter. Enlisted July 12, 1861, aged 37, as Private. Discharged for disability, Annapolis, Md., Jan. 21, 1863. Transferred to Veteran Reserve Corps.

Charles Griffen: Res. St. John, New Brunswick; hostler. Enlisted Aug. 16, 1863, aged 28, as Private and drafted into Co. F. Deserted on Oct. 8, 1863, near Culpeper, Va.

Daniel Hackett: Res. not shown. Enlisted July 12, 1861, aged 20, as Corporal, and deserted the same day at Camp Cameron, Cambridge, Mass.

John J. Hagan: Res. West Cambridge; painter. Enlisted July 12, 1861, aged 18, as Private. Wounded 2nd Bull Run, Va., Aug. 29, 1862. Discharged for wounds June 26, 1863. Transferred to Veteran Reserve Corps.

John Haley: Res. Boston; wheelwright. Enlisted July 20, 1862, aged 35, as Private. Killed 2nd Bull Run, Va., Aug. 29, 1862.

William Haley: Res. Boston; painter. Enlisted July 12, 1861, aged 18, as Private. Re-enlisted Dec. 23, 1863. Prisoner of War, Petersburg, Va., June 22, 1864. Died of disease at Andersonville prison, Ga., Aug. 31, 1864; buried in Grave 7408, Andersonville National Cemetery.

William W. Harding: Res. Charlestown; shoemaker. Enlisted July 12, 1861, aged 38, as Private. Wounded Glendale, Va., June 30, 1862. Discharged for wounds at Washington DC, Oct. 6, 1862.

John Harkins: Res. Somerville; rope spinner. Enlisted July 12, 1861, aged 26, as Private. Discharged for disability Dec. 27, 1862 near Falmouth, Va. Also served in 4th Battery, Mass. Light Artillery.

William Harkins: Res. unknown. Enlisted July 12, 1861, aged 27, as Private. Mustered out July 27, 1864.

Thomas Harrington: Res. West Newton; shoemaker. Enlisted July 12, 1861, aged 19, as private. Discharged Oct. 25, 1862. Subsequent service in Battery H, 1st U.S. Light Artillery; discharged July 1, 1864.

Dennis Hennessey: Res. Cambridge; glass blower. Enlisted July 12, 1861, aged 18, as Private. Mustered out July 27, 1864.

Michael Herron: Res. Boston; billiard maker. Enlisted July 12, 1861, aged 19, as Private. Prisoner of War, Culpeper, Va., Oct. 11, 1862; died of disease in prison, Richmond, Va., Feb. 2, 1864.

Michael Higgins: Res. Boston; packer. Enlisted July 12, 1861, aged 31, as Private. Wounded at 2nd Bull Run, Va., Aug. 29, 1862. Mustered out July 27, 1864.

Dennis Horrigan: Res. Cambridge; glass blower. Enlisted July 12, 1861, aged 22, as Private/ Wounded Gettysburg, Pa., July 2, 1863. Killed Spotsylvania Court House, Va., May 12, 1864.

Edward Hosford: Res. Phildelphia, Pa; civil engineer. Enlisted July 12, 1861, aged 38, as Private. Discharged for disability, Washington DC, March 15, 1863.

James B. Johnson: Res. unknown. Enlisted July 12, 1861, aged 19, as Private. Discharged for disability, Aug. 20, 1861.

Charles Kelly: Res. Boston; printer. Enlisted July 12, 1861, aged 19, as Private. Deserted July 20, 1863.

John Kelly: Res. Randolph; bootmaker. Enlisted July 12, 1861, aged 30, as Private. Discharged for disability, Alexandria, Va., May 30, 1863.

John C. Kelly: Res. Charlestown; currier. Enlisted July 12, 1861, aged 29, as a Private. Promoted Sergeant. Killed Spotsylvania Court House, Va., May 12, 1864.

Patrick Kelly: Res. Woburn; currier. Enlisted July 12, 1861, aged 27, as a Private. Re-enlisted Dec. 23, 1863. Transferred July 11, 1864 to Co. F, 11th Mass. Inf.

John Pitman King: Res. Boston; shoemaker. Enlisted July 12, 1861, aged 21, as a Private. Cpl., Aug. 30, 1861; Sgt., July 20, 1862; re-enlisted Dec. 23, 1863; 1st Lt. Feb. 14, 1864. Wounded Cold Harbor, Va., May 31, 1864. Mustered out July 27, 1864.

Michael King; Res. Boston; shoemaker. Enlisted July 12, 1861, aged 27, as a Private. Deserted Aug. 11, 1861.

Jams L. Lawrence: Res. Otis, Mass.; lumberman. Enlisted July 15, 1863, aged 30, as a Private and drafted into Co. F. Wounded Nov. 27, 1863 at Mine Run, Va. Transferred July 11, 1864 into Co. F, 11th Mass. Inf. Date of discharge not given.

William A. Leonard: res. Great Barrington, Mass.; operative. Enlisted July 15, 1863, aged 20, as a Private and drafted into Co. F. Transferred July 11, 1864 into Co. F, 11th Mass. Inf. Lived in Great Barrington after the war; member of GAR Post 196 (D.G.Anderson), Great Barrington.

William H. Loomis: Res. Sheffield, Mass.; laborer. Enlisted July 15, 1863, aged 24, as a Private and drafted into Co. F. Died of disease Oct. 28, 1863 at Washington, DC; buried at Military Asylum Cemetery, Washington, DC.

James Lynch: Res. Boston; tailor. Enlisted July 12, 1861, aged 20, as Private. Discharged for disability at Boston, May 7, 1863.

Thomas Lynch: Res. Cambridge; farmer. Enlisted July 12, 1861, aged 30, as Private. Re-enlisted Dec. 23, 1863. Transferred July 11,1864 to Co. F, 11th Mass. Inf.

Thomas Lynch: Res. Holliston; currier. Enlisted July 12, 1861, aged 33, as Private. Re-enlisted Dec. 23, 1863. Transferred July 11,1864 to Co. F, 11th Mass. Inf.

Thomas Maloney: Res. Boston; seaman. Enlisted July 12, 1861, aged 21, as Private. Discharged for disability, Aug. 28, 1861.

Hiram C. Manville: Res. Sheffield, Mass.; farmer. Enlisted Aug. 15, 1863, aged 20, as a Private and drafted into Co. F. Transferred on July 11, 1864 into Co. F, 11th Mas.

Inf. Date of discharge not given.

Edward McAndrews: Res. Roxbury; laborer. Enlisted July 12, 1861, aged 18, as a private. Killed June 18, 1862 at Fair Oaks, Va.

John McCabe: Res. Somerville; glass worker. Enlisted July 12, 1861, aged 18, as a Private. Re-enlisted Dec. 23, 1863. Transferred July 11, 1864 into Co. F, 11th Mass. Inf. Mustered out July 14, 1865, at Readville, Mass.

James McCarron: Res. Worcester; currier. Enlisted July 12, 1861, aged 21, as a private. Died of disease at Fortress Monroe, Va., Sept. 10, 1862.

John McCarthy: Res. Chelsea; painter. Enlisted July 12, 1861, aged 20, as a Private. Died of disease at Philadelphia, Pa., Aug. 17, 1862.

Patrick McCarthy: Res. Boston; carpenter. Enlisted July 12, 1861, aged 27, as a Private. Killed June 18, 1862 at Fair Oaks, Va.

Charles McDonald: Res. Charlestown; laborer. Enlisted July 12, 1861, aged 27, as a Private. Discharged for disability March 20, 1863 at Falmouth, Va.

James McLaughlin: Res. Chicopee; hostler. Enlisted Aug. 15, 1863, aged 22, as a Private and drafted into Co. F. Transferred July 11, 1864 into Co. F, 11th Mass. Inf. Deserted from hospital Sept. 30, 1864.

Thomas McNulty: Res. Charlestown; painter. Enlisted July 12, 1861, aged 21, as a Private. Deserted Oct. 6, 1862 at Alexandria, Va.

Edward Mellen: Res. Stoughton; bootmaker. Enlisted Dec. 7, 1861, aged 30, as a Private. Discharged for disability April 6, 1863. Also served in Co., A, 4th Mass. Inf.

Patrick Mullen: Res. Boston; laborer. Enlisted July 12, 1861, aged 28, as a Private. Deserted Sept. 1, 1861 at Camp McClellan, near Baltimore, Md.

Dennis C. Murphy: Res. Roxbury; paper stainer. Enlisted July 12, 1861, aged 19, as a Private. Promoted Corporal. Wounded Fredericksburg, Va., Dec. 14, 1862. Discharged for disability May 26, 1863 at Boston, Mass. Also served in Co. I, 61st Mass. Inf.

Timothy Murphy: Res. Somerville; glass worker. Enlisted July 12, 1861, aged 19, as a Private. Prisoner of War (place & date not stated); paroled City Point, Va., April 16, 1864. Died of disease April 21, 1866 in military hospital.

John F. Murray: Res. Woburn; currier. Enlisted July 12, 1851, aged 18, as a Private. Re-enlisted Dec. 23, 1863. Killed Petersburg, Va., June 20, 1864.

Patrick Neville: Res. Somerville; laborer. Enlisted July 12, 1861, aged 27, as a Private. Transferred July 11, 1864 to Co. F, 11th Mass. Inf. Date of discharge not given.

John C. O'Leary: Res. Charlestown; fur dresser. Enlisted Nov. 27, 1863, aged 35, as a Private. Transferred July 11, 1864 to Co. F, 11th Mass. Inf. Date of discharge not given. Post-war, lived in Charlestown; member of GAR Post 11 (Abraham Lincoln), Charlestown, Mass.

Thomas O'Leary: Res. West Cambridge; currier. Enlisted July 12, 1861, aged 31, as a private. Wounded 2nd Bull Run, Va., Aug. 29, 1863. Mustered out July 27, 1864.

John O'Neal: Res. Lexington; farmer. Enlisted July 12, 1861, aged 33, as a Private. Wounded 2nd Bull Run, Va., Aug. 29, 1862. Transferred Aug. 24, 1863 to Co. A, 9th Veteran Reserve Corps. Mustered out July 18, 1864.

David Orr: Res. Boston; seaman. Enlisted July 12, 1861, aged 18, as Private. Missing in action. Missing at Glendale, June 30, 1862. Deserted near Falmouth, Va., Dec. 14, 1862.

George W. Phillip: Res. Great Barrington; teamster. Enlisted July 15, 1863, aged 20, as a Private, and drafted into Co. F. Wounded May 6, 1864 at Wilderness, Va. Transferred July 11, 1864 into Co. F, 11th Mass. Inf. Date of discharge not given.

George E. Pitts: Res. Charlestown; laborer. Enlisted July 12, 1861, aged 18, as a Private. Mustered out July 27, 1864.

James Powers: Res. Cambridge; glass cutter. Enlisted July 12, 1861, aged 18, as a Private. Wounded Glendale, Va., June 30, 1862; Gettysburg, Pa., July 2, 1863; Wilderness, Va., May 6, 1864. Mustered out July 27, 1864.

John Price: Res. New York City, NY; laborer. Enlisted Aug. 17, 1863, aged 26, as a Private, and drafted into Co. F. Deserted Nov. 26, 1863, near Brandy Station, Va.

Daniel Reddy: Res. Woburn; japanner. Enlisted July 12, 1861, aged 20, as a Private. R-enlisted Jan. 4, 1864. Transferred July 11, 1864 to Co. F, 11th Mass. Inf. Date of discharge not given.

Abraham Richardson: Res. Lowell; shirt maker. Enlisted July 12, 1861, aged 19, as a Private. Discharged for disability June 10, 1862.

Thomas Sharkey: Res. Chelsea; shoemaker. Enlisted July 12, 1861, aged 27, as a Private. Deserted at Camp McClellan, near Baltimore, Md., Aug. 19, 1861.

Stephen Shea: Res. Woburn; shoemaker. Enlisted July 12, 1861, aged 21, as a Private. Mustered out July 27, 1864. Also saw service in U.S. Marine Corps.

Charles F. Stearns: Res. Roxbury; clerk. Enlisted July 13, 1861, aged 19, as a Private. Wounded Fair Oaks, Va., June 18, 1862. Discharged for disability July 30, 1862 at Boston, Mass.

George Steele: Res. Marblehead; cordwainer. Enlisted Dec. 7, 1863, aged 19, as a Private. Transferred July 11, 1864 into Co. F, 11th Mass. Inf. Date of discharge not given.

James Stewart: Res. Boston; printer. Enlisted Nov. 7, 1861, aged 24, as a Private. Deserted from Hospital, Aug. 18, 1863.

John H. Sullivan: Res. Charlestown; shoemaker. Enlisted July 12, 1861, aged 18, as a Private. Discharged for disability Feb. 17, 1864, at Alexandria, Va.

Thomas Taylor: Res. New York City, NY; clerk. Enlisted Aug. 18, 1863, aged 22, as a Private and drafted into Co. F. Wounded May 6, 1864, Wilderness, Va. Deserted June 15, 1864, from hospital.

Reuben K. Thorne: Res. Somerville; teamster. Enlisted July 12, 1861, aged 31, as a Private. Deserted near Washington, DC, May 1, 1863.

Matthew W. Tobey: Res. Auburndale; laborer. Enlisted July 2, 1861 as a Drummer. Deserted Aug. 18, 1861.

Jeremiah Toomey: Res. Cambridge; rope maker. Enlisted July 12, 1861, aged 35, as a Private. Wounded Gettysburg, Pa., July 2, 1863. Mustered out July 27, 1864. Mustered into Co. H, 13th Veteran Reserve Corps, Sept. 19, 1864. Mustered out Nov. 15, 1865 at Concord, NH.

Benjamin Tuck: Res. Woburn Centre; farmer. Enlisted July 12, 1861, aged 36, as a Private. Mustered out July 27, 1864.

George W. Vaughn: Res. Somerville; teamster. Enlisted July 12, 1861, aged 25, as a Private. Corporal, April 13, 1863. Transferred June 15, 1862 to Co. K. Mustered out July 27, 1864.

Patrick Weston: Res. East Boston; cooper. Enlisted July 12, 1861, aged 20, as a Private. Killed June 18, 1862 at Fair Oaks, Va.

Thomas Whalon: Res. Worcester; laborer. Enlisted July 12, 1861, aged 30, as a Private. Wounded June 18, 1862 at Fair Oaks, Va.; died of wounds Oct. 29, 1862 at Alexandria, Va.

Ralph H. Wickham: Res. Stoneham; rubber business. Enlisted July 12, 1861, aged 28, as a Private. Wounded June 30, 1862 at Glendale, Va. Discharged for disability Sept. 30, 1862.

Homer G. Williams: Res. Lee; tailor. Enlisted July 14, 1863, aged 20, as a Private and drafted into Co. F. Transferred July 11, 1864, into Co. F, 11th Mass. Inf. Wounded 1864 (date and place not stated). Date of discharge not given.

Charles Wilson: Born Pennsylvania. Res. Lawrence; laborer. Enlisted July 12, 1861, aged 26, as a Private. Discharged for disability March 12, 1863. Post-war, lived 6th & Race St., Cincinnati, Ohio; died there May 4, 1874, from stomach cancer and buried in Spring Grove Cemetery, Cincinnati, Grave 40-2636,

George E. Wright: Res. Sheffield; clerk. Enlisted July 15, 1863, aged 23, as a Private. Wounded May 6, 1864, Wilderness, Va. Transferred July 11, 1864 into Co. F, 11th Mass. Inf. Transferred May 1, 1865 into 8th Co., 2nd Bn., Veteran Reserve Corps. Discharged for disability Aug. 15, 1865.

****

APPENDIX 3
*

Extracts from the Adjutant-General's Reports for the State of Massachusetts for 1863 and 1864, giving synopses of the service of the 16th Massachusetts Infantry during those years

1863: "The Sixteenth Regiment was recruited at "Camp Cameron", Cambridge, and was composed principally of Middlesex County men. It left the State for the seat of war August 17th, 1861, under the command of Colonel Powell T. Wyman, who was killed June 30, 1862, while bravely leading his regiment to a charge upon the enemy. Colonel Wyman was succeeded by Colonel Thomas R. Tannatt, who being transferred to the Fourteenth (now First) Regiment of Heavy Artillery, was followed by Colonel Gardner Banks. The regiment was engaged in most of the principal battles of the Army of the Potomac. The regiment is now under command of Lieutenant-Colonel Merriam, who has forwarded the following narrative of its year's service:-

HEAD-QUARTERS SIXTEENTH MASSACHUSETTS VOLUNTEERS
 Camp near Brandy Station, Va., December 14, 1863
GENERAL: In compliance with your circular of November 27th, I take great pleasure in furnishing you with a brief narrative of the history of this regiment from November 12th, 1862, the date of my last report, instead of December 14th, as stated in your circular.

November 18th, marched by way of Manassas to Wolf Run Shoals, bivouacked three days. 25th, marched to camp near Falmouth, arriving the 28th.

December 10th, broke camp and took position in front of Fredericksburg. 12th, crossed the river. The only part we took in this engagement was as a reserve to the picket line below the town, sending out two companies at a time to relieve the skirmishers. Our loss was - enlisted men killed, 3, wounded, 10.

On the night of the 13th we recrossed the river and went into our old camp on the 14th. January 20th, 1863, broke camp and marched up the line of the Rappahannock, for about seven miles. This is commonly known as the "mud march"; and on the 28th, we returned to camp, the campaign being abandoned on account of bad weather.

April 28th, again broke camp to participate in the campaign resulting in the battle of Chancellorsville. May 1st, crossed the Rappahannock at United States Ford. At dusk of the 2d, the Second Division of the 3rd Corps, to which we are attached, were ordered in to the support of the Eleventh Corps, and the firing which was desultory during the whole night, was commenced in hot earnest at daylight. We were in the midst of the dense woods of the Wilderness, and the fight was bitterly contested, till, with the rest of the division, we were forced back to our supports. Casualties in this engagement - officers killed, 1; wounded 7 - total, eight. Enlisted men killed, 10; wounded, 55; missing in prisoners, 9 - total, 74.

May 5th, at night recrossed the river, and arrived at camp near Falmouth, on the afternoon of the 6th. June 11th, broke camp and marched to Beverly Ford, twenty nine miles, arrived the next day. Held the ford till night of the 14th, when we marched towards Manassas Junction, arriving the afternoon of the 15th. On the 17th, marched to Centreville; on the 19th, to Gum Springs.

June 25th, marched to Edwards Ferry; crossed the Potomac; marched up the Maryland bank of the river to the Monocacy, where we bivouacked after one of the hardest marches ever made by the regiment. June 26th, to Point of Rocks. 27th, to Jefferson, thence to Burkettsville and Crampton's Pass, South Mountain, where, with one other regiment and a section of artillery we were stationed at the top of the mountain, holding the pass. On the 28th, marched through Middletown to Frederick, and bivouacked. 29th, through Walkersville to Taneytown. This march was made through a friendly country, and the hearty enthusiasm of the people tended much to cheer the troops worn out by their long and toilsome marches.

July 1st, through Emmettsburg to Gettysburg, where we arrived about midnight. On the 2d and 3d, we were engaged in the fight, the details of which having become such a matter of history, it is unnecessary for me to dilate upon. Never have I seen the regiment fight so well and steadily. The casualties were about one-third of the number engaged. We lost three tried and skilful officers killed on the field, and one died of wounds. Officers killed, 3; wounded, 4 - Total, 7. Enlisted men killed, 11; wounded, 50; missing, 14 - Total 75.

July 7th, the regiment left the field so nobly won, under command of Captain Donovan, of Lowell, the senior officer present. Marched through Emmettsburg to Mechanicsville, and bivouacked. 8th, to Frederick. 9th, through Middletown, and encamped on South Mountain. On the 10th, to near Boonesboro'. On the 11th, crossed Antietam Creek to near Hagerstown. On the 12th, into position, expecting an engagement. On the 13th, marched through Sharpsburg. On the 16th, to Pleasant Valley, near Maryland Heights.

On the 17th, crossed the Potomac at Harper's Ferry. On the 18th, marched to Hillsboro'. 19th, Snicker's Gap. On the 20th, Upperville. 23rd, to Manassas Gap. On the 24th, we skirmished through the Gap without loss to Front Royal. Then withdrew through the Gap to Markham. On the 25th, marched via Salem to Warrenton, arriving the 26th.

August 1st, marched to Beverly Ford, on the Rappahannock. Went into camp, where Lieutenant-Colonel Merriam again took command on the 16th. September 16th, crossed the river at Freeman's Ford; marched to Culpepper and went into camp on the 17th.

October 8th, marched with the division to James City, near the Rapidan, to support Kilpatrick's cavalry division. 10th, returned to camp at midnight. 11th, marched to and guarded Freeman's Ford. 13th, marched all day and night. 14th, halted at Greenwich, two hours and marched to Centreville. 15th, to Union Mills. 19th, to Bristow Station. 20th, to Greenwich. 21st, to Catlett's Station, on the railroad. October 30th, marched to Bealeton Station.

November 7th, broke camp and marched to Kelly's Ford; crossed without loss, and bivouacked in line of battle. On the 8th, the enemy had retreated, and we marched in his rear to Brandy Station, where we went into camp. November 26th, broke camp at an early hour and marched to Jacob's Ford; crossed the Rapidan and bivouacked. On the 27th, while endeavoring to make connection with the Second Corps, we met the enemy, and our brigade being in advance, in the afternoon we became engaged in the fight known as Locust or Orange Grove. Casualties, enlisted men, wounded, 15; missing 3 - Total, 18.

On the 28th, we marched to Robertson's Tavern. 30th, in line of battle all day, expecting to charge the enemy's works which were exceedingly ugly to look at; at night we were withdrawn.

December 1st, marched to Parker's Store, on Plank Road, to support Gregg's cavalry. December 2d, recrossed the Rapidan at Culpepper Ford, 3d, marched to old camp at Brandy Station.

Casualties since November 12, 1862

Battle	Killed		Wounded		Missing & Prisoners	
	Officers	Men	Officers	Men	Officers	Men
Fredericksburg	-	3	-	10	-	-
Chancellorsville	1	10	7	55	-	9
Gettysburg	3	11	4	50	-	14
Wapping Heights	-	-	-	-	-	-
Orange Grove	-	-	-	15	-	3
Totals	4	24	11	130	-	26

Casualties since organisation

Time	Killed		Wounded		Missing & Prisoners	
	Officers	Men	Officers	Men	Officers	Men
To November 12, 1862	4	19	7	153	2	90
To December 14, 1863	4	24	11	130	-	26
Totals	8	43	18	283	2	116

Number of missing was finally reduced to 98

The number joined from missing in action is undoubtedly larger, but the regimental papers, for the Peninsula Campaign in 1862, are lost.

Died of wounds, since organization, to Nov. 12, 1862, 15 enlisted men; to Dec. 14, 1863, 3 officers and 57 enlisted men - total, 75.

Died of disease and other causes, to Nov. 12, 1862, 23 enlisted men; to Dec. 14, 1863, two officers and 34 enlisted men - total, 61.

Discharged for disability and other causes, to Nov. 12th, 1862, 16 officers and 81 men; to Dec. 14th, 1863, 10 officers and 192 men - total, 26 officers and 273 enlisted men.

Number deserted to Nov. 12th, 1862, 25 enlisted men; to Dec. 14th, 1863, 41 enlisted men and 49 conscripts; total, 115.

Recapitulation. - Officers killed, 8; wounded, 18; missing and prisoners, 2; died of wounds, 3; died of disease, 1; died of other causes, 1; discharged, 26. Number of men killed, 43; wounded, 283; missing and prisoners, 98; died of wounds, 72; died of disease, 57; died of other causes, 2; discharged, 273; deserted, 115; total, 59 officers and 943 men.

At the date of the last report, Col. Thomas R. Tannatt was in command of the regiment; on the 28th of December he was transferred to the command of the fourteenth Regiment, heavy artillery, and was succeeded by Colonel Gardner Banks, who after long suffering from a painful affection of the knees, was obliged to resign on the 4th of September, 1863; since then the regiment has been under my command.

Out of thirty-eight officers who marched through the streets of Boston, six only remain with the regiment.

Such, in brief, is the detail of a year of hard campaigning and hard fighting, of which many a tale could be told of suffering, hardship and danger.

The yearly retrospection is a mournful one, bringing up, as it does, the recollection of familiar forms and faces, now gone forever. Their memories are enshrined in the hearts of those at home; their names will be remembered with reverence by a grateful posterity. Peace to their ashes.

I have the honor to be, Very respectfully, your obedient servant,
Waldo Merriam, Lieut.-Col. 16th Mass. Vols.
Brig.-Gen. Wm Schouler, Adjutant-General State of Mass."

1864: "This regiment left the state August 17, 1861. It was engaged at Fair Oaks, Glendale, Malvern Hill, Kettle Run, Chantilly and Fredericksburg in 1862, and at Chancellorsville, Gettysburg, and Locust Grove during the year 1863. My report of last year left the regiment December 3, 1863, in camp at Brandy Station, Va.

The following narrative furnished me by Captain Lombard, although it goes over matters contained in previous reports, is at the same time so full of interest that I print it without material alteration or omission. It is an honest story of a gallant regiment which has passed into history.

Having been requested by a number of members of the Sixteenth Regiment Massachusetts Volunteers to write its final report, I must cheerfully comply, - that the last year of its brilliant history may not remain unwritten, - yet rather that the honored dead, whose brave acts and deeds contributed so much to the fair fame of the regiment, may be recorded in the archives of the State, under whose flag they so nobly fell.

Before entering upon a detailed account of the operations, losses, &c., of 1864, I feel it my duty to review the former years' services, giving the names of the officers who have fallen in battle or died of wounds. My object in so doing is that the friends of the deceased officers feel the regiment has not had the justice in former reports which it deserves.

The regiment was organised in July, 1861, under the direction of Colonel Powell T. Wyman, a most efficient and accomplished officer. It left the State August 17, 1861, and proceeded to Baltimore, Md., where it remained until September 1st, when it was ordered to Fortress Monroe, Va. It remained at the latter post until May, 1862, when it triumphantly marched into Norfolk, Portsmouth and Suffolk, it being the first Union regiment which entered those cities. It marched and joined the Army of the Potomac at Fair Oaks, June 13, 1862, and shed its blood on the 18th of the same month in an action known as "Woodland Skirmish". For its gallantry and good conduct at that time, General Hooker complimented Colonel Wyman and the regiment with the remark, "I can trust them anywhere." In this skirmish, Lieutenant F.P.H.Rogers was mortally wounded. From a long and intimate acquaintance with Lieutenant Rogers, I learned the more to esteem him. His whole heart was in the cause he had espoused. All were sad that so good and efficient an officer should thus early fall.

The regiment was next engaged at Peach Orchard, June 25th. 30th, at Glendale, the Sixteenth won for itself true glory. At this time Colour-Sergeant J.F.Capelle distinguished himself in the manner in which he carried the colors in action, and his conduct while there. In the early part of the battle, Colonel Wyman fell. Without a syllable from his lips he passed from this to an unknown world. He was a true patriot and noble commander. All the traits of a good soldier were illustrated in his character. No pen can describe the feelings of officers and men when they knew he was no more. The heart alone knows the bitterness of such a moment. In General Hooker's letter to Governor Andrew on the death of Colonel Wyman, we find the following sentence: "There is no doubt but at Glendale the Sixteenth Massachusetts saved the army."

At Malvern Hill, July 1st; Bristow Station, August 27th, the Sixteenth took part.

August 29th and 30th, were engaged at the battle of second Bull Run. Lieutenants Darricott and Banks were killed. Lieutenant Darricott was a faithful officer, and by his heroic endurance while in feeble health won for himself the respect of both officers and men. Lieutenant Hiram Banks (a brother of General Banks) joined the regiment at Fortress Monroe. His career was indeed glorious. His more than ordinary ability, firmness and decision gave him marked distinction among his fellow officers.

December 12th, 13th and 14th, at Fredericksburg, where Northern blood drenched the banks of the Rappahannock, perhaps no one officer more distinguished himself than the lamented Arthur B. Fuller. Chaplain Fuller was then out of service, having been discharged for disability; but being there, and seeing the heroism of our troops, could not resist the opportunity to prove by his acts his love for the cause, and by example his unfeigned patriotism. No hero deserves a brighter page in history than this departed patriot.

The first battle fought by the Army of the Potomac in 1863 will ever be remembered - Chancellorsville. In this engagement Captain A.J.Dallas was killed, and Lieutenants Hiram Rowe and and Samuel G. Savage mortally wounded. In Captain Dallas' character, strict integrity, morality, and patriotism were most prominent, serving in the army only as a sense of duty. Lieutenant Rowe was promoted from the ranks, a young man of great promise, honest as when a boy he came from the wilds of Vermont, a strict disciplinarian, brave to a fault, and in every sense a good soldier. Lieutenant Savage, one of the few men who "knew himself". He entered the service a Corporal, and by strict attention to duty he won the respect and confidence of his superior, and was promoted for good conduct on the field.

The name of Gettysburg is immortal. We cannot think of the first, second, and third days of July, 1863, without feelings of sorrow, yet mingled with pride. Sorrow for the dead and suffering soldiers, and mourning friends; pride that victory had perched upon our banners. Captains King, Roche and Lieutenant Brown fell upon the field, Captain Johnson mortally wounded, and several other officers slightly wounded. Captain L.G.King was a good officer, true to the cause he so early espoused, never flinching, but always foremost in the fight. He was possessed of great powers of endurance.

Captain David W. Roche was one of Ireland's most noble sons, possessed of the real Irish impetuosity and courage. All who knew him honored him for his devotion to his adopted country and love for our flag, under which he so nobly offered up his life.

Lieutenant Brown was particularly distinguished for modesty, coolness, and true courage. None knew him but to love and honor.

The name of Captain C. Robinson Johnson will awake in the heart of every soldier of the Sixteenth a feeling of respect and love, which can only die when the last patriot of the Sixteenth is no more. His life was so full of noble deeds and heroic acts, that his peaceful death adds to his brilliant record. In camp, on the march, on the field of battle, he was the same. His heroic fortitude, his gallantry, his kindness of heart, reared for him a living monument in the hearts of all soldiers of the command.

(The remainder of the 1864 report, down to muster-out, has, for the sake of continuity of the narrative, been moved from here and printed in historical sequence, above, as Chapter 13, *After Gettysburg.*

****

APPENDIX 4

*

OFFICIAL REPORTS OF THE BATTLE OF GETTYSBURG RELEVANT TO THE ROLE OF THE 16TH MASSACUSETTS INFANTRY

----

(1) Report of Brig. Gen. Andrew A. Humphreys, commanding Second Division, Third Corps (Official Records, Series I, Vol. XXVII, Part 1 [Serial 43])

CAMP, HEADQUARTERS ARMY OF THE POTOMAC, August 16, 1863.

Lieut. Col. O. H. HART.
Assistant Adjutant-General, Third Corps.

COLONEL: I submit, for the information of the major-general commanding Third Corps, the following report of the operations of my division (Second Division, Third Corps) during the recent campaign, up to July 9, on the morning of which day I was relieved from the command of the division, having been appointed chief of staff at the headquarters of this army:

On June 11, about midday, while encamped near Falmouth, Va., orders were received by me from the headquarters of the corps to march at 2 o'clock on the Warrenton road, which order was complied with, the division bivouacking for the night at Hartwood Church.

The march was resumed the next morning at 6 o'clock, my division leading. Upon arriving at Morrisville, I was directed to move to the Rappahannock River, and cover that part of it from Wheatley's Ford, near Kellysville, to Beverly Ford, near the upper forks; to throw up such works and make such defensive arrangements as would render it impracticable for the enemy to cross in my front. It was past midnight of the 12th before my command, after a march of from 22 to 25 miles, was in position at all the fords, it having been posted under my own supervision. Rifle-pits and batteries were thrown up at the crossings, and the railroad bridge was rendered impassable.

On the afternoon of the 13th, the Second Brigade rejoined the division, having been on picket on the 11th, from which it was not relieved until between midnight and morning of the 12th.

On the morning of the 14th, before daylight, it was marched to Kelly's Ford, to relieve the detachments of the Fifth Corps holding that ford.

On the evening of the 14th, in compliance with orders from the corps commander, as soon as it was sufficiently dark to conceal the movement of my troops, the division was concentrated on the railroad, and the march to Manassas Junction was begun.

I reached Cedar Run, near Catlett's Station, between 7 and 8 a.m. of the 15th, where, by authority of the corps commander, the division was halted for rest until 2 p.m., when the march was resumed. It was painful in the extreme, for owing to the long-continued drought, streams, usually of considerable magnitude, were dried up, the dust lay some inches deep on the roadway, and the fields were equally uncomfortable. The suffering from heat, dust, thirst, fatigue, and exhaustion was very great. It was near midnight when the division reached Manassas Junction, after a march varying in the different brigades from 25 to 29 miles.

On the 16th, we remained at Manassas Junction, resting.

On the 17th, marched to Centreville, and on the 19th to Gum Springs, where the division remained until the 25th, when at 10 a.m. it marched to Edwards Ferry, through Fairfarm and Franklinville, and crossing the Potomac on the pontoon bridge about 5 p.m., marched on the tow-path of the canal to the mouth of the Monocacy, reaching that point about midnight, after a march of not less than 25 miles, that portion on the tow-path being rendered very fatiguing and exhausting by a heavy rain that set in at nightfall. The whole command, officers and men, were more exhausted by this march than by that of the 14th and 15th.

On the 26th, the division marched to the vicinity of the Point of Rocks, and bivouacked on the farm of Dr. Duvall, near the summit of the Catoctin Mountain.

On the 27th, marched to the vicinity of Middletown, on the Hagerstown pike, via Jefferson.

On the 28th, marched through Frederick, crossed the Monocacy 3 miles above, and bivouacked for the night 7 miles from that town, on the Woodsborough road.

On the 29th, marched to Taneytown through Woodsborough and Bruceville.

On the 30th, made a short march after midday on the road to Emmitsburg, bivouacking about midway between the two places.

On July 1, marched through Emmitsburg, and halted 1mile out of the town, on the Waynesborough pike. While I was engaged in a careful examination of the ground in front of Emmitsburg, the division was ordered at 3 p.m. to move up to Gettysburg, 12 miles distant, where an engagement had taken place between the two corps of Generals Reynolds and Howard (the First and Eleventh Corps) and the enemy.

A brigade (the Third) and a battery (Smith's) were left, in accordance with orders, in position on the Waynesborough pike. I overtook the head of the division (the First and Second Brigades, with one battery of artillery (Seeley's) 1 mile from the halting ground, and found Lieutenant-Colonel Hayden, assistant inspector-general, Third Corps, with some guides there, for the purpose of pointing out the route the division was to follow. This was on a road nearly parallel to the main road from Emmitsburg to Gettysburg, and about 2 miles west of it.

When half-way to Gettysburg, a dispatch from General Howard to General Sickles, commanding the Third Corps, was delivered to me by Captain McBlair, of the staff, in which the latter general was warned to look out for his left in coming up to

Gettysburg, and about the same time I learned from a citizen, who had guided part of General Reynolds' command, that our troops occupied no ground near Gettysburg west of the road from that town to Emmitsburg.

As we approached the crossing of Marsh Run, I was directed by General Sickles, through a staff officer, to take position on the left of Gettysburg soon as I came up. For reasons that will be apparent, from this statement I concluded that my division should from this point follow the road leading into the main road to Gettysburg, reaching the latter road in about a mile and a half, and at a distance from Gettysburg of about 2 miles; but Lieutenant-Colonel Hayden was positive that General Sickles had instructed him to guide the division by way of the Black Horse Tavern, on the road from Fairfield to Gettysburg. Accordingly, I moved the division in that direction, but, upon approaching the Black Horse Tavern, I found myself in the immediate vicinity of the enemy, who occupied that road in strong force. He was not aware of my presence, and I might have attacked him at daylight with the certainty of at least temporary success; but I was 3 miles distant from the remainder of the army, and I believed such a course would have been inconsistent with the general plan of operations of the commanding general. I accordingly retraced my steps, and marched by the route I have heretofore indicated, bivouacking at 1 a.m. on July 2 about 1 mile from Gettysburg and eastward of the Emmitsburg road.

At an early hour of the morning, my division was massed in the vicinity of its bivouac, facing the Emmitsburg road, near the crest of the ridge running from the cemetery of Gettysburg, in a southerly direction, to a rugged, conical-shaped hill, which I find goes by the name of Round Top, about 2 miles from Gettysburg.

At 9 a.m. the Third Brigade, with Smith's battery, joined the division, having been ordered up by Major-General Meade, commanding the army. It marched by the main road from Emmitsburg to Gettysburg.

Shortly after midday, I was ordered to form my division in line of battle, my left joining the right of the First Division of the Third Corps, Major-General Birney commanding, and my right resting opposite the left of General Caldwell's division, of the Second Corps, which was massed on the crest near my place of bivouac. The line I was directed to occupy was near the foot of the westerly slope of the ridge I have already mentioned, from which foot-slope the ground rose to the Emmitsburg road, which runs on the crest of a ridge nearly parallel to the Round Top ridge. This second ridge declines again immediately west of the road, at the distance of 200 or 300 yards from which the edge of a wood runs parallel to it. This wood was occupied by the enemy, whose pickets were exchanging shots from an early hour in the morning with our pickets thrown out beyond the road on the westerly slope.

The front allotted to me admitted of my forming the First Brigade, commanded by Brig. Gen. Joseph B. Carr, in line of battle, with one regiment of the Second Brigade on its left, the Seventy-first New York (Second Excelsior), commanded by Col. H. L. Potter. The Second Brigade, commanded by Col. W. R. Brewster, was formed in line of battalions in mass 200 yards in rear of the first line, and the Third Brigade, commanded by Col. George C. Burling, was massed 200 yards in rear of the second line, opposite its center. On the east side of the Emmitsburg road, opposite the middle of my line, was a log house surrounded by an orchard. This I occupied with the Seventy-third New York (Fourth Excelsior), Second Brigade, Maj. M. W. Burns commanding. This regiment was subsequently relieved by the **Sixteenth Massachusetts**, First Brigade. A series of peach orchards extended to the left along the Emmitsburg road some distance beyond the point where the road from Marsh Run crosses the Emmitsburg road. This Marsh Run road extends over to the Taneytown road and Baltimore pike, crossing the former just north of the Round Top. The ground occupied by my division and in my front was open. Communication with all points of it had been made easy by removing such of the fences as were in the way. Seeley's battery (K, Fourth U.S. Artillery) was placed at my disposal.

Shortly after these dispositions were made, I was directed to move my Third Brigade to the rear of the right of General Birney's division, and make it subject to his order for support, which was accordingly done. I was at the same time authorized to draw support, should I need it, from General Caldwell's division, Second Corps, and by General Hunt, chief of artillery, was authorized to draw from the Artillery Reserve should I require more.

About 4 p.m., in compliance with General Sickles' orders, I moved my division forward, so that the first line ran along the Emmitsburg road a short distance behind the crest upon which that road lies. At the same time I ordered Lieutenant Seeley to place his battery in position on the right of the log house. As the division moved forward in two lines, as heretofore described, the enemy opened with artillery, which enfiladed us from the left, and subsequently with artillery on our front, both with but little effect. In reply to my inquiry whether I should attack, I was directed to remain in position. Lieutenant Seeley's battery was transferred to the left of the log house, and soon silenced the battery in our front. The position he vacated was immediately occupied by a battery (parts of F and K, Third U.S. Artillery) commanded by Lieut. J. G. Turnbull, sent at my request from the Artillery Reserve. Captain Ransom, Third U.S. Artillery, while engaged in supervising the posting of this battery, was severely wounded.

The division on my left was now engaged with the enemy's infantry, which in my front merely made demonstrations, but did not drive in my pickets.

Colonel Sewell, commanding the Fifth New Jersey Volunteers, of my Third Brigade, reported to me at this time and relieved the pickets of General Graham's brigade (on my left), some of which extended over a part of my front. This regiment had been posted but a short time when a most urgent request was made by a staff officer of General Sickles that another regiment should be sent to the support of General Birney (Graham's brigade), leaving it to me, however, to decide whether it could be sent.

At this moment, Colonel Sewell sent me word that the enemy was driving in my pickets, and was about advancing in two lines to the attack. The demand for aid was so urgent, however, that I sent Major Burns' Fourth Excelsior to General Graham's brigade, and at the same time dispatched one of my aides, Lieutenant Christianny, to General Hancock, commanding Second Corps (General Caldwell's division having been sent to the extreme left), with the request that he would send a brigade, if possible, to my support.

Seeley's battery had now opened upon the enemy's infantry as they began to advance. Turnbull's battery was likewise directed against them, and I was about to throw somewhat forward the left of my infantry and engage the enemy with it, when I received orders from General Birney (General Sickles having been dangerously wounded and carried from the field) to throw back my left, and form a line oblique to and in rear of the one I then held, and was informed that the First Division would complete the line to the Round Top ridge. This I did under a heavy fire of artillery and infantry from the enemy, who now advanced on my whole front.

At this time, Colonel Sewell's regiment returned to the line, having maintained most gallantly its position on picket, with very heavy loss. Seeley's battery remained to the last moment, withdrawing without difficulty, but with severe loss in killed and wounded, including its commander among the latter. His loss was 2 enlisted men killed; 1 commissioned officer and 19 enlisted men wounded; 1 enlisted man missing, and 25 horses killed and disabled.

My infantry now engaged the enemy's, but my left was in air (although I extended it as far as possible with my Second Brigade), and, being the only troops on the field, the enemy's whole attention was directed to my division, which was forced back slowly, firing as they receded. Lieutenant Turnbull fell back with the infantry, suffering severe loss in men and horses, himself wounded. His loss was 1 commissioned officer and 8 enlisted men killed; 14 enlisted men wounded; 1 enlisted man missing, and 44 horses killed.

The two regiments sent me by General Hancock were judiciously posted by Lieut. H. C. Christiancy in support of my right. At this time I received orders through a staff officer from General Birney to withdraw to the Round Top ridge - an order previously conveyed to General Carr, commanding the First Brigade on the right, by General Birney in person. This order I complied with, retiring very slowly, continuing the contest with the enemy, whose fire of artillery and infantry was destructive in the extreme.

Upon arriving at the crest of the ridge mentioned, the remnants of my division formed on the left of General Hancock's troops, whose artillery opened upon the enemy, about 100 yards distant. The infantry joined, and the enemy broke and was driven from the field, rapidly followed by Hancock's troops and the remnants of my two brigades, who took many prisoners and brought off two pieces of our artillery which had been left after all the horses were killed.

Sergt. Thomas Hogan, Third Excelsior, brought to me on the field the flag of the Eighth Florida Regiment, which he had captured. He deserves reward.

It was now near dusk, and the contest for the day was closed. Its severity may be judged by the fact that the loss in killed, wounded, and missing of my division, 5,000 strong, was 2,088, of whom 171 were officers and 1,917 enlisted men. The missing numbered 3 officers and 263 enlisted men, the greater part of whom were probably wounded; some were killed.

I append a tabular list of the loss.

As I have already stated, my Third Brigade was ordered to the support of Major-General Birney, commanding the First Division. The accompanying report of Col. George C. Burling, commanding that brigade, exhibits the disposition that was made of the regiments of the brigade. In succession they, with the exception of Colonel Sewell's regiment, were sent to aid the brigades of the First Division. The Seventh New Jersey, Col. Louis R. Francine commanding, and the Second New Hampshire, Col. Edward L. Bailey commanding, were sent to the support of General Graham's brigade, and the Eighth New Jersey, Colonel Ramsey commanding, the Sixth New Jersey, Lieut. Col. S. R. Gilkyson commanding, and the One hundred and fifteenth Pennsylvania, Major Dunne commanding, were sent to the support of General Ward's brigade.

For the part taken in the engagement by these regiments, I must refer to the reports of the commanders of these brigades. That they did their duty in a manner comporting with their high reputation is manifest from the severe loss they met with-- 430 killed and wounded. Colonel Sewell, Colonel Francine, Colonel Ramsey, and Lieutenant-Colonel Price, officers distinguished for their skill and gallantry, were severely wounded. Colonel Francine's wound proved to be mortal. Colonel Bailey and Lieutenant-Colonel Carr, Second New Hampshire, were also wounded.

The fortune of war rarely places troops under more trying circumstances than those in which my division found itself on this day, and it is greatly to their honor that their soldierly bearing sustained the high reputation they had already won in the severest battles of the war. The fine qualities of many officers were brought out conspicuously. In some instances their gallant conduct fell under my own observation. I wish particularly to recommend to notice the cool courage, determination, and skillful handling of their troops by the two brigade commanders, Brigadier-General Carr and Col. William R. Brewster, and to ask attention to the officers mentioned by them as distinguished by their conduct.

My attention was attracted by the gallant bearing of Capt. Le Grand Benedict, assistant adjutant-general, First Brigade, and of Lieut. E. A. Belger, aide, staff of Second Brigade. Lieut. F. W. Seeley's gallantry, skill, good judgment, and effective management of his battery excited my admiration, as well as that of every officer who saw him. I should not omit to mention the bold and determined manner in which Lieutenant Turnbull managed his battery. Lieut. Manning Livingston, of this battery, was killed during the engagement.

Of my own staff, part of whom had gone through hotly contested fields with me before, I might well use the highest terms of commendation that language admits of, though in speaking of their acts I am painfully reminded that as yet I have been powerless to further the advancement they have won while serving with me. Most conspicuous for gallantry and untiring efforts in aiding me in forming, encouraging, and leading the troops were Capt. Carswell McClellan, of the adjutant-general's department, my special aide; Capt. William Henry Chester, special aide, mortally wounded; and Lieut. H. H. Humphreys, aide, wounded.

I beg leave also to express my sense of the obligations I am under for valuable services rendered me on the field by Maj. Charles Hamlin, assistant adjutant-general; Capt. A. F. Cavada, assistant inspector-general, and my aide, Lieut. Henry C. Christiancy. The judicious disposition by the latter of the re-enforcements he brought me is particularly deserving of mention.

The officers whose gallant and meritorious conduct General Carr brings to my notice are, using the language of General Carr:

Col. Robert McAllister, commanding Eleventh New Jersey Volunteers, twice wounded; Lieut. Col. Porter D. Tripp, commanding Eleventh Massachusetts Volunteers; Lieut. Col. Waldo Merriam, commanding Sixteenth Massachusetts Volunteers, wounded; Maj. Robert L. Bodine, commanding Twenty-sixth Pennsylvania Volunteers; Maj. Philip J. Kearny, Eleventh New Jersey Volunteers, seriously wounded, since dead; Major McDonald, Eleventh Massachusetts Volunteers, wounded; Captain Tomlinson Twenty-sixth Pennsylvania Volunteers, acting lieutenant-colonel; Captain Goodfellow, Twenty-sixth Pennsylvania Volunteers, wounded; and Adjt. John Schoonover, Eleventh New Jersey Volunteers, who was twice wounded, but remained in command of his regiment; and to the following officers of my staff, to whom my sincere thanks are due for valuable services rendered: Capt. Le Grand Benedict, assistant adjutant-general; Capt. George E. Henry, First Massachusetts Volunteers, acting aide-de-camp, and Lieut. John Oldershaw, Eleventh New Jersey Volunteers, acting assistant inspector-general.

Colonel Brewster's mention of those of his brigade distinguished for their conduct is as follows:

The conduct and bearing of both officers and men was so good under the fatigues of the long and tiresome marches, and so gallant, brave, and steady in action, that it is almost impossible to particularize individual acts. It is enough to say that every officer and man in the command seemed determined to sustain the reputation of the brigade, earned on many a hard-fought field, and how well they succeeded is best shown by the loss sustained.

The members of my staff - Adjt. Gen. J. P. Finkelmeier, Capt. George Le Fort, acting assistant inspector-general, and Lieuts J. A. Smith and Belger - were very active in the field, and behaved in the most gallant manner, conveying my orders under the hottest fire. Major Finkelmeier and Captain Le Fort were both wounded, and obliged to leave the field before the action was over. Col. John S. Austin, Third Excelsior, Asst. Surg. Joseph D. Stewart, Fifth Excelsior, and Lieut. Col. C. D. Westbrook, One hundred and twentieth New York Volunteers, were also wounded.

Col. George C. Burling, commanding Third Brigade, expresses himself in relation to the conduct of his brigade in the following terms:

During the two days of fighting, both officers and men behaved with their usual gallantry. I thank Capt. T. W. Eayre, assistant adjutant-general; Capt. J. W. Crawford, acting commissary of subsistence; Lieutenant Bruen, acting aide-de-camp, and Lieutenant Clark, ambulance officer, for their gallantry and promptness in conveying my orders. The last named was mortally wounded, and died on the field.

Colonel Sewell's conspicuous gallantry in the maintenance of his post has been already mentioned by me. He was severely wounded soon after his regiment rejoined the main line.

The enemy having been driven from the field, I formed my division on the left of Hancock's (Second) corps, along the Round Top ridge, where it remained during the night. Parties were at once sent out to bring in the wounded. Lieutenant [William J.] Rusling, ambulance officer, was promptly on the ground.

At daylight on the 3d, the enemy opened a brisk artillery fire upon my division, which, however, soon abated. About sunrise, by order of General Birney, I moved my division to the left and rear, to resupply ammunition, distribute rations, and bring up stragglers. My Third Brigade joined me here. After an hour thus spent, my division was moved to the front again, and massed in rear of the right of the First and left of the Second Corps, a disposition which was soon changed, my division being moved to the left, and massed in rear and support of the Fifth Corps and part of the Sixth Corps, near where the Marsh Run road passes by the Round Top. It remained thus posted until about 4. 30 o'clock, when it was moved rapidly to the right, and formed in mass by battalion in rear and support of the left of the Second and right of the First Corps, several batteries being in position in my front. Here it remained until dusk, losing several valuable officers and a large number of men from the enemy's artillery fire. My special aide, Captain McClellan, was wounded.

At dusk, the position was resumed in rear of the Fifth and Sixth Corps, where my division remained during July 4, 5, and 6, engaged in bringing in the wounded, burying the dead, and collecting arms.

My thanks are due to Capt. G. S. Russell, provost-marshal of the division, for the faithful manner in which the duties of his command were performed in the battle. It was judiciously posted, but from the nature of the ground was subjected to constant fire, causing the loss of several men.

The great distance of the hospital from the field and the necessity of my continued presence with the division prevented my making the visits to it which I had been in the habit of doing. My staff officers were sent by me to see to the wounded.

Surgeon Calhoun, medical director of my division, was placed in charge of the corps hospital, owing to the absence of the corps medical director, and, aided by Surg. C. K. Irwin, acting medical director of the division, and its medical officers, gave every possible attention and skillful treatment to those whom the fortunes of the combat brought upon his hands.

The enterprise and energy of Captain [B. Weller] Hoxie, ordnance officer of the division, entitle him to my thanks, which are also due, for the faithful performance of duty, to Captain [James D.] Earle, commissary of subsistence, and Captain [Thomas P.] Johnston, assistant quartermaster.

At 3 a.m. of the 7th, my division marched on the Emmitsburg road, and bivouacked for the night at Mechanicsville, 9 miles south of Emmitsburg.

At 6 a.m. of the 8th, the march was resumed for Middletown, on the Frederick and Hagerstown pike, by way of Hamburg and the mountain pass in that vicinity, but in consequence of the heavy rains of the night and morning, the roads being nearly impassable, the route was changed to that through Frederick, and the division bivouacked from 2 to 3 miles beyond Frederick, and about 4 miles from Middletown. At midnight I received directions to join the headquarters of the army at Middletown, having been announced in orders as chief of staff of the Army of the Potomac, directions that I complied with at once, turning over the command of the division to Brigadier-General Carr.

In parting from this celebrated division, after having commanded it for the brief period of fifty days, I trust that I may be excused for expressing my admiration for its high soldierly qualities. It is impossible to pass it in review, even, without perceiving that its ranks are filled with men who are soldiers in the best meaning of the term, and that it possesses in the grade of commissioned officers men whose skill, courage, and accomplishments would grace any service. Very respectfully, your obedient servant,

A. A. HUMPHREYS,
Major-General of Volunteers, Commanding Division.

---

(2) Report of Brig. Gen. Joseph B. Carr, commanding First Brigade, 2nd Division, 3rd Corps (Official Records, Series I, Vol. XXVII, Part 1 [Series 43])

HDQRS. FIRST BRIG., SECOND DIV., THIRD CORPS,
Camp near Beverly Ford, Va., August 1, 1863

Maj. CHARLES HAMLIN,
Asst. Adjt. Gen. Second Division, Third Corps.

SIR: In compliance with orders from headquarters Second Division, Third Corps, I have the honor to transmit the following report of the operations of my command from the beginning of the campaign up to and including the 8th ultimo:

On Thursday, June 11, by direction of the division commander, I broke camp, marched my command to Hartwood Church, and bivouacked for the night.

At 6 a.m. on Friday, June 12, took up the line of march toward Rappahannock Station, reaching that point at 7.30 p.m. Here, by order of Major Hamlin, assistant adjutant-general of division, I formed my command in a field, in column of regiments, and soon after moved out and advanced to near Beverly Ford, reaching that place at 10 p.m., establishing picket line along the river and at the ford. During this day's march, nearly 25 miles, many men were compelled to quit the ranks in consequence of exhaustion, consequent upon the excessive heat and unusually dusty roads.

On Saturday, June 13, at 9 p.m., a detail of 200 men reported at brigade headquarters, in accordance with instructions, for the purpose of throwing up intrenchments, but as the tools did not arrive until 2 a.m. on Sunday, June 14, work was not commenced until that hour.

At 9 p.m. moved from Beverly Ford, passing Bealeton at 10 p.m. Monday, June 15, reached Warrenton Junction at 8 a.m., and halted one-half mile from the station.

At 1 p.m. left the Junction and marched to Manassas. This march was one of the most severe in my experience, the air being almost suffocating, the dust blinding, and the heat intolerable. Many men suffered from *coup de soleil,* and a large number sank by the wayside, utterly helpless and exhausted.

At 2 o'clock on the morning of Tuesday, June 16, my brigade halted and went into bivouac. At noon the location of my camp was changed a short distance to the right and rear, where the men were permitted to rest.

At 10 a.m. on Wednesday, June 17, I moved 2 miles in the direction of Centreville, and halted in a grove by the side of Bull Run Creek, to enable my men to bathe.

At 4 p.m. I pushed on to Centreville, and went into camp at 7 p.m. near a fine stream of water.

On Thursday, June 18, at 6 p.m., changed location of camp 1 mile to the right, and established a picket line, with Colonel McAllister, Eleventh New Jersey Volunteers, as officer of the day. At 2.45 p.m. on Friday, June 19, we marched to Gum Springs, reaching that place at 7 p.m., and immediately throwing out a picket detail, consisting of the First and Eleventh Massachusetts Volunteers and Twenty-sixth Pennsylvania Volunteers.

On Thursday, June 25, received orders to be in readiness to move at 5.40 a.m.; moved at 10 a.m., passing through Fairfarm and Franklinville, and crossing the Potomac into Maryland at 5 p.m. Marched along the canal to the Monocacy Aqueduct, halting at 1 o'clock on the morning of Friday, June 26, with about 300 men, the remainder having fallen out during the march, weary and exhausted. Early in the morning I sent back a field officer, who brought up the stragglers at 10 a.m.

At 11 a.m. marched to Point of Rocks, and bivouacked at 5 p.m.

On Saturday, June 27, marched to Jefferson, and halted for two hours.

At 1 p.m. left Jefferson, and marched to Burkittsville, where I relieved a brigade from the ------ Corps, and threw out a strong picket force.

At 9.20 a.m. on Sunday, June 28, left Burkittsville, and marched to Middletown, halting an hour for dinner. Pushed on to Frederick, passing through the city at 6 p.m.; halted just outside the city for supper, and then crossed the Monocacy, going into bivouac at 10.30 p.m.

Monday, June 29, left at 5.20 a.m., and marched to Taneytown, passing through Walkersville, Woodsborough, and Ladiesburg.

At 4.20 p.m. on Tuesday, June 30, left Taneytown, and marched to Bridgeport, going into bivouac at 6.30 p.m.

At 8 a.m. on Wednesday, July 1, left Bridgeport, and marched to Emmitsburg, reaching that place at 1.15 p.m. After a halt of two hours, received orders to move with all possible haste to Gettysburg, as General Howard, commanding Eleventh Corps, had attacked the enemy and been repulsed. General Humphreys, commanding the division, being absent by orders from corps headquarters, for the purpose of selecting a position for the corps, and believing the enemy to be near at hand, I immediately ordered the division under arms, and took up the line of march toward Gettysburg, leaving one battery and the Third Brigade (commanded by Col. George C. Burling) at Emmitsburg.

When about l mile from that town, General Humphreys joined the division, and resumed command. The column was guided by a civilian (a doctor) from Emmitsburg and Lieutenant-Colonel Hayden, assistant inspector-general of the corps. When about 3 miles from Gettysburg, we crossed Marsh Creek and advanced on the left-hand road about a mile, when we were suddenly halted by General Humphreys as a measure of precaution. Lieutenant-Colonel Hayden, who had been in advance with the guides, soon after rode up to General Humphreys, and stated that we were but 200 yards from the enemy's pickets.

General Humphreys rode forward to the Black Horse Tavern, on the road from Fairfield to Gettysburg, and finding the information to be correct, and that the enemy occupied the road in heavy force, and believing that an engagement with him at the distance of 3 miles from the rest of the army, with the enemy between the army and his division, would be inconsistent with the plan of battle, faced the division about, and marched to the rear until striking the main road, upon which we proceeded to Gettysburg, reaching that place and going into bivouac at 1.30 a.m. on Thursday, July 2.

This position I retained until 12.30 p.m., at which hour I was ordered to move to the front and form line of battle on the prolongation of a line composed of the First Division of the Third Corps, connecting on its right. After disposing of my command as above directed, the position I occupied, as nearly as I can judge, was the left center. About 11 a.m. I had sent out a regiment as skirmishers (the First Massachusetts Volunteers, Lieutenant-Colonel Baldwin commanding), and this regiment now covered my front.

At 4.08 p.m., by order of General Humphreys, I advanced my line 300 yards to the crest of a hill, and at the same time **detailed 100 men from the Sixteenth Massachusetts Volunteers** to occupy an old building, situated in an orchard on the left of my line. This detail perforated the house in several places, and materially aided in checking the advance of the enemy. My left first became engaged, and its position was held until the regiment on my left (the Collis Zouaves, of the First Division) gave way, when the enemy advanced in considerable force on my left flank, which compelled me to change my front; but no sooner was it accomplished than the enemy made his appearance on my right flank, pouring in a most destructive cross-fire.

Notwithstanding my apparent critical position, I could and would have maintained my position but for an order received direct from Major-General Birney, commanding the corps, to fall back to the crest of the hill in my rear. At that time I have no doubt that I could have charged on the rebels and driven them in confusion, for my line was still perfect and unbroken, and my troops in the proper spirit for the performance of such a task. In retiring, I suffered a severe loss in killed and wounded.

After I had reached the position designated by General Birney, the brigade was rallied by my assistant adjutant-general and aides, and moved forward, driving the enemy and capturing many prisoners. I continued to advance until I again occupied the field I had but a few moments previous vacated. Here my command remained until morning, the officers and men assisting in removing from the field as many of the wounded as the time and facilities would admit of. I may be pardoned, perhaps, for referring in my report to the conspicuous courage and remarkable coolness of the brigadier-general commanding the division during this terrific struggle. His presence was felt by the officers and men, as the enthusiastic manner in which he was greeted will testify.

At daybreak on the morning of Friday, July 3, the enemy opened with his artillery, and kept up a continuous fire for an hour or more, with but little injury to my command.

At 6 a.m. I was ordered to the rear, where the balance of the corps was in bivouac. After replenishing my supply of ammunition, I was ordered to the front and left of the line, to support a division of the Fifth Corps, which was in the first line.

At 3.22 p.m. I was ordered to the center of the line, to support the Second Corps, which was engaged with the enemy.

As I lay in column of battalions, closed in mass, I suffered severely from the artillery fire of the enemy, losing several valuable officers and a number of men.

At dusk I was ordered to my former position, where I remained until 3.30 a.m. on Tuesday, July 7, at which hour my brigade moved from bivouac and marched to Emmitsburg, where we rested until 1.15 p.m., when we pushed on to Mechanicstown, going into bivouac about 1 mile from the town.

At 6 a.m. on Wednesday, July 8, marched to Frederick, going into camp outside the city at 10 p.m.

At 4 a.m. on Thursday, July 9, Major Hamlin, assistant adjutant-general, turned over to me the command of the division, Brigadier-General Humphreys having accepted the position of chief of staff to the major-general commanding the army.

In closing, I desire to call the attention of the general commanding the division to the gallant and meritorious conduct of Col. Robert McAllister, commanding Eleventh New Jersey Volunteers, twice wounded; Lieut. Col. Porter D. Tripp, commanding Eleventh Massachusetts Volunteers; Lieut. Col. Waldo Merriam, commanding Sixteenth Massachusetts Volunteers, wounded; Maj. Robert L. Bodine, commanding Twenty-sixth Pennsylvania Volunteers; Maj. Philip J. Kearny, Eleventh New Jersey Volunteers, seriously wounded (since dead); Major McDonald, Eleventh Massachusetts Volunteers, wounded; Captain Tomlinson, Twenty-sixth Pennsylvania Volunteers, acting lieutenant-colonel; Captain Goodfellow, Twenty-sixth Pennsylvania Volunteers, wounded; Adjt. John Schoonover, Eleventh New Jersey Volunteers, who was twice wounded, but remained in command of his regiment; and to the following officers of my staff, to whom my sincere thanks are due for valuable services rendered: Capt. Le Grand Benedict, assistant adjutant-general; Capt. George E. Henry, First Massachusetts Volunteers, acting aide-de-camp, and Lieut. John Oldershaw, Eleventh New Jersey Volunteers, acting assistant inspector-general.

Lieut. James Johnson, aide-de-camp and acting assistant quartermaster, and Lieut. James A. Cook, acting commissary of subsistence, are entitled to great credit for the promptness and efficiency displayed in the execution of the duties pertaining to their respective departments.

In justice to the surviving officers and men of the veteran brigade, who have on many hard-fought battle-fields distinguished themselves for gallantry and undaunted courage, I cannot close this report without expressing my admiration for their soldierly conduct on this occasion. At the same time I may be permitted to express my deep and heartfelt sympathy for those who now mourn the loss of husbands, fathers, brothers, and friends, who have sacrificed their lives on the altar of their country in upholding its honor and integrity.

I append herewith a tabular statement of the casualties up to and including the 8th ultimo:

Command	Officers Killed	Men Killed	Officers Wounded	Men Wounded	Officers Missing	Men Missing	Officers Total	Men Total	Aggregate
General staff	---	---	2	---	---	---	2	---	2
1st Massachusetts	1	15	8	75	---	21	9	111	120
11th Massachusetts	1	22	7	89	2	8	10	119	129
16th Massachusetts	3	12	4	49	---	13	7	74	81
26th Pennsylvania	1	29	10	166	---	7	11	202	213
11th New Jersey	3	14	9	115	---	12	12	141	153
12th New Hampshire	1	13	5	62	---	11	6	86	92
Total	10	105	45	556	2	72	57	733	790

I have the honor to be, respectfully, your obedient servant,
JOS. B. CARR,
Brigadier-General

---

(3) Report of Captain Matthew Donovan, Sixteenth Massachusetts Infantry

BIVOUAC IN THE FIELD, July 29, 1863

CAPTAIN: in accordance with circular from brigade headquarters, dated July 27, 1863, asking for a report of the operations of the regiment from the date of leaving camp to July 8, inclusive, I have the honor to transmit the following:

Thursday, June 11, broke camp at 2 p.m.; marched to Hartwood Church; bivouacked for the night.

Friday, June 12, started at 6.30 a.m. and marched to Beverly Ford, on the Rappahannock; distance, 25 miles; bivouacked in woods, within 300 yards of the river.

Saturday, June 13, remained in bivouac all day; saw enemy's pickets across the river; no shots fired. Detail from First brigade to throw up redoubt tonight; great delay caused by not getting intrenching tools until past 1 a.m.

Sunday, June 14, redoubts finished at 5.30 a.m.; the day passed quietly; received orders to be ready to start at sundown; got off at 8.30 and marched all night.

Monday, June 15, arrived at Warrenton Junction at 5 a.m.; bivouacked half a mile below Junction; slept until 12 m.; started at 1.30 p.m. for Manassas Junction, and arrived at 1 a.m. Tuesday June 16; lay down and slept for the night.

At 7 a.m. packed up and marched 1 1/2 miles; stacked arms, and remained all day and night.

Wednesday, June 17, received orders to start at 9.30 a.m.; marched about 3 miles toward Bull Run; halted until 3 p.m., in order to let the men bathe; off again, and marched to Centreville; bivouacked for the night.

Thursday, June 18, changed bivouac half a mile; remained all day and night.

Friday, June 19, received orders to start at 1 p.m.; marched to Gum Springs, arriving about dark; bivouacked for the night.

Saturday June 20, remained in bivouac all day; all quiet.

Sunday, June 21, under arms all day; heard heavy firing in direction of Aldie; changed camp about 300 yards.

Monday, Tuesday, and Wednesday, June 22, 23 and 24, remained in bivouac; all quiet.

Thursday, June 25, received orders to pack up at 4 a.m.; started at 8.30 a.m.; marched to the mouth of Monocacy River (in Maryland) by way of Edwards Ferry, arriving at 1 a.m. of the 26th. on this march we did not have time to make coffee, day or night.

Friday, June 26, started at 9 a.m. and marched to Point of Rocks; bivouacked for the night.

Saturday, June 27, started at 8 a.m. for Jefferson, arriving at 1 p.m.; from there marched to Burkittsville, arriving at 5 p.m.; our regiment ordered on picket on Crampton's Gap, in the South Mountain; passed a quiet night.

Sunday, June 28, received orders to pack up and start for Middletown, arriving at 1 a.m.; remained one hour; started again for Frederick City, arriving at 7 p.m.; marched through the city (bands playing and colors flying), and bivouacked 3 miles outside the city.

Monday, June 29, started at 4.30 a.m.; marched to Taneytown, passing through the villages of Woodsborough and Middleburg, arriving about 5 p.m.; bivouacked for the night in woods in rear of the town.

Tuesday, June 30, the regiment was mustered for pay; started, and marched about 4 miles outside of Taneytown; halted, and bivouacked for the night.

Wednesday, July 1, started about 9 a.m.; marched to Emmitsburg and rested, expecting to stay all night, but got orders to start; marched towards Gettysburg; got on wrong road; about-faced, and marched towards Gettysburg, arriving some 3 miles from it at 1 a.m.; lay down and slept.

Thursday, July 2, up at daylight. At 8 a.m. were ordered into line of battle; lay down behind the stacks; skirmishing going on in front. At 4 p.m. we were ordered to advance in line of battle to an orchard; lay down under the crest of a hill. Soon after, the battle commenced in earnest. We were attacked in front and on the flank. Our men stood it bravely until overpowered by numbers; were forced to fall back a distance of 300 yards, when they again rallied, and drove the enemy back to their original lines. Our regiment lost, in killed, wounded, and missing, 81 officers and men.

Friday, July 3, at 6 a.m., cannonading commenced on our right. Our regiment, with the corps, was marched to a piece of woods, where it drew three days' rations, the first it had had for thirty-six hours. Lay in reserve until 3 p.m., when we were ordered to support a battery, at which time we had 1 officer wounded; firing ceased about 6 p.m.; we were ordered back to the woods; passed a quiet night.

Saturday, July 4, up at 2.30 a.m.; no firing in our front; a little skirmishing on our right the day closed with a report that the enemy were skedaddling.

Sunday, July 5, up early; all quiet, received orders to be ready to start at 6 a.m.

Monday, July 6, remained in woods all day; again received orders to start at 3 o'clock next morning.

Tuesday, July 7, started at 3 a.m.; the roads were in very bad condition owing to late rains; half an hour to get breakfast near Monocacy River; off again, and marched through Emmitsburg; 11.30 o'clock, halted and had dinner; started again, and marched to Mechanicstown; bivouacked for the night.

Wednesday, July 8, started at 8 a.m.; marched to Frederick City, passing through several small villages on the way; heavy rain all forenoon; roads in bad condition; we marched through the city at sundown, and bivouacked for the night 1 mile outside.

Very respectfully, your obedient servant,

M. DONOVAN, Captain, Comdg. Sixteenth Regiment Mass. Vols.

Capt. LE GRAND BENEDICT,

Asst. Adjt. Gen., First Brig., Second Div. Third Corps

****

APPENDIX 5
*
A note on the Flags of the 16th Massachusetts Infantry

The surviving flags of the regiment are held by the Massachusetts State House Flag Collection, State House, Boston, Massachusetts 02133, to whom we are grateful for permission to publish the following accounts written for them by Steven W. Hill, State House Flag Historian.

The regiment received its first two colors (1987.418, 1987.420) in 1861, probably just before departing from the state on August 17. The national color was unmarked; "16th" in yellow paint was added after its return in 1863. The State color has the pine tree shield on its reverse.

Very little is recorded about the colors of the Sixteenth in battle. The staff of the first state color was broken in two at the Battle of Glendale, June 30, 1862, by a cannon ball or bursting shell. The color bearer, 20-year-old Sergeant Jonas F. Capelle of Lexington, was unhurt. He saved the flag and the upper part of the staff (1987.421), and handed the lower part to Major Charles P. Chandler of the First Massachusetts, who was subsequently killed.[310] As the staff was broken off almost exactly at the lower edge of the flag, it is difficult to imagine how the color was carried in the field afterwards.

The Massachusetts Adjutant General issued new colors for the Sixteenth late in 1862. The old colors were returned, and were received by the Massachusetts Adjutant General on February 12, 1863. For purposes of display the state flag was put on an old militia staff, and it is this staff which shows in the 1866 series of photographs. The broken staff was put on display as well; it is not in the 1866 photo, but was noted in the Boston *Globe* inventory in 1885.

The new colors (1987.416, 1987.417) received at the end of 1862 or early in 1863, were used until the regiment was mustered out on July 27, 1864. During their service the national color had its staff broken by a shell about two feet from the top - it was repaired in the field - and the finial shot off and lost. The state color had the blade of its finial shot off as well as much of the silk torn away. Both colors were turned in to the Sergeant-at-Arms on Battleflag Day, December 22, 1865. There is also in the State collection a small fragment of a national color with a tag identifying it as "Piece of Battle Flag 16th Mass. Vols." It may belong to the Sixteenth's second national color, but apart from the tag pinned to it, there is no record of its provenance.

---

[310] Boston *Globe*, December 22, 1885. According to the *Globe*, Chandler "dashed into the fight and was never heard from again." Other sources simply list Chandler as killed, not missing. MSS lists Sergeant Capelle as being commissioned Second Lieutenant on June 26, 1862; presumably the commission had not yet been received in the field by the time of the battle on June 30, or perhaps it was one of those back-dated for pay purposes.

There are therefore 2 National Flags, 2 State Flags, 1 flag fragment, and 1 Broken Staff with finial in the collections; detailed descriptions are as follows:

1987.418   1st National Color; Issued July/August 1861 (the regiment mustered 29 June-12 July, and departed the state 17 August). Received by the State Adjutant General 12 February, 1863. Numerals on middle stripe added after flag's return. Finial type H-1.

1987.420   1st State color. Issued July/August 1861. Staff shot in two at Battle of Glendale, 30 June, 1862. (See 1987.421). Flag returned to State in 1862, put on replacement pole. Pine tree reverse. Label on staff: "This is an old militia staff, the original staff having been cut in two by a shot."

1987.421   Staff with finial H-1. Upper portion of original staff of first state color #1987.420. Lower portion lost in battle 30 June, 1862.

1987.416   2nd National color. Issued 1862. Received by Sergeant-at-Arms 22 December, 1865. Top of pole broken off, finial missing. Staff mended approx 25 in. from top with broad woven tape.

1987.251G   Fragment of National color. Appears to belong to #416.

1987.417   2nd State color. Issued 1862. Received by Sergeant-at-Arms 22 December, 1865. Finial type S-4; blade broken off.

****

APPENDIX 6

*

Subsequent to the completion of the formatting and indexing of the book, six further letters from Johnson came to light. These contain information of considerable importance for the narrative and it was considered essential that they should be included in the book. They therefore follow, as an appendix.

======================

1861
Camp Hamilton
Fort Monroe

Sept. 26
Dear Father,
    I sent you today 3 doz. of Green Figs which I hope may arrive safe though I have my doubt about their keeping good. I would like to have Nellie have a taste of them, if she is not in Boston please send her a few. A Captain's duty to be filled properly requires a diversity of talent, he ought to be a good clerk also be somewhat posted in military law besides his other military requirement. I was president of a regimental court martial this week consisting of three officers, the senior in rank presiding. The court both judges of the guilt and the punishment of the prisoner; we had only three cases; there is now a general court-martial in session. Nellie writes that Mr. Soule is studying Chemistry with Dr. Jackson and is getting along finely which I am glad to hear. Tell Mr. Soule he may hear from me at any time. When you write let me know how much business the firm is doing and how things are generally. I received from you last Sundays papers and also a letter from Nellie. You may see that I don't take much time to write by look of the letter, but if you can read it, it is well written enough. Last evening an Indiana regiment arrived here[311] and this morning and Illinois regiment with rumors that there was still another at the fort. The arrival of troops if they keep a coming in that proportion indicate some early movement from this place either by water or land. The morning here are very damp and the night chilly now, as much so, it appears to me, as it is in Mass. at the same time.
    You must not find any fault with the style & writing of this.
                                                  Truly yours
                                                 Affectionately
                                                 C. Robinson Johnson

---

[311] The 20th Indiana Infantry joined the Department at Fortress Monroe in September, but Dyer shows no Illinois regiment.

P.S.
And compliment ~~of~~ to Stephen & Bradlee also to Mr. Soule & factory men. I received the box which you sent with all the contents, which I shall enjoy exceedingly, last Tuesday & should have written to acknowledge the receipt before if I had not a box of fig to send so waited until I sent them.

****

                                                Camp Hamilton   Nov 22 / 61
Dear Nellie,
    I write this to let you know that I received yours and mother's box yesterday. What! Am I to eat both of those puddings? the big one is nearly large enough for my company. I had my dinner a[t] six o'clock in the evening being on board the frigate Roanoke[312] in the forenoon had four other officers to enjoy it with me Charles having his at one o'clock and was away in the evening. We are having an addition to our force it may mean some thing. I write this in a hurry to let you know I am well.
                                                  From your Affect.
                                                  Charles

****

[Letter undated, but clearly written in the aftermath of, and describing the battle of, Fredericksburg, fought on December 13th. Johnson mentions receiving a letter from Nellie dated the 14th, which presumably took a few days to reach him. The main series has letters from him written to her on Monday 15th and Sunday 21st. It may therefore be suggested that this letter was written towards the end of the week commencing Monday, December 15th]

Camp Near Falmouth Va.

Dear Nellie,
    I have received your favors of 7th, 9th, 11th and 14th also a letter from mother. I am now situated the same and in the same place that I was before we left to cross the Rappahannock. Our regiment was fortunate as to its position Thursday we were out of harm's way, occasionally seeing a rebel shell burst but too distant to do any damage. Friday morning we moved nearly opposite to Fredericksburg where we had a good view of the other side of the river about 3 miles; after we had comfortably arranged ourselves for the night, in fact most of us were asleep, ~~when~~ we were called up to move forward. This march brought us to the river by the ponton's *[pontoon]* bridges where we finished our sleep to awake by the cannonading directly in our front. Again we were in luck, our brigade was divided leaving the 11th N. Jersey & 16th Mass on this side of the river to guard the ponton bridges. We were in a valley formed by the river directly(?); In our rear were high cliffs from which we had a grand view of the strife before us. Our army made several attempts to gain possession of the enemies works to the rear of Fredericksburg and the attempts were continued until after dark when the scene was grand, each flash of musket was distinctly seen resembling on a grander scale a large torch light procession. Sunday morning we left the river and went to the extreme front our regiment doing skirmish work, it was while skirmishing we suffered our lost. Late Sunday afternoon an agreement was made by the pickets not to fire on each other and afterward a flag of truce put a stop to all firing during the armistice. I had a talk with some of the rebel officers found them gentlemanly & polite, one of them said his best friends were North. They felt confident that they could whip us there and well they might. The rebel position was admirable, their batteries were on high hills out of the reach of any guns we could bring on them, in fact it looked like a trap well prepared for us, our generals saw it after they were in it and it was fortunate we succeeding in crossing the river without loss. It was no doubt the

---
[312] See footnote 26

opinion of our commanders that their left (Rebels) might be turned having no idea of the length of their lines, the rebels line were eighteen miles long. David Orr is missing, how I can't explain unless he was shot dead and fell into a ditch   any other explanation than this is impossible, it was my opinion that he had, on the company coming from picket left and gone to the rear, I still hold to ~~my~~ that opinion[313]. I would like to see this war ended and I am seconded by all the officers. Give my regards to all. The mail about to close.

Yours affectionately,
Charley

****

(Part only of a letter, the final page of which is cross-written. In one of the margins is written "July 30, Harrisons Landing, in a probably contemporary hand, undoubtedly that of Nellie or Johnson's father, and presumably because the remainder of the letter had by then already been lost.)

July 30 [1862], Harrison's Landing

... mind back to my old ambition, which is to own a good farm with means to carry it on, an ambition I suppose never to be realized. I am very anxious to see this war ended but I can't see the end, the South are very determined and have a strong hand to control   I dislike the cause *[course]* of the government in not having arrested immediately all deserters. I see by Boston a list of deserters from various camps, they ought to be followed as close as a policeman can follow them, this kind of volunteering is costing the government to[o] much, the majority of men that want to be discharged on account of ....   Jimmy is well and looks first rate I have never seen him look as well as now   Lt Tucker is improving slowly he would improve faster if he had better spirits   they say there are some cases of scurvy in the army although I know of none. The army is well fed and their is no complaints from the men in regard to food. There are still a good number sick which are I believe not serious cases   I received ....
.... and am very much obliged. The pleasant summer weather carry my...
[The final part of the letter is cross-written, but there appears to no continuity of the previous text with the cross-writing, suggesting that there was more cross-written text on the missing page or pages]
... story, you can judge as well as I can the truth of it; no shell (whole) came near enough   pieces flew around thick. I want to caution further against Wickham[314] & Harding[315] both have smooth tongues and would be likely to make father believe they were an honor to the company   they did not receive minor wounds in action, but I have every reason to believe purposely disfigured themselves to escape fighting. Give my regards to all

Charley

****

This undated letter describes Burnside's notorious "Mud March" of January 20-23, 1863, in great detail. Johnson refers to hearing "yesterday" of Burnside's removal from command of the Army of the Potomac, which took place on the 26th. His other letters from this time are dated January 26th and 31st. The news of Burnside's removal must

---

[313] Johnson is partly correct; Orr had in fact deserted on the 14th (see footnote 169), which further indicates that this letter was written several days later.

[314] Private Ralph H. Wickham, from Stoneham, enlisted July 12, 1861, aged 28. He is recorded as wounded on June 30, 1862 at Glendale, Va.. and was discharged for disability Sept. 30, 1862, so Johnson's suspicions cannot be confirmed.

[315] Private William W. Harding, a Charlestown shoemaker, enlisted July 12, 1861, aged 38. He is also shown as wounded at Glendale, Va., June 30, 1862, and discharged for wounds at Washington DC, Oct. 6, 1862.

have spread fairly quickly among the troops. It may therefore be suggested that the letter was written between the 27th and the 30th, and probably closer to the former date. The letter is also valuable for Johnson's comments on the qualities of escaped slaves and Black soldiers which, while to modern eyes uncharitable and - in the light of subsequent experience of the highly creditable battle performance of Black soldiers, even inaccurate - were a reflection of the feelings at this time of many soldiers in the Northern armies, who considered that they were fighting to restore the Union, not to free the slaves, and even less to win them equality with whites.

Camp Near Falmouth [Va.]

Dear Nellie,

     I have intended to have written you in my last a syno[p]sis of the movements of our division in the recent move. We received notice Friday Jan 16 to be ready to move at 1 o'clock the next day. Saturday morning we were notified that the movement had been postponed for twenty four hours. On Sunday morning another 24 hours grace which made us think that something wrong had happened. Monday came finding us disposed to make up our minds to stay yet a little while longer nor was this feeling lessened until 1 o'clock when we were ordered to pack up which order was reluctantly obeyed, now unfortunately the day was cold & threatening snow favorable for a forced march but disagreeable to stand idle in. The column at last was set in motion and moved slowly along until we had proceeded somewhat over a mile with frequent interruptions when we came to a dead halt and after a half hour had been spent by officers & men in trying to keep themselves warm we were notified that we should not move for three hour, consequently everybody made themselves busy in picking up chips to raise a fire to make coffee with it being then our opinion that we should travel all night. And hour and a half had passed rather uncomfortably for us all for we were not only exposed to a cold wind which chilled but had the additional luxury of rain which kept the smoke from rising blinding us occassionally. An hour & half had passed the soldiers were scattered where they could find the best protection against the weather and the readiest means to make a fire when the order fall in was given, We fell in (those that heard the order) about faced and headed for camp. The night was dark and everybody desired to arrive there as soon as possible so we made quick time to camp and proceeded instantly to pitch tents and made ourselves comfortable. On our march back there was confusion owing to the unexpectedness of the order and the suddenness of the start yet they all knew the way and arrived after a fashion. The next morning after a fine sleep we were awakened and told to pack up and fall in right off. There had been no reveille sounded that morning constandly [consequently] but few early risers and there was hurrying to obtain time to take a bite before we left. In a short time we were again in motion over muddy road at a gait which if it werent for an occassional halt made by some stoppage in the roads would have used up all of us, as it was when we arrived at two o'clock to a place where we told we should remain over night the regiment were greatly reduced in number but before night about every body had come up. It requires a dray-horse to take over such roads and at such a gait the load which a foot soldier has to carry, besides his blanket and change of underclothing which he carries in his knapsack, he carries 3 days rations 60 rounds of Cartridges and canteen supposed to be filled with water and gun; in rainy weather with his coat doubly heavy his shoes filled with mud his pants plastered with the same how can you blame a man not well from straggling, yet our men although an occassional growl keep in good spirit and well up as a general thing. There is nothing that takes the spirit out of the troops so much as a hard march and it is a mark of a good general to be able to march his men without using them up. Since we left the peninsula I have seen my severest marches conducted seemingly without method yet we accomplish no more than we used to. On the march from Fairfax Station to our camp near Falmouth we always, unnecessary in my judgement, arrived at our camping ground after dark which prevents the men from making themselves as comfortable as they otherwise would, it being the first object of the men to obtain water & fuel one to make coffee and the other for warmth and to make coffee also, neither of which can be found as well especially in a strange country in the night as well as by day. Another thing was also neglected which was to provide a rough foot bridge over fords too wide to jump yet deep enough to make a man uncomfortable, these bridges might have been made in a short while by the pioneers of which we have plenty by simply throwing logs across. It would surprise any one but a soldier to see how quickly an army of veterans can make themselves comfortable even in the most disagreeable weather especially if they encamp in or near woods. I have been straggling myself from the subject. At two o'clock we arrived in the place where we were told we should stay overnight and the situation was admirable being in the woods with small rivulets running threw it. Hardly had the men been notified that we should remain over night when there instantaneously arose fires here, there & everywhere and the forest was dotted with clusters of shelter tents; how the forest suffered the sound of the axe was ever where trees would fall in front, rear and as you think about on top of you anyway the large oak trees fall with so much stubbordness that the ground shakes when they strike it. It is astonishing rather marvellous that men will cut down trees surrounding with tents with the exception of a narrow strip hardly wide enough for the tree to be placed carefully yet men will take pleasure in falling a tree and having it drop in the only place where it can drop without endangering any one; many a tree have I watched expecting to see it fall on my tent and stood ready to dodge to find that it fell in the right place and nobody hurt. In a very short time I made myself comfortable as well as the rest of them and passed as pleasant a night as usual. Morning came no drums were sounded to disturb us and we laid late in the morning under our shelters listening to the drops of rain as they fell and watching the bright fire at our side. One inconvenience we had, that I did, I sleep without boots or stockings on and after having my stockings dried I am obliged to soap the inside of my boots to have them slide on. After arising we washed eat our breakfast consisting of such thing as we had brought with us, our wagons being left behind and by the way the breakfast was not bad cold biscuits & butter and cold ham, the ham not sugar cured. We generally do well on our first day or two march but after that it is sometimes hard picking I mean in regard to living. After breakfast we smoked a pipe close by the fire or walk around and talk with other officer. At one o'clock we received orders to fall in without arms with our axes. The falling in being accomplished we waded and swam through the mud for two miles and went to cutting trees & brush, carrying them to the road and there using them to make cordurory [corduroy] road. It took twice the time to go and return that we occupied in work. It was on this fatigue party that I first heard that the move had been abandoned. After enjoying a comfortable night rest we were awakened before light and started again without arms to complete the work commenced yesterday. While repairing the road I learnt from artillery officers that although with a guide they got onto the wrong road when they found out the mistake they were obliged to unlimber to turn around & also learnt that the pontoons (?) also were misled besides that they were fast in the mud in all direction, especially those wagons which carried the lumber, I saw myself several wagon some way back from their destination. The story probably is exaggerated although many pontoons were delayed on that account. One more rumor I write which I believe to be correct that the rebel pickets had placed a large board within plain site of our pickets on which was written Burnside stuck in the mud under which was painted a six horse mule team nearly buried in the sacred soil of Virginia. Having finished the roads we returned to camp arriving about one o'clock. We were told that probably we should return to our old camp or where we started from. Now it was my hope that we should remain where we were until the next morning when we could start fresh arrive at noon and have ample time to pitch tents and get ready for night. But notwithstanding the men were tired and muddy we were ordered to fall in with knapsacks packed and at two or thereabouts we started and after a severe march arrived in our old camp very tired with but a small part of the brigade at six o'clock and went to work immediately to get ready for the night. Whilst we were preparing the road I had occassion to see the distress of the poor four-legged animals as they toiled under the application of whip & spurs to do their utmost, if they are able to feel anything for a week or more they must be tough. The artillery had advantage over the wagon trains as they doubled their teams, leaving one half their batteries behind thus a piece ordinary with six horses had ten yet notwithstanding the whips & spurs were used as much in one case as in the other. Officers like myself with no means of arriving at the actual loss in animals to the government make large guesses, I have no doubt that thousand or more animals will perish or be used up in this last move. We all agree that a month will pass before we can take the field against the enemy. We have had heretofore such fine weather that the rebels might reason with some foundation, that providence interfered in their behalf, but we can reason in the same manner. If Burnside had started at the appointed time the rain might have caught us on the other side of the river in front of their batteries, perhaps, with guns fast in the mud and soldier and horses starving for want of rations, as it was a great many horses went twenty four hour without a good meal, and I heard that there were 40,000 soldiers rations brought on the backs of horses not being able to bring them in wagons. Burnside I no doubt is to be pitied I believe he feels it deeply but he had not the power of our little Mac to create enthusiasm, little Mac was always received with cheers wherever he rode Burnside in silence and I heard that in riding through a camp he was saluted with cries of "played out Burnside" it may be true. Any commander taking the command of the Army of the Potomac otherwise than Little Mac will simply have passive men under his command willing to growl & find fault at every little error. There is one thing that the men know that even whilst at Fair Oaks they lived better than they do now at much nearer now our supplies, it may be that the government is economizing. My experience with the colored race is that they appreciate the attempt to free them as much as a wild animal does an attempt to tame him. Negroes are not loved in our army especially by the Irish and I think that a regiment of negroes unless it did all the dirty work might as well go to ---- as to be joined to the Army of the Potomac. We have four or more slaves brought from around Norfolk with us and it is their intention as soon as they can get the money due them by the officers and the passes they will go back to their mistresses they say they do not know where their masters are; you tell them they are free if they remain here it don't make any difference they want to go back Manual an unusually intelligent negro whilst at Washington tried his best to go back to Norfolk but could not obtain a pass. Negroes appreciate the value of money as well as any one, but they are lazy and dont know what freedom means. The President Proclamation has in a measure divided the north & the army. The army hate to think that they are fighting for the negro who if he wish liberty can easily obtain it by fighting as we are doing, if you could see the immense majority they have now in some parts of the slave states a little energy courage & determination would make for us a strong ally but they will never do it unless led on by ambitious white men who will have to scare them into it to see them dissolve before danger as mist before the sun[316]. But what honor would we gain by having them as allies, how it would degrade us as a nation. It was not the intention of the President I suppose to excite servile war but to alarm the south he has failed in that. There are officers very few I am glad to say who say they wont fight for the negro or under the proclamation[317]. My lieut received a letter from Lowell which says

---

[316] Three regiments of Black troops had been raised in occupied territory during 1862, and two more in January 1863, but it was not until about the time Johnson was writing this letter that the famous 54th and 55th Massachusetts Infantry regiments were raised; Johnson's assertion that they "can easily obtain [their liberty] by fighting" missed the point that, at the time, it was virtually impossible for a Black man to join the Union forces. By the end of the war nearly 180,000 Black soldiers had served in the Union Armies and some 19,000 in the Navies, making up an invaluable 10% of the total Union forces, and confounding predictions that they would not be the equal of their white counterparts.

[317] Despite his prejudices, Johnson clearly felt duty bound to obey the spirit of Lincoln's Emancipation Proclamation, issued on January 1, and disapproved of those officers who expressed views to the contrary. However, in company with many others, both at home and abroad - great outrage at Lincoln's supposed last-ditch efforts to foment slave rebellion was expressed in the foreign press - Johnson mistakes Lincoln's motives; there was no intention to incite the slaves to revolt against their masters, and in fact there was effectively no record of any such risings, the slaves behaving with perhaps considerably more restraint than many whites would have done under the same circumstances.

number of officers at home say they wont fight again after the issuing of the proclamation. The only good it has done the army is to give it a subject on which [to] growl. Every negro they pass they shout out "see what we are fighting for." I am glad to say that all this feeling is at present superficial and does little harm, our army being as effective as ever. Wednesday morning, yesterday was unpleasant and rainy in fact since we returned to our camp this last time we have had no steady sunshine, this morning I awoke to find it snowing, the ground wet and sloshy but the trees white with snow, the forests look beautifully. We heard yesterday what you will learn before this reaches you of the removal of Burnside, Franklin[318] & Sumner[319] or rather relieved and Hooker placed in command. Rather need not write that letter as I believe it will be almost useless to try in this direction. I have received yours of the 22nd and unless their be a way to obtain my discharge from Washington I shall have to wait another opportunity. It is still snowing which will prevent any move at present. Give my regards to all. I am writing with my pale ink hope you can make it out.

>Yours
>Affectionately
>Charlie

****

>April 7th 1863
>Camp near Falmouth Va.

Col.,

I have the honor to request a Leave of Absence for the following reasons, Viz: My time of copartnership for five years in the firm of C. & F. W Winchester having recently expired and having been urged by the firm to resign and having had my application returned unapproved for reason, "that no interests of a private nature can be considered with those of the service," and all my future prospects being in the firm which is one of fifty years standing, and having had entire control of the manufacturing dep't before the war, I desire a Leave of Absence to place myself in....
[rest of letter missing]

****

---

[318] William Buel Franklin (1823-1903) led the 6th Corps with distinction, but was accused by Burnside with disobedience of orders at Fredericksburg and thereby partly responsible for the disaster to Union arms at that battle. While Lincoln declined to approve his removal, he was posted to the far west and his army career effectively ended. However, he had a successful post-war career, including being general manager of the Colt's Firearms Company.

[319] Edwin Vose Sumner (1797-1863), known as "Bull-head" because it was rumored that a bullet had once bounced off his head, was a career soldier and the oldest Corps commander in the Civil War. On Hooker's assumption of command after Burnside's dismissal, he asked to be relieved of command. He was assigned to the Department of Missouri, but died in March on the way there.

BIBLIOGRAPHY
*

ANNUAL REPORT OF THE ADJUTANT-GENERAL OF THE COMMONWEALTH OF
MASSACHUSETTS... FOR THE YEAR ENDING DECEMBER 31, 1863 [1864]
[1865]: (Boston, 1864, 1865, 1866]

"ASA SMITH LEAVES THE WAR": American Heritage Magazine 22 (Feb. 1971), 103-5.

THE BATTLE OF FREDERICKSBURG: (Civil War Times Illustrated Special Issue, IV.8,
Dec. 1965)

"Brief Memoranda of our Martyr Soldiers Who Fell During the Great Rebellion of the
Nineteenth Century" compiled by Henry Ingersoll Bowditch: anonymous
manuscript describing Johnson's career, wounding and death, affixed to page
77, published here by courtesy of the Massachusetts Historical Society.

THE CAMPAIGN OF CHANCELLORSVILLE: John Bigelow Jr. (New Haven, Conn., 1910;
Dayton, O., 1973, 1983, 1991; New York, 1995)

CHANCELLORSVILLE: DISASTER IN VICTORY: Brian Palmer (New York, 1967)

CHAPLAIN FULLER: BEING A LIFE SKETCH OF A NEW ENGLAND CLERGYMAN AND
ARMY CHAPLAIN: Richard F. Fuller (Boston, 1863)

CIVIL WAR COLLECTOR'S ENCYCLOPEDIA [Vol. 1]: Francis A. Lord (Harrisburg, Pa.,
1963)

CIVIL WAR NAVAL CHRONOLOGY: W.J.Morgan & R.M.Basoco (Washington, D.C.,
1971)

COMPENDIUM OF THE WAR OF THE REBELLION: Frederick H. Dyer (3 vols - Des
Moines, Ia., 1903; New York, 1959; Dayton, O., 1978, 1984; National Historical
Society, 1987; Wilmington, N. C., 1994)

ENCYCLOPEDIA OF THE CONFEDERACY: editor-in-chief Richard N. Current (4 vols.,
New York, 1993)

GENERALS IN BLUE: LIVES OF THE UNION COMMANDERS: Ezra Warner (Baton
Rouge, 1964 and subsequent editions)

GETTYSBURG – DAY TWO: A STUDY IN MAPS: John D. Imhof (Baltimore, 1999)

GETTYSBURG: Two books on on Sickles' role at Gettysburg were published in 2009, at
too late a stage to be used as sources for the Gettysburg chapter of this work.
Readers may wish to consult them, and an earlier work also cited here, for more
details of the Third Corps' role in the battle:
- SICKLES AT GETTYSBURG: James A. Hessler (Savas Beatie, 2009)
- DEFENDING THE UNION LEFT FLANK: GENERAL DANIEL SICKLES AT THE
BATTLE OF GETTYSBURG: Thomas B. Kopac (PublishAmerica, 2009)
- GETTYSBURG: THE MEADE-SICKLES CONTROVERSY: Richard A. Sauers
(Brasseys, 2003, 2005)

HISTORY OF THE FIRST REGIMENT (MASSACHUSETTS INFANTRY): Warren H.
Cudworth (Boston, 1866)

A HISTORY OF THE SECOND REGIMENT, NEW HAMPSHIRE VOLUNTEER INFANTRY,

IN THE WAR OF THE REBELLION: Martin A. Haynes (Lakeport, N.H., 1896)
IMAGES FROM THE STORM: ed. C.F Bryan et al. (New York, 2001)
THE OFFICIAL MILITARY ATLAS OF THE CIVIL WAR: George B. Davis et al. (reprint New York, 1983)
MASSACHUSETTS IN THE ARMY AND NAVY, 1861 - 1865: (Boston, 1896, 2 vols.)
MR. LINCOLN'S FORTS: A GUIDE TO THE CIVIL WAR DEFENSES OF WASHINGTON: Benjamin F. Cooling III & Walton H. Owen II (Shippensburg, Pa., 1988)
ORDER OF BATTLE: GETTYSBURG, JULY 2, 1863: UNION: THE ARMY OF THE POTOMAC: James Arnold & Roberta Weiner (Botley, Oxford, United Kingdom, 2000)
ORDER OF SERVICES AT THE DEDICATION OF THE CHAPEL TENT OF THE SIXTEENTH REGIMENT OF MASSACHUSETTS *VOLUNTEERS, AT FORTRESS MONROE, VA., DECEMBER 22D, 1861: (Baltimore, 1861)*
16TH MASSACHUSETTS VOLUNTEER INFANTRY, "IRON SIXTEENTH": Website maintained by a grandson of Isaac F. Kennaston, of Johnson's Company F (http://members.aol.com/inf16mavol/16thmass.html)
REBELS RESURGENT: FREDERICKSBURG TO CHANCELLORSVILLE: W.K.Goolrich (Time-Life Books, Alexandria, Va., 1985)
REGIMENTAL STRENGTHS AND LOSSES AT GETTYSBURG: John Busey (Hightstown, N.J., 1980, 1994, revised 2005)
THEY FOUGHT FOR THE UNION: Francis A. Lord (New York, 1960)
TO THE GATES OF RICHMOND: THE PENINSULA CAMPAIGN: Stephen W. Sears (New York, 1992)
UNITED STATES ARMY MILITARY HISTORICAL INSTITUTE: Items in Manuscript Archive on the 16th Massachusetts: Regimental Papers (CWMiscColl); Charles L. Brown (CWTIColl); Charles R. Johnson (HCWRTColl-CocoColl, PrinceColl); Thomas Landers (CWMiscColl); George W. Tainter (CWTIColl); Alonzo K. Worth (CWMiscColl)
WARSHIPS OF THE CIVIL WAR NAVIES: Paul H. Silverstone (Annapolis, Md., 1989)
WAR OF THE REBELLION: A COMPILATION OF THE OFFICIAL RECORDS OF THE UNION AND CONFEDERATE ARMIES: ed. R. N. Scott et al. (Washington, D. C., 1880-1902, 70 vols. in 128 parts; National Historical Society, 1971-2; Wilmington, N. C., 1986, 1992-4; Hicksville, N. Y., 1986; Dayton, O., 1992-3) *[also produced on single CD-ROM, and searchable on Cornell University website http://cdl.library.cornell.edu/moa/moa_browse.html]*

*

INDEX

(Illustration numbers in bold typeface)

Adelaide, steamboat: 14
Alexandria, Va.: **69**, 114-120, 126-127
Amory, William A., Capt., 16th Mass. inf. & Maj., 2nd Mass. Hvy. Arty.: 170, 172
Ashby's Gap, Va.: 168
Balloons, reconnaissance: **70**, 53, 64
Banks, Gardner, Col., 16th Mass. Inf.: **8, 9,** 48, 101, 126, 136, 137, 138, 168, 172
Banks, Hiram B., 2nd Lt., 16th Mass. Inf.: 119
Banks, Nathaniel P., Maj. Gen., USA: 13
Baseball game: 136, 177
Belle Plain, Va.: 138
Berry, Hiram G., Maj. Gen., USA,: **33**
Beverley Ford, Va.: 196, 200
Big Bethel, Va.: 36, 56
Birney, David B., Maj. Gen., USA: **34**, 198
Bixby, Augustus H., Capt., 1st R.I. Cav.: 198
Black troops, Johnson's views on: 256-7
Blaisdell, William, Lt. Col., 16th Mass. Inf.: **10**, 130, 166
Boston, Mass.: 12
Bowditch, Nathaniel, 1st. Lt., 1st Mass. Cav.: 172
Brandy Station, Va.: 196, 198
Bridges, Capt, Benjamin A., 16th Mass. Inf.: 29
Bristoe Station, Va.: 129
Brown, John B., 1st Lt., 16th Mass. Inf.: **11**, 196
Bull Run, Va., Second Battle of: 109-113, 210
Bull's Bay, S.C.,: 28
Burkettville, Md.: 182
Burnside, Ambrose E., Maj. Gen., USA: **72**, 59, 129, 137, 256, 257
Cairnes, James, Pvt., 16th Mass. Inf.: 169
Camp Cameron, Cambridge, Mass.: 12
Camp Hamilton, Fortress Monroe, Va.: 19, 20, 23, 25-62, 209, 253
Camp McClellan, Baltimore, Md.: 12-14,
Capelle, Jonas F., Capt., 16th Mass. Inf.: 198
Carr, Joseph B., Brig. Gen., USA: **35**, 131, 137, 166, 175, 183ff, 243-247
Casey, Silas, Maj. Gen., USA: 77
Catlett's Station, Va.: 198
Catoctin Ridge, Va.: 201
Cedar Run, Va.: 199
Centreville, Va.: 199, 200
Chancellorsville, Va.: **83-84**, 140-159
Charles City Cross Roads: **61**,
Charleston, SC: 32-33
Chantilly, Va.: 114
Chase, Joseph F., Capt., 16th Mass. Inf.: 116

Chickahominy River, Va.: 79
Clifford, Daniel, Pvt., 16th Mass. Inf.: 102
Congress, USS: 44, 45-46
Constitution, USN transport steamer: 40, 41, 43
Cooke, Charles H., Pvt., 16th Mass. Inf.: 201
Copeland, Charles F., 1st Lt., 16th Mass. Inf.: **12,** 128
Couch, Darius, Maj. Gen, USA: 139
Crampton's Gap, Md.: 182
Craney Island, Va.: 22, 43-44, 46, 57
Crozier, Thomas, Asst. Surgeon, 16th & 11th Mass. Inf.: 193
Cumberland, USS: 44, 45, 48
Dacotah, USS: 67
Dallas, Alexander J., 1st Lt., 16th Mass. Inf.: 169, 170, 174, 175
Denton, Charles F., Pvt., 16th Mass. Inf.: 25
Devine, Stephen D., Pvt., 16th Mass. Inf.: 132, 161
Dillon, John, Pvt., 16th Mass. Inf.: 31-32
Donovan, Capt. Matthew, 16th Mass. Inf.: 62, 166, 188, 192, 195, 247-249
E. A. & W. Winchester Company, Lexington, Mass.: 4, 10-11, 27, 42, 79, 169
Edward's Ferry, Va.: 181-182
Emmitsburg, Pa.: 183
Fair Oaks, Va.: 76-77, 80-82
Falmouth, Va.: **79-81**, 132-138, 159-178, 190-196, 253, 254, 257
Farrell, John, Pvt., 16th Mass. Inf.: 25
Flagg, Cassander, 2nd Lt., 16th Mass. Inf.: 23
Flatery, Patrick, Pvt., 16th Mass. Inf.: 31-32, 167
Flynn, john, Pvt., 16th Mass. Inf.: 167
Flynn, Thomas, Pvt., 16th Mass. Inf.: 53
Fortress Monroe, Va.: **49**, 15, 17, 26, 50, 253
Foxhill, Va.: 39
Franklin, Maj. Gen. William B.: 257
Frederick, Md.: 182, 203
Fredericksburg, Va.: **74-76, 82**, 121-125, 132, 134, 140ff, 253
Front Royal, Va.: 72
Frothingham, Ward, 2nd Lt., 16th Mass. Inf.: **13**, 50
Fuller, Arthur B., Chaplain, 16th Mass. Inf.: **14, 15**, 12, 121-125
Galena, USS: 67
Gettysburg, Pa.: **85-91**, 179-203, 236-249
Glendale, Va.: **60**, 83-86,88-90, 94-95, 100
Grover, Cuvier, Brig. Gen., USA: **36**, 76, 77, 81, 84, 196
Gum Spring, Va.: 200-202
Gunn, Neil K., Pvt., 1st Mass. Inf.: 193

Halleck, Henry W., Maj. Gen. USA: 176
Hampton, Va.: **51**, **53**, 21, 23, 39, 46, 51, 54
Hampton Creek, Va.: 59
Hampton Roads, Va.: 50, 52
Harper's Ferry, W. Va.: 119
Harding, Pvt. William W., 16th Mass. inf.: 254
Harrington, Henry S., Cpl., 16th Mass. Inf.: **16**, 39, 166
Harris, Henry A., 1st Lt., 16th Mass. Inf.: 189
Harrison's Landing, Va.: **63-66**, 94-109, 254
Harrold's Mills, Va.: 55, 56
Hartwood Church, Va.: 180, 196
Hatteras, Cape & Fort, N.C.: 15, 16, 209
Heintzelman, Samuel P., Maj. Gen., USA: **37**, 77, 84, 92, 102
Hills, Joseph S., Capt., 16th Mass. Inf.: **17**, **18**, 132, 134, 163, 164, 167, 169, 170, 171, 173, 174, 177, 191, 192
Homer, Charles W., Chaplain, 16th Mass. Inf.: 177
Hooker, Joseph, Maj.-Gen., USA: **38**, 51, 84, 92, 125, 130, 132, 139ff, 171-172, 174, 176, 182
Hubbard, Joseph, Lt., Staff of Gen. Cuvier Grover: 104
Humphreys, Andrew A., Maj. Gen., USA: **39**, 182, 184ff, 236-243
Island No. 10, Miss.: 62
Jamestown, CSS: 59, 67
Jewett, Charles C., Surgeon, 16th Mass. Inf.: **19**, 44, 165, 194
Johnson, Berkeley ("Berk"): 4, 28, 75, 118, 160, 170, 193
Johnson, - , Capt., Naval brigade, USA: 19
Johnson, Charles R.: **1-7**, *passim*
Johnson, Nellie: *passim*
Kelly's Ford, Va.: 171-172
King, John P., Capt., 16th Mass. Inf.: **20**, 171, 173, 175, 193, 194, 195
Kinsley, Joseph W., Pvt., 16th Mass. Inf.: 20
Lamson, Daniel S., Major, 16th Mass. Inf.: **21**, 101, 119, 170
Lawson, Henry T., Maj., 2nd Mass. Hvy. Arty.: 119
Lincoln, Abraham, President USA: **79**, 67, 98, 140, 173, 176
Little Bethel, Va.: 30
Lombard, Richard J., Capt., 16th Mass. Inf.: **22**, 166, 168, 172, 173, 175, 176, 192, 195
Louisiana, Steamboat: 14
Mack, John, F., 5th Mass.Lt. Arty.: 24
Magruder, John B., Maj. Gen., CSA: 23
Malvern Hill, Va.: **62**, 90-93, 100, 102-103, 105-107
Manassas, Va.: 128, 197, 198, 199, 200
Mansfield, Joseph K., Maj. Gen., USA: 27
Mayo, Charles H., 1st. Lt., 16t Mass. Inf.: 12, 24, 25, 31, 32, 34, 36, 38, 40, 66, 75, 79, 81, 98, 100, 101, 103
McClellan, George B., Maj. Gen., USA: **72-73**, 50, 51, 53, 56, 61-62, 98, 102, 129, 130, 191, 256
McDowell, Irvin, Maj. Gen, USA: 57
McKeever, Lt. Samuel, 16th Mass. Inf.: 21
Meade, George G., Maj. Gen., USA: 182ff
Meagher, Thomas F., Brig. Gen. USA: 95, 171-172
Mechanicsville, Va.,: 81
Merriam, Waldo, Col., 16th Mass. Inf.: **23**, 5, 99, 126, 134, 136, 137, 188, 192
Merrimac, CSS – see *Virginia*, CSS
Middletown, Md.: 182
Minnesota, USS: 45, 46
Monitor, USS: 46, 47, 48, 67
Monocacy River, Md.: 181
Mud March, Va.: **77**, 138, 254-257
Murphy, Dennis C., Cpl., 16th Mass. Inf.: 134
Naglee, Henry M., Brig. Gen., USA: **40**,
Naugatuck, USS: 59, 67
New Market Bridge, Va.: 34, 35, 55
Newport News, Va.: 17, 23, 30, 35, 45, 47
Nine Mile Road, Va,: 80
Norfolk, Va.: **57-58**, 67-68, 71, 72
Oak Grove, Va.,: 81
Occoquan River, Va.: 132
Ohio & Chesapeake Canal, Md.: 181-182
Old Point Comfort, Va.: **50**, 13-18,21, 22, 59, 78
O'Hare, Thomas, Capt., 16th Mass. inf.: 184
O'Neal, John, Pvt., 16th Mass. Inf.: 115, 193
Orange & Alexandria RR: 131
Orr, David, Pvt., 16th Mass. Inf.: 102, 253
Ossoli, Margaret Fuller: 13, 122
Pamunkey River: 78
Patrick Henry, CSS: 67
Patterson, Francis E., Brig. Gen., USA: 103
Peninsula Campaign, Va.: **59**, 54 ff, 64ff
Petersburg, Va.: 71
Point of Rocks, Md.: 182
Porter, Fitz John, Maj. Gen. USA: 159-160
Port Royal, SC Expedition: 25, 38
Portsmouth, Va.: 69-70, 210
Putnam, John C., Capt., 16th Mass. Inf.: **24**, 56, 59
Raleigh, CSS: 59
Rappahannock Bridge, Va.: 162-164
Rappahannock Gold Mines, Va.: 163-165
Rappahannock Station, Va.: 196, 197
Regiments, Confederate:
- 8th Alabama Infantry: 35
- 9th Alabama Infantry: 184
- Wilcox's Alabama Brigade: 186
- Perry's Florida Brigade: 186
- -- Georgia Infantry: 164
- Perry's Georgia Brigade: 186
- Barksdale's Mississippi Brigade: 186
- 18th Virginia Battalion Artillery: 68
- 2nd Virginia Infantry: 39

- 4th Virginia Infantry: 164
Regiments, Union:
- 1st Delaware Infantry: 27
- 2nd Delaware Infantry: 137
- 20th Indiana Infantry: 252
- 19th Maine Infantry: 188
- 5th Maryland Infantry: 49
- 2nd Massachusetts Battery, Light Artillery: 14
- 5th Massachusetts Battery, Light Artillery: 54
- 9th Massachusetts Battery, Light Artillery: 199
- 1st Massachusetts Cavalry: 172
- 1st Massachusetts Infantry: 52, 64-66, 78, 83-87, 92-93, 100, 129, 135, 140, 163, 171, 177, 180-183, 193
- 4th Massachusetts Infantry: 21
- 9th Massachusetts Infantry: 50
- 11th Massachusetts Infantry: 78, 80, 83-84, 90, 183
- 12th Massachusetts Infantry: **80,**
- 16th Massachusetts Infantry: **43-48, 85-91,** *passim*, 204-208 (post-Gettysburg), 211-221 (Itineraries), 222-230 (Roster, Co. F), 231-235 (Adjutant-General Reports), 247-249 (Gettysburg), 250-251 (Regimental flags)
- 17th Massachusetts Infantry: 14
- 20th Massachusetts Infantry: 56
- 22nd Massachusetts Infantry: 50
- 24th Massachusetts Infantry: 38
- 29th Massachusetts Infantry: 5
- 33rd Massachusetts Infantry: 175
- 1st Michigan Infantry: 49
- 1st Minnesota Infantry: 188
- 2nd New Hampshire Infantry: 76, 78, 83, 88-92, 102-103, 109-114, 181-183
- 12th New Hampshire Infantry: 183, 188
- 5th New Jersey Infantry: 166
- 11th New Jersey Infantry: 183, 253
- 26th New Jersey Infantry: 180
- 5th New York Infantry: 55, 140
- 20th New York Infantry: 15, 16, 20, 30, 31, 34, 35, 133-134
- 37th New York Infantry: 56, 192
- 38th New York Infantry: 192
- 87th New York Infantry: 50
- 120th New York Infantry: 186
- Naval Brigade, USA: 18, 31
- 26th Pennsylvania Infantry: 78, 83-84, 90, 183
- 58th Pennsylvania Infantry: 49
- 84th Pennsylvania Infantry: 183
- 105th Pennsylvania Infantry: 188
- 1st Rhode Island Cavalry: 198-199
- Batty. K, 4th U.S. Artillery: 186, 188
- 1st & 2nd United States Sharpshooters: 58
- Stannard's Vermont Brigade: 188
Reynolds, George W.M., Chartist: 191
Richardson, Samuel, Major, 16th Mass. Inf.: **25**, 136, 169, 192

Rip Raps, Va.: 19, 35, 61
Roanoke, USS: 20, 45, 253
Roche, David W., Capt., 16th Mass. In.: 171
Rogers, Francis P. H., 1t Lt., 16th Mass. Inf.: 36, 41, 50, 97
Rowe, Hiram, 2nd Lt., 16th Mass. Inf.: 79
Savage Station, Va.: 79, 88
Sea Bird, CSS: 35
Seminole, USS; 67
Seven Days' Battles: 76-93
Sewall's Point, Va.: **54**, 15, 35, 43, 67
Shiloh, Tenn.: 58
Ship Point, Va.: 57
Sickles, Daniel E., Maj. Gen., USA: **41, 42**, 127, 136, 140ff, 172, 177, 183ff
Sigel, Franz, Maj. Gen., USA: 128
Smith, Simeon, Pvt., 16th Mass. Inf.: 47
Smith, Lt. William A, 16th Mass. Inf.: 29
Soule, Langdon, Pvt., 1st Mass. Inf.: 135
Stanton, Edwin M., Secretary of War, USA: 176
Stearns, Charles F., Pvt., 16th Mass. Inf.: 104
Sturgis, Henry M., Lt., 20th Mass. Inf. & staff, Maj. Gen. Hiram A. Berry: **26**, 56
Suffolk, Va.: **78**, 70-75, 210
Sumner, Maj. Gen. Edwin V.: 257
Susquehanna, USS: 67
Taneytown, Md.: 183, 203
Tannatt, Thomas R., Col., 16th Mass. Inf.: **27**, 87, 136, 137
Train, Charles R., Mass. Representative: 34
Tucker, Payson, 2nd Lt., 16th Mass. Inf.: **28**, 20, 24, 25, 36, 50, 58, 79, 80, 81, 88, 99, 102, 118, 169, 254
Tunstall's Station, Va.: 79
Upperville, Va.: 201
Vanderbilt, USS: **67,**
Virginia, CSS: **55**, 44, 45, 46, 47, 48, 57, 58-59, 66, 67, 68, 210
Wade, Benjamin F., Senator, USA: 190
Warrenton, Va.: **71, 73**, 129-131, 181, 194
Warwick River, Va.: 54
Washington, DC: **68**, 125
Weston, Patrick, 26th Mass. Inf.: 24
Whiston, Edward A., Asst. Surg., 16th Mass. Inf.: **29**, 44
White House Landing, Va.: 76, 78
Wiley, John, Capt., 16th Mass. Inf.: 166, 168, 194, 210
Wickham. Pvt. Ralph H., 16th Mass. inf.: 254
Williamsburg, Va.: 69
Willoughby's Point, Va.: 67
Winn's Mills, Va.: 54
Woodbury, Henry T., 1st Lt., 23rd Mass. Inf.: 137
Woodfin, John U., 1st Lt., 16th Mass. Inf.: **30**, 195
Wool, John A., Maj. Gen. USA: 27, 39
Wyman, Powell T., Col., 16th Mass. Inf.: **31, 32**, 70, 85, 95, 99, 101, 165
Yorktown, CSS: 30

Yorktown, Va.: **56**, 20, 21, 60ff, 64ff

ABOUT THE AUTHORS

Albert C. Eisenberg developed his abiding and lifelong interest in the Civil War from growing up in Virginia's Tidewater region. A history major at the University of Richmond, Al moved to Arlington County, Virginia in 1975, and has led a busy life of public service, as a U.S. Senate Staffer, a member of the Arlington County Board, as Deputy Assistant Secretary for Transportation Policy (U.S.), and finally as a member of the Virginia House of Delegates. He is known as a champion for affordable housing, public transportation, public safety, the environment, human rights, and planned development. Throughout the decades, he also passionately pursued collecting original Civil War documents and artifacts, researching and sharing the human stories behind them. Al and his wife, Sharon Davis, live in Arlington, Virginia, and have two sons, Matthew and Alex.

Michael Hammerson, an Englishman, is a Chartered Surveyor and a qualified Archaeologist, and was Planning Policy consultant for the Civic Trust, a national Urban Regeneration charity. He has collected and researched the Civil War for most of his life, and his many other interests including being a community activist on town planning issues. He and his wife Susan live in London. His cat is named Ulysses, for General Grant. He is an Associate Member of the Sons of Union Veterans, and is researching Civil War veterans buried in the United Kingdom, of which there are at least 1,300. He obtained a Veterans Administration Marker for a US Navy Medal of Honor winner buried in London, and is researching the London Branch of American Civil War Veterans. He published a guide to Civil War-related burials in his local cemetery, Highgate, London, which has two Union veterans and a brother of John Wilkes Booth.

*

www.ingramcontent.com/pod-product-compliance
Lightning Source LLC
Chambersburg PA
CBHW070936230426
43666CB00011B/2462